D1071603

Contemporary Pakistan

Contemporary Pakistan:
Politics, Economy, and Society

MANZOORUDDIN AHMED, *Editor*

1980
Carolina Academic Press
Durham, North Carolina

Burgess

DS
384
934
1978

c. 1

Dedicated to
the Memory of the Quaid-I-Azam
Muhammad Ali Jinnah, the Founder of
the Islamic Republic of Pakistan

PIA Pakistan International

with the Compliments of the Pakistan International Airlines,
545 Fifth Avenue, New York, N.Y. 10017

Contents

Foreword

It is a great privilege for me to be invited to write a foreword for this timely volume on *Contemporary Pakistan, Politics, Economy, Society*. The present volume contains a thoughtful selection of scholarly papers which were presented before the Quaid-e-Azam International Conference on Contemporary Pakistan.

By organizing such a Conference and seeking the cooperation and scholarly contribution of so many eminent men of learning, Dr. Manzooruddin Ahmed and his colleagues have indeed set the stage for what will undoubtedly prove to be a fruitful and stimulating experience, not only for the participants but for all those interested in our region and in following developments in countries which face problems similar to our own.

In the present volume various inherently inter-related themes have been judiciously chosen to illuminate key areas, that will contribute to a deeper understanding of "Contemporary Pakistan" and the challenges it faces.

If the present or the contemporary is no more than an evanescent moment in the march of historical time, it also carries the burden of the past, as it presses against the future and indeed foreshadows its unfolding.

The manner in which we see the current setting as linked to past events, will determine the nature and scope of our response for fashioning the future. It is equally the rigour of our reasoning and the intellectual integrity we bring to bear on our problems that will be the measure of the solutions towards which we shall be drawn.

While it is true that detachment and objectivity is an ideal that might be difficult to pursue for those emotionally involved in the destiny of their country, the national tragedies which it has been our lot to endure, demand that we do not flinch from examining our failures, and that we have the courage to face reality and to attempt, in the words of Newman, "to discern the end in every beginning, the origin in every end, the law in every interruption, the limit in each delay."

Approached in this spirit of scientific enquiry, the contribution of so many international personalities from the academic world, trained in the pursuit of knowledge and truth and devoted to these noble aims, is particularly gratifying.

The freshness and originality of minds nurtured in intellectual traditions different from our own will certainly add a new dimension to mutually shared insights and a new orientation to the progress of reasoning towards reality.

So, I welcome with particular warmth and sense of gratitude the contribution of American scholars who lead the world in the field of learning as much as in all pursuits which ennoble life and give it value and meaning.

The eminent contributions to the present volume have truly brought to bear a distinguished tradition of scientific thought, painstaking research, sympathy and indeed empathy for their fellow beings, as also that moral commitment which should form the leaven of all scholarly endeavour. Without it, the life of the mind remains a poor thing, its products dry as dust, its intellectual thrusts fitful and fractured, its anschauung partial and preconceived.

In approaching our subject, as we pick our way, strand by strand, through the various themes of the volume, concerning crucial segments of Pakistan's national life, namely politics, economy and society, we recognize, the interaction between them and also the fact that such distinctions, though unavoidable for academic discussion, are necessarily artificial and even arbitrary —particularly at junction points where the boundaries are necessarily blurred.

While we are aware that the life of a nation—or of an individual—is not lived in fragmented segments but as an organic whole, the process of intellection tends by its very nature to be a series of still pictures or perceptions of things "become", rather than of things "becoming".

Our mental constructs can, therefore, never be more than a rough approximation of the reality we wish to grasp in its ebb and flow, or the phenomenon we wish to represent in its elan and movement. The recognition of this hiatus as a limitation in the operation of the mind is in itself a salutary corrective, for it should put us on guard against dogmatism in our formulations, hubris in our certitudes and distortions in our perspectives.

We recognize equally, on yet another plane, the linkages with developments in other countries, the flow or over-flow of ideas across the borders and the inter-action of external and internal policies in a shrinking and interdependent world.

In comprehending the nature of organic evolution of the inter-related phenomena of politics, economy and society of Pakistan, it is more important than ever that we remind ourselves of the central idea which formed the genesis of Pakistan and reaffirm the principles and values it enshrined, the ideals of which it was the embodiment, and above all the Islamic theme that is its leitmotif and its strongest source of animation.

We must also examine the influence of socio-economic forces at the birth of Pakistan and in the subsequent evolution of its ethos and political history, as these forces are surely fundamental to an understanding of political processes and their future evolution.

It is equally valid to enquire whether the concept of Pakistan, as it germinated in the minds of those who conceived it, and presided at its birth, was subjected to modifications or shifts of emphasis in the interest of personal or political expediency, and with what results.

Apart from these aspects of fundamental philosophy, another consideration central to political evolution in Pakistan has been the relationship between the federal centre and the provinces, starting from the polarization with East Pakistan, that led to the creation of the One Unit and its subsequent transformation into the 4 provinces that form its constituent parts today.

In recent years tension between the centre and the provinces of the North West Frontier and Baluchistan were unnecessarily exacerbated through unwise manipulations, but there is no reason why federal–provincial relations, as defined in the unanimously accepted Constitution of 1973, should not be judiciously handled and harmonized under an over-arching sense of nationhood.

Indeed, the present government has already taken wise and bold steps in that direction to promote national cohesion by not only disbanding the general amnesty to those who had taken to the hills as a protest against actions of the previous regime.

As we dwell on the theme of changing patterns of politics in our country, and its chequered evolution in the last 30 years, we shall be struck, as much by its twists and turns, as the manner in which the democratic ideal has continued to elude us from the very inception of our nationhood.

Whatever the reasons for our past experiments and failures—we have to recall our most recent and painful experience and the sorry pass to which it has brought us.

The details of this sad tale and its unfolding are fresh in the minds of all those who have followed developments in Pakistan since the 5th of July 1977, when the Armed Forces had no patriotic option but to take over the administration of the country which stood at the brink of chaos and disaster.

Indeed, few armies have had to face so thorny and trying an ordeal. It put their morale and discipline to the severest test from which they emerged with credit and recognition, both at home and abroad, for their patriotism, sincerity, restraint and sense of duty.

"The sole aim of the Armed Forces" General Zia-ul-Haq has announced "is to organize free and fair elections, whereupon power will be transferred to the elected representatives of the people." The present government is now engaged in preparing the way for accomplishing this mission which it regards as paramount, after the completion of the present phase of accountability for past wrong doings in order to cleanse the political scene and prevent or deter future lapses of this kind.

A series of other actions are underway in almost all fields of national life, to ensure the maintenance of law and order, to bind the wounds, to restore damaged national institutions, to nurse a shattered economy, to instil discipline in political activity, and generally to create conditions that would facilitate and pave the way for the coming elections and the transfer of power.

This is a truly gigantic task, if we recall the deplorable situation the armed forces inherited in July last year. Within a few years of the promulgation of a unanimously accepted Constitution, we witnessed a remarkable example of all national institutions being neutralized, a representative government becoming an instrument of authoritarian rule, and democracy—with all its norms and values-being transformed into its antithesis.

A similar event occurred across the border, at about the same time, indicating again that a democratic constitution is not an end in itself, and can be subverted and rendered ineffective, unless those who operate it are genuinely committed to the spirit and the principles of democratic freedom which it enshrines.

In all these themes there is material for research and reflection particularly if we expand the scope of our enquiry to cover a comparative study of democratic experiments—as also the fate of popular leaders in the last two or three years—in the countries which emerged from colonial rule in the South Asian region some thirty years ago. The correspondences and homologous relationships of parallel phenomena would indeed form a useful and stimulating field of study that might provide clues for understanding political trends, not only in South Asia, but also in many countries of the Third World as a whole.

Pakistan's preoccupation with the maintenance of its security and the preservation of its territorial integrity has been a major consideration since its birth. As later events were to prove, Pakistan's heightened concern stemmed not from any paranoia against its neighbours but from a genuine anxiety to preserve its independence and sovereignty, in the face of possible threats and hostility. Hence the vigour with which Pakistan defends the right of smaller nations to exist without hegemonic interference of others should suprise no one familiar with the history of our region.

Even today, with fewer borders to defend, the security concern remains paramount. Pakistan can be expected to supplement its efforts at building a credible defence posture with diplomatic initiatives aimed at fostering preventive rather than remedial measures. The establishment of a nuclear-weapon free zone in South Asia or a regime of balanced and reduced forces between India and Pakistan are examples in point.

Pakistan's singular attachment to the right of self-determination was not born with the Kashmir dispute nor is it confined to that area alone. Owing its very existence to the exercise of that right and having advocated it for the subjugated people of other continents, Pakistan cannot do otherwise for the people of Jammu and Kashmir.

Our close relationship with Arab nations pre-dates the affluence of that region and transcends the ordinary norms of interstate communication. It is an integral part of our ethos. This nexus will always be a permanent feature of Pakistan's foreign policy because it is not sustained by the prevailing socio-political systems or governmental direction, but by a clearly articulated desire of the peoples to have brotherly relations with each other. Our total support of the Arab struggle in the Middle East recognizes this essential ingredient as also the justice of the demands for the return of territories taken by armed aggression and the exercise of the right of self-determination.

Similarly, our relationship with Iran and Turkey, though formalised by a treaty and an alliance, finds its strenth in the geographical proximity and cultural identity whose roots extend far into antiquity.

Another key aspect of our foreign policy has been its pragmatism. It has assiduously sought to develop a one-to-one relationship with each major power avoiding any attempt at playing one against the other or to taking sides in their disputes. In fact, where possible Pakistan has helped to establish dialogue, contact and understanding between erstwhile adversaries. The bridge it formed between the United States and China was as much a manifestation of this policy as it was a demonstration of close relations with America and special friendship with China. We believe that a true understanding between the major powers will help greatly in resolving a large number of problems amongst their allies and thus contribute to peace and stability in a troubled and tormented world.

In the end, I would like to add a few words of personal appreciation for, Dr. Manzooruddin Ahmed, the editor of this volume, who has been doing good work at Columbia University in effectively projecting Pakistan in North America and promoting Pakistan Studies in North American Universities and colleges. To the contributors, I would say, may your endeavours be crowned with the success and satisfaction you shall Insha Allah deserve and may the fruit of your labours contribute to a deeper understanding of our country and the high destiny that undoubtedly awaits it.

** * * * * ***

H.E. Sahabzada Yaqub Khan
The Ambassador of Pakistan
to the United States of America

Preface

Scholarly articles included here in this Quaid-e-Azam Memorial volume were orginally presented at a major conference on CONTEMPORARY PAKISTAN at Columbia University in the City of New York held on March 9 throu₄h 11, 1978. This conference was organized under the auspices of Pakistan Center of the Southern Asian Institute of Columbia University to commemorate the Centennial of the Birth of Quaid-e-Azam (The Great Leader) Mohammed Ali Jinnah, the founding Father of the Islamic Republic of Pakistan.

The conference was a unique event in the history of Pakistan Studies in North America insofar as it was the biggest ever held, and was truly international in character. About forty-five prominent scholars including three from Pakistan, and one from Europe participated in the deliberations. Besides, it was attended by a large number of prominent Pakistani residents and students from the eastern coast of the U.S.A. and many American scholars of South Asian Studies.

The conference was inaugurated by His Excellency Sahabzada Yaqub Khan, formerly Pakistan's ambassador in the United States of America whose inaugural address appears in this volume as the Foreword. The other articles were presented before its sessions on politics, economy and society of contemporary Pakistan. The text of the learned address on the Constitution of Pakistan delivered by Professor K.J. Newman of the University of Cologne, Germany, presently Visiting Professor of International Affairs at the Quaid-e-Azam University, Islamabad, is reproduced in this volume in its section on Politics. The sessional chairmen have contributed brief introductions to each section. The editor has taken the liberty of adding a general Introduction with a view to provide readers a broad historical outline of Pakistan's evolution. However, no effort has been made to present all the details. It is hoped that it will help the reader to locate each article of topical interest in the overall configuration of Pakistan's politics, and facilitate his comprehension of the sequence of continuities and discontinuities inherent in the historical evolution of Pakistan. However, it is left for the readers to judge for themselves whether Pakistan has attained any measure of political development or has undergone 'political decay' in the recent years. To sum up it may be asserted with a fair amount of certainty that Pakistan provides a fascinating case study in comparative politics and political development.

The editor would like to express his deepest sense of appreciation to all the contributors who volunteered to rewrite, revise, and update the substance of their scholarly papers. He also wishes to take this opportunity of thanking eminent American scholars of South Asian Studies like Messrs. Ralph Braibanti, Director, Center for Islamic and Arabian Development Studies at Duke University, Durham, N.C., Norman D. Palmer, professor of Political Science at the University of Pennsylvania, Philadelphia, Pa. and Stanislaw Wellisz, professor of Economics of Columbia University who readily agreed to write introductory observations for each section.

The editor should be failing his duty if he does not acknowledge the generous financial support of the Government of Pakistan received through the courtesy of His Excellecy Sahabzada Yaqub Khan. His Excellency's personal patronage, kind guidance, and his moral and material support has always been a permanent source of inspiration. The editor is equally indebted to the kind support that he always received from Mr. Hayat Mehdi, the senior Minister at the Pakistan Embassy in Washington, D.C. In this connection, a word of appreciation must formally be recorded for all the personal care, support, and cooperation which was received by the editor from Mr. Sajjad Haider, who was until recently Educational Attache in the Education Division of the Pakistan Embassy in Washington, D.C.

In New York, the editor received moral support from Mr. Aziz Khan, formerly Consul General, Mr. Tariq Fatemi, Vice Consul, and Mr. Khalid Ali, the Press Attache in Pakistan Mission at the UN, and therefore, this opportunity is availed of for placing on record his appreciation for all these gentleman.

At Columbia University, the editor wishes to acknowledge the kind support that he received from Professor Howard Wriggins, presently American ambassador in Sri Lanka, Associate Dean Ainslee Embree, now holding an important diplomatic assignment in New Delhi, and Professor Theodore Riccardi, Jr., Acting Director of Southern Asian Institute. The editor must also acknowledge his personal indebtedness to his former teacher, Professor J.C. Hurewitz, Director of the Middle East Institute who has always been a source of inspiration.

The editor also wishes to express his appreciation for the Pakistan International Airlines establishment in New York for their generous financial support in organizing the Quaid-e-Azam Conference last year, and in the publication of the present volume. Equally the editor is indebted to National Bank of Pakistan, Habib Bank, and United Bank Limited in New York for their financial contributions towards organizing last year's conference. The editor also likes to place on record his gratitude for generous grants received from the Southern Asian Institute of Columbia University, and the American Institute of Pakistan Studies.

A special word of thanks must be expressed for Mr. Norman Sauvage, aerospace artist who has contributed a thoughful artistic design for the title cover.

At the end the editor gratefully acknowledges his personal indebtedness to the Ministry of Education, and the University Grants Commission of Pakistan for their moral and material support.

Manzooruddin Ahmed,
Quaid-e-Azam Distinguished Professor
of Pakistan Studies.

Pakistan Center, SAI, Columbia University,
New York, June 3, 1979

Contemporary Pakistan

Introduction

Pakistan, literally, *Land of the Pure,* is a predominantly Muslim state in the South Asian region. Its name was coined by Chaudhri Rehmat Ali, one of the proponents of the idea of a separate Muslim state on the Indian subcontinent. The word, Pakistan, is derived from the names of its component regions: the "P" of the Punjab (Land of the Five Rivers); the "A" of Afghania (Northwest Frontier Province); the "K" of Kashmir; the "S" of Sind (the southern province named after the Indus River); and the "TAN" of Baluchistan (the province bordering Iran and Afghanistan).

Today, Pakistan has been catapulted into international prominence because of events in neighboring countries, such as the widespread resistance movement against the Pahlevi dynasty by the Iranian people and the Soviet-sponsored *coup d'état* in Afghanistan. Pakistan is now regarded as an important link in what United States National Security Advisor Zbigniew Brzezinski describes as the "arc of instability"[1] or what *Time Magazine* portrays as "the crescent of crisis"[2]—that is, the countries stretching from Bangladesh to South Africa.

Now, as in earlier times, the area that constitutes Pakistan has geopolitical significance. It is important to look at some basic geographical and historical facts to assess its contemporary prominence. Pakistan extends from the northern Himalayan ranges down to the southern coast of the Arabian Sea; in the west, the country is demarcated along the mountain ranges of Koh Sulaiman from Afghanistan by an internationally agreed political boundary known as the Durrand Line; and in the southwest, from the Iranian section of Baluchistan. In the east, the country is separated from India along the Punjab Valley and the deserts of Rajhastan, and the Rann of Kutch on the basis of an agreement which led to the partition of the subcontinent in 1947. In the north, the Kashmir Valley is divided along a cease-fire line in accordance with a United Nations formula, and remains a disputed territory between

3

India and Pakistan. This still constitutes a source of conflict between the two neighboring countries. Pakistan's border issues with China, in the north, were amicably settled in 1962. Pakistan's northern frontier is also separated from the Soviet Union by a narrow stretch of Afghan territory.

The country, has a total area of 310,403 square miles, or 810,408 square kilometers. Its total estimated population is 64,892,000 [1972].

Given its location, Pakistan occupies a vital position in the geopolitical configuration of the world island, as described by geographer Halford Mackinder, insofar as it constitutes the southernmost flank of the Iranian Upland.[3] The famous passes of Khyber and Bolan provide the historic routes for invasions from the northwestern heartland into the river valleys of the Indian subcontinent. The Makran coast on the south provides a natural outlet into the Arabian Sea. Pakistan's importance in the global configuration arises from the fact that for centuries, its land was targetted by Czarist Russian and subsequently by the Soviet state, as a land route access through its natural harbors into the Indian Ocean. Within the past few years, moreover, Pakistan's security problems have become heightened. The emergence of Iran under the Shahinshah as a pivotal regional military power with its highly modernized military establishment and naval build-up in the neighboring naval bases of Bandar Abbas and Chahar Abbas provided a defense umbrella to Pakistan; but with the destabilization of Iran, Pakistan now stands completely exposed to a military thrust from the northwest. Pakistan's security, however, is strengthened by the Silk Route, built jointly by Pakistani and Chinese engineers in the north, which provides a strategic link with its friendly neighbor, China. The recent conclusion of a treaty of Friendship and Defense between the Taraki government of Afghanistan and the Soviet Union has already set the stage for an incident similar to the one in 1971 where India, supported by the Soviet Union intervened against Pakistan. This culminated in the tragic dismemberment of Pakistan by which East Pakistan became an independent Bangladesh. This time, Afghanistan backed by the Soviet defense treaty may conveniently at some opportune moment intervene in Pakistan on the pretext of protecting its ethnic brothers—the Pakhtuns, and the Baluchis who have remained in a state of insurgency against the central Pakistani government for some time.[4] A further destabilization of Pakistan or its dismemberment would undoubtedly constitute a potential threat to the whole region of South Asia, the rich states of the Gulf, and Saudi Arabia. Therefore, it may be a timely exercise to examine and analyze the forces and factors which shape the internal as well as the external policies of Pakistan. The internal politics of the country is in a state of flux; and the external situation is complicated by Pakistan's delicate interaction with neighboring India and Afghanistan, on the one hand, and with the super-powers: the United States, the Soviet Union and China, on the other.

I

The demand for a separate state for the Indian Muslims was first proposed by Sir Dr. Muhammad Iqbal, the Poet-Philosopher, in his presidential address at the Annual Session of the All India Muslim League in 1930 at Allahabad, a city in the heartland of Hindu India. Iqbal, dilating on the future course of Muslim politics in India, observed:[5]

I would like to see the Punjab, Northwest Frontier Province, Sind, and Baluchistan amalgamated into a single state. Self-government within the British empire or without the British empire the formation of a consolidated North-West Indian Muslim State appears to me the final destiny of the Muslims at least of North-West India.

However, it took a decade before the concept of a Muslim state could be formally articulated as a specific political demand of the Indian Muslims in the form of the Lahore Resolution at the Annual Session of the All-India Muslim League on March 23, 1940 under the dynamic leadership of the Quaid-i-Azam (the Great Leader), Muhammad Ali Jinnah. The Lahore Resolution, also popularly known as the Pakistan Resolution, states:[6]

Resolved, that it is the considered view of this session of the All-India Muslim League that no constitutional plan would be workable in this country or acceptable to the Muslims unless it is designed on the following basic principles, viz., that geographically contiguous units are demarcated into regions which should be so constituted with such territorial readjustments as may be necessary that the areas in which the Muslims are numerically in a majority as in the North Western and Eastern Zones of India should be grouped to constitute "Independent States" in which the constituent units should be autonomous and sovereign.

The demand for a separate state for Muslims was based on the 'Two-Nations Theory' which was put forward by Iqbal, and later elaborated into political and legal terminology by the Quaid-i-Azam, Muhammad Ali Jinnah as a counterargument against the viewpoint of the All India National Congress which believed that all Indians, irrespective of their religion, race, language and caste constituted a single political nationality. The Muslim League leaders were convinced that the All-India National Congress would not agree upon a federal scheme acceptable to all parties as an ultimate solution for the chronic Hindu-Muslim conflict. From 1940 to 1947 many federal schemes were considered, but none could satisfy both parties.[7] Consequently, on the eve of partition, an interim government composed of the representatives of the Congress and the League was set up. The Mountbatten Plan[8] (named after the then Governor General of India) was accepted as the basis of partitioning the subcontinent into the two sovereign states of India and Pakistan. The partition took place in the wake of a widespread communal bloodbath leading to a near total exchange of population between the two countries in the province of the Punjab. Thus, Pakistan came into existence as an independent Muslim state on August 14, 1947. The Government of India Act of 1935, with necessary modifications, together with the Independence Act of India were adopted as the Interim Constitution of the Pakistani state. The Quaid-i-Azam, Muhammad Ali Jinnah, was sworn in as the first Governor-General; and his lieutenant, the Quaid-i-Millat (the Leader of the Nation), Liaquat Ali Khan, was nominated as the first Prime Minister. In accordance with the Interim Constitution, a system of federal parliamentary government was organized with its federal capital at Karachi, a major seaport city in the province of Sind. The members of the Muslim League, who were elected members of the Constituent Assembly during the general elections held in 1946, were organized into the first Constituent Assembly of Pakistan. That Assembly functioned in a dual capacity: first, as a federal legislature; and second, as a constitution-making body. At the same time, League governments were set up in the provinces of East Bengal, Sind, Punjab, and North-West Frontier Province with their provincial capitals at Dacca, Hyderabad, Lahore, and Peshawar, respectively, major cities of the newly created state.

In the initial stages, the Pakistan Muslim League remained the politically dominant party, both at the national level as well as in the provinces. The power of this party rapidly eroded as a dominant political force in the country after the death of its founder, the Quaid-i-Azam in 1948, and after the assassination of its first Prime Minister in 1951. A serious political void developed which could not be effectively filled either by the new group of national leaders or by a stable party system. The Pakistani nation, consequently, has continued to grope through a series of diverse crises during the past thirty-one years of its political existence.

A useful way to study the history of Pakistan is to examine it in six different periods:

a. 1947-1954—transition from colonialism to independence;
b. 1954-1958—parliamentary government, multi-party system and coalition politics;
c. 1958-1969—first Martial Law regime: the Ayub Khan era;
d. 1969-1971—second Martial Law regime: The Agha Muhammad Yahya Khan era; federal crisis and secession of Bangladesh;
e. 1971-1977—the Zulfikar Ali Bhutto era;
f. 1977-   ?—third Martial Law regime: the General Zia-ul-Haq era.

II

1947-1954: Dilemmas of Constitution-making

Pakistan in its early stage of evolution was beset with numerous problems, such as the organization of an effective system of government and administration at the federal capital in Karachi and in the provincial capitals, refugee rehabilitation, reorganization of defense forces, formulation of foreign policy, and laying the foundation for a viable economic system.[9] This was a period of transition from colonialism to independence.

Sitting in the first Constituent Assembly (C.A.), Pakistan's leaders engaged themselves in the most arduous task of drafting a Constitution for the country. Early in March 1949 in the C.A., Prime Minister Liaquat Ali Khan introduced the Objectives Resolution outlining the fundamental principles of the new republic—its ideology, character, and form. Islam was adopted as its ideological foundation. Federalism was adopted as it was recognized as the very basis of the Lahore Resolution of March 1940. The form of government was to be based on the British parliamentary model with a Prime Minister and a responsible Cabinet. Fundamental rights were to be guaranteed, the rights of minorities were to be safeguarded, and the independence of the judiciary was to be secure. The Objectives Resolution was adopted after much heated debate. In the course of subsequent constitutional debates, a number of very crucial issues were raised. These debates occasioned much controversy, both inside and outside the C.A. over specific questions such as the following:

1. The nature of the Islamic state: the manner in which the basic principles of Islam concerning state, economy, and society were to be incorporated into the Constitution.
2. The nature of federalism: questions of provincial autonomy vis-à-vis federal authority with emphasis on the problems of representation on the basis of population and the equality of the federating units; the structure of the federal legislature—unicameral or bicameral.
3. The form of government: whether it was to be modelled on the British or American pattern—parliamentary or presidential.
4. The problem of the electorate: serious questions of joint (all confessional groups vote in one election) versus separate (each confessional group votes separately for its own candidates) electorate.
5. The question of language: both national and regional.

Since 1949, these very fundamental issues have divided the political elites of Pakistan into warring factions and seriously impeded the process of constitution-making in the early years of national independence. These issues, moreover, also obstructed the smooth development of a viable state and the sense of an integrated community and a cohesive nation.

After much debate, the Constituent Assembly was able to prepare a final draft of the Constitution in 1954 which visualized an Islamic Republic of Pakistan with a parliamentary system and a federation of five units, each with a bicameral legislature. It seemed that the constitutional draft could have been adopted in the C.A. by the majority of the League members; but it was not approved by the ruling elites, that is to say, the members of the bureaucracy and the feudal elements of West Pakistan.

For the first time, consequently, *a coup d'état* was brought about by some senior members of the civilian bureaucracy in 1954.[10] The then Governor General, Mr. Ghulam Muhammad, a senior member of the Indian Audit and Accounts Service, backed by Chaudhry Mohammed Ali, another key figure in the administrative machinery of Pakistan, dissolved the C.A. and dismissed Prime Minister Khawaja Nazimuddin, a Bengali. Perhaps this was the first step towards ultimate bureaucratization and consequent militarization of Pakistan's political system. This political development understandably created a legal, political, constitutional and administrative crisis. Both the dissolution of the Constituent Assembly and the dismissal of the Prime Minister were challenged in the courts of law. The dominant political party of the country, the Muslim League, suffered a serious setback from within and from outside the party. The precarious relations between the central government and the provincial governments, particularly that of East Pakistan, were undermined, creating fissures between the Bengalis and the West Pakistanis. Pakistan, with bureaucratic leadership, was given a new direction insofar as the merger of the provinces of West Pakistan was initiated in order to transform a federation originally based on five units into a bipolar federal system. This would ultimately imply perpetual confrontation between East and West Pakistan, and led, in 1971 to the secession of East Pakistan, now known as Bangladesh, from the federation.

III

1954-1958: Coalition Politics

The second phase of Constitution-making in Pakistan began with the installation of a new Constituent Assembly after East Pakistan provincial elections in 1954. The political configuration had already radically changed. A new United Front Party had emerged in East Pakistan bringing into political prominence the representatives of the regionalist elites instead of the former centralist leadership of the Muslim League which had been completely routed in the general elections in East Pakistan. In West Pakistan, a new political party—the Republican Party—was created with the backing of the bureaucrat-politicians. These spectacular developments set the stage for renewed political activity and constitution-making. The questions of forming new governments for the nation as a whole and for the provinces came to be entangled with the problem of constitution-making and led to hard bargaining.

Despite all handicaps, however, a new Constitution was ultimately adopted by the Second Constituent Assembly and promulgated in 1956.[11] This Constitution provided for a federal structure composed of two units, East and West Pakistan. The parliamentary form of government was adopted, and of course, Islamic principles were incorporated into the Constitution. The unicameral legislature was based on the principle of parity of representation between the two wings of the country.

It was expected that the general elections would take place in 1958 in accordance with provisions in the new Constitution, but after a period of unstable coalition politics, the civilian-military coalition of power elites brought about the military *coup d'état,* abrogated the Constitution, and imposed Martial Law with the Commander-in-Chief of the Armed Forces, Mohammed Ayub Khan, later to be named a Field Marshal, as the Chief Martial Law Administrator (CMLA). Soon thereafter the CMLA dismissed the then Governor General, Iskander Mirza, another senior member of the Civil Service and assumed the presidency. This act marked the transformation of the bureaucratic state system into a military regime in which the bureaucrats came to play a subservient rather than a dominant role.

IV

1958-1969: The Ayub Khan Era

Ayub Khan and his colleagues began to reshape the political system of Pakistan in order to ensure much needed political stability.[12] This was done in order to facilitate economic planning and development and to promote military security. They devised a system of Basic Democracy: an indirectly elected system of local government as the foundation upon which they were to erect the superstructure of the political system. The 80,000 indirectly elected members (known as Basic Democrats) were to elect the members of the National and Provincial Assemblies and also the President of the country.

They adopted the American presidential system in place of the British parliamentary system. The Constitution of 1962 was drafted on the basis of the recommendations of the Constitution Commission which had been named by the President. Thus, this new Constitution was not drafted by any elected Constituent Assembly, as had been done in the past. For this reason, it came to be known as a Constitution of one man, promulgated by one man, and perhaps designed for one man, in accordance with the theory of Controlled Democracy which was already propounded by a group from within the civil bureaucracy and particularly espoused by General Iskander Mirza, the dismissed Governor General. The new Constitution, in its much watered down formulations, recognized Islamic principles, a presidential form of government which lacked the necessary checks and balances, and a federal structure which formally provided for a maximum degree of provincial autonomy in the legislative sphere. The federal structure was offset by the unitary character of organization of the executive authority insofar as the President was to appoint provincial governors who would, in turn, form the provincial cabinets without being responsible to the provincial legislatures. The provincial governments, consequently, would be directly responsible to the president of Pakistan.

The Ayubian system was neither presidential nor federal, nor truly representative either in form or in substance. In fact, what it did was to provide for an authoritarian political system which could be geared to the process of economic development and modernization—or militarization of the political system in the wake of Pakistan's alliance with the West within the framework of the Central Treaty Organization (CENTO) and the Southeast Asian Treaty Organization (SEATO). This system survived until 1969 when Field Marshal Mohammed Ayub Khan, under pressure from a popular upheaval, felt compelled to leave the political scene. Ayub handed over power to his successor, the Commander-in-Chief, General Agha Muhammad Yahya Khan, who, after abrogating the Constitution of 1962 imposed Martial Law on the country.

V

1969-1971: The Agha Muhammad Yahya Khan Era

On assuming the presidency, General Agha Muhammad Yahya Khan and his colleagues acceded to popular demands by abolishing the One-Unit System. This was the system that had merged all the provinces of West Pakistan into one unit. He restored autonomy of the old provinces of Sind, the Punjab, and the North West Province, and created the new province of Baluchistan. He also declared that elections would be held on the basis of one man, one vote. One must give due credit to Yahya Khan for having organized fair and impartial elections in December 1970.

The election results truly reflected the ugly political reality: the existing polarization of the Pakistani electorate along regional lines. The Awami League of Sheikh Mujibur Rahman (popularly known as *Banga Bandhu,* a friend of the Bengalis) swept the polls in East Pakistan (now Bangladesh) obtaining an absolute majority in the National Assembly; the Pakistan Peoples Party (PPP) of Mr. Zulfikar Ali Bhutto emerged as the single largest party in West Pakistan with majorities in Sind and the Punjab; and the National Awami Party together with their political ally, Jamiat-ul-'Ulama-i-Islam (the party of a traditional Muslim cleric, Maulana Mufti Mahmud), got clear majorities in Baluchistan and the North West Frontier Province. The Awami League had fought the elections on the basis of their Six Points Formula,[13] which committed them to restructure the existing federal system in order to ensure maximum political autonomy for East Pakistan. Under this formula, only two portfolios—Foreign Affairs and Defense—would be retained by the central government. The Pakistan Peoples Party (PPP), on the other hand, was not willing to dilute the authority of the central government in spite of assuring full provincial autonomy for all the provinces of Pakistan. The National Awami Party (NAP)-Jamiat-ul-'Ulama-i-Islam (JUI) coalition sided with the Awami League (AL) so that they might obtain maximum autonomy for their own provinces, i.e., Baluchistan and the North West Frontier Province.

Thus, the general elections of 1970 produced a new political configuration with three distinct centers of power:

1. the AL in East Pakistan;
2. the PPP in Sind and the Punjab; and
3. the NAP-JUI in Baluchistan and the NWFP.

Of course, at the top of all this was the fourth center of power, the armed forces with their spokesman, Yahya Khan. The basic problem before the Yahya Khan regime was: to whom should they hand over power in view of the fact that there were two major claimants—Sheikh Mujibur Rahman and Mr. Zulfikar Ali Bhutto? The problem was further complicated because of a clash of personalities as well as by the divergence in their political views regarding the future constitution of Pakistan. Among the generals there appeared to be serious differences over the question of the transfer of power. A section of them advocated and ultimately successfully persuaded Yahya Khan to negotiate with Sheikh Mujibur Rahman, the newly elected leader of the AL, in order to reconcile the Six Points Formula with the regime's Legal Framework Order[14] for installing the Sheikh as Prime Minister. This formula retained the presidency for their own nominee—in this case, Yahya Khan, himself.

By early January, it appeared that they had almost agreed upon a formula
somewhat along these lines. However, the negotiations seriously hampered
any prospect of direct political understanding between the two contenders for
political power: Bhutto and the Sheikh. But it also appears that another
group of hawkish generals was not willing to transfer power to the Sheikh
lest he might utterly destroy the very foundations of the defense forces and
weaken the central government to the vanishing point. Therefore, this group
conveniently found itself on the same wave-length as Bhutto and his PPP and
therefore they collaborated with each other in order to bring counter-pressure
on Yayha Khan so that he might "get tough" with the Sheikh over the Six
Points Formula. On February 28, 1971, while in Lahore, Mr. Bhutto was
demanding the postponement of the opening of the National Assembly
session at Dacca. Meanwhile, in Karachi, Yahya Khan who had arrived from
Islamabad en route to Dacca for the purpose of inaugurating the National
Assembly session scheduled for March 3, 1971 announced his decision to
postpone this session in a statement read by his spokesman over radio and
television. This unexpected turn of events cannot be explained in any other
way than to view it as a virtual inner *coup d'état* by the hawkish generals who
successfully displaced the pro-Sheikh generals as close advisors to Yahya
Khan. Consequently, Yahya Khan began acting on their suggestions in his
negotiations with the Sheikh at Dacca. It is now a well-known fact that the
March 1971 negotiations in Dacca with the Sheikh were a smokescreen for
gaining time for Yahya Khan to airlift supplies and military personnel to
Dacca for subsequent military operations. The Governor, Admiral Ahsen,
was dismissed and the General Officer Commanding Lt. General Sahabzada
Yaqub Khan resigned. General Tikka Khan took over as the new GOC of the
Dacca garrison. It was against this background that the Awami League
organized its Civil Disobedience Movement[15] which later developed into a
war of national liberation.

The military intervention by the Indian Security Border Force in the
wake of the Indo-Soviet Treaty of Friendship completely upset the military
situation in East Pakistan. As a result, Pakistani forces had to surrender to
the Indian Army, and almost over 93,000 military personnel were taken as
prisoners of war on December 16, 1971.

Mr. Bhutto's friends among the hawkish generals called him back from
New York where he had been defending Pakistan's case before the United
Nations General Assembly. Among the generals, once again, there seemed to
be a deep cleavage about the future course of action. The generals close to
Yahya Khan wanted him to stop transferring power to the then Commander-
in-Chief, General Abdul Hamid Khan. The hawkish generals, such as Gul
Hasan and Air Marshal Rahim Khan, however are rumored to have prac-
tically forced Yahya Khan at gun point to transfer power to Mr. Bhutto, who

thus became the first civilian to take over as Chief Martial Law Administrator and President of Pakistan. Such was the background of events against which the Bhutto era of Pakistan's political history began on December 20, 1971.

VI

December 20, 1971—July 5, 1977: The Zulfikar Ali Bhutto Era

It is interesting to observe that Bhutto assumed authority during a state of acute crisis after the tragic dismemberment of Pakistan and was ultimately forced to quit the seat of power, leaving the country in a still more acute political crisis. Another common element in the dramatic appearance and still more grotesque exit of Bhutto from the Pakistani political scene was the fact that he assumed power from one general and finally lost it to another one.

In assessing the role of Mr. Bhutto in the government and politics of Pakistan, the most crucial question that arises is: to what extent was he responsible for the tragic dismemberment of Pakistan in 1971? This aspect of his political career will surely be debated in the years to come by observers and historians of Pakistan. Generally, Mr. Bhutto has been blamed for having forced the secession of Bangladesh. The advocates of this view argue that Mr. Bhutto commanded only 82 seats out of the more than 300 seats in the National Assembly, representing only the Punjab and Sind, whereas the Sheikh received an absolute majority of 169 seats. Therefore, in accordance with the theory and practice of parliamentary government, the Sheikh and his Awami League had the legitimate right of forming a government and framing a constitution. Thus, people argue that Mr. Bhutto, as a democrat according to his own profession, should have agreed to occupy the opposition benches. But Mr. Bhutto was of the view that in a federal system, any one constituent unit could not thrust upon the others a constitution of its own making, and therefore, he felt justified in demanding the postponement of the convening of the National Assembly session scheduled for March 3, 1971 at Dacca, the provincial capital of East Pakistan. He feared that the Sheikh would enact a constitution for Pakistan based on his Six Points Formula which could demolish the authority of the federal government, thus leading to the ultimate disintegration of the country.

With the secession of Bangladesh, the situation in West Pakistan was simplified for Mr. Bhutto since his Pakistan People's Party (PPP) had emerged as the single largest party. Therefore, as the majority party leader, Mr. Bhutto was in a position to form his own government at the center. But Bhutto's PPP majorities were confined to only two provinces—the Punjab and Sind; in the North West Frontier Province (NWFP) and in Baluchistan, the National Awami Party (NAP) leader, Wali Khan, and the Jamiat-ul-'Ulama-i-Islam (JUI) leader, Maulana Mufti Mahmud had clear majorities. Consequently, in Baluchistan and in the NWFP, the NAP-JUI coalition governments were formed after the ban on these parties was lifted. Maulana Mufti Mahmud, the elected leader of the religio-political party, JUI, was nominated Chief Minister of the NWFP. This was a politically significant development. A traditional Islamic cleric had emerged as the Chief Executive of the tribal province of the NWFP.

But the political situation was greatly complicated. The NAP-JUI refused to join the central government as a subservient partner of Mr. Bhutto's PPP. Mr. Bhutto, in his anxiety to cushion his regime at the center against the NAP-JUI coalitions in the other two provinces, invited Mr. Khan Abdul Qayum Khan of the Convention Pakistan Muslim League, an arch opponent of the NAP-JUI in Baluchistan and the NWFP, to join him in the central government as a coalition partner and assigned the most important portfolio of Interior and Tribal Affairs to him. Perhaps Mr. Bhutto did so in order to use Mr. Khan Abdul Qayum Khan against Mr. Wali Khan as a political counter-poise. This was, in fact, a political blunder on the part of Mr. Bhutto, as it gave an initiative to Mr. Qayum Khan to generate and accentuate provincial/central government conflict in order to promote his political interests in those provinces where he had a fair degree of local influence. Thus, Mr. Qayum Khan was placed in a pivotal position to play Mr. Bhutto's PPP against the NAP-JUI in those provinces.

Another error of judgment committed by Mr. Bhutto was to have agreed with the NAP-JUI coalitions to have their own governors in these provinces so that he could nominate his own party men as governors in the provinces of Sind and the Punjab. Perhaps, his main objective was to use both the offices of the governors and the Chief Ministers for consolidating his party's political influence and authority in his provinces. But he had to pay the price of conceding the same privileges to the NAP-JUI in the provinces of Baluchistan and the NWFP so that they were in an equal position to consolidate their political authority in these provinces. However, this arrangement was, both in theory and in practice, inconsistent with the principles of federalism since it tended to disturb the precarious federal balance by aggravating the state/center conflict.

In theory, the governor of a province, besides acting as the nominal executive head of the provincial government was also to serve as an executive link with the federal authority insofar as he acted as its representative. Now, under the agreed arrangement, since both governors and the Chief Ministers belonged to the same ruling party of the provinces, the channel of executive linkage between the province and the federal authority was compromised as both acted in unison to promote their party interests in the provinces, and thus, for all practical purposes, the provincial governments were placed virtually in a position to flout the authority and jurisdiction of the federal government. These arrangements created anomalous situations in two ways. Firstly, Mr. Qayum Khan, as the Interior Minister of the federal government, did not lose any opportunity to ignite frictions and conflicts between the provincial governments and the federal authority, thereby accentuating the existing PPP/NAP-JUI political differences. This led to a sharpening and deepening of the federal crisis in Pakistan once again after the tragic debacle in the Eastern wing of the country in 1971. Secondly, the federal crisis was further aggravated in the sense that the PPP-dominated provinces of Sind and the Punjab were poised against Baluchistan and the NWFP under the NAP-JUI. This situation implied a twofold confrontation: firstly, a political one between the PPP and the NAP-JUI; and secondly, administrative friction between the provincial authorities of Baluchistan and the NWFP, and the federal government.

Subsequently, the death of the PPP leader in the NWFP, Mr. Hayat Mohammed Sherpao, as a result of a bomb explosion at the NAP-dominated campus of the Peshawar University deepened the federal crisis and provided a pretext for Mr. Bhutto to retaliate against the NAP by banning it. On the other hand, in the province of Baluchistan, the NAP-JUI government led by the Governor, Mr. Ghaus Bukhsh Bizenjo, and the Chief Minister, Atuallah Mengal, were accused of organizing a para-military militia which was being used against the PPP forces, particularly in the Las Bela District on the Mekran coast. Therefore, the NAP-JUI government was dismissed and was subsequently replaced by the PPP minority government. In sympathy with the dismissed NAP-JUI coalition government of Baluchistan, the Mufti government in the NWFP resigned as a token of protest. Thus, once again, the Pakistani political system was confronted with an acute federal crisis. Ever since, the province of Baluchistan has remained practically in a state of insurgency; the situation in the NWFP was also critical. In addition, Bhutto opted for a policy of military operations against the insurgents.[16] The Bhutto government initiated the Hyderabad Trials against the NAP leaders of the NWFP and Baluchistan, alleging that the banned NAP leaders were guilty of high treason against the state. These measures went a long way in precipitating politico-military confrontation between the smaller provinces of Baluchistan and the NWFP, and the Punjab and Sind. In fact, Bhutto's policy towards the NAP in Baluchistan and in the NWFP could ultimately prove fatal for Pakistan.

Insofar as the provinces of Sind and the Punjab were concerned, Mr. Bhutto treated them as merely administrative units. He controlled them both as party chairman and in his capacity as the Prime Minister of the central government. In Sind, Mr. Rasul Bukksh Talpur was removed as

Governor, and in the Punjab, both Governor Mustafa Khar and the Chief Minister, Hanif Ramay, were replaced by more docile and loyal party leaders. From these instances, once can draw a conclusion that Mr. Bhutto had utterly failed to create a healthy and balanced federal political system in Pakistan. It is indeed an irony of fate that a person of his accomplishments and educational background missed the great opportunity of rebuilding Pakistan into a viable democracy.

Mr. Bhutto and his associates from Sind in the central government gradually initiated policies which ultimately led to creating fissures between his home province and the Punjab. The government of Sind adopted the Sindhi language as the official language of the province. This occasioned language disturbances and ethnic tensions between Sindhis and non-Sindhis, including Indian migrants, and the Punjabi settlers in the province. As might have been expected, the language bill was introduced in the province with the active backing of the Bhutto government. However, the PPP Chief Minister of the Punjab, Mr. Mustafa Khar, took serious note of the language disturbances and sent a provincial delegation to Sind to assess the extent of losses to the Punjabi settlers.

In a separate, well calculated move, the Bhutto regime, in order to assuage the feelings of discontent prevalent among educated Sindhis, initiated a policy of lateral recruitment of civil servants through which many, Sindhis were recruited into different cadres of the civil services of Pakistan. This in turn caused discontent among non-Sindhi bureaucrats.

Mr. Bhutto further decided to resort to a large-scale screening of government officials, who were in many cases non-Sindhis. His talented cousin, Mr. Mumtaz Bhutto, took drastic action against many senior Punjabi officers of the Railways, Communications, and Shipping Agencies. He is also said to have engaged in providing exclusive patronage to the Sindhi militant youth organizations such as Jiye Sindh.[17]

Mr. Bhutto carefully purged the armed forces of Pakistan. As a result, many senior officers of the Army, Navy, and the Air Force were retired and replaced by hand-picked junior officers. Many of the senior officers were sent off on diplomatic assignments. This policy generated disaffection and frustration among the rank and file of the armed forces. One may only refer to an abortive *coup d'état* by some officers who were later court martialed.

Within the PPP, Mr. Bhutto consistently discouraged the democratic process and stifled dissent in order to consolidate his personal, autocratic leadership. He did not pay attention to the problems of reorganization within the PPP, and during the past years no party elections were ever held. Many sincere and devoted workers left the party in utter disgust and frustration. New, opportunistic elements were allowed to join the party ranks and were given key positions. Thus, the party organization remained in disarray.[18] At all levels, factionalism became rampant. The core of party leadership at all levels—provincial, district, and local—were engaged in a tussle for power. As a party leader, Mr. Bhutto failed to mediate intra-party feuds. He also failed to hold together ideologically disparate segments of his party, particularly the left and the right wings. Initially, perhaps, he was able to preserve the balance between the left and the right, but gradually he came to lean towards the right wing for support. As a result, he alienated the left wing. Confidently, from his place in the saddle of power, Mr. Bhutto did not hesitate to eliminate somewhat critical left wing leaders from the party ranks and consistently pursued a ruthless policy of persecuting them. The party's Secretary General, a former Indian civil servant, Mr. J.A.R. Rahim, one of the founding fathers of the PPP was subjected to humiliating treatment; Mr. Mairaj Mohammed Khan, a young labor leader from Karachi, whom Mr. Bhutto had acclaimed as his right-hand man, was imprisoned and tortured. At a later stage, Messrs. Khurshid Hasan Mir, Hanif Ramay, Dr. Mubashir Hasan, and Mustafa Khar of the Punjab PPP were forced out of the party. In his own province of Sind, he mistreated, humiliated, and threw out his Sindhi colleagues Rasul Bukksh Talpur and Ahmed Ali Talpur.

It was against this background of intra-party bickerings that a young lawyer from Kasur in the Punjab, Mr. Ahmad Raza Kasuri, fell out with Mr. Bhutto, and formed a one-man opposition within the PPP, turning into a vehement critic of the government on the floor of the National Assembly. Due to his continuous and loud criticism, Mr. Bhutto got fed up with him, and is alleged to have instructed Mr. Masood Mahmood, Director of the newly created para-military force known as the Federal Security Force, to eliminate this opponent within his own party ranks. Several attempts were made on Kasuri's life. Ultimately, in one such attempt, while Mr. Kasuri was returning by car from a marriage party in Lahore in the company of his father and other members of his family, he was ambushed and shot at. His father was killed although he himself was the alleged target. Mr. Kasuri filed his first information report with the police station and accused Mr. Bhutto of having plotted the whole incident. This case was suppressed during Bhutto's regime. However, it was the origin of the subsequent Bhutto Murder Trial after the July 5, 1977 military *coup d'etat* by General Zia-ul Haq.

The Bhutto Regime

Politics of "Revolutionary Reforms"

The almost five and a half years of the Bhutto era of Pakistan's political history will go down in the years to come as the most controversial ones. At this moment, the Pakistani nation is sharply divided into those who admire

and love Bhutto and those who hate and curse him. Therefore, it is difficult,
if not impossible at this juncture of emotional tension immediately after his
execution, to make an objective assessment of the failures and successes of the
Bhutto regime. However, it would not be far from wrong to observe that
Bhutto, with his mass-oriented PPP, his populist style of politics and
socialistic program, after assuming power in the wake of the dismemberment
of Pakistan, had launched a massive program of what he fondly called
"revolutionary reforms" in different walks of life—land tenure, economy,
society, and politics. To what extent these reforms were revolutionary may be
a valid subject for scholarly investigation by the future historians of Pakistan.
The other legitimate question for investigation would be to determine precisely
the nature, substance, and effects of his multi-dimensional reforms. This
would necessitate a thorough and critical analysis of the theory and practice of
these reformist measures.

One obvious conclusion that may be drawn from a very cursory review of
the Bhutto regime is the fact that most of these reforms were conceived in
great haste and without prior planning. It is true that at the time of preparing the Foundation Papers of the Pakistan Peoples Party, some of the salient
goals were debated and discussed in detail. Also at the time of preparing the
Election Manifesto, most of these issues were thrashed out. But it appears
that these early discussions were sketchy, vague, and therefore party goals
were couched in ambiguous language simply because Bhutto, in organizing
his party on broad-based support, was endeavoring to aggregate the conflicting interests and demands of the diverse elements of Pakistani society. It was
against this political background that Bhutto had adopted four basic principles as the ultimate slogans of his party:

1. Islam is our Faith
2. Democracy is our Polity
3. Socialism is our Economy
4. All power to the People

The major weakness of his reforms arose from the fact that they were
politically motivated rather than based on any firm ideological conviction.
Perhaps, it was for this reason that most of the reforms were conceived and
enforced on an *ad hoc* basis without a framework of any long range policy
goals. Quite early in his regime, on January 17, 1968 while addressing a Bar
Association meeting, Bhutto had aptly described the over-all objective of
organizing his new party: "Our task is to bring a general understanding
between all the parties of the left and of the right. The PPP can form a great
bridge, because we have come with a clean slate." Islamic socialism was
adopted as the goal of the party, but no effort was made to define its basic
principles, methods, and approach. Therefore, in adopting nationalization
measures, Bhutto was motivated by pure political considerations rather than
by a genuine sense of ideological commitment. How can we explain his

subsequent measures of nationalizing cotton ginning, rice husking, and flour mills? These measures were merely directed either to subdue or to eliminate the emergent entrepreneurs.

The methods employed by Bhutto to introduce large-scale reforms in Pakistani society, with its serious socio-economic and political cleavages, were neither rational nor sensible. At first, under the cover of martial law, major reforms were promulgated by martial law regulations, and were subsequently provided with constitutional protection. At a later stage, after the enforcement of the new Constitution of 1973, the reforms were introduced either by hasty legislation or by presidential ordinance. Thus, it may be noted that in promulgating and enforcing the reforms authoritarian tactics were used, whereas in a democratic society, fundamental changes through legislation are brought about by a process of consensus building. However, Bhutto, in promulgating basic reforms, had alienated the volatile urban middle classes, the newly emergent industrial elites, the religious elements, and the feudal lords who were the traditional power brokers. Thus, we do observe that Bhutto's reforms had ultimately brought about political polarization of the worst kind between the PPP and the Pakistan National Alliance (PNA), which was subsequently expressed in the form of mass agitation and violence organized by the PNA against the ruling PPP.

There are generally only two approaches to inducing social change in contemporary societies—either revolutionary communist models as in the Soviet Union and the People's Republic of China, or the British model of reform through legislation. In contrast with both of these models, in Pakistan, reforms have been generally introduced by authoritarian techniques of using either military sanctions, or bureaucratic power, or by manipulating legislatures, or by a combination of any of these methods. In the case of Bhutto, we do notice that he unscrupulously used all these tactics. Therefore, these reforms rested on very fragile grounds, and tended to generate forces of reaction and social tensions which could not be contained within an authoritarian political framework under the guise of constitutional democracy.

Apart from the faulty style and methods of Bhutto's "revolutionary reforms," there was also another inherent weakness of a substantive nature within these reforms insofar as Bhutto had utterly failed to anticipate and avert adverse social, economic, and political consequences of these measures. Therefore, these reforms ultimately exerted destabilizing effects on the politics, economy, and society of Pakistan, and nothing could be done about it. Consequently, these reforms tended to aggravate social discontent and class conflict which were subsequently expressed during the mass upheaval against the Bhutto regime immediately after the general elections of March 1977.

Another serious drawback of these reforms arose from ineffective and discriminatory implementation. For example, the two sets of major land reforms of 1972 and 1977 could not be implemented either in letter or in spirit. There were many instances where party colleagues were allowed to circumvent land reforms by using legal loopholes. These examples have been cited in the *White Papers*.

Most of the reforms introduced during the Bhutto regime may be broadly categorized into three major areas, namely, government and politics, economy, and society. Some of these reforms with far reaching consequences are discussed below.

Constitution

Perhaps by far the most spectacular achievement of the Bhutto era was the enactment of the Constitution of 1973 based on a broad consensus within the National Assembly as well as outside of it. After assuming power in 1972, Bhutto introduced an interim Constitution which was basically a rehash of the old Government of India Act of 1935. According to the *White Paper on the Performance of the Bhutto Regime*, "Mr. Bhutto continued to be the President and chief executive under a hybrid system which combined presidential rule at the centre with a parliamentary form of government in the Provinces."

However, within a year, a new Constitution was adopted by the National Assembly through a Constitutional Accord between the ruling and opposition parties. This constitution provided for Islamic, parliamentary, and federal structure. With the promulgation of the Constitution, Bhutto descended from the presidency to become the Prime Minister of Pakistan, and a senior PPP leader from the Punjab, Mr. Chaudhry Fazl Elahi, took over as the constitutional President. Perhaps, this could be regarded rightly as the major achievement of all political parties. However, Bhutto paid only lip service to the Constitution, as whenever political expedience required, he could amend the Constitution with his absolute majority in the National Assembly. There is substantial truth in the general accusation against him by the opposition leaders that the Constitution was never implemented in letter and spirit. For example, the Constitution provided for provincial autonomy, but Bhutto dealt with the provincial governments with highhandedness, as in the case of Baluchistan and the NWFP, mentioned earlier. It may not be wrong to observe that Bhutto completely ignored the Constitutional Accord, the real basis of the Constitution, and unilaterally amended it without consulting the opposition leaders. The *White Paper* rightly concludes, "Most of the amendments were introduced to meet the need of the regime for more and more arbitrary authority against the citizen, the opponents of the party in power and higher judiciary."[20]

The *White Paper*, itself, constitutes a monumental indictment of the Bhutto regime for the dictatorial manner in which the fundamental state institutions—the Parliament, the Executive, the Judiciary, and the Administration were treated by the ruling party.

Administration

In order to streamline public administration, the Administrative Reforms were announced on August 20, 1973. The traditional classification of civil servants was abolished, and a new unified graded structure offering equality of opportunity on the basis of professional and specialized competence was introduced. The system of lateral entry for professional and qualified persons from industry, trade, and other fields was initiated. A National Pay Commission was set up to review the existing pay structure. However, it may be observed that these reforms were not implemented in spirit. The lateral entry system turned into a spoils system, opening a Pandora's box for corruption, nepotism, and favoritism. The intended professionalization of bureaucracy could hardly be achieved. On the contrary, efforts were made to subdue, coerce, and politicize civil servants of Pakistan through screenings and large scale dismissals and subsequent recruitment of officials having party affiliations. These measures went a long way in demoralizing the bureaucracy and one could notice beneath the surface strong currents of resentment and discontent prevailing among the civil servants.

Economy: Industry

In the economic sector, major reforms were introduced in respect to industry, agriculture, land tenure, and labor. The ten basic industries—vegetable oil; steel and basic metals; heavy engineering; heavy electrical goods; fertilizers; automobiles, trucks, and tractors; petroleum refining; petrochemicals; heavy and basic chemicals; cements and public utilities like gas and electricity were nationalized. Subsequently, life insurance, banking, shipping, and petroleum distributing companies were also nationalized. The administration of these nationalized industries was placed under the newly created Management Boards and Councils manned by civil servants. The fourth volume of the *White Paper*, in a critical evaluation of these measures, observes, "no one could imagine execution of such an important measure in a cavalier fashion and without a debate in the parliament. Even the ruling party was not consulted on the details."[21]

Further, it maintains, "Subsequent experience provided clear evidence to support the view that the primary motivation for nationalization of industries was political in the narrowest sense of the word," perhaps, because "Nationalization of industries was intended to break the economic potential of any possible opposition." Consequently, the whole experiment backfired and the level of production sharply declined, and according to the *White Paper* assessment respecting Pakistan Valika Chemicals, Synthetic Chemicals, and Ravi Rayons, huge accumulated losses were incurred up to 1977-1978.

After the military take-over by General Zia-ul Haq, a Commission was appointed to review the functioning of the nationalized industries. The findings of the Commission provide authentic evidence regarding the deteriorating financial and physical performance of state enterprises. In conclusion, it may be observed that the policy of nationalization in a developing society may not be necessarily regarded as a magic palliative for all economic and social backwardness. In order to insure positive results, it may be essential to proceed cautiously and gradually towards nationalization of industries.

Agrarian Reforms

The *White Paper* (Vol. IV) in assessing the agrarian policies of the Bhutto regime observes that[22]

Agricultural production of major crops had been rising steadily throughout the sixties at an annual rate of 6.4 per cent . . . With the advent of the Bhutto government on the scene, however, there was a reversal of this trend and during the five year period ending June, 1977, performance of the agricultural sector was most disappointing

since

during the period 1972-73 to 1976-77 the growth rate came down to 2.0 per cent registering a decline in per capita agricultural production of about one per cent per annum.

The authors of the *White Paper* ascribe this decline to

a systematic weakening and in some cases destruction of institutions which were built over a period to support and help increase agricultural production.

With a view to accelerating agricultural production and stimulating modernization of cultivation, it was considered necessary to adopt genuine measures of land reform in order to achieve, within the shortest possible time, eradication of traditional feudalism. Earlier, half-hearted measures were adopted during the Ayub regime by reducing ceilings of landholdings. The Ayubian land reforms were regarded by Bhutto as merely fake, "a subterfuge" designed "to fool the people in the name of reform," and therefore, he visualized more radical measures to "effect the eradication of the curse of feudalism."[23]

In order to achieve this objective, Bhutto introduced reforms in two instalments. The first instalment of massive agrarian reforms was introduced in March 1972; the other was announced on the eve of the general elections in 1977. Under the first round of land reforms, the ceiling on individual holdings was reduced from 500 acres of irrigated land or 1000 acres of unirrigated land plus numerous generous exemptions, to 150 acres or 300 acres, respectively, plus only one exemption for tractors and tubewells. Under this reform, land was appropriated without compensation and given free to the tenants. Many other privileges were granted to the tenants. According to the second land reform program of 1977, the ceiling on individual land holding was reduced further from 150 acres of irrigated land and 300 acres of unirrigated land to 100 acres and 300 acres, respectively, on the basis of the price index units, and all exemptions to these ceilings were nullified. In addition, holdings up to 25 acres of irrigated and 50 acres of unirrigated land were exempted from agricultural taxation. Thus Bhutto claimed,[24] "In the past five years we have, through these measures, brought the end of feudalism in an orderly manner without the social convulsion experienced in other countries and with the considerable economic benefit to the nation as a whole." But it is this claim which has been seriously questioned by the authors of the *White Paper.* According to them, the findings of the Special Committee reviewing the whole range of land reforms revealed a different story. The *White Paper* observes:[25]

The Committee report brings out that largely for political considerations the implementation of the reform was tampered with to a degree as to make them ineffective. The reforms were largely vitiated by leakages in implementation, deliberate flouting of the law by influential landlords, mostly belonging to the ruling party otherwise favoured by those in power, and arbitrary application of the law to suit the political interests of the rulers or to carry out Mr. Bhutto's will.

In this connection, one may only refer to Donald Herring's paper on land reform included in this volume. In this painstaking scholarly article, Herring has provided us a critical review of the theory and practice of land reforms in Pakistan, with special reference to a more detailed analysis of land reforms of the Bhutto era. Admitting the soundness of the conceptual foundations of the land reforms, Herring points out the lapses in the implementation of ceilings and alterations of agrarian structure, and observes:[26]

When translated into law, the reform deviated somewhat from the principles of the election manifesto. The *de jure* ceilings was set at 150 acres of irrigated land (or equivalent) though the *de facto* ceiling (calculated in terms of Produce Index Units) was considerably higher, particularly for farmers who purchased tubewells or tractors to take advantage of the bonus provision. The relatively high ceiling would seem to be a political compromise in favour of "feudal" elites, but even so represented a significant reduction of Ayub's ceiling.

Herring also refers to many loopholes in respect to land transfer, evasions, and many other malpractices. Herring's evaluation, in fact, tends to confirm the findings of the Special Committee referred to above in the *White Paper.*

Banking and Insurance

In fulfillment of the PPP Manifesto (1970), life insurance was nationalized in 1972. Later, on January 1, 1974, the Government announced the nationalization of the banking sector with the exception of foreign banks.

Nationalization of banks was carried out without consulting the State Bank of Pakistan. Thus, the whole fabric of the banking system, including the State Bank, was brought under direct political control of the ruling party. The *White Paper* devotes a whole chapter to this, carefully scanning the range and degree of interference in the affairs of banks by the federal ministers, directly or through the intermediary of the Pakistan Banking Council, in respect to advances, credits, and appointments. Thus, the autonomy of the State Bank was seriously compromised. The *White Paper* gives some details of cases of nepotism in appointments, and manipulation in obtaining credit lines from banks for party influentials, loans to hotels, and granting agricultural credits to relatives of ministers. Similar serious irregularities have been pointed out in respect to ports and shipping, which were taken over by the Government on January 1, 1974.

In making an overall evaluation of the level of performance of the Bhutto regime, one may also refer to the recently published *White Paper,* volumes I[27] and II,[28] which have examined in great detail specific allegations against "Mr. Bhutto, his Family and Associates." Volume III[29] deals with numerous examples of "Misuse of the Instruments of State Power," such as state agencies like the Prime Minister's Secretariat, Cabinet Division, Outposts in the Provinces, Intelligence Bureau, and finally, the Federal Security Force to serve his personal and political ends. Bhutto has been charged with organizing the murders of political opponents, abduction and torture, organized violence and suppression. All volumes of the report highlight the despotic and fascist style of the Bhutto regime.

However, it may be only fair to observe that all these allegations and charges have been vehemently and persistently denied and refuted by Bhutto himself, in a series of rejoinders which he had written from his death cell at Kot Lakhpat Gaol. Reference may be made to two major documents:

1. his rejoinders to General Zia-ul Haq re: Constitutional Petition of Begum Nusrat Bhutto challenging the constitutionality of the military takeover and imposition of martial law by General Zia-ul Haq on July 5, 1977,[30] and

2. a 319 page statement[31] written by Mr. Bhutto in his appeal to the Supreme Court of Pakistan against the Lahore High Court Judgment condemning him to death in the murder trial.

In these statements, Bhutto has denied all charges against himself and his tenure in office as the Prime Minister, and has levelled counter-charges against the military regime of General Zia-ul Haq.

It is certain that in the years to come all these documents for and against Bhutto will be subjected to searching investigations by future historians and political analysts in order to sort out fact from fiction and truth from falsehood. However, despite all his weaknesses and faults, one fact stands out clearly—Bhutto was quite successful in the art of mass politics in Pakistan. He was a politician *par excellence*. He had, himself, observed quite early, writing for the *Pakistan Observer* of Dacca, dated January 12, 1976 on "My Debut in Journalism":[32]

It is politics above all that inspires and kindles in me the flame of a lasting romance. Politics is a superior science and a fine art . . . Too many people are understandably suspicious of politics. In many ways, the politicians have failed badly. Tragically, we have played politics with politics. We have soiled a great art. No longer people will repose confidence in politicians who exploit their sentiments and abandon principles at the wink of favours.

General Elections of March 7, 1977

After consolidating his party rule during the five year period, 1972-1977, Bhutto took the most momentous decision of his political career regarding holding general elections. The National Assembly was dissolved on January 10, 1977, and thereafter, Bhutto announced the dates of general elections—March 7, 1977 for the National Assembly and March 10, 1977 for the provincial assemblies. This came as a big surprise because the term of the National Assembly was due to expire on August 14, 1977. Two months were assigned for the election campaigns. Perhaps the decision to hold early elections was taken by Bhutto on the faulty assumption that the ideologically disparate political parties belonging to the Opposition would never unite to form a united front against his Pakistan Peoples Party. However, perhaps, it came as a rude shock to him when shortly after the announcement of the election dates, all the opposition parties formed a grand anti-Bhutto coalition known as the Pakistan National Alliance which was composed of nine political parties.

After hectic national campaigning, the elections were held as scheduled on March 7, 1977. The announcement of the election results stunned the opposition leaders because against all their assessment and calculations the PPP received a landslide victory, obtaining an absolute majority of 155 in a house of 200, leaving only 36 seats to the Pakistan National Alliance.[33] The detailed analysis of the background, election campaign, issues, and all other aspects of the March elections have been covered quite extensively by Sharif al-Mujahid in his article on elections included in this volume and, therefore, it is not necessary to dilate upon the elections here. However, al-Mujahid could not cover all the materials contained in the *Government White Paper on the Conduct of the General Elections in March, 1977*,[34] as it was issued after his paper was delivered. The *White Paper* is a bulky document with its substantive part covering 405 pages plus 1044 pages of annexures establishing the allegation of the Pakistan National Alliance that Bhutto had, himself, masterminded election rigging on a massive scale. Therefore, it may be appropriate to reproduce some of its salient findings on the question of election rigging as a necessary supplement to Sharif al-Mujahid's treatment of the March 1977 elections.

The *White Paper* treats the subject matter of election rigging under ten separate chapters and a brief epilogue. Some of its conclusions may be summed up as follows:

1. At first, in its chapter on "Blue Print," the *White Paper* uncovers, through a minute examination of documentary evidence, a premeditated plot meticulously prepared by Bhutto and his aides in the Prime Minister's Secretariat. They had prepared a Model Election Plan which was also known as the Larkana Plan. The sole purpose of this exercise was to insure the electoral victory of the PPP.

2. In its chapter on "Election Commission," the authors of the *White Paper* have tried to establish that Bhutto's efforts were directed toward control of the Election Commission so that his party could manipulate large-scale rigging in the elections.

3. The *White Paper* further asserts, on the basis of specific examples, how Bhutto manipulated the "Delimitation of Constituencies" in favor of his party's candidates.

4. The other important finding of the *White Paper* was the fact that Bhutto successfully employed members of the civil bureaucracy to the advantage of his party candidates.

5. The section on "The Mobility Factor" sharply focuses on the careful planning for providing transportation to the polls by utilizing all resources of government agencies.

6. In a chapter on "Image Making," the *White Paper* unfolds the manner in which propaganda and publicity agencies of the government were employed for election purposes according to a preplanned scheme.

7. In another section on "Election Funds," the *White Paper* points out how Bhutto received large sums of money from a foreign head of state and how he diverted the State's Secret Service funds for party purposes.

All these and other allegations were denied by Bhutto in his 319 page typewritten statement which was smuggled out of Pakistan for subsequent publication. In this document Bhutto tries to establish his counter-charges that he was made a target of an international conspiracy.

After the general elections were over, the Pakistan National Alliance mounted a nationwide movement against Bhutto and his party demanding dismissal of his government by alleging that it was illegal and demanding the holding of fresh elections under the supervision of the armed forces and the judiciary. Gradually, the movement picked up momentum in most of the urban centers of Pakistan. The Army was called in, and major cities were brought under martial law. Large numbers of people were killed, wounded, or thrown into gaols. All efforts to quell the mass upheaval failed, and Bhutto had to yield to open negotiations with the PNA leaders through the good offices of the Saudi Ambassador in Pakistan. The protracted negotiations continued until July 4, 1977 with no signs of any political settlement. It almost appeared that the country was on the verge of a bloody civil war. Therefore, against this background, General Zia-ul Haq took over the reins of government by dislodging Bhutto and his associates on July 5, 1977. This brought to an end the Bhutto era of Pakistan's political history.

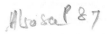

VII

The General Zia-ul Haq Regime

Accountability and Islamic Revival

General Zia-ul Haq, Chief of Staff of the Army of Pakistan, through a bloodless *coup d'état* on July 5, 1977 toppled the Bhutto government at Islamabad and imposed martial law throughout the country. In justifying his action, General Zia, in his address to the nation, asserted:[35]

When the political leaders failed to rescue the country out of a crisis, it is an inexcusable sin for the armed forces to sit as silent spectators, it is primarily for this reason that the army had to intervene to save the country.

Further stating his limited objective of military intervention, General Zia said emphatically,[36]

I want to make it absolutely clear that neither I have any political ambition nor does the army want to be detracted from its profession of soldiering. I was obliged to step in to fill in the vacuum created by the political leaders. I have accepted this challenge as a true soldier of Islam. My sole aim is to organize a free and fair election which would be held in October this year.

General Zia became the Chief Martial Law Administrator (CMLA) and the administration of the country was placed under the Supreme Council of military leaders. However, the Constitution of 1973 was not abrogated, but for the time being, some of its provisions were suspended. Choudhry Fazl Elahi, the President, remained in office, thus providing the much needed legal and constitutional continuity. On assuming power, General Zia made it absolutely clear that the primary object of martial law in the country was to hold elections within ninety days, and restore constitutional democracy. He had also promised strict neutrality of the armed forces towards national politics. In the article contributed by William L. Richter, "From Electoral Politics to Martial Law" which analyzes the background of the military take-over on July 5, 1977, the writer has aptly observed,[37]

Paradoxically, the "consolidating" elections had led to the deconsolidation of Bhutto's regime; the "popular leader"—Quaid-e-Awam as he styled himself—had been weakened by a popular movement and displaced by an army he had assiduously attempted to contain and bring under civilian control.

According to the proclamation issued by Chief Martial Law Administrator General Zia-ul Haq, the Prime Minister and his colleagues were dismissed, and the National Assembly, the Senate, and the Provincial Assemblies were dissolved, and other necessary measures were promulgated. The deposed Prime Minister and some of his colleagues were taken into protective custody. Likewise, all prominent leaders of the PNA were also taken into custody.[38] On July 14, once again, General Zia reiterated his resolve to hold fair and free elections and promised no action against the politicians.

On General Zia's instruction, Pakistan International Airlines chief, Air Marshal (Rtd.) Nur Khan met with Bhutto and with PNA leaders in Murree on July 13. On receiving encouraging reports from him, General Zia dashed to Murree to meet all the detained leaders personally.[39] Thus, it appears that events were moving in the right direction and consequently, all political leaders were released on July 28 and electioneering started with full swing.[40]

After release, Mr. Bhutto and his colleagues came under heavy attack from different quarters, including news media and opposition parties. Rumors were afloat about his likely arrest before the elections. However, Bhutto had his second meeting with General Zia on August 28, 1977.[41] Soon thereafter, on September 3, 1977, Bhutto was arrested in connection with the 1974 murder of Mr. Ahmad Raza Kasuri's father.[42] Along with this, numerous legal cases were instituted against Bhutto and his colleagues. Thus, this phase of the martial law regime may rightly be described as a period of legal confrontation. It was against this background that the elections were postponed for an indefinite period of time until the process of accountability would come to an end.

The high-water mark of this phase of legal confrontation came at the time when Begum Nusrat Bhutto, wife of the former Prime Minister, filed her petition before the Supreme Court of Pakistan under Article 184 (3) of the Constitution of 1973 challenging the constitutionality of General Zia's military *coup d'état*[43] and all his subsequent actions including Martial Law Order 12 detaining Mr. Bhutto and his colleagues. This case will go down in the judicial history of Pakistan as one of the most important. The Constitutional Petition was admitted for regular hearing on September 25.[44] Mr. Yahya Bakhtiar, the counsel for Begum Bhutto, in expounding his views strongly pleaded that the imposition of martial law by General Zia was a grave violation of the constitutional stipulations, that it was an act of brazen usurpation, and was treasonable.

During the hearings on this case, frequent references were made to the earlier Dosso case which was overruled subsequently in the Asma Jilani case by the Supreme Court.[45] According to Mr. A.K. Brohi, counsel for the Federation, the Dosso case could be applicable insofar as in essentials it laid down that "'successful revolution' created a new law-giving factor." In this connection, Mr. Brohi also defended the military *coup d'état* on the basis of Hans Kelsen's doctrine of "revolutionary legalism," which holds that revolution creates its own legal order. Mr. Bakhtiar, however, based his arguments on the precedents established in the Asma Jilani case and the provisions of the Constitution of 1973, which had clearly left no scope for military take-over. At a later stage, on behalf of the Federation, Mr. Sharifuddin Pirzada, subsequently appointed Attorney General, justified the military coup of July 5 and the subsequent actions of the CMLA on the grounds of the doctrine of necessity. After a prolonged hair-splitting debate over the question of constitutionality of the martial law regime, finally the Supreme Court gave its verdict dismissing the petition of Begum Bhutto and upholding the act of imposition of martial law, while partially suspending the Constitution on the grounds of the doctrine of necessity, but at the same time giving directives to the CMLA to arrange for the early holding of elections.

Accountability

In the initial phase, General Zia and his colleagues were preoccupied with the task of organizing the general elections in fulfillment of their promise to restore constitutional democracy. They even showed respect to Bhutto and also seemed to believe that ultimately the PPP might get elected as a majority party. However, this attitude of respect and conciliation gradually gave way to a more aggressive stance by the military regime towards Bhutto, his associates, and party. Most probably it was in reaction to Bhutto's intransigence. It appears that Bhutto and his associates were reluctant to cooperate with the military regime and preferred to go on the war path. Meanwhile, General Zia and his colleagues discovered a huge mass of documentary evidence against the excesses of the Bhutto regime. Therefore, the elections were postponed,[46] and the process of accountability of the old regime was initiated in deference to the general demand by the opposition leaders. In this connection, several steps were taken by the regime:

1. General Zia proceeded to set up special military tribunals composed of judges and military officers for trying members of the Bhutto regime. Many of Bhutto's party men and former ministers were, as a result of these trials, disqualified and punished.

2. A Special Tribunal headed by Justice Shafi-ur-Rahman of the Lahore

High Court was instituted to investigate all specific charges of corruption, abuse of power, and misuse of government funds against the deposed Prime Minister, Bhutto.

3. In addition, several investigative committees were charged with the responsibility of preparing a series of *White Papers* regarding the Bhutto regime. So far, six volumes of these *White Papers* have been released by the Government. These *White Papers* focus on the "Conduct of General Elections," "Misuse of Media," the personal conduct of "Mr. Z.A. Bhutto, his Family and Associates," "Treatment of Fundamental State Institutions," "Misuse of the Instruments of State Power," and an assessment of "The Economy" during the Bhutto regime. The findings of these *White Papers* have already been referred to in an earlier section in greater detail.

4. A murder trial of Mr. Bhutto was reopened in the Lahore High Court. The murder trial, itself, was the most spectacular event of General Zia's regime up to that time, therefore, it may not be out of place to sum up the trial which led to the tragic end of the most eventful political career of Mr. Zulfikar Ali Bhutto.

A reference has already been made in an earlier section to this criminal case against the deposed Prime Minister during his regime. We had noted that the case was filed, and the report of Justice Shafi-ur-Rahman on the case was suppressed. After the military take-over by General Zia, the accused, Messrs. Zulfikar Ali Bhutto, Mian Mohammed Abbas, and Ghulam Mustafa, and others were challenged by the Federal Investigation Agency for conspiracy to assassinate; for assault against Ahmad Raza Kasuri, Member of the National Assembly, a vehement opponent of the deposed Prime Minister, on the night of November 10-11, 1974 in the city of Lahore. The deposed Prime Minister was arrested on September 3, and released on bail on September 13. However, on October 10, his bail was cancelled by order of the Lahore High Court, and the hearing of the murder trial began. It dragged on until March 8, 1978 when finally the Lahore High Court gave its judgement.[47] Mr. Maulvi Mushtaq Hussain, the Chief Justice of the Lahore High Court, in a 134 page unanimous judgment concluded,[48] "All the offenses with which the accused are charged are thus proved to the hilt." Therefore, the Chief Justice pronounced conviction of the principal accused, Mr. Bhutto, and the others under relevant sections of the Pakistan Penal Code, and passed death sentence on all five accused in the trial. The team of lawyers led by Mr. Yahya Bakhtiar, former Attorney General of Pakistan, filed an appeal on behalf of Mr. Bhutto before the Supreme Court of Pakistan, the highest judicial body of the country. After a seven month hearing, the Supreme Court, on Tuesday, February 6, 1979, in a majority opinion, dismissed the appeals of Z.A. Bhutto and the others, and upheld the unanimous judgment of the Lahore High Court. The main judgment, written by the Chief Justice, covered 825 pages. The other three judges agreed. The dissenting judgments were given separately by two other judges, and the third judge agreed with them. Mr. Anwarul Huq, the Chief Justice, observed on the question[49] of sentence that

the facts which had been proved beyond any doubt established that Bhutto used the apparatus of the Government namely, the agency of the Federal Security Force for a political vendetta. This was a diabolical misuse of the instruments of state power as the head of the administration. Instead of safeguarding the life and liberty of the citizens of Pakistan, he set about to destroy a political opponent by using the power of the Federal Security Force, whose Director-General occupied a special position under him. Ahmad Raza Kasuri was pursued relentlessly in Islamabad and Lahore until finally his father became the victim of the conspiracy, and Ahmad Raza Kasuri miraculously escaped. The power of the Prime Minister was then used to stifle proper investigation, and after to pressurize Ahmad Raza Kasuri in rejoining the Pakistan Peoples Party.

In upholding the Lahore High Court Judgment, the majority judgment of the Supreme Court further concluded,

In these circumstances there is absolutely no support for the contention that the present case was politically motivated, or was the result of international conspiracy. The case having been registered almost three years before the ouster of the appellant from power, and a clear indication being available as to the possible identity of assailants not only in the kind of ammunition used in both incidents, but also in the Report of the Shafi-ur-Rahman Tribunal, the investigation was deliberately allowed to be stultified. It is, therefore, futile to urge that the prosecution of the appellant is politically motivated, or a result of international conspiracy.[50]

In his dissenting judgment, spread over 441 pages, Mr. Justice G. Safdar Shah expressed the view that certain statements of Masood Mahmood were in the nature of hearsay and were not admissible as evidence. Secondly, this approver (state witness) was not reliable. Therefore, he concluded that he was convinced that the case had not been proved to the hilt by the prosecution. Accordingly, in his view, the prosecution had failed to prove the existence of a criminal conspiracy between Zulfikar Ali Bhutto and Masood Mahmood. Therefore, he concluded that the prosecution had failed to prove the case against Bhutto and Mian Abbas, and the conviction against them should be set aside.[51] In an independent judgment given by Mr. Justice Dorab Patel, disagreeing with the majority opinion, he maintained that neither the existence of a conspiracy between Bhutto and Masood Mahmood could be established, nor could the evidence of Masood Mahmood be accepted, as he was not a reliable witness.

The whole nation and the world at large had been in a state of suspense for many months over the fate of the deposed Prime Minister of Pakistan. The confirmation of the death sentence by majority decision of the Supreme Court almost stunned the world. Pressures for clemency came from most of the heads of states and governments, including those of the super-powers and the United Nations' Secretary-General Kurt Waldheim, as well as from within Pakistan. But General Zia, in keeping with his word, preferred to set an example in pursuance of the Islamic principles of justice by ordering Bhutto's execution. According to General Zia-ul Haq, the rule of law should apply equally to all, whether high or low.[52] At this moment, it is premature to make any observation concerning the possible political repercussions of the historic execution of Zulfikar Ali Bhutto. But in general, there has not been any widespread agitation or cases of violence except for a few sporadic instances here and there.

To what extent, if any, Bhutto's execution may influence the outcome of the forthcoming general elections scheduled for November 17, 1979, it is difficult to assess. But one thing seems to be quite evident. The Pakistan Peoples Party happens to be in the grip of a major leadership crisis. The political void caused by the exit of its charismatic leader can hardly be filled by any other party leader. At the moment, the party, its organization, leadership, and ideology have been thrown into a vortex of confusion, frustration, and uncertainty. Perhaps, some of the devoted workers of the party may still be willing to pull together the muscles of the party under the leadership of Begum Nusrat Bhutto, or Banazir Bhutto, or even Murtaza Bhutto. However, it is doubtful if all the groups of the PPP would be willing to work under their leadership. It is also likely that the PPP may join hands with other like-minded political parties in order to form an electoral coalition. If such a coalition is formed on a broad political spectrum, it may pose a serious challenge to other political groups in the country, as Bhutto's execution will continue to be the major focus of the election campaign.

Islamization

Since the establishment of Pakistan, there had been a growing popular demand for incorporating Islamic principles into the Constitution and for the Islamization of laws and society. The Constitutions of 1956, 1962, and 1973 all have provided Islamic foundations. At the same time, with the exception of a few minor political groups with secular orientations, almost all parties do agree and recognize that in spite of their mutual differences regarding details, there is an urgent need for the reconstruction of Pakistani society on the basis of Islamic ideology. This universal consensus is itself a unique achievement of the past thirty years. However, if we examine in detail the policies of past regimes, we would, of course, discern a changing pattern of policy orientation toward the implementation of Islamic ideology. These differences of orientation arise from the diversities of social background, economic status, and educational credentials of the ruling elites. The secularists, educated in Western institutions, brought up in the upper strata of society, although they form a minor segment, have always insisted on building Pakistan on European models. The liberal reformists, constituting the bulk of the ruling elites, have endeavored to bring about a synthesis between European traditions and Islamic principles. On the other hand, the traditionalists and fundamentalists from among the middle and lower classes have demanded a return to the pure Islamic societal ideal. Muslim League leaders, during 1947-1954 were anxious to evolve a synthetic model the bureaucrats and military generals of this period were less enthusiastic about Islamization, and therefore, adopted a policy of using Islam as a religious symbolism for the purpose of mass mobilization in support of their policies of modernization, as they did during 1955-1971. However, since 1970 the thrust towards Islam had been eroding as new political parties with socialist orientations gained electoral support. The emergence of the Pakistan Peoples Party under the leadership of Zulfikar Ali Bhutto in the western wing, and the Awami League of Sheikh Mujibur Rahman in the eastern wing (formerly East Pakistan, now Bangladesh) had shifted public attention from Islam to socialism. Therefore, their policy was geared to Islamic ideology for symbolic purposes only, and some of their ideologues had evolved what came to be popularly called "Islamic socialism." But during these successive periods of Pakistan's political history, the votaries of the Islamic ideology of traditional and fundamentalist orientations, such as Jamaat-e-Islami, Jamiat-ul-'Ulama-e-Islam, and later, Jamiat-ul-'Ulama-e-Pakistan and other such groups have been engaged in educating the rural masses and the urban middle class through the traditional channels of mosques, preaching, literature, and training. Throughout these past years, they have exerted both positive and negative influences over the ruling elites in preserving the ideals of an Islamic state as live and active forces in national politics.

During the period of constitution-making (1947-1956) it was due to their political pressure that the basic principles of Islam were incorporated into the Constitution of 1956. Similarly, during 1958-1969, they continued to keep the Ayub regime under constant pressure to reassert the Islamic principles which were diluted in the Constitution of 1962. And lastly, during the Yahya regime and subsequently during the Bhutto regime, too, they acted successfully as agents of political pressure for retaining Islamic ideology. But all this while they never had the opportunity of securing enough electoral support to capture political power in order to utilize state authority in implementing Islamic ideology in its true spirit. Lately, they have been successful in mobilizing mass support for Islamic ideology, particularly during the post-election anti-Bhutto mass upheavals. The Pakistan National Alliance, the anti-Bhutto front, during their agitation against the Bhutto regime, had sharply focussed on what is popularly called "Nizam-e-Mustafa" (Prophetic Order) as a positive political slogan. Due to the failures of the successive ruling elites of the past to solve the basic social, economic, and political problems of the people, there were widespread feelings of disenchantment, frustration, and disaffection against the slogans of modernization, westernization, capitalism, and socialism. Therefore, it was against this background that the people have turned their attention towards Islamic ideology and the 'ulama, as its custodians, for leadership. Among the military elites as well, a new generation of officers with a conservative religious bias have emerged in the top hierarchy. General Zia and his colleagues belong to this generation. Thus, we do notice that General Zia is sharply different from his predecessors like Sandhurst-trained Field Marshal Mohammed Ayub Khan or General Yahya Khan. He is known to be a devout and pious Muslim in his everyday life. This also explains the identity of outlook, behavior, and ideology among the present military elite and the leaders of the Pakistan National Alliance.

After the postponement of the elections in October 1977, the PNA welcomed the offer made by General Zia to join him in helping to form a civilian government at Islamabad. In fact, according to their own pronouncements, they had joined the government with the specific purpose of insuring an early introduction of "Nizam-e-Mustafa" in the country, as well as for securing a final but firm date for holding the general elections. This is why, as the process of accountability led to the execution of Bhutto, and after General Zia had announced the introduction of Islamic measures and declared November 17, 1979 as the date for holding general elections, that the PNA cabinet decided to withdraw from the government in order to prepare themselves for these elections. At present, a new cabinet composed of both civilians and military officers has been sworn into office.

Perhaps the first measure towards Islamization was taken when it was decided to introduce separate electorates as the basis of the forthcoming elections. According to this system, voters belonging to different religious persuasions were to exercise their franchise only for their own candidates. For this, a constitutional amendment was introduced. Some political parties have not approved of this idea.

The next step in the direction of Islamization was taken on December 2, 1978 (the first day of the hijri [Muslim] year 1399) when General Zia, in his address to the nation, announced measures to enforce Nizam-e-Islam (Islam Order).[53]

1. Directives were issued to government departments to arrange for the offering of prayers during office hours and enjoining respective departmental heads to lead the prayers, or at least to join in the prayers, themselves.

2. Similarly, people were enjoined to say their Friday prayers, and for the period of prayers, all shops and business centers were obliged to close.

3. In respect to public laws, General Zia announced that steps were being taken to revive the Islamic institutions of Zakat (poor tax) and Ushr

(tax on agricultural produce). A committee was set up to examine all aspects of these institutions, and to submit their recommendations.

4. Another important measure for Islamization of Pakistan's economic system was the early abolition of "the curse of usury" and as a beginning towards this end, it was decided that 1. no interest would be charged on advances from government sources for buying bicycles; 2. no interest would be charged on loans to government servants from grades 1 to 15 (excluding grades 16 to 23) for house building; and 3. National Investment Trust would, as its future strategy, make investments on the basis of equity participation and not on the basis of interest.

5. According to General Zia's announcement, immediate steps were being taken to set up, in addition to present courts, a Sharia Appeal Bench at the Supreme Court level. There would be no court fees for filing an application with the Sharia Bench. Each Bench would be composed of competent 'ulama (religious scholars) and lawyers. The decisions of these Benches could not be challanged in the Supreme Court, the High Court, or in any other Courts.

6. The latest announcement of the second instalment of Islamization was made by General Zia in his address to the Nation on February 10, 1979 (birthday of the Holy Prophet):

(a) The new measures included detailed arrangements for the organization of the collection of Zakat and Ushr, and its proper utilization. These regulations will not apply to non-Muslims. The Zakat Fund was instituted with an initial capital of Rs. 2250 millions in addition to generous donations from Saudi Arabia and the United Arab Emirates. For the purposes of collection and the proper utilization of Zakat, local, provincial, and central accounts will be opened, and at the local level, the matter will be entrusted to the local bodies, after election to such bodies are completed. For the administration of provincial and central accounts, a Provincial Zakat Council and a Central Zakat Council will be set up.

(b) In respect to the policy of nationalization, General Zia, referring to Islamic Injunctions observed, "There were many factors responsible for the wrecking of national economy. The policy of nationalization which was applied indiscriminately also played a major role in it. Islam confers the rights to possess property both on the citizen and the state. The public and private sectors are wheels of the same cart. Unless the two wheels move in unison, the nation cannot move towards progress and development."[54] In view of such an Islamic philosophy, according to General Zia, "The present government has, therefore, adopted several measures to motivate the private sector to play its due role in the national economy. But certain industrialists still apprehend that the present or the future government may nationalize their properties without any justification or compensation. To allay these fears, we are giving them a constitutional safeguard, which is being announced today. It is being guaranteed that in future no industrial concern would be nationalized without appropriate compensation."[55]

(c) The other important aspect of Islamic economy aims at elimination of "the curse of interest," and therefore, General Zia announced certain measures as modest beginnings towards the achievement of this goal. From the next fiscal year, The House Building Finance Corporation will provide assistance on the basis of sharing of income accruing from rent in the cases of houses having not more than 2250 square feet, and the maximum ceiling of a loan will be 100,000 rupees. Similarly, the National Investment Trust, and the Investment Corporation of Pakistan will operate on an equity basis instead of charging interest. These measures will ultimately lead to the development of interestless banking system, and interestless economy.

(d) General Zia also announced certain important measures concerning "the punitive aspect which form part of the Islamic code of life." The Islamic punishments, technically known as "Hudud" are prescribed distinctly for only four kinds of offenses, namely; drinking, adultery, theft, and imputation of adultery (Qazf). Total prohibition was enforced except for non-Muslims for purposes of religious ceremonies, and for foreigners within the confines of their embassies and residences. At the same time, the manufacture, possession, purchase or sale, and import or export of alcohol has also been prohibited. Similarly, other offenses were also declared punishable. Islamic punishments have been enforced for these offenses as a deterrent.

(e) In order to insure effective enforcement of these measures, it is naturally necessary to provide for an efficient system of enforcement. Thus, certain important measures were announced for reeducating the police in the light of Islamic teachings, the country's constitution and laws. For this purpose a comprehensive code of ethics has been formulated. Among related reforms, it has been provided that in the future, prosecution of criminal cases will not be the responsibility of the police, but will be entrusted to an autonomous body.

(f) For the purpose of simplifying the process of law, a Law Commission has been appointed. Also provision has been made to establish a Faculty of Sharia (Islamic law) at the Quaid-e-Azam University in Islamabad for both teaching and research.

(g) The Council of Islamic Ideology has been made an autonomous body, and it has been entrusted with the task of examining all aspects of Islamization of law and society.

(h) The Islamic Research Institute has been entrusted with the task of conducting research in Islam.

(i) In consonance with the new educational policy, steps have been taken to revise textbooks, and replace English by Urdu as the medium of instruction from next year onward. At the same time, the mass communication media has been projecting a definite Islamic viewpoint.

Thus it may be noted, in the light of the massive program of Islamization initiated by General Zia, that this constitutes the cornerstone of his policy.[56] Also, it is fairly evident that the present military leaders have successfully launched their program of Islamic revival in Pakistan for two basic reasons. Firstly, the 'ulama, and all other opposition parties had created a general public demand for an Islamic Order during the election campaign of 1977 and subsequently during the mass upheaval in the country. Secondly, they have also been inspired by the global resurgence of Islam, particularly since it appears that Saudi Arabia and the Gulf states have also encouraged interest in the Islamic revival movement. But at the same time, it may be fair to say that fundamentally, their concern for Islamization arises from their deep faith in the Islamic ideology.

Toward Democracy

At present, General Zia has a new cabinet which has replaced the former civilian cabinet of the PNA. It is composed of competent generals, civilians, and technocrats. The basic purpose of this cabinet is to undertake the great responsibility of preparing the ground rules for the forthcoming elections on November 17, 1979 and to conduct these elections with utmost fairness and impartiality. On a number of occasions, General Zia has reiterated that the elections will be held on time, as scheduled. However, it appears that before elections are held, General Zia is anxious to ensure positive results. For this purpose, he has recently initiated a dialogue with political leaders to clarify some very fundamental issues:

1. Firstly, the present military leaders are of the view that the elections of local bodies should be held before the general elections in the month of November because democracy can be built only from the grass roots level. They have already announced restoration of the three-tier system of local self-government. But at the same time they have made it abundantly clear that this does not imply restoration of the Ayubian system of Basic Democracy and would not serve as an electoral college. The general response of the political leaders has been consistently negative, although, there have been some voices heard in its favor during General Zia's visit to Baluchistan. In order to agree on a common program, it has been suggested that a Roundtable Conference be held. This suggestion, too, has been received coolly in political circles.

2. The generals have expressed their opinion that the present constitution needs an amendment in order to provide for a better balance of powers between the President and the Prime Minister. The political leaders seem to agree with their view, but they are of the opinion that any amendments should be left for the elected parliament to decide, and that before the election is held, no

amendment should be made lest it may open a Pandora's Box for other amendments such as one on the provincial autonomy question.

3. General Zia and his colleagues have expressed their opinions in favor of providing a constitutional role for the Armed Forces. This, again, is a highly controversial issue.

In dealing with these questions, it may be of vital importance to adopt a final course of action through a process of consultation with political leaders. Perhaps, it may be more advisable to broaden further the scope of political discussions so as to cover the whole range of problematic issues which have perennially marred the political evolution of Pakistan since its birth in 1947. In order to to do so, one has to identify the basic issues, analyze them in their true historical perspective, so that one may proceed cautiously towards finding permanent solutions. It appears that the most vital aspects which deserve immediate attention are the following:

1. How does Pakistan propose to reconstruct the existing political structure in order to avoid recurring "federal crises"?

2. How can the constitution be restructured to ensure the steady growth of democratic institutions?

3. What constitutional measures should be adopted to ensure development of a balanced party system?

Federalism

A federal system, defined politically as a power-sharing arrangement, and constitutionally as a union of fully autonomous federating units, can work effectively only in a multi-unit federal society such as the U.S.A., the U.S.S.R. or Australia, for examples. But in Pakistan so far, federal experiments have miserably failed to contain the opposing forces of regionalism and nationalism. Consequently, during the past thirty years, Pakistan's federal system has failed to achieve its balance because it has been torn asunder by the polarities of extreme centralization and peripheralization.[57] One of the basic reasons for its failure arises from the fact that most of its constituent federating units are artificial creations from colonial days. Secondly, these units lack inner balance due to differences in size, resources, population, and level of socioeconomic developments. Thirdly, during 1955-1969, the bipolar federal structure generated federal-provincial conflict which was fraught with the potentiality of secession. Therefore, in the light of the past experience, in order to provide for guarantee against federal crises, it may be suggested that the existing provincial boundaries should be redrawn so that the existing unequal units are transformed into a genuinely multi-polar federal structure with units of approximately equal weight. With a view toward achieving this objective, the following suggestions may be considered:

1. A high powered Commission should be set up to recommend redistributing existing provinces on the basis of language, socio-economic characteristics, and administrative requirements.

2. To achieve this end, the existing units may be broken up to constitute ten units: the Punjab, 2 or 3 the North West Frontier Province, 2; Baluchistan, 2; Sind, 2; and Kashmir, 1.

3. The Senate should be constituted on the basis of principle of equal representation, and the lower house on the basis of population. In certain specified matters, the Senate and the Assembly should share equal powers.

4. The provincial governors, nominated on non-party basis, should always be responsible to the President.

5. Matters of exclusively provincial concern should be left to the jurisdiction of the provinces, and all subjects of exclusively national concern should be assigned to the federal authority.

6. An Inter-provincial Coordination Council should be created for the management of matters of inter-provincial concerns.

7. In addition, a Federal-provincial Council should be created to review revenue allocations, grants, and aids, and to oversee planning and development.

8. Both provincial and national languages should be made compulsory in schools.

Democracy

General Zia's concern for balancing the powers of the President and the Prime Minister seems to be quite valid in the light of past experience. Pakistan has not been able to achieve this desired balance because it had inherited a hybrid constitutional system through the Government of India Act of 1935 which was vice-regal in its nature, and after 1947, this Act was adopted as a model for constitution-making purposes. Therefore, either there were too strong Prime Ministers, or autocratic Presidents. Therefore, the following suggestions are submitted for consideration:

1. In order to achieve a balance, the method of electing the President is of great importance. This could be done by either of the following ways:

    a. the President is directly elected on a non-party basis; or

    b. is indirectly elected by members of the National and the Provincial Assemblies, or

    c. is indirectly elected by a specially constituted electoral college.

2. The President should have sufficient powers to act as a constitutional umpire rather than merely as a figurehead;

3. The President should be invested with "emergency powers" for a specific period of time and under specified conditions, to be approved subsequently by the National Assembly;

4. He should also be invested with authority of exercising his discretion to determine who commands the confidence of the majority of the house—that is to say, who should become the Prime Minister;

5. He should be given powers to dissolve the National Assembly in case of crisis or whenever there is no majority party leader to form a government; and;

6. He may be provided with powers *to call the Armed Forces* to step in during periods of constitutional crises, in order to conduct elections within a definite time-limit.

Party System

The failure of democratic process in Pakistan may well be ascribed to the lack of a stable party system. The party system has suffered from two basic faults—(i) it has been invariably 'personality' oriented, and hence, failed to become institutionalized in the political life of the country; and (ii) political parties, in the past thirty years, have tended to oscillate between a one dominant party system and a multi-party system. For these reasons, a balance was never achieved. At best the system can generally be described as political factionalism rather than party system in its strict sense. In order to promote the development of a healthy competitive party system, the following measures may be considered:

1. The fundamental issues of ideology, territorial integrity and independence, security and defense, the sanctity of the constitution, and permanent elements of foreign policy should be declared above all political controversy among the political parties.

2. The system of compulsory registration of political parties should be introduced, so that a party candidate, once elected on his party ticket cannot change his party affiliation. He would automatically lose his seat in the Assembly if he decides to change his party affiliation.

3. In order to discourage mushroom growth of parties, it may be provided that only political parties which are able to secure at least 10-20 per cent votes in a general election should be allowed to function. A party should be recognized as such in the Assembly if it can secure at least 10 per cent of the total seats of that body.

4. In order to discourage growth of regional, parochial political parties, it should be provided that all parties to be recognized as such should have a national organization, ideology, leadership, and following; and therefore, any party confined to a region or locality should not be recognized as a political party. Similarly, provisions should be made to discourage the growth of sectarian or tribal parties.

5. In order to insure the growth of democracy, it may be further provided that all political parties be required to hold periodic elections within their party organizations.

6. In order to insure adherance to all such provisions, a permanent Commission of a purely autonomous character and composed of retired judges should be set up to constantly review the functioning of political parties with the provision that any individual citizen, or a group of citizens may challenge the genuine political character of a party.

In conclusion, it may be observed that in a developing society like Pakistan, there are no short-cuts to political development. The processes of building its community, statehood, and nationhood must go hand in hand. Only a common ideology can hold its diverse elements together and weld them into a prosperous, and robust Islamic democracy.

Notes

1. *U.S. News & World Report,* January 15, 1979, pp. 24-25, Dr. Brzezinski observed, "Today the area of crisis is a group of states on the shores of the Indian Ocean—literally an arc of instability, which can be drawn on a map from Chittagong in Bangladesh, through Islamabad, all the way to Aden . . . Persian Gulf, Iran, all the way down to South Africa."

2. *Time Magzine,* January 15, 1979, see cover page picture, and the inside report: 'Crescent of Crisis: Troubles Beyond Iran', pp. 18-25.

3. Sir Halford J. Mackinder, *Democratic Ideals and Reality* (New York: Henry Holt And Company, 1910, 1942), p. 74.

4. *U.S. News & World Report,* January 15, 1979, pp. 32-33, see a report entitled, "Turbulent Fragment, A Colonized Baluchistan yearns for autonomy", it may be noted that the author describes Baluchistan as a "country", and recognizes Baluchis as a "nation", or "tribal nation without defined border"; see also Selig Harrison's article, "Nightmare in Baluchistan" in *Foreign Policy,* New York, The Fall, 1978, pp. 136-160.

5. Jamil-ul-din Ahmad, *Historic Documents of the Muslim Freedom Movement* (Lahore: Publishers United Ltd., 1970), pp. 121-137; see also Sir Maurice Gwyer and A. Appadorai, *Speeches and Documents on the Indian Constitution,* (Bombay, London, New York: Oxford University Press, 1957), Vol. II, pp. 435-443.

6. *Ibid.,* p. 382; see also Gwyer and Appadorai, *Speeches and Documents . . .,* Vol. II, p. 443.

7. Gwyer and Appadorai, *Speeches and Documents . . .,* pp. 444-467; see also for details, Sharifuddin Pirzada, *Evolution of Pakistan* (Lahore: All Pakistan Legal Decisions, 1963).

8. *Ibid.,* pp. 670-680.

9. Richard Symonds, *The Making of Pakistan* (London: Faber and Faber, 1949, 1951) reproduced later by National Book Foundation, Islamabad, 1976, Part II, pp. 81-198 essentially an excellent account of the first two years after independence, for later period, see G.W. Chowdhury, *Constitutional Development of Pakistan* (Lahore: Longmans, 1959).

10. Khalid B. Sayeed, *The Political System of Pakistan* (Boston: Houghton Mifflin Company, 1967), pp. 70-71, for further details, see Keith Callard, *Pakistan, A Political Study* (London: Allen & Unwin, 1957); it has been described here as a *coup d'état* chiefly because it was brought about by a few civilian bureaucrats against the established rules of law and constitution, and later Justice M. Munir of the Supreme Court had to justify it, see legal aspects in Sir Ivor Jennings, *Constitutional Problems in Pakistan* (Cambridge: at the University Press, 1955).

11. *The Constitution of The Islamic Republic of Pakistan* (Karachi: Government of Pakistan Press, 1956).

12. For this period reference may be made to Karl von Vorys, *Political Development of Pakistan* (Princeton: Princeton University Press, 1965); Lawrence Ziring, *The Ayub Khan Era, Politics in Pakistan, 1958-1969,* First Edition (Syracuse: Syracuse University Press, 1971); see also Herbert Feldman, *Revolution in Pakistan, A Study of The Martial Law Administration* (London, Lahore: Oxford University Press, 1967), and *From Crisis to Crisis, 1962-1969* (London: Oxford University Press, 1972) see also Field Marshal Mohammed Ayub Khan's First broadcast to the Nation, October, 1958, *The Constitution, A Study,* reproduced for the Bureau of National Reconstruction by the Department of Films and Publications, Government of Pakistan, also see his broadcast, *My Manifesto,* March 23, 1962 published by the Bureau of National Reconstruction in which he observed, "Our second objective must be the security and stability of Pakistan . . ." see also G.W. Chowdhury, *Democracy in Pakistan* (Dacca: Green Bookhouse, 1963); for Islamic aspects, see Manzooruddin Ahmed, *Pakistan, The Emerging Islamic State* (Karachi: Allies Book Corporation, 1967) particularly the chapter on "The Islamic Aspects of the New Constitution".

13. Sheikh Mujibur Rahman, *6-Point Formula: Our Right to Live* (Dacca: The Awami League, 1966), in substance, these were aimed to achieve a confederal relationship with the western wing of the country.

14. Fazal Muqeem, *Pakistan's Crisis in Leadership* (Islamabad, Karachi, Lahore: National Book Foundation, 1973), pp. 34-36; see also G.W. Chowdhury, *The Last Days of United Pakistan* (Bloomington: Indiana University Press, 1974); see also Rounaq Jahan, *Pakistan: Failure in National Integration* (New York: Columbia University Press, 1972); see also Kalim Siddiqui, *Conflict, Crisis, and War in Pakistan* (New York: Praeger, 1972).

15. *Ibid.,* pp. 56-57.

16. *The White Paper on Baluchistan,* issued by the Government of Pakistan, Rawalpindi, October 19, 1974; see also Selig Harrison's article referred to above, "Nightmare in Baluchistan", pp. 138-140.

17. *Jiye Sindh,* literally meaning "Long Live Sind" is primarily a regionalist political group of Sindhi youth which vociferously demands complete autonomy for the province of Sind. They have also been dubbed as secessionists with their political links with the Sindhu Desh (Independent Sind) movement.

18. See a recent interview with Mr. Khurshid Hasan Mir, formerly Secretary General of the Pakistan Peoples Party in the Weekly, *Akhbar-i-Jahan* (The World News), Karachi, Jung Publications, Vol. 13, No. 23 dated May 28–June 3, 1979, pp. 12-13 in which Mr. Mir has succinctly pointed out some of the major weaknesses of the PPP and of Bhutto's policies.

19. Overseas Weekly *Dawn,* dated September II, 1977, p. 2.

20. *White Paper on the Performance of the Bhutto Regime,* Vol. II, "Treatment of Fundamental State Institutions" (Islamabad: Government of Pakistan, January, 1979), p. 5.

21. *Ibid.,* Vol. IV, "The Economy", p. 37-39.

22. *Ibid.,* pp. 9-10.

23. Zulfikar Ali Bhutto, "Address to the Nation", March 1, 1972 reprinted by Government of Pakistan, Department of Films & Publications, (Karachi: 1972), p. 3.

24. *Ibid.,* p. 1.

25. *White Paper,* Vol. IV, p. 13.

26. Donald Herring, "Good Land Lords, Bad Landlords, Parasites and Entrepreneurs: The Policy of Land Reforms in Pakistan" article included in this volume.

27. *White Paper,* Vol. I, "Mr. Z.A. Bhutto, His Family And Associates" (Islamabad: Government of Pakistan, January, 1979).

28. *White Paper,* Vol. II, "Treatment of Fundamental State Institutions" (Islamabad: Government of Pakistan, January, 1979).

29. *White Paper,* Vol. III, "Misuse of the Instruments of State Power", (Islamabad: Government of Pakistan, January 1979).

30. Rejoinder to the reply of the Respondent re: Constitutional Petition of Begum Bhutto, 104 pages, dated October 10, 1977 submitted by Ghulam Ali Memon, Counsel for Begum Bhutto; see also another rejoinder of Zulfikar Ali Bhutto of 126 pages, printed by Musawat Press Ltd.

31. Zulfikar Ali Bhutto's rejoinder of 319 pages typewritten was reproduced with necessary editing, and an additional anonymous Introduction by *Executive Intelligence Review,* New York, supplement January, 1979, New Solidarity International Press Service.

32. Zulfikar Ali Bhutto, *Politics of the People,* Vol. 2, pp. 26-27, *Awakening the People,* edited by Hamid Jalal and Khalid Hasan (Rawalpindi: Pakistan Publications, n.d.)

33. Overseas Weekly *Dawn,* March 13, 1977, pp. 1-2.

34. *White Paper on The Conduct of the General Elections in March 1977,* (Rawalpindi: Government of Pakistan, January, 1979).

35. Overseas Weekly *Dawn,* July 10, 1977, pp. 1-2.

36. *Ibid.*

37. William I. Richter, "From Electoral Politics to Martial Law", article included in this volume.

38. *Op. cit., Dawn,* July 11, 1977, p. 2.

39. *Ibid.,* July 24, 1977, p. 3.

40. *Ibid.,* August 7, 1977, p. 3.

41. *Ibid.,* September 4, 1977.

42. *Ibid.,* September 11, 1977, p. 1.

43. *Ibid.,* October 16, 1977, p. 3.

44. *Ibid.,* September 25, 1977.

45. *Ibid.,* October 9, 1977, p. 4, there are references to two earlier cases in which the question of the constitutionality of Martial Law was raised. In the Dosso case, the Court had upheld it, whereas in the latter case of Asma Jilani, it was declared unconstitutional. In the Dosso case, the Supreme Court of Pakistan had held that successful revolution through military *coup d'état* gives rise to a new legal order, and therefore, it does not owe its legal authority to the established constitution. This view is based on a well known theory propounded by Hans Kelsen, a reputed authority on jurisprudence and international law. However, in the year 1973 in the Asma Jilani case, the Supreme Court reversed its earlier ruling, and did not follow Hans Kelsen's theory of successful revolution. They had found that the revolution, though successful, cannot become a source of legal order if it does not conform to the basic law of the country, i.e., the constitution made by the elected representatives of the people. But in such situations where normal legal institutions have totally failed to function resulting in absolute chaos and confusion, there must be some authority which should be responsible for restoring law and order in the country, and if in such situations, revolution takes place, then that revolution could only be justified to the extent that it had taken measures and performed acts for good government in the larger interests of the country, such acts could be condoned for the reason that they were not made by a lawful authority. This view is based on the doctrine of necessity, by this it is implied that all other acts of a usurper or a revolutionary regime could not be given any legal validity or sanctity.

46. *Ibid.,* pp. 1-2.

47. *Lahore High Court Judgment in Murder Trial;* State vs. Zulfikar Ali Bhutto and others, (Lahore: The Pakistan Times Press, 1978).

48. *Ibid.,* see para 618, p. 132.

49. *Summary of the Supreme Court Judgment:* Zulfikar Ali Bhutto & others vs. The State (Islamabad: Ministry of Information and Broadcasting, Directorate of Films & Publications, Government of Pakistan, 1979).

50. *Ibid.,* pp. 3-4.

51. *Ibid.,* pp. 11-12.

52. Daily *Dawn,* Karachi, February 8, 1979, page 1 refers to President General Zia-ul Haq's interview with Sandy Gall of Independent Television, telecast in London.

53. President General Zia-ul Haq, Address to the Nation, *Measures to Enforce Nizam-i-Islam,* (Islamabad: Directorate of Films & Publications, Ministry of Information and Broadcasting, Government of Pakistan, 1979), pp. 1-10.

54. President General Zia-ul Haq, Address to the Nation, *Introduction of Islamic Laws,* Islamabad, February 10, 1979, (Islamabad: Ministry of Information & Broadcasting, Directorate of Films & Publications, Government of Pakistan, 1979), p. 16.

55. *Ibid.*

56. *Ibid.,* pp. 16-21, for details see Annexes A-1 to A-54.

57. Manzooruddin Ahmed, "The Nature of Federal Crisis in Canada and Pakistan", in *Political Science Review,* Karachi, 1973, Vol. 1, No. 1, pp. 14-34 in which the concept of 'federal crisis' has been defined in terms of systems analysis and comparative federalism.

Changing Patterns of Politics in Pakistan:
An Overview
NORMAN D. PALMER

Pakistan's political history has been a troubled one. As one of the largest of the many new nations that have emerged in the postwar era, and as the second largest Muslim nation in terms of numbers of devotees of the Islamic faith within its borders (prior to the second partition in 1971), Pakistan seemed destined to play a much more active and influential role in both regional and international affairs than it has in fact played. It has, instead, been perhaps the least known and least effective of the larger nations of the world. The reasons for this failure to live up to its apparent potential are to be found mainly in the country's internal divisions and weaknesses, complicated by its proximity to and tense relations with a much larger and more influential neighbor and by its failure to establish the kind of relationship to which it aspired with its fellow-Muslim nations to the west.

Pakistan's Political Traumas

It is probably unfair, and certainly unkind, to refer to Pakistan, as a prominent Indian journalist did in 1977, to "Pakistan's failure as a modern state."[1] Few, if any, of the developing nations that have emerged in recent years have been able to achieve the status of "a modern state." Each of them is a mixture of tradition and modernity. Almost none seems to have been able to organize its political, economic, and soical order in such a way as to cross the threshold of modernity on more than a limited number of fronts. But there is considerable basis for Professor Ralph Braibanti's considered judgment that "no other new nation which gained independence after 1947 has experienced the variety or the intensity of traumas that Pakistan has suffered."[2]

Braibanti mentions eight of these traumas:

(1) Pakistan is unique in having had four constitutions in a quarter of a century. . . .(2) No other new state has rearranged the crucial relationship of space, power, and culture four times—from five provinces to two . . . then again to five provinces and, with the secession of East Pakistan, to four provinces. (3) No other state outside the communist

system has tried to depart from the colonial heritage of local government and the global ideological suasion of community development theory by devising a structure —Basic Democracies—that, while not totally original, was an ingenious adaptation to cultural content. . . . (4) Pakistan was also the major exemplar of an effort to sedate the participation explosion while building institutional capability. . . . (5) Nor has any other new state changed its basic structure of government from a parliamentary to a presidential system, then returned to a parliamentary form and simultaneously adjusted from a unicameral to a bicameral legislative system. (6) As though these major changes in polity and power were not enough, there was also a long period in which both the legislative and political party processes were suspended. (7) These changes occured within the context of two periods of martial law, three wars with India, including the only successful war of secession among the new states in the post-independence period. (8) Further, few nations . . . have had such a massive infusion of technological and economic aid from the United States or allied themselves in foreign policy so closely with that country. Nor have many new nations so shrewdly and intelligently adjusted their foreign policy to a highly multilateral set of relations coupled with a renaissance of Islamic connections, once the futility of exclusivity with the United States was realized.[3]

This is a formidable, and probably unique, list of "traumas". Moreover, several others could be added. For example, probably no other new state— certainly no other large new state—has tried so many different kinds of political experiments, all of which, after some temporary successes, have eventually broken down and have been succeeded by other and different political experiments. At least five of these abortive political experiments can be identified, interspersed with three periods of martial law and direct mili- tary rule.

"Crises of Political Development": The Pakistani Experience

More than almost any other new state Pakistan has experienced to an intense degree all of the "crises of political development" that were identified and analyzed by the Committee on Comparative Politics of the Social Science Research Council in the United States. These are the crises of identity, legitimacy, integration, penetration, participation, and distribution.[4]

1) *The Identity Crisis*. With almost no historical roots, with its two major divisions separated by a thousand miles of Indian territory, with major religious, ethnic, linguistic, regional, and tribal groups whose loyalties were often more parochial and regional than national and often were in real or apparent conflict with the sense of larger national identity, Pakistan's identi- ty crisis, even after the seccession of East Pakistan in 1971, has been particularly severe.

2) *The Crisis of Legitimacy*. Several governments in Pakistan have suc- ceeded in establishing their legitimacy, almost beyond question, but only for limited periods of time. This was true when Mohammad Ali Jinnah and his

chief lieutenant and successor in effective power, Liaquat Ali Khan, were in office, and during the heyday of the rule of Ayub Khan and of Zulfikar Ali Bhutto; but Jinnah died about a year after Pakistan's independence, and Liaquat was assassinated three years later, Ayub Khan's hold on the country began to slip in the latter part of the 1960s and he was eased out in early 1969, and Bhutto, the architect of Pakistan's recovery from the traumas of division and defeat in 1971, after a spectacular electoral victory in March, 1977, which seemed to reconfirm his legitimacy and his unchallengeable postion in the country, experienced the supreme humiliation of a growingly effective and increasingly violent resistance movement which in early July, 1977, led the military to depose him and assume control, and which a few weeks later led to his arrest and trial on changes of murder and other crimes and in early 1978 to the handing down by the Lahore High Court of a sentence of death by hanging.

Thus, except for the great founders of the nation, no other political leaders of Pakistan and no other governments have been able to establish and maintain their legitimacy for more than brief periods of time. For nearly half of its existence Pakistan has had either weak governments whose legitimacy was almost constantly in question or has been under martial law or various forms of military rule when the legitimacy of the regime was always in doubt, even though it could not be successfully challenged at the peaks of emergency rule. Since the sudden fall of Bhutto the country has experienced another of these eras of military rule, when in effect the political system has been in abeyance while the leaders of the interim military regime try to figure out how to restore more normal political processes, with some form of democracy invariably being the announced if not always the real objective, without the danger of chaos in the country and without jeopardizing their own professional future or even their survival.

In view of these difficulties in establishing, and especially in maintaining, legitimacy there is considerable basis for Professor Anwar Syed's assertion that "of all the crises that have afflicted Pakistani politics, that of legitimacy is the most inclusive and far-reaching."[5]

3) *The Crisis of Integration.* The search for national integration has been another elusive one for Pakistan. It is clearly related to the crisis of identity, and to the problem of building a nation out of a group of disparate peoples, within borders that have no historical foundations and with geographical and other divisions that caused the country to be described as a "geographical absurdity" and that eventually led to the break-up of the nation in the form in which it had existed from 1947 to 1971. Even within the more limited, more logical, and more cohesive borders of the post-1971 period Pakistan has been unable to resolve the problems arising from a variety of ethnic, regional, and other divisions.

Pakistan has twice struggled to achieve national integration. The first effort was eventually a failure. The results of the second try are still quite uncertain. Pakistan's survival as a nation for more than three decades is a truly impressive achievement. It has had rather remarkable success in state-building, even though it eventually lost the larger part of its former population; but it has had only limited success in nation-building. Much of its political future depends on its ability to deal with this problem.

4) *The Penetration Crisis.* The penetration crisis "involves the problems of government in reaching down into the society and effecting basic policies."[6] In traditional societies the gap between the ruling elite and the masses of the people is conspicuously wide. That gap also exists in transitional societies. In a sense it is an even more complicating factor, for the leaders of such societies are compelled to attempt to achieve more effective and extensive penetration of the political and social system, as a necessary means of securing acceptance and legitimacy and of achieving developmental goals.

In Pakistan, a major transitional society, the gap betweeen rulers and ruled is still alarmingly wide, and the efforts of the ruling groups to penetrate the society have varied greatly in extent and in results. Mohammad Ali Jinnah was an elitist par excellence, but his hold on the people of Pakistan was such that he did not have to be concerned about legitimacy or popular support. Ayub Khan was in the same position, for different reasons and under different circumstances, in the early years of his rule, but later on he tried to develop institutions and practices, notably the system of Basic Democracies, which would reach down to the local levels, identify the people with his regime, and enlist popular participation in and support for his regime and for the development programs that were necessary to give the country a more viable economic as well as political system. Bhutto, an aristocrat, was the first top political leader of Pakistan who resorted to the politics of populism as a means of entrenching himself and his regime and of moving the country forward in a more "progressive" direction. For a time the politics of populism seemed to work well. While it was used by Bhutto in ways that eventually led to his downfall, it did give him a base of popular support that was not completely eroded after he lost out in the political arena or even after he had been tried, found guilty, and sentenced to death by hanging. Bhutto, in other words, was able to penetrate the political and social system more pervasively than perhaps any other outstanding political leader in the brief history of independent Pakistan. As Professor Sharif al Mujahid points out, "he had a unique opportunity to institutionalize parliamentary democracy, . . . and to establish a viable political system which is congruent with the country's political culture. But . . . he thoughtlessly threw away that unique opportunity, if only for the sake of institutionalizing his personal rule in Pakistan."[7]

5) *The Crisis of Participation.* Closely related to the crisis of penetration,

and in many respects of even greater importance, is the crisis of participation. This "occurs when there is uncertainty over the appropriate rate of expansion and when the influx of new participants creates serious strains on the existing institutions."[8] This crisis is also related to the crisis of legitimacy, for legitimacy often becomes difficult to maintain either under conditions of limited participation—the "normal" experience in most of the new states—or under conditions of widespread participation. Most authoritarian rulers seek what they allege to be mass participation in the systems over which they preside, but mainly for the purpose of marshalling support for themselves and their regimes and seldom for the purpose of giving the masses of the people any real say in their own government, even though this seems to be a *sine qua non* for any form of democracy that is not a travesty on the term.

Many of Pakistan's political problems inhere in the difficulty in finding ways to resolve the participation crisis. On the whole Pakistan has been a limited participation state. This may account in large part for its failure to evolve a satisfactory political system and to develop an accepted base for political viability. One of the announced purposes of Ayub Khan's system of Basic Democracies was to broaden the base of political participation and to give the people of Pakistan a greater voice in shaping their own destiny; but in actual operation, and probably in the inmost intentions of its sponsor, the system was used more as an instrument for marshalling support for Ayub Khan than for genuine participation. The same observation might be made of the populist politics and the appeals to "Islamic socialism" of Zulfikar Ali Bhutto. These seemed to widen the base of the political system greatly, but, to paraphrase Sharif al Mujahid, they were used more to institutionalize Bhutto's personal rule than to develop a more genuinely democratic system, based on more genuine and more widespread political participation.

Political participation may assume many forms, some of which are more symbolic than effective and may in fact be mere facades for limited participation and authoritarian manipulation and control. But no genuinely democratic system, whatever its form, can exist without widespread and meaningful political participation. Two of the major agencies or institutions of such participation are political parties and elections.

Pakistan's experience with both parties and elections has not been a happy one. There has been a plethora of political parties at various stages of Pakistan's history, and a few, such as the undivided Muslim League in the early years of the country's existence, the Awami League in East Pakistan, and the Pakistan People's Party, have been effective and successful for limited periods. But political parties have not fared well in Pakistan, and nothing even close to a real party system has emerged.

Pakistan's experience with elections has been even more limited and disappointing.[8] Elections of various kinds on the subnational level, and even so-called national elections on the basis of a very limited franchise, especially under the Basic Democracies system, have been held rather frequently; but no nationwide elections on the basis of universal adult suffrage were held in the first twenty-three years of Pakistan's existence, and only two such elections—in December, 1970, and March, 1977—have ever been held. Instead of giving greater stability and integration of the Pakistan political system, the two truly national elections led quickly to conditions of turmoil and division. The question that Professor Richter poses is quite relevant: "Why . . . should free democratic elections be such a difficult and troublesome feature of Pakistan's politics?"[9] Surely the answer is that unless and until Pakistan is able to evolve a genuinely democratic system, that will be consistent with its political culture and that will be able to meet "the test of performance," the environmental and systemic conditions for successful democratic elections will not exist.

An underlying theme in all the chapters in this section is that of political participation. Sharif al Mujahid is concerned with the March, 1977, national elections, which represented an expansion of political participation, whatever its limitations and aftermath. William L. Richter moves from the participant experience of elections to the experience under martial law, representing, among other changes, a definite limitation on political paticipation. And Philip Jones, in his analysis of the changing party structure, with particular attention to the Pakistan People's Party and the Pakistan National Alliance, the main contenders in the 1977 national elections, calls attention to the embryonic nature of the party structure, and to the weaknessess of both the PPP and the PNA, which proved to be rather amoral and even dangerous agencies of mass mobilization and participation.

6) *The Distribution Crisis.* In all developing countries there is much talk about equity and distributive justice, both between developing and developed countries, and within the developing countries themselves. As a crisis in political development the distribution crisis "involves questions about how government powers are to be used to influence the distribution of goods, services, and values throughout the society."[10] Most leaders in most developing countries—especially those who use the rhetoric of populism, like Mrs. Gandhi in India and Zulfikar Ali Bhutto in Pakistan—insist that greater equity and distributive justice are central objectives of their programs; but in spite of the rhetoric and in spite of many programs of sweeping economic and social reforms very little has in fact been done to distribute "goods, services, and values" more equitably "throughout the society."

All of these "crises of political development"—and many more—have bedeviled Pakistan throughout its brief and troubled history, and not one of them has been satisfactorily handled, not to mention resolved. The forms which these crises have assumed in Pakistan, the kinds of policies and solutions that have been pursued, the reasons for the failure to resolve any of these crises—or, in some instances, apparent success in dealing with them, usually followed by failure—and the probabilities of greater success or greater failures in the future are subjects of absorbing interest to all friends of Pakistan, to all who are concerned with the prospects for democracy or for any viable political systems in developing countries, and to all students of political development. Again we are reminded that Pakistan is an especially large and significant laboratory of political development and social change, which has received far less attention than it richly merits.

Differing Interpretations of Pakistan's Political History

Pakistan's historical experience and political development are even more difficult to evaluate adequately because from the very beginning there have been many different interpretations of major aspects of the country's political history, even of the reasons for its creation. Let us begin with the central question: "Why Pakistan?" As Wayne Wilcox observed several years ago, "general interpretation of Pakistan's development must begin with the realization that differing interpretations about the roots of the state had important consequences after its creation."[11] Wilcox suggested five different hypotheses, without attempting to treat any of them in detail or to evaluate their relative validity and significance. These he called the "pull" hypothesis, the "push" hypothesis, the "secular interests" hypothesis, the "divide and rule" hypothesis, and the "party leaders competition" hypothesis.[12]

After the abrogation of the democratic constitution and the parliamentary system in 1958, there was a prolonged debate on the reasons for the failure of the parliamentary form of government in the pre-1958 period. Some argued that it failed because it was never given a chance to succeed. In 1961 a Constitution Commission, appinted by President Ayub Khan in 1960, consisting of eleven distinguished private citizens from both "wings" of the country, concluded that "the real causes of the failure of the parliamentary form of government in Pakistan were mainly the lack of leadership resulting in lack of well-organized and disciplined parties, the general lack of character in the politicians and their undue interference in the administration."[13] This was by no means the final word on this very intriguing question.

Different interpretations have also persisted regarding Ayub Khan's most innovative political experiment, which came to be known as the system of Basic Democracies. If it is interpreted as one of the most significant of the various experiments in "democratic decentralization" and of popular participation in government, administration, and development in developing countries, it deserves continuing and special attention, even though it was not a very successful experiment along these lines. If, on the other hand, it is viewed as a thin facade for mobilizing popular support for Ayub's authoritarian regime, by using the "Basic Democrats'—originally only 80,000 in both "wings," and later only 100,000—as the "electoral college" to elect the President of the nation, it must be pronounced an immediate success and an eventual failure. But the real failures of the system rest in the limitations that were placed upon it from the beginning, the lack of real popular response, and, above all, the basic weaknesses of the "Ayub system" generally.

The 1977 Crisis and Alternative Political Futures

Professor Richter's contribution advances six different interpretations of what happened during the first six months of 1977, the "six months between Bhutto's announcement of the elections and his downfall, which, as he states, "must rank among the most eventful and crucial periods in Pakistan's troubled political history."[14] He offers the insightful comment that "In a very real sense, how we understand the next stage in Pakistan's political history will depend very much on which interpretation we give to the crisis by which it began."[15]

All of the papers in this section throw light on these eventful six months. Together with the background analyses that are necessary, relating to Pakistan's historical experience and political development, the reasons for its successes and failures, and the differing interpretations of major periods and aspects in its history, these papers suggest several possible alternative political futures for Pakistan, although they do not, and cannot, indicate which of these alternatives will in fact be Pakistan's destiny.

Notes

1. Girilal Jain, "Search for a Scapegoat: Absurd Charges Against Mr. Bhutto," *The Times of India*, Sept. 7, 1977.

2. Ralph Braibanti, "The Research Potential of Pakistan's Development," Chap. 15 in Lawrence Ziring, Ralph Braibanti, and W. Howard Wriggins, eds., *Pakistan: The Long View* (Durham, N. C.: Duke University Press, 1977), p. 438.

3. *Ibid.*, pp. 438–440.

4. See Lucian W. Pye, *Aspects of Political Development* (Boston: Little Brown, 1966), pp. 62–66; and Leonard Binder, et al., *Crises and Sequences in Political Development* (Princeton, N. J.: Princeton University Press, 1971).

5. Anwar H. Syed, "The Pakistan People's Party: Phases One and Two," Chap. 4 in Ziring, Braibanti, and Wilcox, eds., *Pakistan: The Long View*, p. 73.

6. Pye, *Aspects of Political Development*, p. 64.

7. Sharif al Mujahid, "The Pakistan Elections: An Analysis," in this volume.

8. See Norman D. Palmer, *Elections and Political Development: The South Asian Experience* (London: C. Hurst & Company, 1975), pp. 178–190.

9. William L. Richter, "From Electoral Politics to Martial Law: The Political Crisis of 1977," in this volume.

10. Pye, *Aspects of Political Development*, p. 66.

11. Wayne A. Wilcox, "The Wellsprings of Pakistan," Chap. 2 in Ziring, Braibanti, and Wriggins, eds., *Pakistan: The Long View*, p. 25.

12. *Ibid.*, pp. 27-37.

13. *Report of the Constitution Commission, Pakistan* (Karachi: Manager of Publications, Government of Pakistan, 1961), p. 13.

14. Richter, "From Electoral Politics to Martial Law," in this volume.

15. *Ibid.*

The Constitutional Problems of Pakistan

KARL J. NEWMAN

Students of South Asian Affairs are prone to complain these days: "events in Pakistan are getting less and less transparent; it is becoming more and more difficult to discern any kind of pattern of political and constitutional processes". This is true in as much as the present military rules of the country, very different from the Martial Law Administration of President Ayub Khan, have so far proclaimed their desire to limit themselves to their task of an interim, a trustholder government. Unlike their predecessors in 1958, they have not abrogated the Constitution of 1973, and they have clearly indicated that they wish to maintain the powers of the judiciary, in particular, the right of judicial review and interpretation of the Constitution. They have temporarily limited and strongly restrained the political parties, but have not dissolved them, including Mr. Zulfiquar Ali Bhutto's Peoples Party.

On the other hand, it is undeniable that the greater power and wealth which the oil has brought to some of the orthodox Arab countries and to Iran, has not only led to a greater emphasis on Muslim solidarity throughout the world; there has also been a stronger impact of Islamic orthodoxy on countries such as Pakistan, whose *raison d'etre* is, after all, its origin and existence as an Islamic state. This trend has become so powerful there that whichever groupings or parties might find themselves in charge of its destinies would have to assure the masses of the conformity of the Constitution with the laws and the tenets of Islam. This is no easy task for the judiciary, as guardians of the Constitution; but perhaps not an insoluble one, when you consider that it has always been the task of constitutional judges, (no matter if I think of the U.S. Supreme Court, or the German Supreme Constitutional Court), to overcome the contradiction which positive law, produced by legislation, often presents in comparison with what is right, in terms of legal philosophy.

To give a clearer picture of the elements of evolution, which are and will be operative in constitutional thought in Pakistan, some fundamental presuppositions will have to be elucidated. First, a note of caution. I consider it wrong to evaluate the situation in Pakistan in such terms as many contemporary writers apply to conditions of the developing countries of the Third World in general, and which reads somewhat like this: "constitutional democracy is a luxury reserved for the prosperous countries of the West with long traditions of free institutions. In countries without the economic and cultural infrastructure we must be lucky if we can rely on some kind of enlightened authoritarian rule willing to preserve national independence intact, and prepared to promote the economic uplift of society.[1] That such generalisations are untrue is proved by the upsurge of the masses of Pakistan against the attempt by the PPP (Pakistan Peoples Party) (during the first half) in 1977 to establish single party rule; and even more by the revolt originating from the suspicion that the results of the elections of March 1977 did not accurately express the manifested will of the people; just as much as the violent upsurge of the masses in neighbouring India, against the attempt of reducing the democratic essence of the Indian Constitution by means of emergency rule—which led, for the first time in Indian history, to the defeat of a Congress Government during the last general elections. This justifies the assumption that not only in India, but also in Pakistan, there persists *sense* amongst the masses a strong sense of political and constitutional legitimacy, which any government can dare to ignore only if it is ready to risk its own political survival. Confirmation of this hypothesis is offered by a quite analogous process recently observed in the state of Sri Lanka, also influenced by similar traditions and forces.

The historical roots of this phenomenon cannot be so easily discerned. For thousands of years the Subcontinent was continuously exposed to deeply-rooted monarchic, even despotic influences, just as were the surrounding areas of the Middle East, South East Asia and the Far East. Traditions of an initial village democracy can offer only a very small part of the explanation. More influence, perhaps, should be placed on the heterogeneity of religions, races, cultures and legal systems which, through their coexistence, necessitated a certain amount of what may be called "liberty through variety", the need for toleration, or the history of the freedom to be different as Martin Buber put it. This habit of living with a variety of structures defies any attempt at novelty. The Mogul Emperor Akhbar had already found that generosity to all was the necessary condition for successful government. It is a phenomenon which is well known in the West. The liberty of the Western World goes back to the fact that neither State nor Church could ever achieve a monolithic structure. On the other hand, one has to remember that the early Muslim Kings of India had as their model the Abbaside Cakiphate[2], which had long turned its back on simple democratic customs as they had *democracy in Islam* existed in the days of the Holy Prophet of Islam and his successors. Mughal Government, in some ways related to the post-Renaissance states of Europe, was a very powerful autocratic government. It was, nevertheless, influenced as much by the interpretation of moral and political conduct as by its theology.

While it is undeniable that the army has always played, and still does play, a very important part within the political traditions of Muslim states, it is also true that their role has often been a transitional one. This means a takeover during a real emergency in the interest of legitimacy, sometimes also in the interest of constitutionalism; a fact which can be particularly clearly discerned in the history of Turkey, as for instance in the case of Menderes, who, having come to power by constitutional means, was not prepared to allow the opposition a legal chance to regain power.

I have in some other papers pointed out the important role which the impact of British institutions[3], with the aim to educate people gradually for self-government (a sort of democracy by installments), had for the entire Sub-continent. Less through their system of education, but much more through the introduction of the legal system of Common Law, the principles of constitutional government were able to strike deep roots in the whole Sub-continent because all lawyers were *ab initio* trained to represent the rule of law, and even fight for it when necessary. This disposition of the legal profession stands out as its decisive feature.

Thus on the Sub-continent, the legitimacy of constitutional government is so strongly entrenched that no one dare challenge it. It is in the dialectic of the relationship between Islamic Law on the one hand, and constitutional law on the other, that the whole personality and work of the founder of Pakistan, Mohammad Ali Jinnah, must be understood; an achievement for which the philosopher and poet Iqbal had laid the philosophical, theological and theoretical foundations. In this way a synthesis between Islam and constitutionalism was imbibed by all Pakistanis. It means that no one is allowed to question the foundation of Islam without becoming suspect of subverting Constitutional Democracy, and that no one is allowed to turn away from Democracy without becoming suspect of subverting or neglecting the tenets of Islam. This synthesis has made much difference in the conduct of politics in Pakistan compared with the attitude to political power in some countries of the Middle East. It has modified the long prevailing trend of thought put forward by famous Arab scholars such as Al Ghazali and Ibn Jamaa, who stressed the fact that there is no genuine theory of resistance against unjust rule in Islam. It may be demonstrated by the quick reversal of public opinion against all those who proved insincere to either the tenet of Islam or constitutional rule.

Now as to the trends of thought which are still active today, it is necessary to distinguish the four different stages through which the constitution making process in Pakistan went, because residues of thought appertaining to these various stages are still today active in the minds of people.

1) With the help the Government of India Acts of 1919 and 1935, the British Government accustomed the people of the Sub-continent to self government, while maintaining bureaucratic-hierarchical structures, fashioned according to the French system of administration by Prefects. As it operated with the help of an elite of public servants, they always stood by to take over

this task from elected representatives as soon as it became obvious that the party structure was too weak, or that politicians were not responsible enough to make parliamentary government work. An integral part of this system was the strong prerogatives of the Viceroys and Governors, later the Pakistan Governor Generals and Presidents, and far-reaching emergency powers (which were also used elsewhere, e.g. in India). These British acts constitute the basic framework in Pakistan even today.[4]

2) The second model is based on the pure Whitehall system of Parliamentary Government, aimed at by the Pakistan Muslim League, the Awami League, and other parties in the time between 1947 and 1958. It found expression in the First Constitution of Pakistan in 1956. This partly demolished the dualism of British legislation for India by making the President a figurehead, vesting all power in the Prime Minister and his Cabinet, while maintaining largely the safety valve of emergency provisions. Still, the President maintained the important right to dismiss the Prime Minister, if, in his opinion, he had lost the confidence of the majority of the members of the unicameral legislature. It is true in Pakistan that there was up to 1958 a considerable instability of the Executive, comparable to the Third and Fourth French or the German Weimar Republic. Politicians thirsted for power and sought pleasure in constantly repeating the game of making and unmaking cabinets.[5] Frequently they left the Government party (to which they owed their election) only because they had not received a job in the Cabinet, or because they hoped to receive a post from the opposition if they crossed the floor. Yet political habits die slowly, and the President was not ready to accept the dignified symbolic role which the Constitution had provided for him, and was ready just as in the case of President Mirza to move against Prime Minister Suhrwardy. Not that the latter would have shown more tolerance against parties other than his own. So it can be said that the main drawback of the constitution of 1956 was instability of Cabinets, selfishness of party leaders, and intolerance towards opposition groups. Because of the setback which the Muslim League had received in East Pakistan, its weakening through secularist, liberal and conservative parties, such as the Awami League and the Republican party, there remained no well organized parties. Their politics consisted of cheap slogans and clustered around personalities. On the other side, there stood a caste of civil servants educated in a spirit of elitism. The elite turned against the Constitution whenever there was a real possibility that it would function. It can be said that the Constitution of 1958 was abrogated just as there was going to be the first general election which might have tested its substance.

Now the Constitution of 1962 was not decided by the Constituent Assembly, but decreed by President Ayub Khan. It introduced the Presidential form of Government, but without the separation of powers, which is the precondition for the democratic nature of presidential government in the U.S. These 156 members of an unicameral legislature were elected by 80,000 basic democrats (an electoral college) via indirect elections. The President selected and dismissed his Cabinet Ministers and Governors, he presided over the Council of Ministers, similar to the 5th French Republic which stood as a model. The position of the judiciary was weakened. There were to be no political parties. Yet one of the "non-existing political parties", the Muslim League, won an absolute majority in the elections.

This outcome could be expected from a largely conservative electorate which still believed sufficiently in democratic traditions to enforce some sort of return to the party system. Yet President Ayub Khan accepted the verdict, appointed his ministers mostly from members of his own Muslim League and finally split this party, after he joined it, thus making it a personal domain. This proved to be a fatal decision, as far as the Muslim League was concerned, as the future was going to show. Not different from his model De Gaulle, Ayub Khan allowed himself to be elected by plebiscite in this case against the candidature of the sister of the founder of Pakistan, Fatima Jinnah. She, more than anyone else in Pakistan, represented the true spirit and moral heritage of the Muslim League which was condemned to weakness as a result of confusion and division. It should be frankly admitted that Pakistan experienced in the 12 years of the Ayub Khan era its greatest economic prosperity and uplift. The country gained respect in the world, and fought a partly successful war against India in 1965. Yet in the course of these years the submerged intrinsic and basic factors gradually surfaced. The people were missing the legitimacy of rule in both parts of the country. The disqualified politicians took vengeance in the name of Democracy. This led in East Pakistan ultimately to secession, and in West Pakistan to the emergence of a new move towards the left orientated party, under Ayub Khan's former Foreign Minister, Z. A. Bhutto. His Pakistan Peoples Party in 1970 swept the polls in the first free election, and took over power from President General Yahya Khan, after India's victory over Pakistan in the war over the secession of Bangla Desh. Bhutto then advocated a new democratic constitution for what was left of Pakistan, and after a short time he presented Parliament with a Draft which became the Constitution of the Islamic Republic of Pakistan on April 12th, 1973. It is noteworthy that although the Pakistan Peoples Party had a two-thirds majority in Parliament, the Constitution was accepted unanimously.

If the Constitution of 1956 had the British House of Commons as its model, the Constitution of 1962, with its indirectly elected Parliament and directly elected President (both by an electoral college), resembled the French Fourth Republic, except that there was no directly elected Lower House and no Prime Minister. The Constitution of 1973 again was nearer to the Basic Law of the German Federal Republic, in its most characteristic aspects.

Article 91 of the Pakistan Constitution resembles Article 63 of the Bonn Fundamental Law, in as much as the Prime Minister is not nominated by the President, but elected by the National Assembly, and the system of his election is almost identical with the German system. Likewise (as in Germany) it is the Prime Minister who appoints the other federal ministers.

Yet the most decisive feature is the integration of Articles 67 and 68 of the German Fundamental Law, the so-called Constructive Vote of No-confidence, in articles 93 and 96 of the Pakistan Constitution. This means that no Vote of No-confidence can be moved against the Prime Minister and his Cabinet unless at the same time an alternative candidate is offered by the opposition for the post of Prime Minister to be elected by the National Assembly. These provisions meant to preclude cabinet instability, so typical of the Pakistan Parliaments between 1947 and 1958 (just as they meant in Germany to make impossible the reoccurrence of Parliamentary decay of the twenties and thirties when there was a new Prime Minister every six to nine months). But even in Germany, with its powerful opposition parties, this novel provision has caused the Federal Chancellor and the Chief Ministers of the Laender to become almost irreplaceable. The existence of a third party ready to make coalitions with another major party has made a change in power possible only once in a decade or so. Moreover, Germany's ballot system of Proportional Representation presents a truer picture of public opinion, so that the major opposition parties are never condemned to complete frustration.

In Pakistan, the strong position of the Prime Minister, embedded in the Constitution, was reinforced by the British type of electoral system of relative majority in single member constituencies, which tends to increase the power of the majority and condemns the small party to insignificance. Moreover, the Pakistan Peoples Party was left as the only thoroughly organised hierarchical party, led by a cadre of paid political workers, many of them favourites of Mr. Bhutto who combined the office of Prime Mnister with a very strong party-chairmanship. This should have been sufficient to assure him undisturbed power for many years. Nevertheless, he proved himself even in respect of the existing insignificant, small parliamentary minorities to be anything but self-assured. Even wings and factions in his own party, he hardly viewed with favour. One would have thought that he might have been interested in an effective opposition to his own party, with an opportunity to criticise while being unable to overthrow his government. But he surprised everybody, also including the friends of Pakistan in other countries, by his constitutional amendments. The first, in 1974, strengthened his power for dissolution of political parties. The third, in 1975, increased the possibilities for preventive custody of dissenters; and the fourth and fifth curtailed the power of the judiciary to help those in protective custody.

It is true, however, that the opposition was not always particularly selective in its choice of methods, as it has always been one of the most difficult lessons in the art of democratic government (this is true of both government and opposition) to differentiate between constructive opposition and destructive obstruction. If Mr. Bhutto's Government mistrusted even a very minute opposition hampered by its weakness to play its role, the specter of a united, sizeable, and active opposition (as was seen in its formative process during the electioneering of March 1977), must have appeared to him utterly intolerable. Most people in Pakistan able to judge impartially agree that even without the irregularities ascribed to the Pakistan Peoples Party, they might have easily won 40% of the votes. But even the conquest of 40% of the mandate by the opposition, considering the spirit of those governing and those governed, would have adversely affected the working climate of Parliament—to judge according to the electioneering campaign which preceded it; though in other countries stormy electioneering campaigns are often forgotten, once the parties take their seats in the chamber.

Still one should not forget that in countries of the third world, which do not possess as yet the infrastructure of industrialized states, the reaction of the masses increases even more violently where they are made to suffer from economic depression, than in the industrial north of the world, because existential fear and death cannot be channelled into the legal receptacle of an existing parliamentary opposition. Under such conditions the extra-parliamentary opposition is bound to grow quickly. Moreover, in Pakistan with its relatively narrow middle class, and its predominant village structure, theologians have retained much of their influence on the masses, as was the case in Europe till the end of the 19th century, and in South America even later. Mr. Bhutto's Pakistan Peoples Party had partly grown in defiance of former more religiously orientated parties, such as the Muslim League. Bhutto's Party grew into a largely secular party and was opposed not only by Muslim Leaguers but also by those groups inspired by uncompromising theologians, such as Maulana Maudoodi. Perhaps Mr. Bhutto was not careful enough to avoid shocking the pious by condoning a fast liberalisation of public morality. When his mixed economy, neither capitalism nor socialism, but private enterprise strangled by bureaucracy, did not bring about the promised economic miracle the same masses who had acclaimed him now condemned him.

Thus if we are to analyse past experience and present and the prospect of the present Constitution in the future, it must be said that the Constitution of 1973 in trying to remedy the faults of its predecessor of 1956 overshot its mark exaggerating stability into rigidity. Of course, the old wisdom is still valid in that the success of a constitution depends largely on the way in which it is handled—and there can be no shadow of a doubt that its stabilising elements were exploited for establishing virtual one party rule. On the other hand, it cannot be denied that some of the members of the opposition used methods for combating the government of which Mr. Ali Jinnah as Speaker of Parliament and as a thorough expert on Parliamentary procedure, certainly would not have approved.

The most striking factor is that none of the parties in opposition achieved any strength or effectiveness till they joined the P.N.A., and became more known for what they opposed than for what they wanted to achieve. Still, the people of Pakistan must be credited with much political maturity. Many were prepared against what must have appeared to them as being the beginning of dictatorial rule, even if it were backed by an overwhelming parliamentary majority. Still it is true that if autocratic measures are backed by even 95 percent of a parliament this cannot be called Democracy. In this sense, General Ziaul Haq can hardly be considered as one of the many military rulers (who today in the U.N. have achieved an astonishing measure of respectability), but rather as a disciple of Marshal Badoglio or even Count Stauffenberg who ruled constitutionally in the interest of the values for which the Constitution was made. Still, even today Bhutto's Pakistan Peoples Party has certainly many supporters, particularly amongst the working classes who were promised an equal slice of the cake. However, even a party having no regard for others is a force if it has millions to follow them. On the other hand, the trends toward Islamisation must not be understood as a trend leading back into the stage of medieval scholasticism. On the contrary, Justice Cheema, Chairman of the Council for Islamic Ideology, spoke of the democratic requirement of Ijtihad, this is individual self-determination. The demands of the Shariat Law have much in common with Western concepts of Natural Law.

General Ziaul Haq must partly be considered as a hard taskmaster in accustoming parties and their members to a system of fair play (in the British tradition), but also as a champion of a stern Islamic ethical code. True, there are some phenomena, such as harsh punishments administered in virtue of the Islamic penal code that horrify standards of liberals throughout the world. Yet, the Third World has standards of conduct, which were once familiar in the West, but which have been abandoned since World War II. To these standards correspond sanctions which were also practised in the West long ago.

Last but not least, our judgment has become blurred by self-deception. In large parts of the world, we condone political violence, as long as it is committed in the name of "progress", however illegal these deeds might be. Pakistan has chosen stern methods to safeguard the rule of law. These might not find the approval of the West, but the alternative might well have been chaos and anarchy.

Notes

1. See also Karl J. Newman: *Die Entwicklungsdiktatur und der Verfassungsstaat*, Frankfurt, Bonn, 1963, p. 16.

2. See: Newman, "Papst, Kaiser, Kalif und Basileus" in *Politische Vierteljahrsschrift*, 1963, Heft 1, pp. 21, 32–37.

3. See: E. I. J. Rosenthal, *Political Thought in Medieval Islam*, Cambridge, 1958, pp. 32, 40 and 44.

4. A. B. Rudra, *The Viceroy and the Governor General*, London, 1940.

5. K. J. Newman, "Pakistan's Preventive Autocracy and Its Causes" in *Pacific Affairs*, New York, March 1959.

The 1977 Pakistani Elections: An Analysis
SHARIF AL MUJAHID

Introduction

Everywhere in the world, elections are regarded among the most tangible, formal and demonstrable acts of collective decision in the political process.[1] Though by no means an uncomplicated process, elections are "at the centre of politics everywhere."[2]

The elections are not only central to the political system itself; they also provide an index to the nature of political systems, as well as to the total political and social environment of the country. They also provide clues to the measure of linkage between politics and government. The electoral process tends to bring into sharp focus the nature of political culture, the crosscurrents of nationalism and subnationalisms, and the continuing impact of pressure and interest associational groups. They indicate, as perhaps nothing else does, whether or not the congeries of political groups in a given country are on the way to becoming a political community, whether the "nation" is edging toward political development or political decay in the Huntington's sense.[3] Indeed, so central are elections to the political systems that often the electoral process is equated with the political process itself.[4]

The elections may be either "truly meaningful" or merely ritualistic acts. If meaningful, they would promote popular participation in a democratic society; but if merely ritualistic, they give the people only "the illusion but not the reality of participation"[5] and provide legitimacy to an already entrenched regime. While free and competitive elections produce a stabilizing effect, ritualistic elections, being inherently only a smokescreen for democracy, tend to bring about systemic destablization.[6]

The elections in Pakistan, India and Sri Lanka held within six months of each other, could be regarded "critical" as termed by V. O. Key[7] or "realigning" as used by Augus Campbell.[8] However, in the case of India and Sri Lanka, the elections have produced, at least for the time being, stabilizing effects, but elections in Pakistan have brought about systemic destabilization by causing polarization, agitation, violence, anomie, and disruption, climaxing in yet another spell of martial law, though of a diluted type, to "avert" a civil war that had been looming large in the Pakistani political landscape.[9]

63

The fact that the elections in Pakistan in sharp contrast with those held in India and Sri Lanka did not produce similar effects may be attributed partly to the relative inadequacies of the electoral system, and also to the prevailing incongruencies between the political culture and the political system of Pakistan. In this paper, we offer an empirical analysis of such variables that account for the existing inadequacies of the electoral system of Pakistan. For this purpose, the actual working of the electoral process will be examined in the light of demographic data and such other socioeconomic variables which determine the parties' appeals, the voters' choice and their seeming eventual frustration (as indicated by the extent and intensity of post-election agitation and violence). We shall also analyze the programs, manifestoes, strategies, campaigns, nature and style of leadership, and expectations, whether real or imaginary, of the ruling and the opposition parties.

Since the 1977 Pakistani elections are by no means an isolated incident or act, an attempt would also be made to examine them in a "systematic context," in the context of the totality of Pakistan's political and social processes and its past electoral records. The elections can be studied, according to Professor Palmer, as either dependent or intervening or independent variables.[10] However, in the present paper, the emphasis would be for the most part on the elections as dependent variables, since they are primarily conditioned by the overall political environment of the society. But still, the elections as intervening and independent variables cannot be altogether ignored while discussing, though briefly, the post-election developments. Finally, the present study is based on news reports, participant observations, interviews (mostly with journalists), and analysis of aggregate data and published materials.

II. The 1977 Elections: Background

a) Past Electoral Experience

During the past 30 years, Pakistan's experiment with democracy has been rather brief, erratic, fragmented, and crisis-laden, often disrupted by long periods of authoritarian rule. However, experience in electoral politics has been even more erratic, bewildering, frustrating and destabilizing. For one thing, elections have not yet become a part of Pakistan's political culture in the course of its political evolution.

Since 1947 in Pakistan there had been held four provincial elections (Punjab, March 1951; NWFP, December 1951; Sind, May 1953; and East Bengal, April 1954) on adult-franchise basis; two national and provincial "elections" (1962 and 1965) and the presidential election (1965) under President Ayub Khan's (1958-69) ingenious Basic Democracy (BD) system of indirect elections, and the December 1970 national and provincial assembly elections on adult-franchise and "one-man one-vote" basis.[12] All these elections were conducted by an election machinery set up by the government; but the 1970 elections were the only ones in which the regime was not directly involved as an interested party. Hence the 1970 elections, often considered Pakistan's first general elections, were also the only free and fair elections to be held under a neutral regime. But the prime significance of the March 1977 elections lay in the fact that—as often claimed by Prime Minister Zulfikar Ali Bhutto (1971–77)—these were the first elections to be held by a "popularly-elected government."

b) Election Preliminaries

The preliminaries to the 1977 election may be briefly noted here. The Peoples' Representation Bill was finally passed by the National Assembly (NA) on December 17, 1976. A three-member Election Commission (EC), headed by a retired Supreme Court Judge, Mr. Justice Sajjad Ahmad Jan, was assembled, and entrusted with the task of conducting elections and preparing the ground rules for it. In the political arena several parties were competing for leadership of each of the three broad right, centre, or left-oriented segments of the electorate. Also, conflicts of personal ambitions of some of its leaders had kept the opposition divided. Therefore, all attempts at forging a single opposition platform were thwarted during most of Bhutto's five-year rule. However, the United Democratic Front (UDF; founded March 1973) under Pir Pagaro, at times seemed to be nearly successful in achieving much desired unity. It is in this context that the formation of the newly combined opposition electoral front, called the Pakistan National Alliance (PNA) was the most significant event. Formally launched on January 11, 1977, it offered itself as an alternative national platform as against the ruling PPP.

A PNA Coordinating Committee (consisting of leaders of nine coalescing parties and Begum Wali Khan, the wife of the defunct NAP leader under detention) was formed to draw up a single, mutually agreed slate of opposition candidates in order to avert any eventuality of suicidal fragmentation of votes—as it happened in the 1970 elections.

The parties comprising the PNA were: (1) Rtd. Air Marshal Asghar Khan's Tehrik-i-Istiqlal (TI); (2) Mian Tufail Muhammad's Jamaat-i-Islami (JI); (3) Maulana Mufti Mahmud's Jamiatul-Ulema-e-Islam (JUI); (4) Maulana Shah Ahmed Noorani's Jamiatul-Ulema-i-Pakistan (JUP); (5) Pir Pagaro's Pakistan Muslim League (PML); (6) Sardar Sherbaz Mazari's National Democratic Party (NDP); (7) Nawabzada Nasrullah Khan's Pakistan Democratic Party (PDP); (8) Khan Muhammad Ashraf Khan's Khaksar Tehrik (KT); and (9) Azad Kashmir Muslim Conference (AKMC), headed by

Sardar Abdul Qayyum, President of Azad Kashmir (1972–75), who was removed by Bhutto and put under detention without any warrant of arrest or charge during the Azad Kashmir election of 1975. The JI, JUI, and the JUP are rightist fundamentalist parties; the PML and PDP are centrists; the TI is left of the center; and the NDP, a successor to the defunct National Awami Party (NAP), is leftist in orientation. These are the only parties which really mattered, commanding support either in particular regions or across the country; the other three minor parties were included in the opposition front to further augment its strength.

The grand Alliance represented almost the entire spectrum of current political thinking and ideological orientation in the country. While this was obviously a source of tremendous strength for the PNA to put up a tough fight against the PPP, in a sense it could also be a source of weakness. For, in contrast with an incredibly monolithic PPP organization and Bhutto's charismatic leadership, the PNA, with a semblance of unity under its collective leadership, was plagued by interpersonal rivalries of its leaders and differences of political interests and ideologies.

In any case, the three most baffling problems confronting the PNA were: (1) how to remain united, at least during and after the election campaign; (2) how to resolve the problem of filling top PNA offices; and (3) how to draw up a coherent compromise plank which would, on the one hand, satisfy rather disparate viewpoints within the Alliance and, still on the other, have enough appeal for the voters. All these complex problems were to be tackled discreetly by them, without having much time and without the benefit of an inspiring political *guru* and arbiter of a national stature like Jaya Prakash Narayan in neighboring India.

Surprisingly enough, the claims and counterclaims for offices were somehow amicably settled, and ultimately, on January 16, Mufti Mahmud (JUI), and Rafiq Bajwa (JUP) were unanimously elected President and Secretary General respectively. The Mufti was acting leader of the opposition in the outgoing NA. Bajwa, a comparatively younger man, who had earned a reputation as a successful lawyer for fighting cases of the newspapers suppressed during the Bhutto regime, had, perhaps, played the key role in bringing about unity among the opposition parties. The PNA resolved to boycott election in Baluchistan, presumably as a measure of concession to the NDP, which, like its predecessor (NAP), had for long demanded the return of the army to barracks in troubled Baluchistan. A nine-stared green flag, representing the nine coalescing parties, was adopted as the party flag, and the plough as its election symbol.

While the opposition parties successfully maneuvered to join a grand alliance, another significant development in the political arena was the breakup of a five-year alliance between the PPP and the PML simply because Bhutto did not concede an adequate number of seats to the PML in the Frontier, and instead resolved to put up his own party candidates. This further weakened the already shaky position of the PPP in the Frontier because Qayyum Khan had a considerable political influence in that region.

Both the PPP and the PNA formally launched their election campaigns on January 23. The PPP started its campaign from Rawalpindi, a nerve center of its political influence. On the other hand, the PNA concentrated on Karachi which has long been a center of opposition politics. On January 24, the PPP manifesto was published but the PNA failed in producing its own manifesto. This motivated Bhutto to jeer at the opposition for having entered into the arena of electioneering without a manifesto of its own. The PNA reacted sharply by announcing its manifesto on February 8.
on February 8.

In such circumstance, the PNA manifesto at best reflected compromises which were expediently worked out ideologies of its component parties. Even so, the very fact that the opposition parties were able to forge a grand Alliance and working within a framework analogous to a federation were fairly successful in producing a collective leadership, an election manifesto and a set of uniform policies and program during the election campaigns was substantial evidence of their political prudence, robust pragmatism, the political sagacity and the height of patriotism. In short, it was a unique achievement in the context of the political environment.[13]

III. Bhutto: His Political System, Style and Strategy

Bhutto, as a keen student of history and politics, seems to have carefully studied political biographies of men like Napoleon, Hitler, Mussolini, Lenin, Mao, Soekarno and others who has mastered the art of mass mobilization. Therefore, he tried to emulate them in developing his new style of mass politics. The political system he sought to evolve through the 1973 constitution truly reflected his style of politics.[14] The constitution, adopted almost by consensus, was still heavily tilted in his favor as it carefully managed to legalize, consolidate and perpetuate the existing configuration of power. At the same time the constitution was amended and mutilated by the two-thirds majority of the PPP in the NA to suit Bhutto's thinking and style. In fact, Bhutto was chiefly concerned with a constitution which might insure for him a semiauthoritarian system with a facade of democracy. For example, the constitution claimed to provide for a genuine federal system, but in practice, Bhutto had virtually transformed it into a highly centralized one, to the extent that like Ayub, he directly controlled all provincial matters.[15]

The Ayub regime, measured in terms of Karl Deutsch's categories,[16] was a typically totalitarian or authoritarian system. However, Ayub ultimately failed to command national support primarily because he had ignored the task of social mobilization of the masses through populist slogans. Bhutto, despite his recurring and untiring rhetoric against his former mentor, closely followed and improved upon Ayub's techniques, tactics, methods, and philosophy. He successfully augmented the regime's regulative and extractive capabilities through a series of measures like the creation of the controversial Federal Security Force (FSF; a sort of Mukti Bahini, responsible to him personally), the frequent use of emergency powers under the Defense of Pakistan Rules (DPR), the curbing of the press and the curtailment of the powers of the judiciary. He also ingeniously coined populist slogans like *Roti*, *Kapra* and *Makan* (bread, clothes and shelter), and promised a new era of distributive justice and of an egalitarian order[17]—all of which he skillfully exploited in his 1970 election campaign to secure a majority in West Pakistan. And, once in power, Bhutto effected "reforms", designed to benefit the have-nots, and initiated a systematic program of mass mobilization. Simultaneously, he extended patronage on a massive scale to both the underprivileged and the privileged classes in a concerted attempt to build up vast reserves of support for the regime in both urban and rural areas. He linked, *a la* Ayub again but in a more systematic and effective way, the rural elites and notables (i.e., wealthy landowners and powerful rural-based families) to the political system (chiefly as his "vassals"). At the party level, he had organized the PPP on a hierarchical basis,[18] restaffing it with his henchmen by elbowing out, committed leftists, critical democrats and troublesome individualists,[19] so that he could emerge as the sole authority responsible for filling offices even at the local level. The bureaucracy was put in its "proper" place by first humbling and then politicizing it through "threats, massive dismissals, and lateral entries." The armed forces were likewise first humiliated, then purged of "undesirable" elements, and, still later, were put under command of loyal generals, and General Tikka Khan, advisor on defense, was entrusted with the task of overseeing the rank and file of the armed forces.

Along with these measures, Bhutto also began exploiting the mass media on an extensive scale for consolidating his position in the public eye. At first he raised "socialist slogans", but as he realized that these were becoming counterproductive, he switched over to "Islamic cliches". A series of measures were adopted both on the domestic and international plane, with a view toward conciliating, if not endearing, him to the religious-minded people of Pakistan. Thus he tried to project himself as a dedicated servant of Islam and as a great champion of Muslim unity.

Professional classes and the "intellectuals" like lawyers, journalists, teachers, writers, entrepreneurs and the managerial classes were systematically recruited into the serried ranks of the party "faithfuls." In this manner Bhutto consistently tried to mobilize public opinion for his party among the city dwellers, an aspect which was totally neglected by the Ayub regime. The policy of Adnan Manderes to rule Turkey with the support of a largely rural political base was aborted by the alienated urbanites; and for the same reason Ayub had become the target of attack. Although Bhutto was also primarily concerned with the welfare of the rural peasantry at the expense of the city dwellers, perhaps because it is usually easier to govern docile peasantry, yet he was shrewd enough not to neglect city dwellers altogether for maintaining a minimal level of support for his regime among them who are politically more conscious, volatile, and active.

Consequently, it may be observed that no previous regime had ever attempted to bring about social and political mobilization[20] of the masses on such a scale as Bhutto did, and in this regard, his achievements were phenomenal.

a) Social Mobilization

Social and political mobilization can be effected only when a single message is relayed across the national wavelengths to the complete exclusion of all other messages, with only one theme being repeated *ad nauseum* through both the spoken and the written word. Bhutto faithfully observed this basic principle of social mobilization. This explains why after assuming power, he maintained the tempo of campaign even after the election.

He periodically went on extensive meet-the-people tours of the various provinces, arranged officially at public expense. These tours were characterized by a "barnstorming quality".[21] The ubiquitous section 144 and the loudspeaker ordinance prevented the opposition from holding public rallies and meetings to present their viewpoint. Even closed-door meetings of the opposition were disrupted, opposition relief camps for the flood victims were raided and dismantled. The opposition parties were obstructed in setting up their offices. Within a year, the two non-PPP governments in Baluchistan and the N.W.F.P. were toppled, artificial PPP majorities were contrived, and PPP governments were installed. At the top of all this the regime freely indulged in self-adulation on state-run radio and television, *a la* Ayub but on a much larger scale. The government carefully controlled and regulated news management, and adopted a carrot-and-stick policy in cajoling the national press into agreement with the official policies, and dissident views were repressed.

While the UDF was made ineffective within months of its founding, the NAP was finally banned in February 1975 on the pretext of Hayat Khan Sherpao's murder. Beginning in 1972, a series of political murders, (Khwaja Rafiq, Dr. Nazir Ahmad, Moulvi Shamshuddin, Abdus Samad Khan Achakzai, to name only a few of the more prominent leaders), attempts at assassination of some top opposition leaders (including Wali Khan and Asghar Khan) and jailing of yet others signalled how hazardous could be any opposition to the regime.[22]

In this manner the stage was set where the PPP could be identified with the entire nation to the extent that its election symbol was incorporated in the Presidential flag; and the party anthem was telecast on August 14, 1973 after the Prime Minister's speech. It was also included in programs of youth gymnastics. The main centers and roundabouts in Karachi, Lahore, Rawalpindi-Islamabad were decorated with PPP party colors during the visits of foreign heads of state such as King Khalid, President Ceausescu and others. The party colors were also chosen for the uniforms of boys and girls participating in youth gymnastics and festivals and even for the title cover of the special numbers of publicity magazines, for example the December 1973 issue of *Pakistan Pictorial*. This systematic deification of party symbol, party flag and party colors, and the progressive development of a "Bhutto cult" represented a trend toward "political narcissism." To top it all, Bhutto adopted a "De Gaulle-like streak": "if the People's Party was strong," he claimed, "Pakistan was also strong and stable."[23]

Since the summer of 1976, Bhutto accelerated the process of social and political mobilization by refurbishing his progressive and populist image. In a surprise move, he nationalized flour mills, rice husking units and cotton ginning factories on July 17. From October 1, the regime initiated celebration of several weeks in the same way as Ayub had celebrated his "Decade of Development" in 1968. The labor week was inaugurated on October 1 with much fanfare, a number of labor leaders under detention were released and at a tripartite labor conference, Bhutto reiterated his oft-repeated promises to work for the amelioration and welfare of labor.

The first inter-provincial Bhutto 'Youth Sports' festival was inaugurated in Islamabad on October 20; the women's week was inaugurated on October 18 by Begum Nusrat Bhutto and a 19-point "declaration" on the rights of women was announced on October 23, extending them complete equality with men. The distribution of 2,243,185 acres of land resumed under the 1972 land reforms among 100,000 landless peasants on September 17; and the extension of the date for the five-marla plots' applications in the villages was announced on December 11. During the Peasants' week, announcing an eight-point national charter for peasants on December 18, the Prime Minister promised "an accelerated transfer of all state lands, with full ownership rights, to landless cultivators."[24]

The Prime Minister inaugurated the five-day Jurists' International Conference at Karachi on December 8 and the week-long International Congress on Quaid-i-Azam at Islamabad on December 19, and laid the foundation stone of the Islamabad sports and cultural complex on December 20, and of the Quaid-i-Azam museum on December 25. The news about the rich oil strikes at Dhodak in Dera Ghazi Khan (which were later found to be highly exaggerated) was announced on December 21, and the second phase of land reforms was made public on January 5. The new reforms reduced the ceiling from the 1972 ceiling of 150 irrigated acres to 100 acres, and from 300 unirrigated acres to 200 acres—i.e., from 1,200 produce units in 1972 to 8,000 produce units. Simultaneously, it was decided to replace the traditional land tax with a tax on agricultural income for 25-plus irrigated and 50-plus unirrigated farms.[25] Actually the reforms were chiefly designed to outwit the TI and NDP, which had called for a lower ceiling, as their "campaign issue." Pension increases for all retired civil and military personnel were announced on January 6. Friday was declared the weekly holiday from July 1 and the following day the dates of general elections were announced.

In short, all these measures were taken for mobilizing public opinion in favor of the ruling party. Thus Bhutto had prepared himself, his party, and the electorate for the general elections and had systematically created, step by step, the "proper" climate to ensure for his party a landslide victory.

This assertion is further confirmed by the fact that during 1975–76, inspired reports of mass entry of people from various sectors of life into the PPP were published in the national press. These reports were matched, if at all, by stories of mutual differences, suspicions, and bickering among the "divided opposition" and the utter failure to agree upon a common leader and a common platform.

While Bhutto had meticulously prepared every detail of a successful election campaign for ensuring a massive PPP victory, he somehow miserably failed in his calculations insofar as he could not visualize the possibility of being suddenly confronted with a united opposition. Hence Bhutto was caught napping when the opposition, in a surprise and sudden move, decided to offer a united front in the elections. Yet, initially Bhutto was supremely confident that this "hodge-podge" of an electoral coalition would neither last long, nor make any effective impact on the electorate. In this prognostication, however, Bhutto, as we shall see later, was utterly unrealistic, and was to be sorely disappointed.

V. NA Seats, Nominations, Candidates

a) Province-wise Distribution

At stake in the NA elections were 200 seats, which were distributed among the four provinces in proportion to their respective population per-

TABLE I
Province-wise Distribution of Population, NV Seats, Registered Voters and Voting Percentage

Provinces	Population/ percentage of total pop.	No. of seats/ percentage seats	Av. No. of persons per seat	Regd. voters/ percentage of pop.	Av. No. of Regd. voters per seat	Votes polled percentage of Regd. voters
1. Punjab[a]	37,743,404 (58.10%)	116 (58%)	325,374.17	18,903,344 (50.08%)	162,959.86	12,806,586 (67.5%)
2. Sind	14,007,701 (21.56%)	43 (21.50%)	325,760.49	4,412,411 (31.50%)	102,614.21	2,761,667 (62.5%)
3. N.W.F.P. (incl. Tribal Areas)	10,811,252 (16.64%)	34 (17%)	317,978	3,753,940 (34.72%)	110,410	1,780,903 (47.4%)
a) NWFP (excl. Tribal Areas)	8,325,385 (12.82%)	26 (13%)	320,207.12	3,674,967 (44.14%)	141,344.88	1,760,716 (47.91%)
b) Federally Administered Tribal Areas	2,485,867 (3.83%)	8 (4%)	310,733.38	78,973 (3.18%)	9,871.63	20,187 (25.56%)
4. Baluchistan	2,401,154 (3.7%)	7 (3.50%)	343,022	491,132 (20.45%)	70,161.71	145,593 (29.6%)
Total	64,963,511	200	324,817.56	27,620,827 (42.52%)	138,104.14	17,494,949 (63.3%)

centages (see Table I). Punjab with 58 percent of Pakistan's total population was given the largest number of seats (116), followed by Sind (43), NWFP (34), and Baluchistan (7). The average number of persons represented by each NA seat ranged between 318,000 and 343,000 with the mean of 324,000. However, the variance in the average number of the registered voters per seat between the various provinces was much higher: 163,000 in the Punjab to about 70,000 in Baluchistan, excluding the federally-administered tribal areas where the score was about 9,900 per seat.

The EC had decided that it was "committed to hold a fair election" and claimed to be "doing its utmost and taking all possible measures to ensure clean elections" and to appoint persons "who commanded respect and inspired confidence."[26] The EC set up some 13,800 polling stations, each one with a presiding officer (Punjab, 9,200; Sind, 2,200; NWFP, 2,000; and Baluchistan, 400), and appointed some 50,000 assistant presiding officers, 100,000 polling officers and 182 returning officers (since 19 candidates had been returned unopposed).

TABLE II
Nomination for the National Assembly by Party and Region

	Punjab	Sind	N.W.F.P.	Saluchistan	Total
Total Seats	(116)	(43)	(34)	(7)	200
Pakistan Peoples Party (PPP)	116	28 + 15[a]	25	3 + 4[a]	191
Pakistan National Alliance (P.N.A.)	115	27	26	—	168
Pakistan Muslim League (Qayyum Group)(QML)	17	1	17	2	37
Other minor parties[b]	11	4	2	4	21
Independents	133	33	155	3	324
Total:	392	108	225	16	741
Average number of candidates per seat	3.38	2.51	6.62	2.29	3.71

a) Elected unopposed.

b) Minor parties include NAP (Pakhtoonkhawa) 3 seats in Baluchistan only; Jamiat-i-Ulama-i-Islam 9 seats (Punjab 4, Sind 2, NWFP 2, Baluchistan 1); Pakistan Inqilabi Nahaz 3 seats in Punjab only; Pakistan Workers Party 3 seats (Punjab 1, Sind 2); Pakistan Socialist Party, Tahaffaz-i-Islam Party and Jamaat-i-Alia Mujahedden one seat each in Punjab only.

Nominations totalled 741 which works out to 3.71 candidates per seat (see Table II). The largest number of candidates per seat was in the NWFP (6.62) while the lowest was in Baluchistan (2.29). The PPP nominated candidates to all the seats (excepting the eight seats in the tribal areas where political parties do not function); but the rejection of the PPP contestants' nomination papers (Peshawar 1; NA 1) left 191 PPP candidates in the field. Some 168 candidates contested the elections on PNA's ticket; but in view of the PNA's charges of some of their candidates having been prevented from filing nomination papers through kidnapping and other devices, the actual number of PNA nominations must be a little higher. Province-wise, they contested 115 of Punjab's 116 seats, 27 in Sind and 26 in NWFP, but boycotted the elections in Baluchistan. The QML candidates numbered 37; and other minor parties put up 21 candidates. There were in all 324 independents, a number of them contesting from NWFP, with the largest average number of candidates per seat.

It may be interesting to observe that in a comparison with the 1970 elections, during the last election there was a considerable decline in the number of major parties contesting the elections, in the number of nominations, in the number of independents, and in the number of candidates per seat. For, in 1970, there were 12 major parties, and a total of 801 candidates (including 210 independents) for West Pakistan's 138 seats, which works out to 5.8 candidates per seat. In part, this decline signalled a trend towards emergent stable political parties, in fact a healthy trend in terms of development of a democratic polity.

b) Candidates' Background

For the PPP tickets, there was, of course, a stampede since a PPP ticket was considered a sure win. After all, the regime had "managed" to win every by-election, including all but two in disaffected Baluchistan and alienated NWFP. Forty of the 100 PPP sitting NA members (including the party's Secretary-General and at least one minister) were denied tickets. Many dedicated party workers were not given tickets, and instead members of "the old wealthy families" and fresh recruits were issued party tickets simply because they were considered "electable." The infusion of such new elements into party ranks frustrated and alienated old party workers of leftist orientation.[27]

On the contrary, the PNA candidates were largely drawn from amongst (a) the opposition members of the outgoing NA and PA's; (b) opposition-oriented lawyers who had been active in bar politics; (c) the clerics' ulema representing various schools of thought; (d) former student leaders; and (e) trusted political workers. In fact, most of the PNA candidates came from a middle-class background with a long record of affiliation with the opposition, but most of the PPP candidates were recruited from either the land-owning, or the industrial, or the business classes, or politically influential families (like the Noons, Daulatanas, Qureshis and the Gilzais) who had always been on the side of the establishment.

Under such circumstances, Bhutto and his party went for the elections overconfident of their eventual sweeping victory; but the PNA entered the arena skeptical and uncertain because Bhutto had all the cards in his hand while they had none. The ruling party's intentions of employing the governmental machinery for ensuring victory of its candidates was sufficiently evidenced by the fact that 19 NA and 66 PA candidates of the PPP were declared "elected unopposed." They included the Prime Minister as well as all four Chief Ministers.[28]

But in view of the fact that only one candidate was elected unopposed in 1970, the long list of those "elected unopposed" looked incredible, and proved counterproductive; it only lent credence to the opposition charges of the kidnapping of Jan Muhammad Abbasi and Mian Ehsan Bari, who were rivals of Bhutto and the Punjab Chief Minister, Sadiq Husain Qureshi. Similarly, the PNA openly charged that their many candidates were prevented from filing nomination papers.[29] There were also charges of foul play on the part of both administration and the Returning Officers (RO's), involving some 81 NA and PA constituencies. The EC, anxious to demonstrate its neutrality, set aside some of the RO's decisions; but because of its limited powers skirted around the alleged Abbasi kidnapping case and dismissed his appeal on technical grounds. From then on, the government's sincerity to hold, and the EC's competence to ensure free and fair elections became even more suspect.

VI. *The Issues*

a) *The Manifestoes*

In Table III are shown various issues contained in the respective manifestoes of the PPP and the PNA in accordance with their relative preferences. The PPP manifesto referred to the inherited political problems, dilated at length on the "fulfillment" of its numerous promises, and delineated its future plans for consolidating the already achieved "gains" and ushering in an "egalitarian" order through a comprehensive socioeconomic program. In his "Foreword", Chairman Bhutto promised "to carry forward the task" of building a more prosperous and glorious Pakistan" and sought the people's support to face "the challenge of the future."[30]

The PNA manifesto, on the other hand, focused attention on the dismantling of the democratic institutions, the distortion of the 1973 consti-

TABLE III

Main Political Themes and Their Relative
Frequency in the Manifestoes and Major
Addresses of the PPP and PNA leaders
(in percentage)

Themes	P.P.P.		P.N.A.	
	Manifesto	Bhutto & Major leaders[a]	Manifesto	Council[b] Members
1. Democratic Institution; Constitution	4.91	(c)	5	5.545
2. Civic rights	4.31	—	25.46	51.201
3. Inherited pol. problems	6.10	(c)	—	—
Total (Political)	(15.32)	(13.92)	(30.46)	(56.74)
4. Socioeconomic problems and reforms	61.06	17.40	46.37	15.73
5. Islamic Ideology	4.46	2.954	8.18	17.730
6. Foreign policy and defence	15.92	4.008	10.45	0.237
7. Miscellaneous	3.14	17.51	1.82	9.534
8. Negative Approach	—	44.198	2.72	70 (approx)

a) Major PPP leaders include, Abdul Hafeez Pirzada, Mumtaz Ali Bhutto and Kausar Niazi, while PNA leaders include all the members of the PNA Coordinating Council (Mufti Mahmud, Asghar Khan, Mian Tufail Muhammad, Shah Ahmad Noorani, Sherbaz Khan Mazari, Nawabzada Nasrullah Khan, Malik Muhammad Qasim, Ashraf Khan, Sardar Sikandar Hayat, and Rafiq Ahmad Bajwa), besides Ghafoor Ahmad and Begum Nasim Wali Khan, who addressed major meetings together.

b) Contents or materials which are either anti-regime PPP or anti-PNA have been computed under "Negative Approach" head.

c) Contents under the two heads cannot be easily separated.

tution, the curtailment of the powers of the judiciary, the denial of civil rights, the abuses of power, press curbs, the bureaucratic red tape, the failure of so-called "reforms", high prices and the growing unemployment in the country. In regard to foreign policy, it promised to quit CENTO, disowned the Simla agreement and resolved not to repay unproductive foreign loans.[31]

b) The Campaign Themes

In the face of numerous hindrances in fighting an already entrenched regime, the opposition, from the start of its campaign, forcefully articulated the anti-Bhutto sentiments which could not be expressed by people for reasons of fear of political vengeance. They exploited skillfully the widespread discontent (arising chiefly from reactions against the regime's "excesses", continuing price hikes, mounting corruption in high places, grievances and indignities). They were remarkably successful in arousing popular enthusiasm. Soon enough, the PNA flags, which so far could scarcely be seen, became a common sight everywhere. Consequently, the initial psychological thrust created by the PNA kept the PPP on the defensive until the end of the campaign.

The massive offensive mounted by the opposition and the surprisingly enthusiastic response of the people ultimately forced Bhutto to shed "his calm demeanor", and adopt his usual fiery posture in the course of the election campaign.

Interestingly, the claims and counter-claims, the charges and counter-charges proffered by both the parties were reminiscent of the Ayub-Miss Jinnah duel in 1964. Like Ayub, Bhutto fought on the strength of his past record, referring tirelessly to his numerous socioeconomic "reforms", to his "signal " contributions toward promoting unity of the Muslim world and the solidarity of the Third World. Again like Ayub, Bhutto sharply focused on foreign policy as the main plank of his election,[31] aiming at capitalizing on his personal "prestige" and "accomplishments" in the international field. But the opposition refused to walk into his booby trap. Therefore, foreign poicy themes which were originally given a 16 percent weightage in the PPP manifesto dropped to about four percent in the major addresses of Bhutto and his chief lieutenants (see Table III).

The main theme of the opposition campaign related to the regime's record; but the stress was on its seamy side, its "spectacular failures", "unscrupulous squandering" of the national wealth, its excessive expenditure on administration and its suicidal economic policies, its failure to check price spiralling and the worsening law and order situation, the widespread corruption, politicising of the bureaucracy, and misuse of government or government-aided agencies for party purposes, creation of the FSF as a counterblast against the armed forces and for using it against the opposition, its curtailment of the powers of the judiciary, its muzzling of the press, its "brutal trampling" of basic human rights, its sellout on Kashmir in the Simla Accord, and, above all, its identification of the party with the state.[33]

c) Charges and Counter-Charges

In a society like Pakistan, highly fragmented both horizontally and vertically, the issues presented are bound to be in terms of black and white, with no shade of grey in between. Thus the PPP presented itself as a united, progressive, stable, forward-looking and experienced body while accusing the PNA of being disunited, retrogressive, unstable, backward-looking and inexperienced. As in the 1964 election, during the recent election also the ruling party confronted the voters with the Hobson's choice of "stability vs. chaos", and the opposition emphasized "democracy vs. authoritarianism." The opposition, as did Miss Jinnah in 1964, also charged that the regime had created an atmosphere "laden with fear and reeking corruption"; on the contrary, Bhutto, like Ayub, challenged the capacity of the opposition to lead the nation.[34]

Bhutto went about charging that most of the PNA's constituent parties were against the very creation of Pakistan, and they were still hobnobbing with Mujib against him and against Pakistan. He asserted that the opposition parties were responsible for the trouble in Baluchistan and were still bent upon undoing Pakistan. The opposition counter-charged that in the first place Bhutto was resonsible for the dismemberment of Pakistan in order to achieve his personal ambitions. They also vehemently criticized Bhutto's refusal to put Yahya on trial and to release the Hamoodur Rahman Commission report.

As "the level of personal trust was low", and because "the political process was viewed as a life-and-death conflict", little surprising that the six-week debate was characterized by a lack of moderation and by increasing bitterness. The opposition was dubbed an agency of disruption, whereas the PPP government was accused of being an engine of oppression. For both the ruling party and the opposition, the stakes seemed too high; the rival party too dangerous.

d) Political Adjustments

Interestingly, both the PPP and the PNA, conceding to political realities, made significant adjustments. Bhutto preempted the opposition's Islamic plank, with a long list of his services to hold aloft the banner of Islam in Pakistan and elsewhere. The PNA on its part tried to preempt the PPP's socioeconomic plank. The PPP spokesmen and advertisements dropped all direct references to socialism, replacing it by "Masawat-i-Muhammadi"; the PNA promised not to denationalize any of the nationalized industries except the agro-based, micro rice milling, flour husking and cotton ginning factories, and held out an assurance of a better deal to labor, peasantry, the shelterless and the poor. Although still firmly committed to progressive socioeconomic goals and a more egalitarian order, the PPP mainly stressed, in the course of the election campaign, that they were more capable of serving Islam and the Islamic cause in Pakistan and elsewhere. Bhutto, on his part, was determined to defeat the PNA on the ideological ground, denying at the same time the civic rights of the people.

On the contrary, the PNA, promising an early enforcement of an Islamic system in Pakistan, mainly stressed the restoration of civic rights. Thus it may be observed that neither Islam nor socioeconomic matters were the real issues, but in fact restoration of civic rights and democracy were made the central theme of the acrimonious debate (see Table III). Therefore, naturally, vindication of the citizens' self-respect which, according to the PNA, had been "badly bruised" and "systematically trampled upon" by the PPP regime, became the most explosive issue of the campaign.[35]

The recurring "negative approach" throughout the campaign (see Table III) provides a reliable index of the level and measure of mutual acrimony and distrust, almost bordering on deadly enmity. This is also borne out by statistical analysis of election speeches of the party leaders. Approximately 44 percent of all speeches of PPP leaders were devoted to scathing criticism of the opposition leaders, their past affiliation, their subversive role, and their future "designs"; in contrast, about 75 percent of the campaign speeches of the PNA leaders were directed against Bhutto, and the "iniquitous" system that he had thrust upon the country.

e) Campaign Strategy

The opposition's main problem was how to convey their viewpoint to the electorate, given a short period of the campaign, persistent denial of access to mass media[36] and extremely limited coverage of their viewpoint in the national press, with the sole exception of the *Nawa-i-Waqt* (Lahore). Therefore, they used the strategy of holding meetings at all important places, organizing public rallies and taking out impressive processions.[37] They organized a 125-mile march from Rawalpindi to Gujranwala along the Grand Trunk Road which was joined in a various stages by hundreds of thousands of people from far-off places, holding in their hands ploughs and lanterns, the PNA election symbols. The high point of all this election fanfare was a marathon led by Asghar Khan, a 20-mile long procession from the Karachi airport to the main center of the old city covering almost 12 hours on February 20. It is estimated that nearly one million people had joined the procession. Consequently, Asghar Khan, as de facto leader of the PNA, was able to project forcefully his image in the public eye as a national leader, and

TABLE IV
Distribution by Frequency of Major Mass
Rallies, Addresses to Special Croups and
Statements of Major PPP and PNA Leaders[a]
from January 1, to March 5, 1977

Nature of Audience	Bhutto & Major ppp leaders[a]	PNA leaders
Public rallies and processions	5	16
Radio addresses	4	—
Press conference releases	15	12
Total	24	28
Bar Association	—	1
Ulema	1	—
Official functions	4	—
Party workers/conventions	6	—
Students	1	1
Peasantry	3	—
Journalists	4	1
Minorities	2	1
Total	21	4

a) Major PPP leaders include Z.A. Bhutto, Abdul Hafeer Pirzada, Mumtaz Ali Bhutto and Kausar Niazi, while PNA leaders include mostly its coordinating council members.

SOURCE: *Nawa-i-Waqt* (Lahore) and *Musawat* (Karachi)

an effective substitute of Bhutto. Of course Bhutto, never at a loss to present a riposte, also organized a marathon procession in Karachi a week later, but this procession, like other PPP processions, was a state-managed affair.

In Table IV details are shown regarding the frequencies of major rallies, processions and addresses to special groups and press conferences of major leaders of both ruling and opposition parties. Table V shows the regionwise distribution of public meetings of the PPP and the PNA. Both tables clearly bring out how the PNA relied most heavily on the tactics of organizing public meetings and rallies, for the sake of winning electoral support.

Interestingly, the PPP counter-offensive was launched almost the same day as Asghar led perhaps the most memorable procession in the recent history of the subcontinent. It began with Bhutto's "give-them-hell" speech at Gol Bagh in Lahore, which put heart into PPP's sagging morale. Asghar's

TABLE V

Distribution by Region and Audience of Major
Public Meetings addressed by Major PPP leaders,
and PNA leaders from January 1, to March 5, 1977

Provinces	Bhutto & major ppp leaders(a)	PNA leaders
Punjab	58	50
Sind	20	67
N.W.F.P.	7	25
Baluchistan	1	1
Total	86	143

a) Major ppp leaders include Z.A. Bhutto, Abdul Hafeez Pirzada, Mumtaz Ali Bhutto and Kausar Niazi, while the PNA team includes chiefly its coordinating council members.

SOURCE: *Nawa-i-Waqt* (Lahore) and *Musawat* (Karachi)

controversial statement at the press conference on February 21 to the effect that the NAP case would be referred back to the Supreme Court and that the NAP would be given facilities for defending itself (which were allegedly denied during the 1975 Supreme Court reference) was seized upon by the PPP to exploit the prevalent Punjabi suspicions about Wali Khan's bona-fides. Consequently, the PNA campaign seemed to have lost some of its tempo during the last two weeks.

From February 27, barely a week before the elections, the incidence of violence sharply increased. The PNA charged the PPP of trying to browbeat the PNA workers and supporters through its "local toughs." According to incomplete reports in the newspapers, 10 people died, 71 were injured, and 397 PNA workers were arrested under the DPR during the February 27–March 5 period. Besides, there were 29 other cases of reported violence in major cities. Incidents were reported from some 16 places, including all the major cities.[38] Even processions led by Sherbaz Mazari in Karachi and Asghar Khan in Rawalpindi were fired upon. In protest, the PNA gave a call for strike on February 28, and subsequently the strike was highly successful in eight places, including Karachi, Hyderabad, Multan and Lyallpur and partially successful in Lahore, Rawalpindi and a few other places.

The PNA also charged the regime for misusing the government apparatus and administrative machinery for "unfair practices", and for "torturing" and "humiliating" opposition candidates in Sind; and for the leakage of the ballot papers and for the printing of forged ballot papers.[39] Therefore, the PNA demanded that the EC should be given legal, administrative and financial powers and that the election officers should be chosen from the judiciary and the armed forces, in order to restore the people's confidence in the conduct of the elections. All these charges were, as usual, brushed aside as "fake" and all their demands were dismissed as "unconstitutional." In consequence, the EC's competence to conduct clean and honest polls came to be increasingly debated, and the PNA, especially Asghar, gave notice of launching a countrywide movement in case the results were manipulated as appeared most likely. The PPP, on its part, charged that the PNA was doing so only in order to cover up its imminent defeat at the polls.

VII. The Results

The results were bewildering to almost everyone—except perhaps Bhutto. The reaction on both sides was admirably summed up by the BBC correspondent covering the March 8 press conferences of both Asghar and Bhutto, when he remarked that "neither did the winners look like having won, nor the losers like having lost." For the results gave the PPP a "landslide victory" of 136 out of 173 seats under contest, plus another 19 "uncontested" seats (see Table V). The PNA was conceded only 36 seats and the QML could get only one.

According to official results, a total of 17,494,749 votes were cast, which works out to 63.0 percent of the total registered votes. But this voting percentage can be misleading in view of the 19 "unopposed" seats and the PNA boycott of polls in Baluchistan. When the votes for the 19 "unopposed" seats (about 20 percent) and the 9.4 percent drop in polling in Baluchistan compared to 1970 polling (in view of the PNA boycott) are accounted for, the total registered voters for the contested seats may be computed at approximately 22,050,496. On this basis, the voting percentage comes to 79.55 percent of the registered voters in the contested constituencies. Considering the fact that the voting percentage in the U.S. Presidential elections (1976) and the Indian (Lok Sabha) elections of March 1977 were respectively 53.3 percent and 60 percent, the "official" Pakistani percentage seems rather too high.

More astonishing was the PPP's score of 58.1 percent as against PNA's 35.1 percent of the total votes cast (see Table VII). Still more astonishing was PNA's score of only eight out of 116 seats in the Punjab which was by all indications tilted toward the PNA by at least a small margin (see Table VI).

All the more incredible do the results look in view of the PPP's 1970 performance. In 1970 when it was "riding at the crest of its popularity", and was "suffering from no backlash", with all the pluses on their side, the PPP

TABLE VI

National Assembly Results: Party Position

Provinces	Total seats	PPP	PNA	QML
Punjab[a]	116[a]	108[a]	8	—
Sind	43	32 (17 + 15[b])	11	—
N.W.F.P.	34 (28 + 8[c])	8	17	1
Baluchistan	7	7 (3 + 4[b])	—	—
Total	200	155	36	1

a) Includes Islamabad's one seat.
b) Elected "unopposed."
c) Tribal Areas' seats which went to independents.

could not secure more than 39 percent of the votes cast. And now after a "controversial" five years in office, confronted by a united opposition and in the face of mass discontent, its latest score of 58 percent votes calls in question the entire conduct of the elections and their results (see Table VII). By the same token, how could the united opposition secure only 35 percent of the votes while these parties together had obtained 48.7 percent votes in multicornered contests in 1970?

One revealing feature was the early announcement on radio and television networks of results of rural constituencies like those of Tharparkar 1 (NA-173) and Sukkur 11 and 111 (NA-152 and 153) with total votes cast ranging from 125,758 to 139,157. Those results were announced on the television network by 7:30 P.M.—while the results from key constituencies in cities with better communication facilities like Karachi were withheld till about 5 A.M. the next morning. Even otherwise, how could some 140,000 ballot papers in each constituency be unfolded and counted, and the aggregate results tabulated and communicated to Rawalpindi-Islamabad within a matter of three hours after polling is stopped at 4 P.M.? All this seemed to give credence to rumors[40] that the statistics had been preset and issued directly from the Prime Minister's office.[41]

Without going into too many details, one may refer here to an analysis of the official "results" by a senior Pakistani journalist,[42] who has pointed out instances of incredible voting patterns, and given interesting conclusions. The rural Sukkur 111 (NA-153) constituency registered an 85 percent turn-out while it ranged from 64.5 percent to 47.5 percent in the highly polit-

TABLE VII

Performance of PPP and Other "Opposition" Parties in 1970 & 1977
Elections in Terms of Vote Percentage and Seats Won

Contesting Parties	Percent of votes in favor		Seats Won	
	1970	1977	1970	1977
PUNJAB				
PPP	41.66	60.12	62	108
Other parties excluding Independents	35.38	34.75	20	8 PNA
SIND				
PPP	44.95	63.00	18	17
Other parties excluding Independents	34.94	30.00	9	11 PNA
N.W.F.P.				
PPP	14.28	37.00	1	8
Other parties excluding Independents	73.70	48.00	17	17 PNA
BALUCHISTAN				
PPP	1.88	43.00	—	3
Other parties excluding Independents	48.38	33.00	4	—
WEST PAKISTAN (POST 1971 PAKISTAN)				
PPP	38.89	58.1	81	136
Other parties excluding Independents	48.66	35.4	42	35 PNA

icized and hotly contested Karachi metropolitan area. At polling station No. 55, (Primary School Area) the vote cast (1,608) exceeded the number of registered voters (1,580), while polling station No. 53 showed 100 percent voting, which means "that nobody in the area covered by the polling station has died between the preparation of the electoral rolls and the polling day, that nobody felt like not to exercise his right of franchise."[43] The voting trend showed that polling was generally higher where the PPP candidates had won. showed that polling was generally higher where the PPP candidates had won.

The figures of rejected votes given officially present a bizarre pattern. At least there were two constituencies (Quetta 11/NA-195 and Multan-1/NA-3) where the number of invalid votes was higher than the margin between the first two leading candidates. In Yahya Bakhtiar's (Attorney-General) constituency (Quetta 11), the rejected votes totalled 10,993 while the winner had a margin of only 1,489 votes over his leading rival. While Sahiwal VI (NA-137) registered no invalid votes, its neighbouring Shaiwal IV (NA-135) registered 4,003 out of 128,652 votes. Likewise, Rahim Yar Khan 1 and 11 (NA-147 and NA-148) had 4,417 and 4,070 invalid votes respectively, while Rahim Yar Khan IV (NA-150) registered not a single invalid vote. It is interesting to note that most of these rejected votes bore two stamp marks— one each against the name of both candidates.

On the basis of the data presented in his article, Burney concludes:[44]

The Election Commission has conceded that (a) "hair-raising" malpractices have been committed (b) samples of ballot papers were leaked out in Karachi; (c) allegations that ballot paper books were despatched on 8.3.1977 (March 8, 1977) were brought to its notice; (d) tampering with election results was attempted at least in one constituency by as high a functionary as the Deputy Commissioner of Mardan; (e) it is possible to clear up "all this mess' within six months.

Under an ordinance promulgated by the President of Pakistan on March 30 conferring the powers of an Election Tribunal on the EC, it held preliminary inquiries, sealed and sent for the polling record of at least 26 constituencies including those of five federal ministers, and pronounced judgment in six cases till April 26. However, when the newly sworn-in PPP government found that the Chief Election Commissioner (CEC) meant business this time and that the inquiries blasted the regime's claims of having held a free and fair election, it withdrew suddenly the powers earlier conferred on the EC. However, the cases already scrutinised showed, according to the CEC, that the polls had been "vitiated by grave irregularities." One has only to refer to the EC's judgment in the case of Sargodha V, NA-57, (PPP's Hafizullah Cheema vs. PNA's Zafarullah Khan) to note to what extent even federal ministers went to manipulate results in their favor. Even Prime Minister Bhutto, while stoutly denying having any hand in the rigging or manipulation of results, had conceded before the National Assembly on March 28: " . . . there might have been irregularities in some places . . . ;" but defended them saying, "it happened even in civilised countries like the U.S.A." More concrete evidence of rigging has come in the recent Supreme Court judgment in Begum Nusrat Bhutto's case against her husband's detention.

Finally, even Mr. Justice Sajjad Ahmad Jan, former CEC, had admitted the rigging charge in unequivocal terms.[45] In his last press interview before he fell a victim to gas poisoning at PPP's Nasrullah Khan Khattak's residence last November, he admitted that[46]

The failure of the electoral process was by and large due to the candidates of the ruling party who exploited their position and the party machine and succeeded in hoaxing the officials in charge of the elections and thus destroying the sanctity of the ballot box.

He also admitted that the "Election Commission had no resources to stop rigging without the active and earnest support of the Government in power and its agencies", and that the March last elections were "a complete hoax."[47]

In his March 8 televised press conference, Bhutto perfunctorily dismissed charges of a systematic and massive rigging of polls, made earlier that afternoon by Asghar Khan, and asserted that if the people felt cheated by the election results, they would take to the streets to show their resentment. The nation responded to that challenge by boycotting the PA elections on March 10 and observing a complete hartal the following day in all the big cities and towns, and still later, from March 14 onwards, by launching a movement which, in its duration, its intensity and its resilency, outmatched any other movement in the recent history of the subcontinent.

Again, Bhutto's claim in the same press conference that the womenfolk as a group had voted PPP *en masse* was later to be controverted massively by the women[48] themselves who injected fresh enthusiasm into, gave a momentum to, and sustained the PNA's movement for the cancellation of the discredited March polls and the holding of fresh polls under neutral agencies.

VIII. Conclusion

The tragedy with Bhutto was that he was too sure of himself. He considered himself a man of crisis, deliberately creating one and then managing it with immense relish. But unfortunately for him, when he decided, as has been amply demonstrated, to rig the polls, or when he disdainfully rejected the PNA's initially moderate demands, he did not realize at all that his highhanded conduct would ultimately precipitate a crisis of such a magnitude and intensity that would defy disentanglement and diffusion. Perhaps he did not imagine that his own hand-picked generals could dare topple him from the pinnacle of power. Thus he was a victim of his own overconfidence, complacency, miscalculation, and lust for power. It is indeed a misfortune that a man of unusual accomplishments like Bhutto should have acted Borbourn-like. Had he been a little less ambitious, and less ruthless and a little more tolerant toward his political opponents, he would still be very much at the pedestal of power. Ayub had also manipulated the 1964–65 presidential election results, but was careful enough not to manipulate them to the extent Bhutto did. Ayub had conceded his rival a 36.4 percent vote even in an indirect election, but Bhutto would not concede the united opposition more than 18 percent of the NA seats. Had Bhutto only conceded the PNA about 70 seats, the rigging charge would not have struck so heavy and so fast, nor would the PNA have been able to organize and carry on a mass movement on such a scale for almost three months. Bhutto was sustained in office during the last three months of his rule by the rather unstinted, though inexplicable, support of the armed forces which he tried to use and did use to suppress the PNA movement so long as he could. But one who tries to ride a tiger ends up by being swallowed or mauled by it.

Bhutto had a unique opportunity to institutionalize parliamentary democracy, to found and strengthen democratic institutions, and to establish a viable political system congruent with the country's political culture; but he thoughtlessly threw away the unique opportunity, if only for the sake of institutionalizing his personal rule in Pakistan. Tragic as this was, his greatest disservice to Pakistan (which itself was created on the basis of the ballot box) lay in abusing the sanctity of the ballot box. And in doing this in such a crude way, he almost shattered the nation's faith in elections.

Notes

1. The author acknowledges his debt to Professor Norman D. Palmer's definitive work, *Elections and Political Development: The South Asian Experience* (London: C. Hurst & Company, 1975), for the insights and clues it provided while writing the present paper; (all references to Palmer, unless otherwise stated, are to this work). While the "Introduction" draws upon Palmer heavily for its theoretical framework in the first chapter, the following four articles on the Indian and Pakistani elections published in *Asian Survey* XVII:7 (July 1977) were also found extremely useful: Lawrence Ziring, "Pakistan: The Campaign before the Storm," pp. 581-98; M.G. Weinbaum, "The March 1977 Elections in Pakistan: Where Everyone Lost," pp. 599-618; Myron Weiner, "The 1977 Parliamentary Elections in India," pp. 619-626; and Norman D. Palmer, "The Two Elections: A Comparative Analysis," pp. 648-66.

2. W.J.M. Mackenzie, *Free Elections: An Elementary Textbook* (New York: Rinehart and Company, 1958), p. 175, cited in Palmer, *op. cit.*, p. 4.

3. *Ibid.*, p. 12.

4. For instance, see Betty B. Burch and Allan B. Cole (eds.), *Asian Political Systems* (New York: D. Van Nostrand Company, Inc., 1968) wherein the present author's two studies on the 1965 elections, published earlier, and Ayub Khan's 1965 election manifesto have been included under the section entitled "Political Processes," pp. 415-40.

5. Palmer, *op. cit.*, p. 214.

6. *Ibid.*, p. 7.

7. According to Prof. Key, a "critical election," is one "in which the depth and intensity of electoral involvement are high, in which more or less, profound readjustments occur in the relation of power within the community, and in which new and durable electoral groupings are formed." V.O. Key, Jr., "A Theory of Critical Elections," *Journal of Politics*, XVII (1955), pp. 3-18. See also Palmer, *op. cit.*, pp. 15-16, for a discussion on the classification of elections and for specific examples of each type.

8. See Angus Campbell, Philip E. Converse, Warren E. Miller, and Donald E. Stokes, *Elections and the Political Order* (New York: John Wiley and Sons, 1966), Chapter 4, "Classification of Presidential Elections."

9. Armed clashes had frequently occurred between PPP and PNA supporters since April 14, 1977, when Bhutto addressed his party workers in Punjab Governor's House and tried to put heart into their sagging morale. Arms licences had been issued on a large scale since April 1977: the MNAs were given 100 licences and MPAs 50 licences for their supporters. The Law and Order Committee, headed by Yahya Bakhtiar (see below) noted at its June 27 meeting that some of these licences were even sold to the opposition (*Dawn*, October 11, 1977, p. 10). Arms and ammunition shops were also broken open and their contents stolen. Both parties, it seemed, were arming themselves to the teeth. Renewed clashes occurred when the PPP-PNA dialogue ran into a deadlock. Tearing of PNA banners by a procession headed by Ghulam Mustafa Khar led to a serious clash in Sheikhupura on June 30 in which firearms were freely used (*Nawa-i-Waqt*, July 2, 1977, p. 2: July 5, 1977, p. 2). Several persons were hurt in a PPP-PNA clash in Lahore on June 24. Later, on July 4, an armed PPP procession attacked PNA supporters in Anarkali, Lahore. The present author was told that but for the army takeover on July 5, there would have been a serious explosion in Lahore that day.

The Law and Order Committee at its June 11 meeting recorded that "the prospects of maintaining law and order in the eventuality of a breakdown of talks are bleak;" for details see *The State vs. Z.A. Bhutto: Lahore High Court Judgement and Two Supreme Court Judgements* (Karachi: Maz Publications, 1978), p. 44.

Since his appointment as Personal Assistant to the Prime Minister on June 17, Khar began making extremley bellicose speeches inciting PPP followers to violence—e.g., see his June 30 Sheikupura speech (*Dawn*, July 2, 1977, p. 3; see also *ibid.*, June 27, 1977, p. 1 and *Jang*, July 5, 1977, p. 1). During his June 21 visit to Peshawar, Khar had reportedly brought three truckloads of arms and ammunitions from the tribal areas and sent them on to Lahore for distribution among the PPP workers; (the Law and Order Committee minutes of July 2 took note of these rumors: see *State vs. Z.A. Bhutto, op. cit.*, p. 45).

10. Palmer, *op. cit.*, p. 2.

11. The leading papers along with party papers and weeklies (like *Masawat*, the official PPP daily; *Mayar, Al-Fatah*, and *Viewpoint*, PPP oriented weeklies; *Islami Jamhuriyah, Afrasia*, and *Chatan*, pro-PNA weeklies) were consulted in preparation of the present paper. Among dailies, *Nawa'i-Waqt* (Lahore) was the only pro-PNA paper. While the National Press Trust's papers (like the *Pakistan Times*, Lahore and Rawalpindi *Morning News*, Karachi; *Mashriq*, Lahore, Karachi, Peshawar and Quetta; *Imroze*, Lahore and Multan) were the "drum beaters" for the regime and the PPP, papers like *Dawn* (Karachi), *Jang*, (Karachi, Rawalpindi and Quetta), and *Hurriyet* (Karachi), though under independent management, were tilted in PPP's favor; it was only after the PNA's election campaign had shown a demonstrated capacity for calling forth mammoth crowds that the last category of papers began to give somewhat better coverage to PNA's meetings and rallies. For instance, compare *Dawn*'s and *Jang*'s coverage of PNA's first election meeting at Karachi with their reports of Asghar's February 20 epoch-making procession; *Dawn*, 24 January 1977, p. 1, and February 21, 1977, p. 1; *Jang*, January 25, 1977, and February 22, 1977, p. 1.

12. For the Bhawalpur elections, see Masud Hasan Shahab, *Bhawalpur ki Siyasi Tarikh* (Bhawalpur: Maktaba-i-Ilham, 1977) and Wayne Ayres Wilcox, *Pakistan: The Consolidation of a Nation* (New York: Columbia University Press, 1963), pp. 129-133. For the four provincial elections in the 'fifties see Keith Callard, *Pakistan: A Political Study* (London: George Allen & Unwin, 1957), pp. 55-59, and Mushtaq Ahmed, *Government and Politics in Pakistan* (Karachi: Pakistan Publishing House, 2nd ed. 1963), pp. 172-73. For the 1965 presidential and assembly elections, see Karl von Vorys, *Political Development in Pakistan* (Princeton: Princeton University Press, 1965), Chapter 12, "A Guided Democracy in Action: Managing Reelections;" Sharif al Mujahid, "Pakistan's First Presidential Elections," *Asian Survey*, V:6 (June 1965), pp. 280-94; and "The Assembly Elections in Pakistan," *Asian Survey*, V:11 (November 1965), pp. 538-53) (these two articles have been included in Burch and Cole, *Asian Political Systems, op. cit.*, pp.

415-37). For the 1970 elections, see Sharif al Mujahid, "Pakistan: First General Elections," *Asian Survey,* XI:2 (February 1971), pp. 159-171; Craig Baxter, "Pakistan Votes—1970," *Asian Survey,* XI:3 (March 1971), pp. 197-218; Javed K. Bashir, *N.W.F.P. Elections of 1970: An Analysis* (Lahore: Progressive Publishers, 1973); and Iftikhar Ahmed, *Pakistan General Elections: 1970* (Lahore: South Asian Institute, 1976). Surprisingly, over 80% of Ahmad's 12 pages on the 1965 elections are a verbatim reproduction of the present author's articles, cited earlier.

13. See Mujahid, "Pakistan: The First General Elections," *loc. cit.,* p. 164.

14. Some clue of Bhutto's political style may be gained by noting his heroes which included Napoleon, Hitler, Mussolini, Nasser and Soekarno; see Oriana Fallaci, *Interview With History,* tr. John Sheplay (Boston: Houghton Mifflin Company, 1977), p. 184; "We Must Hear [Sardar Khair Baksh] Marri," *The Punjab Punch* (Lahore), Vo. 3: 33, August 19-26, 1973, pp. 1,4.

15. For instance, see the charges levelled by both Mustafa Khar and Hanif Ramay at the joint press conference, Lahore, October 21, 1975: *Nawa-i-Waqt,* October 22, 1975, pp. 1,6.

16. See Karl W. Deutsch, "Cracks in the Monolith: Possibilities and Patterns of Dis-integration in Totalitarian Systems," in Harvey Eckstein and David E. Apter (eds.), *Comparative Politics: A Reader* (New York: The Free Press, 1968), pp. 497-508.

17. See *Election Manifesto of The Pakistan People's Party 1970* (Karachi: Vision Publications Limited, 1970); *The Pakistan People's Party: Foundation and Policy* (Lahore: Pakistan People's Party, n.d.; but 1968). For an analysis of Bhutto's appeal and campaign posture in the 1970 elections see Mujahid, "Pakistan: the First General Elections," *loc. cit.,* pp. 67-170.

18. Interestingly, all of the four committees set up at the Party's first convention in 1967 had Bhutto as its chairman. "Throughout this period (1967-1974) the party developed as a Bhutto Party and no democratic structure was evolved. It was the will of the Chairman to retain any office holder . . . The result was democracy not as an expression of the will of the people but *as an eexpression of the will of one man"* (italics for emphasis). Abdullah Malik, "New Compulsions and the PPP," *Outlook,* (Karachi), Vol. 3: 10, June 8, 1974, p. 13.

19. On Secretary-General J.A. Rahim's exit, the outspoken *Outlook* (Vol. 3:14, July 6, 1974, p.3) remarked, "It is curious that from amongst the prominent persons who attended the first convention of the People's Party at Lahore on November 30, 1967, only Dr. Mubashir Hasan, Khurshid Hasan Meer and A.W. Katpur have managed to survive. The others, apart from those who never mattered, have been put on the chopping block." Meer was elbowed out in December 1974. Again for instance, Bhutto himself was reportedly behind the campaign launched by PPP MPAs Yaqub Mian, Nawab Khakwani, Raja Munawwar, Khalid Ahmad and Abdul Qayyum against Chief Minister Khar. Otherwise, I was told by well-informed journalists in Lahore, neither would they have dared to unleash the campaign against Khar, nor would their statements have been so prominently published in the Trust papers. Bhutto obviously wanted to bring the soaring, self-appointed "Quaid-i-Punjab" down to earth like a deflated balloon. Actually, Bhutto used to shift his patronage periodically, from one group to another, with a view to preventing any one group from becoming too entrenched or too powerful.

20. Cf. "Social mobilization can be defined . . . as the process in which major clusters of old social, economic and psychological commitments are eroded or broken and people become available for new patterns of socialization and behavior." Karl W. Deutsch, "Social Mobilization and Political Development," in Eckstein and Apter, *Comparative Politics: A Reader, op. cit.,* p. 583.

21. Editorial, "The Perils of Narcissism, "*Outlook,* Vol 2: 43, January 26, 1974, p. 3.

22. According to Wali Khan, the PPP government in NWFP contacted some undertrial prisoners accused of murder and promised to release them on condition that they would be used as political murderers; (interview to Yusaf Lodi in *Outlook,* Vol 3: 14, July 6, 1974, pp. 8-9). Similar charges have been levelled against PPP governments in other provinces. Numerous references to political murders, arrests and harassment occur in "The Muffled Sobs," *Outlook,* Vol 2: 37, December 15, 1973, pp. 8-13; M.H. Shah, "Sanghar: A Study in Tyranny," *ibid.,* Vol 3:12, June 22, 1974, pp. 6-8; "Witch Hunt in D.G. Khan," *ibid.,* Vol 2: 31, November 3, 1973, pp. 5-6; Yusaf Lodi, "The Strange Case of Zahur Ilahi," *ibid.,* Vol 2: 44, February 2, 1974, pp. 5-7; "Twilight of Justice," *ibid.,* Vol 2: 45, February 9, 1974, pp. 9-12; Asrar Ahmad, "Language of

Bullets," *ibid.*, Vol 1: 52, March 31, 1973, pp. 4-5; "Asghar Khan's Ordeal," *ibid.*, Vol 2: 37, December 15, 1973, p. 5; S. Nayab Husain, "Asghar: a lonely knight," *ibid.*, Vol 3: 12, June 22, 1974, p. 4; and "The Trail of Violence," *ibid.*, Vol 2; 28, October 13, 1973, pp. 4-5.

23. "The Perils of Narcissim," *loc. cit.*

24. Under the Peasants' Charter, over 10 million acres of land were to be distributed to some one million landless or less-than-subsistence-level peasant families. See M. Masud, "National Charter for Peasants," *Dawn*, January 8, 1977, p. 7.

25. Interestingly, the loophole in the 1972 law, which defined ownership by individual rather than by family basis, also plagued the 1977 law, thus enabling large landowners to retain their most fertile holdings through subdivision among their immediate family members. Actually, the reforms were chiefly designed to rob the TI and NDP, which had called for a lower ceiling, of a "looming campaign issue." It has also been alleged that many landlords had been "tipped off during the previous spring" and "had long since gotten under the revised limits." Weinbaum, *loc. cit.*, p. 604.

26. *Dawn*, February 18, 1977, p. 1.

27. See Abdullah Malik, "Elections 77: What Will Be the Bhutto Strategy," *Viewpoint*, Vol. II: 26, February 4, 1977, pp. 15-16; "PPP and the Alliance," *ibid.*, Vol II: 24, January 21, 1977, p. 9; "Sargodha: PPP Workers Disappointed," *ibid.*, Vol II: 27, February 11, 1977, p. 12.

28. Bhutto's "unopposed election" was greeted by the national press by featuring on the front page of the leading dailies on January 20, 1977 an identical three-column photograph, under almost identical captions: "the supreme leader, the undisputed leader, the great leader."

29. For Jan Mohammad Abbasi's account see *Dawn*, January 24, 1977, p. 8; and *Nawa-i-Waqt*, January 24, 1977, p. 1. For Ahsan Bari's account, see *Mayar* (Karachi), June 11-18, 1977, pp. 20-22; *Nawa-i-Waqt*, 14 February 1977, p. 2. For other cases of harassment, see *Dawn*, January 25, 1977, p. 10.

30. *Pakistan People's Party Manifesto,* (Rawalpindi: Pakistan People's Party Central Secretariat, 1977), p. 4.

31. See *Manshoor Pakistani Qaumi Ittihad* (Rawalpindi: Jamiat Tulba-i-Islam, 1977); text in *Dawn*, February 10, 1977, p. 4, and February 11, 1977, p. 8.

For an incisive analysis of the two manifestoes, see A.T. Chaudhri, "The Battle of Manifestos" in two parts, *Dawn*, February 14 and 17, 1977. Safdar Mir's two-part article on PPP manifesto in *The Pakistan Times* (January 27 and 28, 1977) is much too partisan.

32. Since 1976, Bhutto has published several papers outlining his thoughts on various aspects of foreign policy and international relations. These were published in full in all Pakistani papers and were also produced as pamphlets for wider circulation. See *RCD: Challenge and Response* (April, 1976); *The Third World: the Imperative of Unity* (September, 1976); and *Bilateralism: New Directions* (October, 1976); also *Zulfikar Ali Bhutto and the Third World's Struggle for New Economic Order* (Karachi: Institute of International Affairs, 1976). A White Paper on Kashmir was also issued in January 1977; see *The Pakistan Times*, January 16, 1977, p. 1. All these papers were obviously designed to bolster Bhutto's image as a world statesman.

33. Interestingly, there was a good deal of similarity in the campaign themes and techniques of PNA and Janata on the one hand and in the claims and tactics of Bhutto and Indira Gandhi on the other. Palmer ("The Two Elections," *loc. cit.*) brings out some of these similiarities; but an in depth comparison of the campaign themes, postures and techniques in the two elections may provide the clue as to why, despite so much in common, the results of the elections were so divergent. For a rather raw narrative of Indian elections, see Anirudha Gupta, *Revolution Through Ballot: India January–March 1977* (New Delhi: Ankur Publishing House, May 1977).

34. For instance, Bhutto, as was his wont, asked sarcastically, "If, God forbid, Mufti Mahmud became the Prime Minister and if a summit was held, how would he respond to the speeches of the Shah of Iran, President Boumouddin or to President Ceausescu of Rumania?" *Masawat* (Karachi), February 1, 1977, p. 6. Ayub had likewise accused Miss Jinnah of lacking "experience in statecraft," and of not making "the grade," even "if a bottom standard was set." See Mujahid, "Pakistan's First Presidential Elections," *loc. cit.*, p. 291.

35. See, for instance, Begum Naseem Wali Khan's speech at Peshawar on January 30: *Islam Jamhouria* (Lahore), Vol 7: 26, February 7-13, 1977, p. 8.

36. Radio and television even refused to broadcast the main points in the PNA's manifesto on a commercial basis. More atrocious, for a long time they referred to PNA not by its nomenclature in English or Urdu but as "the group of nine parties," and sometimes as "the gang of nine parties." See PNA's protest, *Dawn*, February 15, 1977, p. 8. Despite the High Court and Supreme Court ruling, the state-run media did not give adequate coverage to the PNA's campaign.

37. Table IV details the relative frequencies of major rallies and processions, addresses to special groups and press conferences of major PPP and PNA leaders while Table V shows the distribution of PPP and PNA public meetings by region and audiences. These two tables indicate the emphasis laid by the opposition for reaching wider audiences through more numerous rallies, and public meetings.

38. Figures based on news items published in *Jang* (Karachi) and *Nawa-i-Waqt* for the period February 25-March 4, 1977. See opposition's apprehensions about the ruling party's "designs," *Viewpoint*, Vol II: 27, February 11, 1977, p. 10.

39. The only action taken was to suspend a staff member of the Security Printing Press, Karachi. The CEC's explanation was that the EC "would be justified in reprinting the ballot papers . . . only *if it was established* that the ballot papers were taken out with some fraudulent intention or on a considerable scale" (italics for emphasis). Facsimile of the ballot paper prestamped in PPP's favor and bearing the official stamp and code of the EC, and allegedly "forged" officially and distributed to ruling party men were published in *Nawa-i-Waqt*; also in *Impact International* (London), Vol 7-6, March 25-April 7, 1977, p.6.

40. In view of an unofficial ban on certain types of communication, rumors have claimed widespread credibility and respectability at least since Ayub's rise to power. During Bhutto's regime in particular, they had a field day. In part, rumor-mongering may be attributed to what a progovernment daily calls the "information gap created by Government agencies themselves;" editorial, "Rumours," *The Pakistan Times* (Lahore), October 3, 1971, p. 8.

41. In many constituencies there was a discrepancy between voting figures announced by the radio and the actual count. Therefore additional ballot papers were allegedly printed on the night of March 7/8 and ballot boxes refilled to remove the discrepancy. Interestingly 12 books of ballot papers for constituency No. NA 146 were dispatched at 1:30 P.M. on March 8 from the printing press and received by the Deputy Election Commissioner, Punjab. The PNA Secretariat claimed to possess the voucher, showing the dispatch of the books, and the time and date. See *Impact International* (London), Vol 7:6, March 25-April 7, 1977, p. 7; and I.H. Burney, "March '77 Elections: An Analysis," *Pakistan Economist* (Karachi), Vol 17:30, July 23, 1977, p. 17.

42. *Ibid.,* pp. 13-23.

43. *Ibid.,* p. 22.

44. *Ibid.,* pp. 22-23.

45. See *Dawn*, April 6, 1977, p. 1; April 7, 1977, pp. 1, 8; *Nawa-i-Waqt*, editorial, April 8, 1977; *Chatan* (Lahore), May 23, 1977; and *Millat* (Karachi), May 6, 1977. Interestingly, even Bhutto, while stoutly denying having had any hand in the rigging or manipulation of results, still conceded before the National Assembly on March 28: ". . . there might have been individual excesses," but defended them saying, "it happened in most civilized countries" like the U.S.A. See *Dawn*, March 29, 1977, p. 8.

46. For E.C.'s judgement, see *Dawn*, April 1, 1977; p. 1; *PLD 1977, Journal* 64, p. 176.

47. *Dawn*, November 29, 1977, p. 1.

48. According to government sources 248 women processions were taken out during the first nine weeks, March 14-May 17. This was the first time women had participated in a political movment in such a substantial and significant way. See *The State vs. Z.A. Bhutto, op. cit.,* p. 43.

From Electoral Politics to Martial Law:
Alternative Perspectives
on Pakistan's Political Crisis of 1977
WILLIAM L. RICHTER

On July 5, 1977, the five year reign of Zulfikar Ali Bhutto and his People's Party Government came to an abrupt end. Bhutto was ousted in a bloodless military take-over headed by Chief of Army Staff, General Zia-ul Haq. Only six months earlier, Prime Minister Bhutto had been at the pinnacle of his power. In early January, when he announced that general elections would be held in March for national and provincial assemblies, Bhutto could claim that Pakistan was the "most democratic country in South Asia." His recent tours of the country had persuaded him that his political stock was high and he perceived the elections both as an opportunity to consolidate the reforms of five years of "People's Government" and as a crowning achievement in his reconstruction of the new Pakistan following the debacle of the 1971 war. The elections were to be the first under the 1973 Constitution and, more importantly, the first in Pakistan's thirty year history in which an incumbent government submitted itself to the judgment of the direct popular vote of the people.

The six months between Bhutto's announcement of the elections and his downfall must rank amoung the most eventful and crucial periods in Pakistan's troubled political history. In January and February, Bhutto found himself faced with an unexpectedly stiff challenge from a united and powerful coalition of opposition parties, the Pakistan National Alliance (PNA).[1] When the national assembly elections were held March 7, Bhutto and the PPP won heavily, but were immediately charged by the PNA with having "rigged" the elections. The PNA boycotted the March 10 provincial elections and undertook a sustained agitation calling for the prime minister's resignation and the holding of new elections under army supervision. Bhutto denied any wrongdoing and indicated a willingness to discuss opposition grievances, but warned his critics that his "chair" was strong and safe from their attack, and that he would use the full force of state power to counter any disruption. During the next three months, however, the protest grew to dimensions greater than the anti-Ayub movement of 1968-69 and surpassed only by the

92

holocaust of the 1971 Civil War.[2] Though negotiation between the weakened government and the opposition moved haltingly toward an agreement during June, the army intervened early on the morning of July 5 with the declared purpose of restoring order and creating the conditions by which new elections could be held and democracy restored. Paradoxically, the "consolidating" elections had led to the deconsolidation of Bhutto's regime; the "popular leader"—Quaid-i-Awam as he styled himself—had been weakened by a popular movement and displaced by an army he had assiduously attempted to contain and bring under civilian control.

These developments might be interpreted and explained in a variety of ways, ranging from social science models of violence and praetorianism to popular conspiracy theories. Some explanations of what happened in the first half of 1977 in Pakistan are fairly obvious, others less so. Though alternative interpretations of this crisis are not entirely mutually exclusive, they do lead in several instances to quite different assessments of specific events as well as quite different expectations for the future course of Pakistan's politics. Moreover, delineation of these different perspectives should highlight certain specific empirical questions and thereby facilitate future inquiry into this crucial transitional period.

Political Decay

From one perspective, the events leading to the 1977 military intervention in Pakistani politics constitute almost a classic case of political decay and praetorian takeover.[3] They also conform quite well to current models of relative deprivation and violence.[4] The March election campaign mobilized large numbers of Pakistanis. Both sides organized massive public meetings and demonstrations. One PNA procession was reportedly 132 miles in length,[5] and Prime Minister Bhutto and the PNA's Air Marshal Asghar Khan competed with one another to see which could turn out the largest crowds of supporters in demonstrations in Karachi. Despite the fact that fewer seats were at stake and fewer parties competing than in 1970, just as many votes were cast in the 1977 elections.[6]

Inspired by the public response to their campaign, PNA leaders declared even before the balloting that anything short of a PNA victory would be unacceptable and clear evidence of rigged elections. In the absence of any nation-wide public opinion polls or other reasonably accurate measures of voter sentiment, People's Party aspirations were also expressed in strongly optimistic terms, though at the same time Bhutto and his followers pulled no punches in meeting the strong PNA challenge.

In this atmosphere of mobilized participation and uncertainty, the election results of March 7 came as a severe blow to the PNA partisans, who could only interpret the result as a massive rigging designed to thwart public sentiment and maintain the control of the incumbent prime minister. While there clearly were widespread instances of malpractice in the elections, it seems equally clear that the significance of these events were greatly magnified by the suddenly apparent gulf between PNA expectations and the election returns.[7] No longer accepting the legitimacy of the ruling party or governmental institutions, and no longer perceiving any alternative channel for public protest, the PNA resorted to the well established procedure of civil disobedience.[8]

The agitation against Bhutto began rather modestly. During March, Karachi had outbreaks of violence and curfew, but elsewhere in Pakistan the protest consisted largely of daily or weekly processions, often with no more than six people in each (just enough to violate the terms of section 114 prohibiting congregation of five or more people). In early April, however, the tempo picked up. The major intensification of the conflict came on April 9, when demonstrators in Lahore marched on the provincial assembly building to protest the convening of the newly elected assembly. Police reaction was harsh and several demonstrators were killed and several more injured. In retaliation, banks and other buildings were burned and new demonstrations organized.

April 9 was a turning point in the agitation in several respects. First, this was the first major outbreak of violence within Punjab. Most of the earlier problems had centered in Karachi, Hyderabad, and Sukkur, all in Sind. Karachi and Hyderabad were acknowledged to be opposition strongholds, while the shift of the agitation to the Punjab capital constituted a major threat to the very heartland of the Bhutto support. Secondly, at about this same time, other sources of support for the Bhutto regime began to crumble. Taj Mohammad Langah, Khurshid Hasan Meer, and other leftists, many of whom had been long time active members of the Pakistan People's Party, met on April 9 and formed the Pakistan Awami Jamhoori Party.[9] Other resignations further eroded the regime's legitimacy. PPP General Secretary Mubashir Hasan resigned from his post, ostensibly for health reasons. Pakistan's ambassadors to Greece and Spain, Lt. General Gul Hasan and Air Marshall Rahim Kahn, both of whom had been among the Coterie of generals who had handed power over to Bhutto in late 1971, resigned in protest over the government's treatment of demonstrators. Sardar Shaukat Hayat and six other members of the national assembly, as well as ten PPP members of the Punjab assembly, also resigned from the party and from the assemblies in sympathy with the protest movement.[10]

Public order quickly deteriorated and within days the Prime Minister was forced to call in the army to restore order in five cities in the provinces of Punjab and Sind. Bhutto attempted several different tactics in an attempt to check the movement and force its leaders to negotiate their grievances with the government.[11] Eventually he succeeded in this endeavor in late May and PNA and government negotiators began a lengthy series of meetings to work out a mutually agreeable settlement to the dispute. PNA leaders were released from jail and agreed to call off demonstrations while negotiations continued. Throughout the month of June the talks appeared to move haltingly toward an agreement. In early July it was announced that both sides had agreed in principle on all major matters, but when the PNA negotiators submitted the draft agreement to their general council, it was rejected.

It was at this point, when an agreement was so near and yet so far, that General Zia-ul Haq stepped in and took control. The failure of the government to maintain public order and the danger of a renewed outbreak of violence appeared to have been the precipitants of the takeover. As Eric Nordlinger notes, reasons for military intervention often

are to be found in the civilian government's performance failures and their resulting loss of legitimacy. Performance failures (eg. the inability to preserve public order) strengthen the officers' resolve to act upon their interventionist motives in so far as they come to hold the incumbents in greater or lesser contempt the officers can more easily rationalize and justify their coups when acting against incumbents whom they see as incompetent or worse. More important, performance failures lead to the deflation of governmental legitimacy within the politicized stratum of the civilian population. It is this factor that encourages and allows the officers to act upon their interventionist motives. Despite the enormous power enjoyed by the military, there are several reasons why it is almost never used against civilian governments unless (or until) they have lost their legitimizing mantle. Legitimacy deflations are crucial in facilitating the transformation of interventionist motivations into coup attempts.[12]

The army's own explanation of its intervention in Pakistan on July 5 corresponds closely to this interpretation of events. On the evening of July 5, General Zia explained in a nationally televised speech the reasons for the military takeover and announced the arrangements which would be followed under martial law. He noted that the alleged rigging of the March 7 election had led to "a movement which assumed such dimensions that people even started saying that democracy was not workable in Pakistan." Even during this period he added, "the armed forces resisted the temptation to take over during the recent provocative circumstances inspite of diverse massive political pressures. The armed forces have always desired and tried for the political solution to political problems. That is why the armed forces stressed on to the government that they should reach a compromise with their political rivals without any loss of time. The government needed time to hold these talks. The armed forces bought them this valuable period of time by maintaining law and order in the country." He then added, "it must be quite clear to you now that when the political leaders failed to steer the country out of a crisis, it is an inexcusable sin for the armed forces to sit as silent spectators. It is primarily, for this reason, that the army, perforce had to intervene to save the country." He "saw no prospects of a compromise between the People's Party and PNA, because of their mutual distrust and lack of faith. It was feared that the failure of the PNA and PPP to reach a compromise would throw the country into chaos and the country would thus be plunged into a more serious crisis. This risk could not be taken in view of the larger interests of the country. The army had therefore to act as a result of which the government of Mr. Bhutto has ceased to exist; martial law has been imposed throughout the country."

Zia further announced that his purpose in seizing power was a temporary one, that his "sole aim" would be "to organize free and fair elections which would be held in October," and then to return power to the "elected representatives of the people." Towards this end, he announced that the 1973 constitution would be kept in effect, with only "the operation of certain parts of the constitution . . . held in abeyance," and that President Fazal Elahi Chaudhry would continue as President of Pakistan.[13]

Even though the October 1977 elections were ultimately postponed, at least into late 1978, General Zia has continued to maintain that his main goal in seizing power was to restore order and ultimately to return power to the people's representatives.[14] Several months later, the same argument was made before the Supreme Court of Pakistan by Zia's attorney general Sharifuddin Pirzada and his counsel, leading constitutional lawyer A.K. Brohi. Responding to a petition from Begum Nusrat Bhutto challenging her husband's detention under martial law orders, Brohi submitted a 31 page written statement to the court detailing the development of events the election campaign and the military takeover. In addition to what has already been noted, he revealed that arms licences had been issued during the height of the agitation to large numbers of people recommended by Peoples Party MNAs and MPAs.[15] Bhutto he alleged, had made other preparations for a potential renewal of violence. Meanwhile, he argued, "the dialogue between the PPP and the PNA, which had been prolonged by Mr. Bhutto for his own 'mala fide' purposes had reached an impasse. The nation had clearly reached a critical juncture. The spectre of a civil war loomed ahead. The necessity for the army to act had become imperative. "Martial law was imposed," he summarized, "not in order to displace a constitutional authority, but in order to provide a bridge to enable the country to return to the path of constitutional rule."[16] After extensive argumentation from both sides, the Supreme Court of Pakistan unanimously agreed.

The proclamation of Martial Law on the 5th of July 1977, appears to be an extra-constitutional step necessitated by the complete breakdown and erosion of the constitutional and moral authority of the government of Mr. Z.A. Bhutto, as a result of the unprecedental protest movement launched by the Pakistan National Alliance against the alleged massive rigging of elections to the National Assembly, held on March 7, 1977. It was a situation for which the constitution provided no solution, and the armed forces had, therefore, to intervene to save the country from further chaos and bloodshed, to safeguard its integrity and sovereignty, and to separate the warring factions which had brought the country to the brink of disaster. [17]

There are a few difficulties with this familiar interpretation. The most obvious, perhaps, is that declaration of martial law came, not when governmental authority was at its lowest in April and May, but after more than a month of peaceful negotiations which appeared to be nearing a successful completion. Whether the negotiations were delayed by Bhutto (as Brohi suggested), by the PNA (as press reports in late June and early July seemed to indicated), or even by General Zia (as Bhutto later alleged), [18] it is quite reasonable to speculate that government and opposition would have signed their draft agreement if the army had not been available to step in when it did. [19] A second related difficulty lies in General Zia's statement that he decided on his own, and at the last minute, to intervene. The efficiency with which the operation was carried off gave little indication of its being a last-minute snap decision. There are several other unanswered questions, but many of these will be encountered as we look at other interpretations of the recent crisis.

Military Equilibrium

One theoretical difficulty with the political decay model is that it assumes political order as a norm and praetorianism as a deviation. But if the nearly fourteen years in which generals have ruled Pakistan are taken as the norm and the Bhutto phenomenon as the deviation, 1977 can be interpreted more as a return to a well-established authoritarian equilibrium. This theme, too, is not an unfamiliar one in Pakistan. When the second nation-wide martial law occurred in 1969, Wayne Wilcox wrote that Pakistan was "once again at the starting point." [20] Lawrence Ziring echoed the same theme:

Events in Pakistan have come full circle. In March 1969, as in October 1958, the military declared Martial Law. Once again a general has taken up the reins of government. Now, as then, a prevailing constitution has been abrogated. Now, as then, there are intentions to write a new constitution, reconstitute the political system, purge the corrupt bureaucrats and resolve socioeconomic inequities. Now, as then, there is the ubiquous promotion of modernization schemes.

It is all so familiar, it seems strange that there should be so much talk about a new beginning—or is it a return to an old beginning? [21]

These same comments, with some modification, could as easily be used to describe the return to Martial Law in 1977. Unlike his predecessors, General

Zia did not abrogate the 1973 Constitution, but he also did not specify which parts of the Constitution remained operative and which were being held in abeyance. In fact, his legal counsel Mr. Brohi argued before the Supreme Court that Zia's declaration of Martial Law on July 5 created a "new legal order", entirely supplanting the old legal order established under Bhutto except for those portions which it found convenient to maintain in force.[22] Like his predecessors, Zia has been persuaded by circumstances to remain in power longer than originally planned and, though his reforms differ from theirs somewhat in flavor, he is no less active either in his reform or in his purging of political and bureaucratic corruption.[23] One might very plausibly consider the developments of the first half of 1977 in Pakistan as a return to military business as usual.

This perspective not only suggests parallels between the present Martial Law regime and those which preceded it, but also dictates more consideration of the military's active role in Pakistan's politics. Rather than considering the army as a neutral "savior" stepping in an institutional vacuum to restore order, one would need to ask to what extent it manipulated events in order to return to control.

According to this point of view, Bhutto's five years in office were a concerted but ultimately unsuccessful attempt to break the "vicious circle" of recurrent military rule.[24] When Bhutto was given power by the disgraced generals in December of 1971, he was in a better position to assert civilian control over the military than any Pakistani civilian ruler since the early 1950s.[25] During the following half decade, Mr. Bhutto worked first as President and chief martial law administrator and then as Prime Minister to erect further safeguards against the return of military rule. The 1973 constitution provided that its abrogation or subversion was to be considered high treason and an oath was prescribed for members of the armed forces in which they promised to uphold the constitution and not to engage "in any political activities whatsoever."[26] Bhutto reorganized the command structure of the armed forces and created a joint chiefs of staff system under what was designed to be strong civilian control. He retired many higher officers and passed over others in making appointments in order to ensure that the top leaders would be obligated to him and therefore loyal.[27] When language riots in July of 1972 necessitated the use of governmental coercion, Bhutto created a Federal Security Force (FSF) to maintain internal security and avoid leaning too heavily upon the military. In addition to these actions taken by the Prime Minister, the Supreme Court of Pakistan, in the 1972 Asma Jilani case, reversed an earlier decision justifying military intervention and declared that the Martial Law regime of General A.M. Yahya Khan (1969-71) had been an unconstitutional usurpation of power.

After the March 1977 elections, Bhutto was not able to avoid using military support, but he still attempted to keep a rein on the generals. He required the three service chiefs and the chairman of the joint chiefs of staff to sign a joint statement declaring their full agreement with the policy of the government in its response to the PNA agitation. He also appointed as his defense minister retired General Tikka Khan, the "Butcher of Baluchistan," who had distinguished himself for his ruthless use of force both against the tribals of Baluchistan and against the Bengali rebels in 1971.

Zia commented, in his July 5 televised speech, that the army had been subject to criticism from various quarters for its role during the disturbances of April and May.[28] He did not elaborate on this point, but it is possible to identify at least a few of the pressures to which General Zia, as army chief of staff, was subjected during that troubled period. Most publicized were the appeals from the PNA agitators. Asghar Khan called publicly for the army to disobey the orders of the Prime Minister, an act which Bhutto branded as treasonist. PNA women appealed to the soldiers not to fire upon their husbands and sons. The distinctly Islamic tone of the PNA agitation further served to undermine army resolve to quell the rebellion. Less publicized were pressures from within the military itself. Lower ranking soldiers were rumored to be pressuring their superiors against firing upon fellow Pakistanis. Retired Lt. General Gul Hasan, who as noted above resigned his embassy post in Athens over the conflict, reportedly sent to General Zia a blistering letter impugning the latter's honor for serving as Bhutto's lackey.[29] In addition to all of this, both the military and the government came under legal attack in the provincial high courts of Sind and Punjab for their role in the selectively imposed martial law in five cities in April. The Sind high court agreed that the use of the army for these purposes was in support of the civil power and was therefore constitutional. The Punjab high court, however, declared the army actions to be unconstitutional and both cases were taken to the Supreme Court and were being argued there at the time that Zia seized power. Whether these cases had anything to do with the army's intervention, the July 5 takeover made the whole question moot.

If the army did have, as this model would imply, other than altrusitic motives in seizing power, the impending agreement between the government and the PNA in early July may well have been viewed as a "last chance" to strike before Bhutto began to rebuild his political credit. This also could have been a factor in the last minute PNA refusal to sign the agreement which their negotiators had worked out with the government.[30] General Zia may have taken an even more active and more longer term role in this matter, however. According to Mr. Bhutto's testimony before the Supreme Court, General Zia was "the artist and the architect of the mosaic events within the country in the critical months of April, May, June and July, 1977." Bhutto reported that as early as April 9, Zia had told him in Lahore "that the army would not accept the settlement if the special court of Hyderabad was not allowed to proceed with the case against Wali Khan and others and the army in Baluchistan was recalled to barracks. With the passage of time, the respondent and all the corps commanders became more rigid on these two conditions and reiterated them persistently in every meeting called by me and attended by them." Zia, he argued, "was responsible for the delay in the progress of negotiations between the PPP government and the PNA." Moreover, he alleged that Zia had "manipulated the events to aggravate the situation" by utilizing Operation Wheel Jam, an army contingency plan for promoting civil commotion in the event of a hostile government coming into power. To support his contention, Bhutto mentioned a meeting of army officers in Karachi addressed by Foreign Minister Aziz Ahmed which ended in pandemonium. "This was apparently an engineered affair," Bhutto concluded, "as all officers are very disciplined and do not resort to rank insubordination of this nature. This incident could not have happened but for the instigation of the respondent (Zia)."[31] Bhutto also asserted that Zia had secretly collected data concerning election malpractices until this came to the Prime Minister's notice and he reprimanded the General for it.[32]

The military equilibrium interpretation of recent developments in Pakistan is at least for the moment more difficult to document than the political decay model, though future historical research may provide more substantial answers to some of the questions raised here.[33] Among the questions which remain are why Zia waited so long to seize power and why, if Bhutto was aware of Zia's conspiratorial activities during April and May, he did not then relieve him of his duties.[34]

Authoritarian Continuity

Both the political decay and military equilibrium models emphasize the differences between Bhutto's parliamentary regime and the Martial Law regimes which both preceded and followed it. Alternatively, one might question whether even the Bhutto era was a deviation from the continuity of authoritarian rule in Pakistan. Although Bhutto created for himself and his party a wider base of popular support than any earlier Pakistani politician, he too used the same tools of authoritarian control which Ayub and the civilian rulers of the 1950s had developed, and even devised some additional ones his predecessors had not tried. A good portion of Bhutto's legitimacy lay in the majority support his party had secured in the west Pakistan elections in 1970, but his actual succession was received from the hands of Ayub Khan's council of generals much as Yhaya had succeeded Ayub Khan in 1969 and Ayub had displaced Iskander Mirza in 1958.

By emphasizing the similarity between civilian and military regimes in Pakistan this perspective highlights not only the similar control mechanisms, succession processes, and other parallels, but also points to more fundamental characteristics of Pakistan's political culture. Why, for instance, should free democratic elections be such a difficult and troublesome feature of Pakistan's politics? As Wayne Wilcox said of Bahawalpur, few countries have been "as innocent of democratic politics" as Pakistan.[35] The March 1977 elections were not the first in Pakistan to be rigged, nor probably the last. It would be fair to say that no ruler in Pakistan has conducted elections except under conditions favorable to his own interest.[36] Some have miscalculated, such as the Muslim League in Bengal in 1954 or Yhaya Khan in 1970.[37] Others have postponed elections when conditions were not favorable, and still others have "rigged" the outcome in one way or the other.[38] When nation-wide elections have been held, they have been followed by disastrous consequences, most notably by the 1971 war and the 1977 civil disturbances.

Is this unwillingness of rulers to risk their power by holding free and fair elections stronger in Pakistan than in other countries? If so, can it be traced to patterns of traditional authority which have existed among people's of the Indus Valley for centuries? Alternatively, is there something in Pakistan's Islamic ideology and culture which militates against the dispersion of political power required by open elections?[39] Or finally, is it simply that political and cultural cleavages within Pakistan's society run so deep that the stakes in an election are too high to allow for the possibility of defeat? All of these questions, suggested by the observed continuities throughout Pakistan's political history, propose interesting lines of inquiry for future research.

When elections did not function as mechanisms for succession, other processes took their place. The most prominent in Pakistan has been that used to replace both Ayub and Bhutto: the weakening of governmental authority by sustained agitation, followed by the displacement of the incumbent ruler, followed by a dismantling of the ousted leader's structure of power.[40] Whether the transition is from military to civilian ruler, civilian to military, or military to military, the press and the general public seem quite able to shift gears rapidly in accordance with the familiar phrase, "the king is dead; long live the king." The repeated success of such methods of replacing rulers no doubt enhances its popular legitimacy and increases its probability of future use.

The main utility of the authoritarian continuity perspective lies in its drawing attention to the similarities between the fall of Bhutto and the fall of Ayub. Beyond this, it is perhaps not as useful as in interpreting the distinctive characteristics of the 1977 political crisis as the earlier approaches discussed above.

Conservative Reaction

All three of the foregoing perspectives on Pakistani politics emphasized the dynamics of elite interaction, although the third one does raise some broader cultural questions. A focus upon the dynamics of class conflict, however, suggests at least two other interpretations of the events of 1977. The first of these emphasizes parallels between developments in the 1970s in Pakistan and in the neighboring South Asian countries of India, Bangladesh, and Sri Lanka. In all four countries, a popular leader (Bhutto, Indira Gandhi, Sheikh Mujibur Rehman, Sirimavo Bandaranaike) utilized personal charisma and a well organized political party (PPP, Congress, Awami League, Sri Lanka Freedom Party) to gain impressive electoral victories in 1970 and 1971. Each translated such power into constitutional changes which strengthened the leader's powers, combined socialist rhetoric with middle class support and authoritarian methods, created special security forces and other mechanisms of state control,[41] crippled the opposition and the press, boosted the political role of family members, indiscriminately jailed political opponents, and weakened civil liberties and the courts.[42] Patterns varied slightly from country to country, but the parallels are obvious and it is possible in some instances to trace the diffusion of ideas and practices from one South Asian country to another. Sheikh Mujib was overthrown by a military coup in mid-August, 1975, and the other three leaders were toppled in 1977, Mrs. Gandhi and Mrs. Bandaranaike by election defeats and Mr. Bhutto by military coup. All four successors—General Zia-ul Haq in Pakistan, General Ziaur Rehman in Bangladesh, Morarji Desai in India and J.R. Jayawardene in Sri Lanka—are more conservative than the "socialist" leaders whom they replaced. Each has attempted to dismantle or unravel the "excesses" of the previous government. In Pakistan, this has taken the form of denationalization of certain industries which Bhutto had nationalized, disbanding the federal security forces, cancellation of arms licenses and ration depot licenses (which had been disproportionately allocated to PPP supporters), widespread transfer of bureaucratic officials, review of lateral entry and promotion procedures, restoration of certain press freedoms, release of political prisoners, and the institution of a large number of "accountability" procedures.[43]

What light does this comparative perspective throw on Pakistan's 1977 political crisis? Perhaps the most interesting was the interplay between the Indian and Pakistani general elections, both held in March 1977.[44] Mrs. Gandhi's announcement of March elections followed shortly after Mr. Bhutto's and the Pakistani Prime Minister boasted at various points in the spring campaign that he had goaded Mrs. Gandhi into going to the polls. The results of the two elections, however, backfired on Mr. Bhutto. By the time the Indian elections were held in the third week of March and the results of Mrs. Gandhi's defeat became known in Pakistan, the PNA agitation over the "rigged" elections had been underway for approximately two weeks. The results of the Indian elections served to strengthen the opposition and further undermine Mr. Bhutto's legitimacy. Pakistanis questioned, "If India can conduct free elections, why can't we?"

Another interesting development, though one not as crucial to the 1977 crisis as the elections, was Prime Minister Bhutto's decision to hold a referendum in May. Only a few days before, General Ziaur Rehman in Bangladesh had held a plebiscite and had received overwhelming support of more than 90% of the votes cast.[45] For Bhutto, the idea of a plebiscite came as an opportunity to counter the opposition demand for his resignation. He offered to resign and hold new elections if the people of Pakistan voted against him. A constitutional amendment was passed authorizing this extraordinary procedure despite the fact that only a few weeks earlier PPP spokesmen had dismissed proposals for new elections on the grounds that such would be unconstitutional and too costly. Nonetheless, the plebiscite proposal served two useful functions for the government. It challenged the PNA claim to represent the majority of the people and it forced the PNA to shift ground on their definition of the central issue of their agitation.[46] Ultimately, the course of negotiations between the government and the PNA precluded the holding of the plebiscite, and in retrospect it appears only to have been a minor interlude in the overall drama of the 1977 crisis.

By noting the parallels between the transitional events of 1977 in Pakistan and comparable developments in neighboring countries, between India's Janata Party and Pakistan's PNA, between Pakistan's General Zia and Bangladesh's General Zia,[47] this perspective is suggestive of many potentially fruitful lines of scholarly inquiry. It should also serve as a corrective to the dominant tendency to treat each country as an isolated unit without consideration of political factors and ideas which filter across international boundaries.

Middle Class Islamic Movement

A slightly different class-based analysis of the 1977 political crisis would treat the July 5 military takeover as not so much the restoration of an earlier status quo, but as the successful conclusion of a middle class revolution with a highly religious content.[48] This perspective would direct our attention to (1) the tremendous resurgence in 1977 of Islam as a political symbol and area of public policy;[49] (2) the relationship between Islamic resurgence and class conflict; (3) the internal class dynamics of the Pakistan National Alliance; (4) similarities and linkages between the PNA and General Zia's military regime; (5) differences between Zia's distinctive Islamic fundamentalism and the "modernist" approaches to the religious question by earlier martial law rulers.

For obvious historical reasons connected with the very origin and birth of Pakistan as a nation, Islam has always been a central issue in its politics.[50] Religious parties have also been prominent throughout the country's history, most notably the militant Jamaat-i-Islami. However, the extent of Islam's centrality as a public issue have varied greatly over the country's thirty-year history. Its renewed recent prominence is related to several factors, including the search for a new identity following the loss of East Pakistan, the rise in wealth and importance of the Middle East in the 1970s, and increased diplomatic activity among Muslim states. In Pakistan the dynamics of party competition and class conflict have also served to reinforce these trends. In 1977, Islam became a central issue in the spring election campaign. The Pakistan National Alliance used mosques and religious leaders to spread their political doctrine, both in the spring campaign and in the agitation which followed the elections, to the extent that the antigovernment movement took on the spirit of a *jihad.*

The vague but potent slogan, *Nizam-i-Mustafa,* or the call of an Islamic social, political and economic system, became the broadest ideological base on which the diverse parties in the PNA could agree. The prominence of the Islamic issue indicated the ascendency within the alliance of the "Islam-Pasand" jamaats over the more secular National Democratic Party and Tehrik-i-Istiqlal. It also showed that the more predominantly middle class elements within the more fundamental Islamic parties had gained at least some dominance over the more elitist Pakistan Muslim League. These and other cleavages within the Pakistan National Alliance surfaced repeatedly during 1977. In campaign meetings prior to the fall elections, for instance, heated arguments arose between old line Pakistan Muslim League leaders, who preferred to allocate PNA tickets to landed notables as in the past, and Jamaat-i-Islami spokesman who demanded greater representation of middle and lower class candidates. The old elite, whose disdain for the maulvis, fondness for drinking, and preference for keeping politics within the hands of the "well bred," were subjected to pressures within the alliance to broaden their political base and join in the demand for Nizam-i-Mustafa in order to capture political power.[51] Why should the Islamic appeal of the PNA have received such a strong positive response from the general public? Not long before, it seemed that the politics of religion had been superseded in Pakistan by the politics of class, that the mobilization of the masses under the slogan of socialism had defined the new political formula by which Pakistani leaders would be chosen.[52] More detailed explanation of this transition in public sentiment is needed, but one explanation offered by a local level Muslim League politician seems persuasive:

During the first ten years, Pakistan was capitalistic. The upper class tortured workers. Big land lords could get people arrested when they wanted. The lower class developed a hatred for capitalism. Then came the demand for socialism. Bhutto came, but he couldn't solve the problems facing the country. Now the people see Nizam-i-Mustafa as a possible answer. We don't know how it will work, or even if it will work, but we will try.[53]

In other words, the masses mobilized in 1970 by Bhutto's call for socialism were frustrated by the performance of the people's party government in office and looked to a third alternative, making them susceptible to the Nizam-i-Mustafa appeal.

Bhutto made several attempts to undercut this source of PNA political support, particularly during the disturbances in April and May. He reorganized the Council of Islamic Ideology and invited the leaders of the three major Islamic parties to participate within it. In mid-April, he announced and had passed by parliament a series of "Shari' at laws" which included, among other things, the outlawing of alcoholic beverages, gambling, nightclubs, and other "unIslamic" activities, and shifting the weekly holiday from Sunday to Friday. He emphasized his ties with the Islamic states of the middle east and utilized their representatives to intercede with the PNA. That Bhutto, whose fondness for drinking and for Savile Row suits should have been the perpetrator of these Islamic reforms is indicative not only of the strength of the religious issue in 1977 but also of the Prime Minister's need to capitalize on it in his search for political support.

Though the dynamics of party competition and class conflict were important to the resurgence of Islam in the first half of 1977, the military takeover on July 5 did not halt this trend, but rather accelerated it. In his speech of July 5, General Zia praised "the spirit of Islam, demonstrated during the recent movement."

It proves that Pakistan, which was created in the name of Islam, will continue to survive only if it sticks to Islam. That is why I consider the introduction of Islamic system as an essential prerequisite for the country.[54]

Within days, he issued a series of Martial Law regulations prescribing stringent corporal punishments for specified crimes, including amputation of the hand and public whippings. In subsequent weeks, he took numerous other steps to demonstrate his zeal in bringing about an Islamic tranformation of Pakistan's society.[55]

It may simply be coincidental that a General of Zia's temperament and character should have occupied the key position of Army Chief of Staff during this crucial period.[56] In any case, the similarity of his background and policy orientations to the main protagonists within the PNA movement is striking. Unlike earlier military rulers Zia is a Punjabi *muhajir* (refugee from Indian Punjab), an Arain by caste, and a close relative of Jamaat-i-Islami and PNA leader Mian Tufail Muhammad.[57] PNA leaders have found little to criticize in the new Martial Law regime's programs and policies. They could hardly have found among themselves a leader who would so actively work to realize their own social and political goals.

To this point, there has been no clear evidence of actual conspiracy or collusion between the PNA and General Zia in overthrowing the Bhutto regime.[58] As the Martial Law administration has become more firmly established, however, Zia has increasingly abandoned any pretense at impartiality and has thereby lent further credence to the impression that the PNA electoral campaign, agitation, and negotiations and the military takeover which followed all of these were part and parcel of a common movement.

Outside Intervention

A final approach to explaining the political crisis of 1977 portrays the downfall of Bhutto as a conspiracy engineered by outside powers. To a lesser or greater extent, this interpretation is believed by large numbers of Pakistanis who assume generally that Pakistan's politics are thoroughly manipulated by outside forces. Conspiracy theories have always been popular in South Asia in general and in Pakistan in particular, a factor that has tended to exacerbate politics.[59] There may also be something in the Islamic political culture, particularly the belief in an omnipotent Allah by whose will all human affairs are ordered, which reinforces this assumption that public affairs in Pakistan cannot possibly be explained without reference to outside sources.[60]

The clearest and most forceful statement of the external intervention viewpoint appeared in Prime Minister Bhutto's April 28 speech to the National Assembly. Bhutto accused the opposition leaders of having received massive financial assistance from outside Pakistan. He claimed to have direct evidence of outside involvement and, though he did not specifically mention the United States by name, few people doubted which outside country he had in mind.[60] The pro-government press reported the speech under banner headlines and echoed its themes in an outpouring of vilification of the CIA, American foreign policy, and other aspects of American neoimperialism. Why the United States would have an interest in toppling Bhutto was explained in terms of U.S.-Pakistani disagreement over Bhutto's plans to build a nuclear reprocessing plant in Pakistan. The United States, suspicious of Pakistan's motives and fearful of nuclear proliferation, had brought pressure on Canada and France to impede development of the project and former Secretary of State Henry Kissinger had, according to Bhutto, promised to make Pakistan a "horrible example" if he proceeded with the project. Bhutto, it was further argued, had become too forceful a spokesman for third world interests against the exploitation of the western nations.

Mindful of Bhutto's apparent tactical reasons for making such a speech, U.S. Secretary of State Vance issued a moderate reponse indicating a willingness to discuss any mutual disagreements. Pakistani Foreign Minister Aziz Ahmed accordingly carried a long statement of Pakistani accusations to his meeting with Vance in Paris, but, according to Pakistan government sources, had his hotel room ransacked by unknown agents while there. The contents of the governmental statement were never made public. The two most solid pieces of evidence which were publicized were (1) a telephone conversation between two American officials (presumably overheard by means of a wire tap) in which one of the speakers announced with reference to Bhutto's waning political support, "the party's over." (2) The second basis for Bhutto's assertion of widespread outside intervention was a drop in the black market value of the dollar in Pakistan during the PNA agitation, implying a large influx of Amerian currency.

The major difficulty with this interpretation of the 1977 crisis is the failure of its proponents to offer a satisfactory explanation why the United States should have a preference for the PNA or Zia over Bhutto, who was a known political quantity. During the spring election campaign, American officials in Pakistan were prohibited from travel and unofficial Americans were strongly advised not to travel to outlying areas in order not to provide any basis for either side to claim American interference. The American official position was one of strict neutrality, a "hands off" policy. If the United States had to make a choice, it seems much more plausible that it would have supported Bhutto rather than his opponents.[62] This is not to say that the PNA would have refused outside aid if it were available. One PNA leader later confided to me that he had approached the Americans for financial support in late 1976 and had been turned down.

Other pieces of information might be woven into a conspiracy theory of American involvement, such as President Carter's long delay in recognizing Prime Minister Bhutto's reelection, the visit of an American Admiral to Pakistan just after the military takeover, and Zia's having received military training at the U.S. Command and General Staff College at Fort Leavenworth. However, the outside intervention interpretation of the 1977 crisis appears less plausible than explanations based upon the dynamics of domestic politics. Bhutto may indeed believe the accusations which he leveled against the American imperialists, but his speech had clearly apparent domestic purposes and effects: it broke the tempo of the PNA movement and recaptured some of the leftist support which had dissipated after the elections.

Less prominent theories of outside intervention identified the Iranians or the Arabs as prime movers.[63] The role of neighboring Muslim states is clearly worth investigating. The Saudi and United Arab Emirate ambassadors interceded between the government and the PNA ostensibly at the request of the Prime Minister, but they apparently also brought pressure on Bhutto to arrive at a settlement with the PNA.[64] Bhutto's rapid tour of six middle east capitals during the final days of the negotiations is difficult to explain except as a consultation over the acceptability of the tentative terms of the agreement. Similarly, General Zia's frequent diplomatic intercourse with neighboring Islamic leaders, Asghar Khan's trip to consult with the Shah of Iran, and other communication between Pakistan and its middle eastern neighbors would be a subject of potential investigation.

It is probably worth noting that speculation concerning outside intervention in the Pakistani political crisis generally did not include reference to
India. At one point, Bhutto alleged that Indian and Iranian troops were
massing on Pakistan's borders, but this was apparently also done for domestic
political affect.

The outside intervention pespective on recent Pakistani politics should
not be dismissed out of hand. Like all conspiracy theories, it rests upon some
empirical support and a lot of suspicion and conjecture. It is valuable both
because it highlights aspects of the crisis not covered by the previously
related approaches and because it also reveals some deep-seated elements of
Pakistani public opinion.

Summary and Conclusions

Exploring alternative interpretations of a crisis such as the one Pakistan
passed through in the first half of 1977 is valuable not because it makes
possible the confirmation of one interpretation as correct and the others as
false, but because it demonstrates that the same empirical events may lead
quite plausibly to quite different explanations and conclusions.[65] A complete
and accurate explanation of the crisis would probably need to integrate
elements from each of these partial perspectives. Not all of the approaches are
equally plausible, but each identifies different sets of strands in the complex
fabric of events by which one important era of Pakistan's political history has
come to a dramatic close and another has begun.

This exercise in looking at Pakistani politics from different points of view
has also served to raise at least as many questions as it has answered. The roles
played by Zia, Bhutto, and the PNA leaders, relationships between the PNA
and the military, Bhutto's relationship to malpractices in the March elections, and the political dynamics of the PNA, PPP, and the military during
this crucial period are all questions in which further inquiry should help to
clarify our understanding and in some cases to support one interpretation
over others.

Finally, whether one views the events of 1977 as decay or development,
static or cyclical, reactionary or progressive, will determine his positive or
negative evaluation of not only the current military regime but also of future
political developments. For instance, if General Zia is viewed as a disin-
terested caretaker whose only political goal is the restoration of democracy to
Pakistan, then his postponement of the October 1977 elections might easily
be justified on practical grounds. If, on the other hand, he is seen as a PNA
stalking horse or as another Yahya Khan, one might evaluate his actions
quite differently. In a very real sense, how we understand the next stage in
Pakistan's political history will depend very much on which interpretation
we give to the crisis by which it began.

Notes

1. For a detailed account of the election campaign and the elections, see Lawrence Ziring, "Pakistan: The Campaign Before the Storm," *Asian Survey XVII*, No. 7 (July 1977), 581-598 and M.G. Weinbaum, "The March 1977 Elections in Pakistan: Where Everyone Lost," *Asian Survey XVII*, No. 7 (July 1977), 599-618. Norman Palmer compares the Indian and Pakistani elections in "The Two Elecʿions: A Comparative Analysis," *Asian Survey XVII*, No. 7 (July 1977), 648-666.

2. Official figures indicated that "the nation wide agitations led to 22 persons being killed, and 369 injured up to March 7, and 242 killed and 1,227 injured thereafter. In addition, 9 persons of the security forces were killed and another 536 injured. No less than 16,863 persons were arrested, 4,290 processions were taken out by members of general public, 262 by women, 95 by lawyers, 19 Ulema, 283 by students and 68 by children. 1,623 vehicles were destroyed and the same was the case with 18 installations, 42 stores, 31 wine shops, 7 hotels, 58 bank branches, 11 cinemas, 7 factories, 23 railway carriges, 57 offices, and 38 shops. In addition, the national economy ground to a halt during the summer month while the flame of violence spread all over the land." Cf. "Brohi's Statement in Begum Bhutto's Petition," *Pakistan Times*, October 13, 1977.

3. Cf. Samuel Huntington, *Political Order and Changing Societies* (New Haven: Yale University Press, 1968), Chapter 4: "Praetorianism and Political Decay," pp. 192-263.

4. Cf. Ted Robert Gurr, *Why Men Rebel;* Hugh Davis Graham and Ted Robert Gurr, *Violence in America: Historical and Comparative Perspectives* (New York: New American Library, 1969); Ivo K. Feierabend, Rosalind L. Feierabend, and Ted Robert Gurr, editors, *Anger, Violence and Politics: Theories and Research* (Englewood-Cliffs: Prentice-Hall, 1972).

5. *Far Eastern Economic Review.*

6. I.H. Burney concludes that the greater turn out per contested seat was prima facie evidence that ballot stuffing occurred. I.H. Burney, "March '77 Elections: An Analysis," *Pakistan Economist* 17, No. 30 (July 23, 1977), p. 13. It seems reasonable to assume, however, especially considering the observed mass participation in rallies and demonstrations, that a good portion of this increase is attributable to the mobilization of larger numbers of the Pakistani public.

7. The extent and variety of the rigging of the elections is treated most thoroughly in *ibid.*, pp. 13-23.

8. A prominent PNA partisan, retired general and former federal minister, told me in Lahore on March 8 that with peaceful channels of protest blocked by Bhutto, there was no alternative for the PNA but to turn to the streets.

9. Bhutto had for years balanced off leftists and rightists factions within the PPP. For a discussion of some of this process, see Anwar H. Syed, "The Pakistan People's Party: Phases One and Two," in Lawrence Ziring, Ralph Braibanti and W. Howard Wriggins, editors, *Pakistan: The Long View* (Duke University Center for Common Wealth and Comparative Studies, No. 43. Durham: Duke University Press, 1977), pp. 70-116. In his December 1976 reorganization of the PPP and in the distribution of party tickets for the 1977 March elections, however, Bhutto gave much greater preference to the right, particularly the landed local notables. This rightist strategy was apparently in anticipation of the fact that Bhutto's major political challenge in the elections would come from the right. That turned out to be a correct assessment and was successful in the short run, but it alienated large numbers of PPP leftists. Many of these, who could not possibly have voted for the PNA in the March elections, were willing to support the demand for new elections and to join in opposing Bhutto's repression of the protest movement in April. Bhutto spoke out in mid April against what he termed extremists of both right and left.

10. Salamat Ali, "Bhutto feels the heat," *Far Eastern Economic Review* 95, No. 17 (April 29, 1977), pp. 8-9. Salamat Ali also notes in the same article: "the most dramatic aspect of the present strife has been the swift erosion of Bhutto's power, which can be traced to a single, violent event—a clash between demonstrators and police in Lahore on April 9 during the visit there of the Prime Minister." *Ibid.,* p. 8.

11. Two of the most important of these were his impassioned speech before the national assembly on April 28 accusing the protest movement of being financed by foreign money and his enlistment of diplomats from friendly Arab countries to intercede with the PNA leadership. Both of these are discussed in later sections of this paper.

12. Eric A. Nordlinger, *Soldiers in Politics; Military Coups and Governments* (Englewood Cliffs: Prentice-Hall, 1977), p. 64.

13. "Text of General Zia's address to nation," *Dawn,* July 6, 1977, p. 8.

14. I pursue of these post-coup developments in a separate paper entitled "Persistent Praetorianism: Pakistan's Third Military Regime."

15. For the period from March 7 to June 26, the provincial totals were Sind—971; Baluchistan—80; NWFP—13,137; and Punjab—5,321. "Brohi's Statement," *Dawn,* October 12, 1977.

16. *Ibid.*

17. Quoted in Maqbul Sharif "Step covered by doctrine of Necessity," *Pakistan Times,* November 11, 1977, p. 4.

18. See discussion below.

19. I was informed by a former member of Bhutto's cabinet, on the basis of his own personal observation, that Bhutto had a cabinet meeting on July 4, and in the presence of General Zia, told his negotiators to sign any written agreement presented to them by the PNA. Interviews, Lahore, fall 1977.

20. Wayne Wilcox, "Pakistan in 1969: Once again at the Starting Point," *Asian Survey,* 10, No. 2 (February 1970), 73-81.

21. Lawrence Ziring, *The Ayub Khan Era: Politics in Pakistan* 1958-59 (Syracuse: Syracuse University Press, 1971), p. viii. See also Lawrence Ziring, "Militarism in Pakistan: The Yahya Khan Interregnum," in W.H. Wriggins, ed., *Pakistan in Transition* (Islamabad: University of Islamabad Press, 1975), pp. 198-232. Ziring's essay is given a longer title in the table of contents: "Perennial Militarism: An Interpretation of Political Underdevelopment—Pakistan Under General Yahya Khan, 1969-1971."

22. Interestingly, the Supreme Court rejected this argument and held that the Martial Law regime was subject to the demands and conditions which surrounded its establishment in July. Most notably, they declared that the legitimacy of the regime lay in Zia's promise to hold elections and return power to civilian hands. See the court's opinion in *Dawn,* November 11, 1977, pp. 1, 4.

23. Zia has also considered and publicly speculated upon the need for alternative constitutional arrangements. Cf. "Constitutional Lessons: Distribution of Powers Needs Review," *Pakistan Times,* September 18, 1977.

24. As Nordlinger notes, "the most frequent sequel to military coups and government is more of the same. After disengaging, the officers almost invariably play an important political role as moderator-type praetorians. Some successful regimes may be more accurately described as mixed civilian-military regimes. And then sooner or later—usually sooner—the soldiers regularly return to the center of the political stage by overthrowing the civilian incumbents and taking up the mantle of government once again. Where the soldiers have once assumed the highest offices, the most common subsequent pattern is an alternation between civilian and military regimes, with the officers almost always remaining within the political elite as moderator types when the government is headed by civilians. The aftermath of military intervention is military intervention." Nordlinger, *Soldiers in Politics,* p. 207.

25. Fazal Muqeem Khan, *Pakistan's Crisis in Leadership* (Islamabad: National Book Foundation, 1973), pp. 248-249.

26. *The Constitution of the Islamic Republic of Pakistan, 1973*, see *The Gazette of Pakistan*, Islamabad, Sunday, December 31, 1972, article 244, p. 1108, and for the 'text of the oath, see p. 1156.

27. For example, General Zia-ul Haq himself was appointed by Bhutto, the executed PM superseding several senior officers.

28. Overseas Weekly *Dawn*, July 10, 1977, pp. 1-2.

29. Retired Lt. General Gul Hasan had played a prominent role in forcing General Yahya Khan to hand over power to Mr. Bhutto on December 20, 1971.

30. The PNA Council had refused to accept the text of the Agreement which was worked out through it representatives. The Agreement was turned by the Council because of the tough line taken by Rtd. Air Marshall Asghar Khan.

31. See Bhutto's rejoinder to the Statement of the Federation of Pakistan before the Supreme Court.

32. All these assertions are contained in Bhutto's rejoinder to the statement of the federation of Pakistan before the Supreme Court, reported in *Dawn*, October 20, 1977.

33. Cf. Herbert Feldman's extensive documentation of earlier developments in *Revolution in Pakistan: A Study of the Martial Law Administration* (London: Oxford University Press, 1967); *From Crisis to Crisis: Pakistan 1962-1969* (London: Oxford University Press, 1972); and *The End and the Beginning* (London: Oxford University Press, 1976); plus Ziring, *The Ayub Khan Era*.

34. It was also rumored that Zia and nine other top generals were scheduled for removal by Bhutto at the time that the takeover occurred. Bhutto, however, denied this in his Supreme Court testimony.

35. Wayne Wilcox, *Pakistan: Consolidation of a Nation* (New York: Columbia University Press, 1962).

36. This is, of course, somewhat characteristic of a large number of third-world countries, where "it is extremely rare to find instances of one party succeeding another in executive office as the result of an election." Robert E. Gamer, *The Developing Nations: A Comparative Perspective* (Boston: Allyn and Bacon, 1976), p. 39.

37. The 1970 elections are generally recognized to have been the fairest that Pakistan has held, but it is also generally believed that Yahya both expected the vote to be so fragmented that he could broker interests in the assembly and also that he channeled money and support to Muslim League factions which he favored. See Herbert Feldman, *The End and the Beginning: Pakistan 1969-71.*

38. Newspaper comments on the 1952 elections in Bahawalpur state suggested that if future practice in Pakistan were modeled upon the example set by Bahawalpur, the future of democracy in the country was dim indeed.

39. The last two elements of Quaid-i-Azam Mohammad Ali Jinnah's motto, "Faith, Unity, Discipline," would seem to be relevant here.

40. In mid March, when the agitations were just beginning, I was told by a PNA activitist, "we shall bring down Bhutto the same way we brought down Ayub."

41. See Myron Weiner, "India's New Political Institutions," *Asian Survey* 16, No. 9 (September 1976), 88-901.

42. Cf. A.T. Chaudhri, "Changing World of South Asia," *Dawn*, August 9 and 18, 1977.

43. Accountability, most notably the prosecution of former Prime Minister Bhutto for murder, was the major reason for postponing the October 1977 elections. This is discussed more at length in my separate paper, "Persistent Praetorianism: Pakistan's Third Military Regime."

44. Norman Palmer discusses the similarities and differences between these two events in his article in *Asian Survey, XVII*, 648-666.

45. The device of the plebiscite has, of course, been used elsewhere with great effect, most notably by President Ferdinand Marcos in the Phillipines.

46. *Far Eastern Economic Review.*

47. A common quip in India refers to the two Generals as "Zia West" and "Zia East."

48. I am indebted to Stanley Kochanek for his suggestion of this line of inquiry during some of our discussions in Lahore during February and March and during June to August, 1975.

49. I have a separate discussion of this phenomenon in a paper entitled "The Political Dynamics of Islamic Resurgence in Pakistan."

50. Cf. Leonard Binder, *Religion and Politics in Pakistan* (Berkeley: University of California Press, 1961); Donald E. Smith, ed., *South Asian Politics and Religion* (Princeton: Princeton University Press, 1966); Freeland Abbott, *Islam and Pakistan* (Ithaca: Cornell University Press, 1968).

51. These comments are made on the basis of my personal observation of a series of PNA meetings in Bahawalpur and Rahimyar Khan districts in early August, 1977. When future accounts are written of the history of the Pakistan National Alliance, they should certainly include more detailed and systematic consideration of these internal class conflicts.

52. *Pakistan: The Long View.*

53. Interview, Bahawalpur, August 2, 1977.

54. *Pakistan Times,* July 6, 1977, p. 8.

55. Among these were appointment of an educational commission to consider abolition of coeducation in schools and universities, reconstitution of the Council of Islamic Ideology, renaming of streets and cities, appointment of a committee of economists to consider procedures for introducing interest-free banking and other Islamic economic reforms, and several trips to middle eastern countries to reaffirm ties of Islamic brotherhood. These are treated somewhat more at length in my "Persistent Praetorianism" paper.

56. It would be interesting to determine whether Bhutto selected Zia in part because of these personal characteristics, which might have been expected to contribute either to his loyalty and obedience or to his isolation from other officers.

57. *Far Eastern Economic Review,* July 22, 1977, p. 10.

58. It is interesting to note, however, that while Zia specifically denied in his July 5 speech that he was acting in collusion with the Prime Minister, there was no such denial of PNA involvement.

59. Cf. Jamna Das Akhtar, *Political Conspiracies in Pakistan* (Delhi: Punjabi Pustak Bhandar, 1969).

60. In one or another, I encountered this explanation of events between March and July in conversations with both Bhutto supporters and Bhutto opponents, government officials, and individuals from all levels of Pakistani society. One passenger in a railway apartment asserted "It was the Americans who put Mr. Bhutto in office and it was the Americans who removed him." An upper class former state official in Bahawalpur said, "Of course the Americans are responsible for getting rid of Bhutto and they are to be congratulated for it." At the height of the violence in mid April, bewildered embassy officials in Manila questioned "how is it possible for the PNA to muster so much strength without outside assistance."

61. In his inaugural address to the National Assembly earlier in April, Bhutto had raised the same theme, though with less impact. See Salamat Ali, "Bhutto's bid to find an opposition," *Far Eastern Economic Review,* 95, No. 14 (April 8, 1977), p. 13.

62. Interviews with American embassy officials in Islamabad, February, 1977. The subsequent departure of two members of the political section of the U.S. embassy in Islamabad shortly thereafter appeared to observers to be more than simply coincidental, though neither the Pakistan government nor American official sources would confirm any connection.

63. Once column in *Le Monde,* for instance, treated the Pakistani disturbances as part of a right-wing Islamic movement throughout the Middle East.

64. Saudi Arabia is rumored to have offered Prime Minister Bhutto financial assistance sufficient to make up the losses suffered during the PNA agitation if a peaceful settlement could be arrived at through negotiation.

65. Cf. Graham T. Allison, *Essence of Decision: Explaining the Cuban Missile Crisis* (Boston: Little, Brown and Co., 1971).

Changing Party Structures in Pakistan:
From Muslim League to People's Party[1]
PHILIP E. JONES

Political parties in Pakistan have been intermittent and unstable phenomena which the political system has neither been able to work well with
nor operate for long periods without. The overthrow of the Bhutto Government reminds us again that the representative institutions and procedures
of modern statehood—constitutions, parliaments, political parties and elections—have not found easy implantation in Pakistan, despite the endorsement of this path to political modernity by the Quaid-i-Azam, Muhammad
Ali Jinnah. It seems hardly necessary to recount the profound political and
economic damage done to this troubled State by the absence of a legitimate
and durable political order. Not unexpectedly, political parties have come in
for much of the blame for the recurrent political crises in Pakistan's short
history. For students of political development in Pakistan, however, a critical
analysis of the weaknesses of political parties *per se* is only part of the required
effort. Also important is an understanding of how political parties emerge as
"dependent" phenomena in the system. The timing and manner of their
advent, how they organize, and how they perform are aspects largely
dependent on wider environmental factors, among these being: historical
experience, the pre-existing elite setting, the structure of traditional society,
the permeation of central institutions, the strategy of economic development, the patterns and degree of urbanization and industrialization, and the
spread of literacy.

Before proceeding to the Pakistan experience in light of these factors,
perhaps it would be well to note some problems of definition and period-
ization. As institutional requisites of developed political systems, political
parties commonly have a number of salient characteristics. First, and
foremost, they are coalitions of social and interest groups whose primary
rationale is to capture and hold the organs of government. "'Parties,'" as
Weber noted, "live in a house of 'power,' . . . their leaders normally deal
with the conquest of a community."[2] Second, while the levers of power are
also sought for the patronage they bring, political parties do offer policy
programs, usually founded on ideological assumptions, that purport to

benefit the community as a whole. Third, parties are not transient organizations whose existence is tied to the destiny of a single individual, or to the life span of a founding generation. Fourth, political parties are mass organizations, with membership readily available to all citizens. They derive their legitimacy from the democratic principle, variously interpreted, that the common man is a citizen, not a subject, and entitled to certain rights in the ordering of his governance. Finally, as mass organizations, parties function in the system as "a two-way communication channel, processing the demands and interests of the population upward, and simultaneously passing downward to the people as a whole a better understanding of the absolute restraints and the ultimate requirements of the polity as a whole."[3]

Clearly, few of the many organizations in developing countries, Pakistan included, which present themselves as political parties can live up to all the attributes of parties in developed systems, particularly in the matter of durable organization. Nevertheless, the episodic and intermittent conjuctions of social and interest groups that appear in countries like Pakistan, and which do have enormous political effects, are important phenomena. If rigid definitions are to be maintained, we can call them proto-parties or political movements. Their presence indicates the processes of party formation are well under way in a polity, but that the social and economic conditions have yet to exist that will combine to push the society across the threshold to what Lerner has called the "Participant Society."[4] Lerner proposes that modern society is "distinctively industrial, urban, literate and *participant*." It is participant

. . . in that it functions by "consensus"—individuals making personal decisions on public issues must concur often enough with other individuals they do not know to make possible a stable common governance. Among the marks of this historic achievement . . . are that most people go through school, read newspapers, receive cash payments in jobs they are legally free to change, buy goods for cash in open market, vote in elections which actually decide among competing candidates, and express opinions on many matters which are not their personal business.

Contrasted to this is traditional society, which is nonparticipant in that it

. . . deploys people by kinship into communities isolated from each other and from a center; without an urban-rural division of labor, it develops few needs requiring economic interdependence; lacking the bonds of interdependence, people's horizons are limited by locale and their decisions involve only other *known* people in *known* situations. Hence, there is no need for the transpersonal common formulated in terms of shared secondary symbols—a national "ideology" which enables persons unknown to each other to engage in political controversy or achieve "consensus" by comparing their opinions.[5]

Though these models are somewhat artificial in view of the complex reality they attempt to describe, they do point to transformations in the wider environment that have crucial import for the patterns of organization and durability that political parties are able to achieve. It is not necessary for a society to be wholly modern for political parties to become requisite and durable phenomena. At some point in the development processes, the magnitudes of social change—as measured by indices of urbanization, media consumption, voter participation, etc.—are great enough to set the stage for "political take off." In this paper we shall argue that, taken together, the mass movement of 1968-1969 against the Ayub Regime and the election campaign of 1970 marked the passage of Punjabi society across the threshold to the participant society. Further, we shall suggest that one of the primary reasons for the steep decline of the People's Party in Punjab resulted from its failure to follow up on the organizational opportunities and imperatives produced by this historic change.

Social Origins of Parties in Punjab

Political parties, or their antecedent phenomena, tend to emerge in that period in the development of a polity when social groups that are not part of the traditional, pre-industrial ruling elite combine to seek access to the policy-making organs of government. Implicit even in this early stage is a future demand not only for the expansion of the political community, but also for a redistribution of power within it. In Punjabi Muslim society, the first decade of this century saw the first glimmerings of this process in the founding of the Punjab Muslim League by a westernized, urban middle class of lawyers, journalists, teachers, rentiers and government contractors. These "new men" were a propertied urban gentry who, barred from commerce and banking by Hindu monopolization, had found in the legal profession a lucrative occupation and an upwardly mobile status. Partially anglicized by educational sojourns in London or Aligarh, but not uninfluenced by the revived orthodox religious schools, this group was particularly conscious of the educational and cultural backwardness of Punjabi Muslims. Hence their first common effort came in the founding of the Anjuman-i-Himāyat-i-Islam (1886), a welfare association dedicated to education, community uplift and religious reform. These influences and objectives were also strongly felt in the urban *barādarī* and artisan associations, which began to appear in some numbers during the first decade of the twentieth century, and which enabled this new elite to gain status mobility by projecting reformist influences deeper into their own endogamous kinship networks.

Neither the Anjuman nor the barādarī associations were frankly political organizations, though they did lobby gently with the bureaucracy for their interests. Nonetheless, it was only a matter of time before these new men would extend their activities to the political arena. Less able than the rural *ashrāfīya* to rely on customary social authority, they saw in the Muslim community, and in its numbers, their natural constituency. Their participation in the Simla Delegation and in the founding of the All-India Muslim League (1906) and the Punjab Muslim Leagues (1907) was the beginning of their effort to organize Punjabi Muslim opinion around essentially communal issues. It should be noted that this class of urban gentlemen was neither a particularly cohesive or radical group—aspects which inevitably affected the organizational characteristics of the Punjab League. From the very beginning, this organization was never free from conflicting personal and barādarī loyalties. The Kashmiri/Kakkezai-Arain dichotomy fractured the League more than once, and at times the organization tended to become the personal following of powerful figures like Mian Muhammad Shafi or Allama Mahammad Iqbal. For the most part, too, the League gentry made moderate and limited demands on the colonial authorities, and, being men of proven ability and loyalty, were readily co-opted upward into the "Punjab system" —as is demonstrated in the careers of Mian Shah Din, Mian Muhammad Shafi and Mian Fazl-i-Husain. All of this meant that the Punjab League would remain a loose grouping of middle class interests overlying essentially parochial structures, that it would remain dormant for years at a time, and that it would not be inclined to focus on the economic and social needs of the Muslim lower classes. It was only after the disastrous League performance in the 1937 provincial elections that Iqbal would write to Jinnah:

The League will have to finally decide whether it will remain a body representing the upper class of India Muslims or Muslim masses who have so far, with good reason, taken no interest in it. Personally, I believe that a political organization which gives no promise of improving the lot of the average Muslim cannot attract our masses.[6]

Nonetheless, if the germ of Muslim nationalism was inherent in the original demand for separate electorates, this class remained true to its first political impulse and formed the core around which the Pakistan Movement would be organized.

Although ignored by the gentry of the League, the Muslim lower classes were not ignored by another social group that entered (or re-entered) the political arena during the First World War—he urban *ulama*. Significantly, the ulama maintained their political alliances with the Indian National Congress, not the Muslim League. The opportunity to hoist the old banner of "Islam in Danger," came during the joint Satyagraha-Khilafat Movement of 1920, which galvanized the humbler orders of Muslim society in large areas of North Indian. In Punjab, the Khilafat struggle affected the students, minor clerks, small shopkeepers, petty landholders of the heartland districts, and country-town *mullahs,* but it appealed most strongly to the urban artisans. As such, it renewed an older political linkage, visible in the *jihād* of

Sayyid Ahmad Shahid (1826-1831) and the Great Rebellion (1857), between the ulama and the lower middle class of pre-industrial Muslim society, cemented in a radical politics that was at once both religious and social—and anti-British.[7] The Khilafat Movement set off a whole series of secondary religio-political convulsions in the heartland towns and cities of Punjab. The most significant of these were: the *Rangīla Rasūl* riots (1927-1928), the "Kashmir-entry" movement (1931-1933), the sectarian Ahrar-Ahmadiyya controversy (1934-1936), and the Masjid-i-Shahidganj agitations (1935-1938). Figuring most prominently in all these events were the ulama of the Punjab Khilafat Committee, which disintegrated about 1930. Among the organizations which replaced it were two "political parties": the Majlis-i-Ahrar and the Ittehad-i-Millat. Both of these parties produced programs promising radical social reform and revolving around chiliastic concepts of *Hakūmat-i-Ilāhia,* both were rooted in the economically hard-pressed artisan groups, and both did better in the 1937 elections than did the Muslim League.

Although the political organizations of the Punjab ulama have yet to be adequately studied, there is some evidence they relied on the old guild-like artisan associations, a link that was enhanced by the artisan social backgrounds of a large number of urban *maulvis.* It is also apparent that these groups were expert at tapping considerable financial resources through loosely connected masjid associations and touring groups or orators and teachers. For the most part, however, the political organization of the Punjab ulama remained rudimentary. They preferred to rely on tested agitational techniques such as demagogic bazaar oratory and the opportunities to lead processions from the *jūma* prayers. These techniques reached something of an extreme in the 1953 Punjab Disturbances, when the ulama mixed a highly combustible brew of unfounded rumor, violent bigotry, and heretical conspiracy theory with the economic frustrations of the urban artisans and lumpenproletariate. In somewhat moderated form, these techniques also reappeared in the agitations agains the Ayub and Bhutto Regimes. From the standpoint of purposes and organizations, it is interesting to note that agitations usually began on religious issues, but rapidly turned agaisnt the government, and that the original leaders always lost effective control over their followers.

The urban gentry and the ulama were alike in that their organizations were formed outside the established political community. Such was not the case for the third social grouping to emerge as an organized political force in the decades before independence. This was the class of landed notables—*ashrāfī* tribal chiefs and powerful *sādāt* families, whose traditions of local rulership reached back to pre-Sikh times, rising gentry families, whose wealth was secured more under British rule, and the leading *chaudhrī* families of the compact peasant *pattīdarī/bhaichāra* clans and brotherhoods (Jat, Arain, Gujjar) of the heartland districts. The security of British rule in Punjab, and the footing of its paternal administration, had been founded in this class. In return for assistance in the crucial tasks of administration—recruitment to the Army and Police, and participation in the revenue administration—the British secured the ancient feudal privileges of this class and maintained them as an active political force in the countryside. As persons of status and influence within their tribes, the notables were, in effect, heads of patron-client networks. On the one hand, they brokered with the administration to recognize sometimes dubious claims to land, quash indictments, increase water quotas from the canals, lease government land, gain remission of land revenue in bad times, promote their supporters as candidates for the services, and press for the construction of public works. On the other, they used their influence to override the traditional authority of the village *panchāyats* in matters of local disputes and neighborhood factionalism (*sharīqa*). Through their familial and lineage networks, the notable families were uniquely situated to control the flow of criminal intelligence in their neighborhoods. While this made them extremely valuable to the police, it also enabled some of them to maintain *rassāgīrī* (cattlelifting) operations, and to indulge in that venerable Punjabi pastime, the abduction of women. Though these attributes were more characteristic of the lower orders of the gentry than of the chiefly families, they are important because they were effective, if crude, methods of social and political control in the Punjab hinterland. If judged by their continued use, the intervening years have in no way lessened their efficacy.

The colonial policy of working as much as possible through indigenous structures had enormous consequences for Punjab politics and the structure of intermediary political organizations. It not only preserved the economic resources and social authority of the landed notables, it ensured that the political authority of the traditional elite would remain founded on local centers of power. Moreover, the paternalist school of administration, which ultimately dependend on a "symbiotic linkage" between the district administration and the rural notables, gave the latter a strategic position astride the relays of power linking countryside and metropolitan power—a position from which they have persistently risen to major influence in Punjab politics. It is no wonder, then, that when faced with the growing demands of new urban social groups, the British sought to draw the landed ashrafiya into the provincial political arena. This was easily accomplished via the tutelary Councils and restricted Assemblies introduced during the various stages of governmental reform. Ruralist interests naturally dominated these Assemblies and soon collected in an organized form as the National Unionist Party. In a classical British mould, the Unionist Party had its origins in Assembly politics and remained an elite organization of anglicized rural gentlemen.

Mass Movement Politics

It is not our intention here to review the underlying causes that set in motion the tidal shift of Punjabi Muslim opinion in favor of the Pakistan demand. It is, rather, to note that the Pakistan Movement succeeded in this province because it was able to link together all the politically active groups, with the exception of the Ahrar ulama, in a single mass movement organization. Undoubtedly, the individual most responsible for the success of this endeavor was M.A. Jinnah. It was Jinnah who, after the collapse of the Muslim League's election effort in 1937, recognized that the Muslim middle class of the province was altogether too weak in numbers and resources to carry alone the nationalist movement. The Sikandar-Jinnah Pact (1937) implicitly recognized this fact of Punjab politics and set in motion the first steps to bring the rural notables into the League. This effort began to gain momentum with the arrival of a new generation of ashrafi leaders—Mian Mumtaz Khan Daultana, Sardar Shaukat Hayat Khan, and Nawab Iftikhar Hussain (of Mamdot)—who saw their political futures in terms of a new Muslim nation, not in a declining empire, and whose progressive opinions were welcomed by the urban youth and student organizations that had resisted the wholesale incorporation of the Unionists into the League in 1937. The "young Turk" landholders formed the opening wedge for the rural notables to enter the League. In the 1946 elections, many of the Unionist MLAs from the heartland and canal colony districts stood on League tickets, while others from the same class of chiefs, *pīrs,* and rural gentry also acquired League tickets to challenge and widely defeat the Unionist die-hards. By 1946, then, the League had come to represent the landed interests of Punjab. In thus embedding themselves in the nationalist movement, the rural notables had not only secured for themselves a central place in the post-independence structure of power, but had kept the League from moving to arouse the rural masses. At the mass level, the Pakistan Movement was largely an urban phenomenon.

With the passing of both Iqbal and Sir Sikandar Hayat Khan, Jinnah had increasingly assumed the role of arbiter in Punjab politics. An outsider to the province, he was able to persuade disparate interests to submerge their differences in the wider national struggle. His insistence on properly constituted organizations and procedures—despite the fact that he and everyone else knew he ran the League out of his own brief case—enabled him to contain sometimes clashing interests. By 1947, the League held in uneasy suspension most of the diverse elements in Punjab society—the rural notables, with their wider tribal and personal alliances, the old urban gentry and their barādarī associations, radical young lawyers and students, nascent merchant and professional associations, and the urban lower middle and artisan classes, who deserted their traditional religious leaders in response to the radical social program drawn up by the League's left wing. Jinnah's authority thus overrode factional and parochial cleavages in Punjab politics, but it did not fuse them, or change old identities and interests. The appearance and reality of organization in Jinnah's League did not coincide. The technique of stringing together vertically structured patron-client and kinship networks by bringing their leaders together on League Working Committees, made for unstable, fluid and highly personalized organization.

Not unexpectedly, the years after the passing of Jinnah saw both the disintegration of the League and the rise of the rural notables to dominance in Punjab politics. Bred to a life of display, to the indulgence of feudal perquisities, to the suppression of any opposition from below, the landed ashrafi-gentry classes of the Indus Plain were not ones to operate parliamentary institutions in a manner responsible to a citizen electorate. Although there were always important exceptions, too many of the notables acted as if the law, and its agencies (the local *thānadār*), were tools to be used against one's opponents, but bypassed to help one's self and one's clients. In these circumstances, League organizations in rural Punjab were simply extensions of the influence networks of the locally dominant *zamindārs*. Party membership rolls carried the names of their henchmen, barādarī members, tenants, and of enough fictitious enrolees to better the next man's claim to precedence. Control over a large block of votes was deemed essential as a base from which to bargain for party office, patronage, a ticket in the next elections, or for inserting one's self into the entourage of a powerful minister. For their part, the party leaders could hardly afford to ignore those who controlled the vote bank of an area. Political rivalry there was aplenty, but it occurred between competing factions and notables who claimed the dominant influence in the same area.

The basis for a participant social order was emerging in the major cities, where perhaps thirty percent of the males were literate, but this was complicated by a number of factors. Urban barādarī leaders (Arains, Kashmiris, Kakezais, and Sheikhs in Lahore) continued to operate lineage ties as the basis for political organization. They were favored in this by compact tribal residential patterns in the old urban neighborhoods and by the fact that East Punjabi *muhājirs* (partition refugees) and rural to urban migrants used barādarī and family connections, when available, to integrate themselves into the urban setting. Urban party units were under the control of the 1946 MLAs, with their barādarī members as ward and mahallah level workers. The organization of the "new" Punjab Muslim League after partition was, in fact, put into the hands of these established political figures.[8] Those urban elements who were committed to ideological programs and to collective forms of leadership quite rapidly found themselves isolated as a

Progressive Bloc within the League. They soon formed the Azad Pakistan Party outside the League, a party with negligible support at the time, but one which, nevertheless, held within it the antecedents of both the National Awami Party and the left wing of the Pakistan People's Party.

The first decade of independence marked the high tide of notable dominance in Punjab. Local powerholders moved to control the sources of rural credit and water distribution and to manipulate District Board and Market Committee elections through ministerial pressure, bureaucratic agencies and *jhurlū* (armed band) politics. What minimal League organizations that had existed at the District and Tehsil levels either became pocket organizations or simply evaporated. The Punjab League began to fragment under the pressures of factions and shifting group loyalties. Dominant faction leaders assumed policy positions and made personal alliances simply to advance their own careers. The League did not act as a political party in the sense that it organized consistent support for its leaders in government, fashioned programs that were to be implemented by legislation, or served as a channel to communicate popular demands upward to government leaders. It served rather as a hiring hall for prospective ministers, a platform for the disgruntled and a political club for the transient clusterings of patron-client groups that combined, disintegrated and recombined as they sought the quickest route to power. Not surprisingly, as party structures weakened in Pakistan, so also did parliamentary institutions.

One result of these trends was a growing conflict between the bureaucratic elite and the rural notables. Like the latter, the civil elite (as a result of the gradual "Indianization" of the ICS and the Army officer corps after World War One) emerged from Partition as a rising force. Though both elites shared a common and somewhat anglicized social and educational milieu, and though civil servants were at first disposed to serve party governments, they would increasingly find themselves at odds as the decade progressed. In the districts, this conflict grew out of the ambitions of the notables to use the bureaucracy as an instrument of power. In the cities, the bureaucracy found itself called upon to intervene in law and order situations arising out of the conditions of political instability. At the national and provincial levels, however, the conflict was more fundamental. As it became more conscious of the need for planned development, the administrative elite began to press for the concentration of power in centralized institutions. Further, a significant element in the bureaucracy began to see land reform as the best way to end the stagnation of West Pakistan's rural economy. The landed ashrafi-gentry class, the conservative force with the most to lose from any economic or social betterment of the rural population, was not unaware that any such concentration of power would mean the "political expropriation" of its old feudal privileges and the local authority founded thereon. The notables therefore resisted bureaucratic incursions into the political arena, sought to secure a constitutional settlement that legitimized a pluralist political system (they had resisted One Unit), and regularly turned aside any suggestion of meaningful land reform. In this inter-elite struggle, and in the conditions that gave rise to it, can be seen the rationale for the coup d'ètat of 1958.

Changes in the Environment

Between the disintegration of the Muslim League and the rise of the Pakistan People's Party, the social environment underwent substantial structural change. Some of this change—*e.g.,* urbanization and demographic patterns—was cumulative and the result of underlying trends, but much of it resulted from, or was enhanced by, the political and developmental policies pursued by the Ayub Government. This was a government of conservative modernizers who urged rapid economic development, but who were also quick to see the need to expand national authority by rationalizing it in central institutions and, as much as possible, to depoliticize the system of representation by containing it in a restricted, bureaucratically controlled system. As is well known, the Ayub Regime did achieve major economic progress in both the agricultural and industrial sectors, but it failed to appreciate the social impact of this change or that the Basic Democracies system would completely fail to contain it.

Like the British in Punjab, Ayub attempted to secure his rule on a rural base. This he accomplished by aligning with the old Unionist establishment (Kalabagh), attempting to undermine the authority of the League period zamindar-politicians through Elective Bodies Disqualification Order, the operations of the Basic Democracies system and land reform, and by activating the class of middle landlords and their collateral interest groups in the rural-to-town matrix: grain commission agents, transporters and government contractors. These groups, which also had strong representation in the army officer corps, were activated politically in the Basic Democracies system and given access to patronage sources in the development effort produced by the Rural Works Program. As Burki's studies show,[9] the middle zamindars proved to be energetic entrepreneurs. Aided by government subsidies, they were particularly adept in adopting tube well technology—a "strategic innovation" that would later give them ready access to the high yield seed/fertilizer package of the "Green Revolution."[10] The middle zamindars were somewhat eclipsed in the later Ayub years by the politicization of the regime and the return of the zamindar-politicians under the Convention Muslim League (CML). But, having been drawn into the political arena, they would not soon abandon it. It is interesting to note that middle zamindars formed the most substantial social element among the Punjab People's Party representation from Punjab in the Assemblies elected in 1970. (See Table 4.)

In the urban areas, Ayub's institutional reforms worked to restrict the influence and livelihood of important interest groups, such as lawyers and the ulama. The reforms promoted bureaucratic penetration into areas heretofore free of direct government management: the press, religious establishments, universities, cultural institutions, trade unions and professional organizations. The need to deal with an often unsympathetic bureaucracy for the protection of their interests, strengthened the organizational responses of old interest groups and encouraged the formation of new ones. Ayub's policies and methods, particularly those stemming from the martial law period, created an undercurrent of opposition to his regime among groups strategically placed to influence public opinion. These were groups that would work with the regime as long as its grip on power remained secure, but they were interests from which Ayub Khan could expect little support once a viable opposition began to coalesce. It was of no little importance, for example, that the district bar associations gave Zulfikar Ali Bhutto his first public platforms in Punjab after his departure from the Ayub Regime.

The redistribution of power among established social groups was undoubtedly an important factor in setting the scene for the advent of the PPP, but equally important were the social and political consequences of change produced by economic development. The growing concentration of population in the urban centers, the diffusion of technology, the shift in landholding patterns, the rural-to-urban migrations of landless tenants and small peasant holders, the expansion of industry in cities like Lyallpur and its spread to ex-urban sites (Kala Shah Kaku, Sheikhupura Road), the growth of vernacular and electronic media sources, were all part of the wider process of change that accelerated the profound uncertainties already visible in traditional Punjabi society. Indeed, much of the available data on social development (see: Appendix) suggests that large parts of Punjab were well across the threshold to the "participant society" by the end of the Ayub decade. This was certainly the case for urbanization, since Punjab had passed the ten percent urbanization figure early in the Ayub period—ten percent urbanization being Lerner's bench mark indicator of the transition of developing political systems to the politics of participation. Not surprisingly, the new social and interest groups that formed this newly participant sector were crucial elements in the success of the PPP. Among them were: a generation of students whose political consciousness had been formed during the September War with India and radicalized by the pro-China euphoria that followed; teachers in private schools and colleges, many of them being from East Punjabi *muhājir* families who were now demanding economic rewards commensurate with their rising status and ambitions; teachers and medical compounders in the tehsil and *mandī* towns; radical labor fronts (People's Labor Front, Muttahida Mazdoor Mahaz, Taraqqipasand Mazdoor Mahaz, etc.) bent on organizing the large industrial settlements (e.g., at Kot Lakhpat) completed during the latter Ayub years; peasant associations (Thal Mihnat Kash Mahaz); the menial service ranks of the government departments; press workers; tonga, rehra and thela walas; mechanics; the rural-urban migrants of the *kachhī abādīs*; even the wage-slaves of the outlying *bhattās* (brick kilns). These were the heart and soul of the PPP in Punjab. Unlike the older interest groups (urban lawyers), who split in their party support patterns, these groups remained loyal to the PPP.

The surge of this latter grouping against Ayub Khan, captured and extended by the PPP during the 1970 election campaign, represented Punjab's late "coming of age." It was the breakthrough of the mass public into the political sphere, and it signalled a fundamental and irreversible alteration in the relationship between rulers and ruled. In short, the events of 1968-1970 forced open the Punjab political system to the entry of mass-based political parties. Yet, for most developing countries this era of "mass entry" has not been a stable one. This, as Huntington has noted, results because the politicization of social forces far outpaces the growth of middle range or "community political institutions," including political parties, that are needed to organize, aggregate and contain the plethora of burgeoning expectations set off by the rapid downward penetration of political consciousness.[11]

This situation of high politicization and low institutionalization is, of course, fertile ground for the emergence of mass movements which are ridden to power by charismatic figures and their haphazardly organized political parties. These parties tend to be unstable conglomerations of political personalities; patron-client groups, both functional and parochial; and local party organizations rising spontaneously from mass public sectors that are politicized in the movement. The very rapidity of their rise to power militates against the establishment of clear organizational boundaries. This is so partly because, in the swelling tide of popular support, they are not perceived to be a prerequisite for gaining power, and partly because only in a long struggle by dedicated and able party leaders are the conditions met for the breaking down of old identities and pre-existing social compartments and the homogenizing of these under a new party rubric. Moreover, charismatic leaders are often unable to perceive the salience of the social and economic expectations that carried them to power, preferring to trade on their personal appeal, and are unwilling to organize the kind of bounded party that would soon impose constraints on their scope for maneuver.

From Quaid-i-Azam to Quaid-i-Awam

When he left the Ayub Regime in June, 1966, Zulfikar Ali Bhutto was already a national figure. He was a hero to much of the post-independence generation who had been brought up in the domestic vortexes of Pakistan's anti-India nationalism. His assiduous avowal of the China demarche, his hardline stand on the September War with India and the Tashkent negotiations, and his passionately nationalistic speeches at the UN Security Council debates on that war, had won him the adulation of much of the West Pakistani student community. After Tashkent, in every college and university, and in most high schools, multiple new student groups of varying ideological emphases were organized and most of these were pro-Bhutto. On the issues of war and peace, President Ayub Khan was perceived to have knuckled under to foreign pressure, while Foreign Minister Bhutto was a true champion of Pakistan's national interests. Public anger at the diplomatic outcome of the war was thus deflected away from Bhutto, perhaps the prime mover of the failed forward policy in Kashmir—the immediate cause of the war—and was focused on the man who, as President, bore the ultimate responsibility.

The 1965 war and Tashkent were watershed events, the economic and military-political ramifications of which eventually brought down the Ayub Regime. For the pro-Bhutto students, and for the urban intelligentsia, these events confirmed the linkage between foreign and domestic policies which the leftist parties, the old Azad Pakistan Party and the National Awami Party, had always asserted. Pakistan's military and diplomatic weaknesses, they believed, stemmed from the structure of Pakistani society—the hold of the military/bureaucratic elite, its intimate ties to feudal landlords and "comprador capitalists," and its subservience to the "neocolonial powers," by way of exploitative trade, aid, military and intelligence relationships. They also perceived in Ayub's refusal to continue the war with Chinese material aid, the fear that a long war would deeply politicize the lower social orders and thus destroy the elite social base of the Regime. The visible hallmarks of this new political consciousness were anti-Americanism, a Marxist rhetoric and a pro-China euphoria, but beneath all of this was the far stronger current of Pakistani nationalism. Most of the pro-Bhutto students were neither Marxists nor revolutionaries, but ardent nationalists who were committed to the kinds of structural change that would set the nation on the road to economic and military self-sufficiency.

The Tashkent Declaration brought the West Pakistan student community—the new and left groups—into the streets to protest, for the first time, a major issue of national policy.[12] This was the first indication that the students had begun to see themselves as the main center for organized opposition to the authoritarian Regime and its police controls. Like Jinnah during the Pakistan Movement, Bhutto saw the value of an aroused student community as a vanguard force in attacking the Ayubian version of the vice-regal state. Hence, he was prepared to align with the student federations, but he was also aware that student politics could be volatile and episodic. He moved therefore to secure his political future on a wider circle of support groups and canvassed a number of possible alternatives before deciding to form his own political party. These alternatives began with the idea of a forward bloc inside Ayub's Convention Muslim League, went on to the notion of a united front of opposition parties, and ended when his efforts to gain a position of leadership in one of several opposition parties came to naught.

Despite their nonsuccess, however, Bhutto's talks with the opposition parties were an important indication of the direction in which he wanted to move. The fact that he made his most concerted efforts with the Council Muslim League and the National Awami Party is particularly significant, for it suggests that Bhutto had to come to envision the recreation of the Quaid-i-Azam's broad nationalist coalition as the most effective means of countering, even overthrowing, the grip of the vice-regal institutions on the state. Both parties were products of the Pakistan Movement, the CML having the most direct organizational connection, the Punjab NAP tracing its political lineage through the Azad Pakistan Party to the Progressive Group in the old Punjab Muslim League. As representative of social elements in the League, both groupings had been crucial to the success of the Pakistan Movement in Punjab—the centrist Daultana group, because it had brought the dominant social force in the province decisively into the Movement, and the Progressive Group, because it had united key urban social groups (lawyers, students, workers, artisans, the pro-Pakistan section of the ulama) behind the League's radical manifesto of 1946.

Yet, in his contacts with these two parties, it soon became evident that, though both were remnants of the original nationalist coalition, the intervening years had affected both so unfavorably that neither was suitable for carrying out the strategy envisioned by Bhutto. The CML had been irreparably damaged by its political failings during the pre-coup years of League governments. Moreover, it was now little more than an isolated and quarrelsome elite, over-reliant on its rural pocket boroughs, and neither likely nor willing to transform itself into a mass movement. For Bhutto, who was increasingly conscious that the deep ferment in Pakistani society meant that his contemplated reconstruction of Jinnah's rural-urban coalition would have to be founded on a markedly expanded social base, this aspect of the CML was unacceptable. The NAP posed more serious problems for Bhutto. Its internal alliance of provincial autonomists and anti-feudal revolutionists was, in his view, a potential threat to the survival of the Pakistani state. In Pakistan, where the national movement had preceded the now anticipated anti-feudal revolution, the ethnic/linguistic autonomists were seen as a threat to the supremacy of Muslim nationalism. In like manner, the anti-feudal revolutionists were a threat to the key social element in the original state-forming coalition. Should these groups come to power together in a mass movement, or conjoin with the Bengali nationalists of the Awami League, the result might well be the break up of the State or the emergence of an even purer form of bonapartism. It is not that Bhutto was opposed to the anti-feudal revolution. Its advent was, in one form or another, an historical necessity. Rather, it was a concern that the form it would take would have major long-term consequences both for the social and institutional structure of power and for the stability of the State. For Bhutto, then, Pakistan's most basic interests would best be protected if the anti-feudal revolution could be submerged within a strong recrudescence of a wider Pakistani nationalism. This is the real significance of Bhutto's early alliance with J.A. Rahim, the first Secretary-General of the Pakistan People's Party, for in this partnership were the essential elements of a "Jinnahist" coalition of nationalist and radical social elements. Rahim touched on this aspect, as well as on Bhutto's deeper concerns for the security of Pakistan, when he told this student:

Bhutto's own leaning was always very nationalistic. He always emphasized the nationalistic side, while I inclined the other way and emphasized internal social change, believing that we could take the nation, and its existence in the framework of the State, for granted.[13]

Though Bhutto would later be pushed farther to the left by the exigencies of the People's Movement than he would otherwise have been inclined to go, he never lost sight of his original conception. It would later be visible in many ways, but most particularly in Bhutto's quiet, but persistent, courting of the old League *zamindāriāt* in the 1970 elections, and in the fact that it was the People's Party in 1972 that finally put into law much of the Punjab Muslim League manifesto of 1946.

The People's Party as Organization

From its foundation at Lahore on December 1, 1967, the Pakistan People's Party displayed a marked internal dichotomy of factional groupings, programmatic emphases and organizational strategies. In the most general sense, this dichotomy reflected the transitional nature of the times, and of the People' Party as a link between a passing age of elite politics and the new age of mass politics. Although there were core leaders, neither of the clusterings of individuals and subgroups on either side of the dichotomy was immutable. Hence, considerable movement across the divide was possible, and did occur, though for the most part in one direction.

The first of these groupings we may call the "politicals." They tended to be from the higher social orders, to have landed interests, and to have had either personal or familial experience of parliamentary membership. They were in the PPP either because of strong personal ties to Zulfikar Ali Bhutto

(Ghulam Mustapha Khar) or because they saw in Bhutto the one man who could defeat Ayub Khan and become the next leader of Pakistan (Malik Aslam Hayat and, later, Nawab Sadiq Hussain Qureshi). They were interested both in the patronage rewards of power and in general reform to break up the industrial conglomerates and the hierarchical, elitist structure of the civil service, but they had no desire to weaken the legal protection for private property. The "politicals" also desired the break up of West Pakistan into its former provinces, the etablishment of "one man, one vote" parliamentary government, and a mixed economy. They were nationalists who stressed the need for constitutional pluralism, but who also saw Islamic Socialism more as a slogan than an ideological base for the party. Their organizational strategy looked to a duplication of the Muslim League mass movement of 1946-1947. They saw party organization at a "top-down" process of vertical recruitment, which fitted well with the fact that most of them brought their own patron-client groups into the party. The "politicals" preferred the technique of mass meetings as a prelude to elections and naturally, and often in a most paternalist way, promoted the charisma of th Party Chairman, Z.A. Bhutto.

The second general grouping in the PPP was that of the "ideologicals." For the most part, the "ideologicals" came from common social backgrounds and were part of the newly politicized mass sectors. They were generally urban residents, well educated (above F.A.), but many also had rural backgrounds as peasant small-holders (Malik Meraj Khalid, Hanif Ramay, Sheikh Muhammad Rashid, etc.). If they had them, their earlier political identities led back through the National Awami Party (Bhashani Group) to the Azad Pakistan Party and the Progressive Bloc of the old Muslim League (Sheikh Rashid, Khurshid Hasan Mir). For the most part, however, the "ideologicals" were new entrants to party politics and came to the PPP from radical student and labor politics. This grouping was more committed to fundamental, systemic reform. They agreed with the need to break up the industrial conglomerates and the civil service elite, but they also put a major emphasis on deep-going land reform and on new types of rural social and economic structures (agrovilles). They had less concern for the sanctity of private property and supported the nationalization of industry and financial institutions. Part of this group saw Islamic Socialism as a "third way" for Pakistan, looked back to Iqbal for inspiration, and, in highly intellectual study circles, attempted to work out the theoretical underpinnings for their ideology (Hanif Ramay, Dr. Mubashar Hasan). Others (J.A. Rahim) stressed socialism almost exclusively. In terms of organizational strategy, they believed in the need for the party structures to emerge from below. Hence, they supported elected local units and "democratic centralism" and maintained that the party ought to serve as the policy organ for Government. Without access to strong parochial bodies, their political influence depended on the strength of the party organizations they could muster. Thus, they stressed party discipline and were not unwilling to urge the PPP into "revolutionary" confrontation with the Government. They also believed the PPP should organize student, worker/peasant and women's organizations, and acted on these beliefs, thus beginning to operate along horizontal social linkages.

The place of Z.A. Bhutto, as party chairman, above this dichotomy was a most ambivalent one which required considerable political dexterity. It seems clear that Bhutto was more comfortable with the politicals than the ideologicals, and that he was, in fact, their real leader. Among the ideological adherents to the PPP, there was always a group which suspected the PPP was a "fuherist" party founded to advance the political career of its overwhelmingly dominant figure, but they stayed with it as long as they thought they could "use" the PPP to open up the political system. Other ideologicals took heart from the fact that Bhutto's credentials as a third world figure and overseer to the Peking connection were at least as solid as his "one thousand year war with India" nationalism. Though somewhat Fabian, and evidently not thought through in specifically economic terms, Bhutto's commitment to a socialist economy for Pakistan was, in our perception, genuine.[14] So long as the PPP moved in that direction, most ideologicals saw no reason to abandon it simply because it did not move fast enough. In any case, the PPP was their best hope for meaningful change.

The basic contradictions between the groupings are visible in much of the party literature, in the founding convention documents (*Foundation and Policy*), and in the 1970 election "Manifesto." A text analysis of party literature would perhaps prove burdensome, so we will confine ourselves to a quick look at the Interim Constitution of the Party. The views of the politicals are evident in the provisions governing membership and the powers of the chairman. These insured that the party would be open to universal membership and not restricted to individuals of a certain class or previous political affiliation. The chairman was given major powers to appoint and remove the various chairmen of provincial organizing committees and "after consultation with the chairmen of the provincial and lower levels, to expel any member from the Party who is found to deviate from the Party's principles . . ." Needless to say, Bhutto rarely considered the consultation provision a serious necessity. The interests of the ideologicals were protected by the provisions governing the constitution of local party units and that permitting the representation of "active party members from amongst the wokers, the peasants, the youth, the women and the intellectuals." The provisions on local units not only required the election of office-bearers, but granted District and City Organising Committees considerable autonomy in the constitution and certification of local units in their jurisdictions.

In contrast to its swelling popularity, the work of organizing the formal structures of the PPP was remarkably slow, particularly in Punjab. In his first press conference after the founding of the PPP, Bhutto noted

We are not in any hurry and the appointment of mere officebearers is not the main point. We do not want to make our organization a 'party of patronage.' We will do our organization work slowly, gradually and with the consensus and approval of friends.[15]

Interestingly, at the same news conference, he announced the appointment of Organizing Chairmen for Sind and the NWFP, but failed to mention an appointment for the Punjab. Already, in Punjab, factional struggles were under way. An Organizing Chairman for Punjab was delayed for months, until the appointment of Sheikh Rashid was virtually forced by the success of the students in the anti-Ayub campaign. The Punjab Organizing Committee followed soon thereafter (March, 1969), but the PPP Central Committee did not appear until after the general election. Further, several of the projected party institutions—the National Council and the Planning Committees— never saw the light of day. Clearly, Bhutto was in no hurry to establish formal structures.

In the absence of formal structures, Bhutto used highly personal forms of leadership, which operated through an informal hierarchy of access to the Chairman. The inner circle which formed around Bhutto, and which came to be known among the party faithful as the "central cell," was made up of those who had access to Bhutto without first explaining themselves to intermediaries. The internal dynamic of this grouping was founded on sets of intense personal rivalries which grew out of the primary cleavage in the party. Membership in the group was highly restricted and contingent on Bhutto's good will rather than on one's party post. One rising leader in the PPP credited his failure to penetrate the central cell to the personal and political hostility of Ghulam Mustapha Khar.[16] As "door-keeper" to the physical presence of Bhutto, Khar for minor reasons refused to permit this individual in to see Bhutto, despite a prior appointment initiated by Bhutto. A mundane matter perhaps, but these were the kinds of concerns often expressed in interviews with second and third echelon party leaders.

Personalized leadership was, of course, well fitted to Bhutto's remarkable political and intellectual abilities. It gave him a substantial degree of freedom to operate simultaneously at several levels both in the party and in the wider political arena. It had its drawbacks, however. One of these was the fact that it opened up party matters to the darker side of Bhutto's personality—the dismissal of J.A. Rahim in 1974 being only one of a series of unfortunate incidents in which former colleagues were pushed out of the Party. Another drawback was the unreadiness of the PPP to face its first real internal crisis.

This occurred on November 14, 1968 with the arrest of Bhutto. Uncertain of what action to take, and faced with an internal power struggle over the acting chairmanship (J.A. Rahim versus Ali Ahmad Talpur), the PPP discovered just how shallow and disorganized its central institutions were. Moreover, the decision to run Bhutto as a Presidential candidate in the coming BD system elections, taken by Bhutto in prison and announced by Rahim at the Lahore Bar Association, shook the PPP to its foundations and led to the departure of, among others, Malik Aslam Hayat, the original Convener of the party. It was after this painful debacle that Bhutto consented to the appointment of a Punjab Organizing Committee.

The period between March, 1969, when the Punjab Organizing Committee was appointed, and March, 1970, when Bhutto and the politicals moved to curb its powers, marked the high point of the ideological wing of the Punjab People's Party. Despite the Yahya Regime's modified ban on party activity, the young radicals moved to capture the newly politicized mass sectors aroused in the anti-Ayub Movement. Under the wider leadership of Sheikh Rashid, the cities and towns became centers of intense organizational activity. When the ban on political activity was lifted early in 1970 and elections scheduled under the Legal Framework Order, the Punjab Organizing Committee moved to extend its efforts to the countryside and mandi towns of the province. In these areas, as earlier in the cities and district towns, the party workers found the humbler orders of Punjabi society already highly politicized. In many cases, party organization was simply a matter of certifying party units that had already been spontaneously created. By late March, 1970, the ideological wing felt strong enough to attempt a coup of sorts within the party and to assert itself on policy and organizational matters. In a meeting of the Punjab Committee on March 29th., the ideologicals passed a series of resolutions that, among other things, called for a far more radical land reform than the PPP had thus far contemplated. Another important resolution attempted to place curbs on the movement of established political figures (ex-supporters of Ayub's Convention Muslim League) into the PPP. Bhutto's response was a flying visit to Lahore and a bitter confrontation in a meeting at the Hotel Intercontinental in which the ideologicals were verbally beaten into submission. As one participant put it, "We were humiliated in the feudal way."[17]

If the March 29th meeting marked the high point of the ideological's influence in the Punjab PPP, their decline was in no way precipitous. Nevertheless, as the PPP election campaign gained momentum, it was the political wing that gained the most. This was precisely because, in the election campaign, the PPP became a mass movement. The local party units that were organized after July, 1970 showed an increasing number that were organized on a patronclient and barādarī basis. Old political leaders who had at first opposed the PPP, and in some cases had perpetrated violence against the PPP, made quiet approaches to Bhutto, and were accepted into the party along with their groups. Small political parties, such as the Shia Political Party, declared their support for the PPP. What the entry of these and many other groups meant, of course, was that they would have to be accommodated in the distribution of PPP tickets to the National and Provincial Assemblies. These processes triggered a second breakdown in PPP organization and another confrontation between the ideologicals and the politicals. This time the victory of the politicals was more decisive, since the Central Parliamentary Board, which the politicals dominated, took over the ticketing procedure and revoked a substantial number of tickets already given by the Punjab Board to ideologicals. The result was visible in the social make-up of PPP MNAs and MPAs (see Appendix), though also visible here is the substantial change that the PPP nevertheless represented, even as a mass movement.

The election victory did not lessen the growing tensions within the PPP. Fundamental disagreement (again ideologicals versus politicals) over the East Pakistan situation, wrangling over prospective ministries, and divided counsels on how to respond to the quiet counter-revolution being waged in the countryside, enhanced internal strains that could only be superficially ameliorated. The arrival of the PPP into power only enhanced its disorganization. This was to be expected, for in the classic pattern, the top PPP leadership (both ideological and political) was absorbed into the provincial and central governments at the ministerial level. Party affairs were increasingly manipulated through client networks. With the prospect of patronage and influence on policy at stake, control of party organizations became even more essential. Despite the entry of a number of old political leaders and rural notables into the Assemblies via the PPP, many of the party's MNAs and MPAs were "new men" who depended on party organizations, rather than personal or parochial networks, for their local influence with the district bureaucracy. Thus, in the districts which had voted overwhelmingly for the PPP, the years 1972 and 1973 saw a growing number of serious incidents of violence between opposing factions of partymen. The November, 1972 convention of the PPP at Rawalpindi produced a plan (*Tanzim-e-Nau*) to reorganize the party with the object of relieving factional tensions and giving party managers greater control over the volatile and sometimes buccaneering elements within the Punjab PPP. This effort, however, rapidly became absorbed in the growing factional struggle on the provincial level (Khar versus Ramay).

Growing confusion in the PPP, public disaffection over a whole range of issues (Bangla Desh recognition, rapid inflation, corruption in the PPP), the appearance of non-PPP leaders who could serve as a focus for this disaffection (Air Marshal, Retd., Asghar Khan), and the need to the seek a more stable base of support in view of the nationalization of industry and civil service reform, helped to continue the shift in the PPP's social support base which was already visible before the election. This meant that the long-honored principle of rural Punjab politics, *jerā jītā, odā nāl* (loosely: "If you can't beat 'em, join 'em.") came into play as the traditional power groups sought entry into the PPP. For the most part, in return for lipservice to the PPP manifesto and loyalty to Bhutto, they found easy entry into local party units. By 1975, it was becoming evident that old rural notable and gentry families were gaining control over PPP units up to the Tehsil level. Inside the party, the notables, with their local centers of power still essentially intact, their political skills honed by long experience, and their jhurlū techniques, proved adept at manipulating internal factions and operating barādarī networks as election mobilization instruments. Barādarī, which had been swept aside as a factor in the 1970 elections, re-emerged as a mobilization technique in the Narowal and Chak Jumra by-elections (1973).

Some Conclusions

The years after 1972, very much like the years after 1947, witnessed the progressive deterioration of the dominant political party in the Punjab. Both periods of decline followed periods of unity and electoral success produced by a mass movement strategy which focused both on a dominant leader—who was also an outsider to the province,—and on a strategy that combined nationalism with a radical social program. Neither leader was able to dominate Punjab politics by using his party organization. Jinnah, who understood the organizational requisites of representative party politics, did not find in Muslim Punjab the social material out of which a modern political party could be fashioned. Bhutto, who had, in the emergence of the "participant society" in Punjab, the social material out of which organizations are made, failed to adequately appreciate the requirement of political organization in an era of mass participation. Both leaders depended on their charisma to hold their mass movements together, though there were differences in the way each operated. Jinnah threw a cloak of formal organization and exacting principle over a parochial reality and believed in the virtue of consistency, while Bhutto relied on political acrobatics and the calculated use of unpredictability to keep the loyalty of his partymen and the opposition off balance.

As organizations, both the People's Party and the Muslim League (after Jinnah's death) had difficulties maintaining their organizational boundaries or finding mechanisms to solve internal disputes. As particularistic cleavages began to re-emerge, so too did the pattern of playing off powerful intra-provincial interests one against the other, and in both cases this ultimately redounded to the advantage of the rural notables and the bureaucracy. The PPP, however, can be seen as representing a transitional stage to the age of mass politics. Rooted more deeply in Punjab's social fabric, the PPP gave both voice and ideological focus to the aspirations of the lower social classes and political-agitational expertise to their natural leaders. Having seen their votes hoist the PPP into power, these groups will not soon forget the opportunities available through political action, nor their leaders the sumptuary and patronage benefit of party office. The PPP showed a tendency to rely on the support of organized social and interest groups, though it created few formal organizations to maintain these support relationships. It also produced a number of political role types—partymen, power brokers, etc., —that had not much been seen before in Punjab, and, in parts of the province, the party was successful in replacing the rural notables as the crucial link between the peasantry and the administration. Further, as a party which emerged out of a period of ideological polarization in Pakistan, the PPP was far more effective in translating its manifesto into legislation. In its land reforms it advanced the anti-feudal revolution by several notches, and in its civil service reforms broke down the elitist and compartmentalized structure of the bureacracy. Finally, with the wholesale politicization of society, the PPP was more effective than the Muslim League in bridging the historic rural-urban dichotomy in Punjab by linking together the lower social order as a whole under a common political program.

Appendix

TABLE 1
Urbanization in Punjab

	1931[a]	1951	1961	1972
Population (millions):	14	21	26	37
Urbanization (percent):				
Cities over 20,000	3	4	5	5
Cities over 100,000	5	9	11	15
Literacy (percent):	3	13	14	16
Voting (pct. eligibles):	59 (PLA)[b]	50 (PLA)	73[c]	66 (NA)[d]

[a]The 1931 urbanization figure is for the area now in Pakistan's Punjab; otherwise 1931 figures are for Muslims in pre-Partition Punjab.

[b]1937 Punjab Legislative Assembly election held under restricted sufferage. All other figures are for universal sufferage elections.

[c]West Pakistan Union Council elections, 1959.

[d]Elections to the National Assembly, 1970.

TABLE 2
Pakistan: Social Indicators of Development[a]

	1950	1955	1960	1965	1970
Media:					
No. of dailies	35	79	99	88	137
Circulation (000s)	150	716	606	—	643
Circ. (per 1,000 pop.)	2	9	7	—	5
Radio (000s)	62	109	276	549	1,626
Radio trans. power (KW)	137.6	137.6	204	664.5	2,604.5
TV sets (000s)	NA	NA	NA	10	80
TV sets (per 1,000 pop.)	NA	NA	NA	0.1	0.7
TV trans. power (KW)	NA	NA	NA	4	24
Films produced	10[b]	20	42	89	141
No. of cinemas	284[c]	300	361	325	545
Education (pct. total pop.)					
Primary	4.5	4.9	5.4	6.6	7.4[d]
Secondary	1.5	1.6	1.6	2.5	3.1[d]
Vocational	.01	.01	.01	.02	.03[d]
Teacher Training	.01	.01	.01	.02	—
Higher and Univ.	.08	.09	0.2	0.3	0.3[d]
Registered Trade Unions:					
No. of Unions	255	475	666	975	1,082[d]
Membership (000s)	140	139	269	414	556[d]
No. workers/disputes (000s)	16	42	25	125	298[d]

[a]SOURCES: GOP, Central Statistical Office, *25 Years of Pakistan in Statistics, 1947–1972* (Karachi: Manager of Publications, 1972); and United Nations, *Statistical Yearbook, 1951–1972.*
[b]1953   [c]1952   [d]1968

TABLE 3
Assembly Interest Group Representation
Punjab Districts
(Percentage)

Interest	National Assembly			W. Pak. Assembly		
	1955	1962	1965	1956	1962	1965
Landholders[a]	66.7	66.0	57.4	57.8	54.2	43.1
Ashrafi-Pirs	14.3	6.4	8.5	11.6	8.3	11.1
Ashrafi-Other	42.9	14.9	19.1	20.4	8.3	13.9
Gentry	9.5	31.9	21.3	17.7	23.6	13.9
Middle	—	12.8	8.5	8.2	13.9	4.2
Industry/Business	4.8	10.6	14.9	12.9	18.1	22.2
Lawyers	14.3	8.5	8.5	13.6	12.5	12.5
Ulama	—	2.1	—	5.4	1.4	1.4
Military (Rtd.)	—	—	6.4	1.4	—	2.8
Public Ser.	14.3	4.3	2.1	3.4	4.2	9.7
Professions, Other	—	8.5	10.6	5.4	9.7	8.3

[a]Although these categories do not depend solely on the category of landholding size, it is perhaps helpful to note that ashrafi landholders tend to hold more than 500 acres, gentry holders from 150 to 500 acres, middle holders from 50 to 150 acres.

TABLE 4
Assembly Interest Group Representation
Pakistan People's Party
Punjab Districts

Interest	National Assembly 1970	Punjab Assembly 1970
Landholders	61.9	54.8
Ashrafi-Pirs	4.8	2.6
Ashrafi-Other	4.8	3.5
Gentry	14.3	13.0
Middle	30.2	20.0
Rich Peasant	7.9	15.7
Industry	—	0.9
Small Industry	1.6	6.1
Commerce	3.2	14.8
Ulama	1.6	—
Military (Rtd.)	1.6	0.9
Public Ser.	1.6	3.5
Professions, Elite	7.9	4.3
Trans.	1.6	3.5
Lawyers	19.1	11.3

Notes

1. This paper presents some of the perspectives reached by the author during his doctoral research in Punjab in 1973 and 1974. A fuller accounting of this research is available in the author's doctoral thesis: "The Pakistan People's Party: Social Group Response and Party Development in an Era of Mass Participation," unpublished Ph.D. thesis, The Fletcher School of Law and Diplomacy, 1979.

2. *From Max Weber, Essays in Sociology,* trans. and ed. by H.H. Gerth and C. Wright Mills (London: Kegan Paul, 1947), p. 194.

3. Lucian W. Pye, "Party Systems and National Development in Asia," in *Political Parties and Political Development,* ed. by LaPalombara and Weiner, (Princeton, 1966), 372.

4. Daniel Lerner, *The Passing of Traditional Society,* (New York: The Free Press, 1958), pp. 50-51.

5. *Ibid.,* pp. 50-52.

6. "Letters of Iqbal to Jinnah," in *Iqbal: Poet-Philosopher of Pakistan,* ed. by Hafeez Malik, (Columbia, 1971), p. 385.

7. See: Abdullah Malik, *Punjab Ki Siyasi Tehriken,* (Lahore: Nigarshat, 1971).

8. Safdar Mahmud, *Muslim League ka Daur-i-Hakumat, 1947-1954,* (Lahore: Sheikh Ghulam Ali, 1973), p. 82.

9. Shahid Javed Burki, "Interest Group Involvement in West Pakistan's Rural Works Program," *Public Policy,* XIX (1971), pp. 187-188.

10. Gustav. F. Papanek, *Pakistan's Development: Social Goals and Private Incentives* (Harvard, 1967), p. 170.

11. Samuel P. Huntington, *Political Order in Changing Societies,* (Yale, 1968), p. 238.

12. Previous student activism had been directed at educational issues, like the Universities Ordinance of 1962, or at events abroad, like the national liberation struggle in Algeria.

13. J.A. Rahim, private interview at the WPIDC Rest House, Lahore, October 12, 1973.

14. Zulfikar Ali Bhutto, private interview, Rawalpindi, July 17, 1974.

15. *The Pakistan Times,* December 3, 1967.

16. Taj Muhammad Khan Langah, private interview, Lahore, July 21, 1973.

17. *Ibid.*

Some Remarks on Pakistan's Economic System Before, During, and After the Bhutto Period

STANISLAW WELLISZ

The roots of the major economic policy errors committed by the Bhutto regime are deeply imbedded in Pakistan's institutional structure, an unhappy mixture of planning and of free enterprise. In principle, mixed economic systems seem to provide an appropriate setting for the solution of development problems. In Pakistan as in other developing countries there is need for quantitative and spatial planning of public goods which ought to be provided at a rate compatible with the growth of the individual goods' sector. There is room for public enterprise where private initiative is hampered by the assembly problem. There is reason for interference in instances of serious market failure. There is need to correct social inequities. Above all, there is urgency for institutional planning, that is for a deliberate creation of institutions required for the efficient running of a complex, modern economy.

Unfortunately in the case of Pakistan, as in the case of several other developing countries, planners and administrators took upon themselves functions which the market can do better, and neglected tasks which the market cannot readily undertake. Several factors conspired to create this situation. The newly independent Pakistan inherited from the British rule a rudimentary market mechanism and a small managerial and entrepreneurial class. The foundations upon which to build a free market system were, therefore, very weak. On the other hand, there was a strong, well organized civil service, the successor of the Indian Civil Service which included in its ranks highly skilled individuals experienced in enforcing rules and used to assuming responsibility. It was natural, therefore, that the civil service be given a key role in the design and execution of economic development policy.

The Pakistani concept of economic planning reflects the administrative approach, which calls for articulated rules and regulations and is basically inimical to the pragmatism and flexibility of a free market system. Private enterprise is relegated to the role of executor of the plan conceived and controlled by bureaucrats, with only the "unorganized", small enterprise sector left to its own devices.

140

The administrative approach to economic development is aided and abetted by economists who, as employees or consultants, participate in the details of the planning process. On the positive side the economic technicians reduce the irrationality of administrative rulings. In my opinion, however, in the long run the economists' contribution is negative because their alliance with the bureaucrats' delays needed fundamental reforms.

The "captive" economists' freedom of action is necessarily limited, but even if they could do as they please it is by no means obvious that detailed plans drawn by them would be better than the administrative plans. The virtue of economic analysis is that it gives an overview of the system, that it pares economic reality to its barest essentials and deliberately abstracts from the minute detail of the mechanism. The economist does not have to make thousands upon thousands of managerial and marketing decisions because he rightly assumes that in a functioning economy such decisions are made by other agents. Indeed the economist has neither the information nor the motivation to make such decisions; he must abstract from details in order to gain an overview, a global understanding which is useful for the design of an overall strategy and guidance.

The economist does not have, however, any comparative advantage in the preparation of a detailed "menu" of inputs and of outputs for the economy. Highly-praised tools such as input-output analysis insure, at best, plan consistency. Whether consistency is an advantage is a moot point. Inconsistent rules and regulations lead to highly visible waste, to shortages and to surpluses. Visible waste leads to public outcry and, ultimately, to the repeal of the offending regulations. Consistency camouflages waste: such pernicious phenomena as "negative value added" (activities which subtract from, instead of contribute to, national product) are invisible. The public seeks the product, the workers get paid, the owners accumulate profits. The costs are hidden, and even if they outweigh the benefits there is no public pressure for change.

It would be unfair to dismiss entirely the economists' efficiency calculations. Some projects strongly favored by administrative elements were abandoned or modified as a consequence of cost-benefit analyses. Economists also injected elements of optimization into multi-sectoral planning. Common sense fortified by recent theoretical findings indicates, however, that in a price-distorted system, such calculations are at best rough and at worst misleading.

I do not want to give the impression that economic planners are unwilling tools in the hands of bureaucrats. Many economists frustrated with the role of passive observers are all too eager to try their hand at an active, directive role. Their willingness bolsters the administrative approach, and, undoubtedly they learn by doing. Their efforts, in the long run, might push forward the frontiers of economic knowledge, but in the meanwhile Pakistan is one of their victims.

Paradoxically, influential private business elements also support planning of the Pakistani type. Planners and administrators manipulate prices and engage in direct resource allocation so as to create profits and induce private investment in plan priority areas. The plan thus creates a business clientele whose prosperity, and sometimes even whose livelihood depends on the preservation of the system.

A further paradox: the plan is favored by the consortium of donors composed of representatives of countries and of organizations deeply committed to free private enterprise. The donors wish to be shown that the resources they make available are put to good use. They want to know what projects will be financed with their aid, and how the projects fit into the general development scheme. The need to control leads to detailed project design, the incorporation of projects into sectoral and intersectoral plans, and to planning performance monitoring. Such controls reduce the probability that highly wasteful projects will benefit from foreign financing, but they impose on the economy a rigid system devoid of a self-correcting mechanism. Fewer errors may be committed than under a flexible, competitive system, but they weigh more heavily because they are not eliminated.

Foreign aid helped Pakistan in some of its most difficult periods, but it was not an unmixed blessing. The simplest way to demonstrate the "need" for foreign aid is to overspend so as to create a "foreign exchange gap". The availability of aid thus encourages countries to live beyond their means. Foreign aid comes in the form of cheap capital, hence it distorts the domestic factor price ratios and favors investment in capital-intensive projects. Where there are domestic capital-imported capital complementarities, domestic capital is drawn to the foreign-favored projects, draining other sectors of the economy. Last but not least the need to monitor foreign-financed projects employs an inordinately large proportion of the most skilled technicians whose skills could be put to much better use by the country.

In Pakistan (as elsewhere) excessive concentration on detailed planning went hand in hand with inadequate attention to overall development design. Problems of surging population, of job creation, of rural-urban migration, of educational planning, of urban infrastructure planning, or agricultural extention—to mention at random just a few issues, were given the most cursory treatment in the successive national plans, while industrial structure was investigated in painstaking detail. The desire to modernize at a rapid pace, the need to prepare detailed project blueprints, the availability of foreign capital (hence of foreign capital goods) at concessionary rates all conspired to favor industry over agriculture, large-scale projects over small ones, capital-intensive over labor intensive methods. As a consequence the growth of output outpaced the growth of employment, and the growth of profits outpaced the growth of wages. There was a rapid and highly visible rise in economic activity without a corresponding increase in the general level of well-being.

To be sure large masses benefitted from many important improvements, but the rise of expectations outpaced the increase in opportunities. Improved transport and communications lead to greater spatial mobility and to rural-urban migration. Most of the migrants settled in bustees, and only a small proportion of the labor force participants obtained jobs in the "organized" sector. It may be argued that a poor urban family is better off than a poor rural family, even if the former's principal bread winner has only casual work. The successes had, however, a negative "demonstration effect": opportunities which seem to be within reach, but which are in fact unavailable, breed discontent. The poor rural family comes into contact with other rural poor. The poor urban family sees every day workers who have well-paying steady jobs, not to speak of the newly-enriched bourgeoisie. Another, even more vociferous group of discontented consisted of the newly-educated who, for lack of adequate manpower planning, could not find jobs commensurate with their aspirations. The discontented also included the small entrepreneurs who eked out a precarious existence at the edge of the plan, and who survived only because they were permitted to pay lower wages than the "organized" sector.

The forces of economic discontent found their champion in Bhutto, who took direct measures to rectify the social inequities. What he attempted to do, and how and why he failed is expertly described and analyzed by Messrs. Burki and Gustafson whose papers appear in this section. Bhutto's regime nationalized large-scale industry and wiped out the major source of accumulation of private fortunes. It sought to improve workers' conditions by extending the coverage of labor protection laws to smaller economic units. It attempted to create new jobs. It speeded up land reform. In short, it strove to foster the interests of the economically disadvantaged and to reduce inequality.

The Bhutto regime did nothing, however, to change the basic priorities of development or to reform the structure of economic administration. Large-scale capital-intensive projects received the same priority as before, but, under public ownership they were less ably managed than under private owners. The situation of the small-scale, labor-intensive sector became even more precarious because of the new minimum wage and labor condition obligations. Make-work projects proved to be costly and ineffectual. What happened to the land reform is something of a mystery, but no one could have expected any dramatic positive economic results.

The most charitable appraisal of Bhutto's economic policies is that he purchased a modicum of social justice at the cost of increased productive inefficiency. I fear that the post-Bhutto regime will strive to increase efficiency at the cost of social equity. Yet, because the situation is "Pareto inefficient" it should be possible to institute reform leading to greater efficiency and to greater justice. To achieve such a goal it would be necessary to overhaul the system by taking a series of bold but judicious steps. Unfortunately, the basic system seems to be as deeply entrenched as ever: the political issue is in whose benefit it should be operated, not whether it should be scrapped and replaced by something better. Yet we should not despair, for history teaches us that human enterprise and ingenuity always manage at the end to overcome the most perfidious administrative design, and that societies manage to prosper in apparent violation of the most basic economic laws.

A Review of the Pakistani Economy Under Bhutto

W. Eric Gustafson

With the proclamation of Martial Law on 4 July 1977 ended the five-and-a-half year rule of the leader of the Pakistan People's Party, Prime Minister Zulfikar Ali Bhutto.[1] Given the slow pace at which the Martial Law Regime is moving toward new elections, and the seriousness of the many allegations made against the ex-Prime Minister, we are unlikely to see any quick return of Bhutto to power. It may be a good time to attempt a preliminary assessment of the performance of the economy under Bhutto, and the achievements of his Government in trying to alter things for the better. At the same time the paper will give an account of what the Martial Law Regime of General Zia ul Haq has done as it has changed its status from a caretaking regime with its bags not even unpacked to one which was clearly going to be in office for a while.

Whatever we say about the economy in the 1970's must be said against the backdrop composed of three things hardly under the control of Bhutto's Government: the separation from Bangladesh in 1971, the sharp rises in world prices (especially of course that of oil) in 1973–74, and the world slump in the cotton trade at roughly the same time. The Government would certainly have had its hands full dealing only with these matters, without trying a major program of economic and social reforms at the same time.

The economy appears to have gone into a tailspin in the last half of the Bhutto regime, after a brave start in the early years when the simultaneous arrival of the world commodities boom and high prosperity in the Middle East pushed Pakistan's exports to new peaks and more than compensated for the loss of the Bangladesh market. Things began to sour in 1974. Table 1 gives the summary figures.[2] The final year's performance (or non-performance) was of course a function of the political disturbances, and tells us nothing at all about the fundamental health of the economy.

The basic figures to watch are those for large-scale industry and for major crops. One could be elaborately critical of the way in which those numbers are collected, but they are good enough to sustain the use made of them here: to give broad trends of production in the two major sectors. The Gross National Product figures looks too good, however, partly because it includes small-scale industry, services, wholesale and retail trade, and transport. One could politely describe the estimation methods for these sectors as fiction: the numbers are not firmly anchored in year-to-year reality, but drift upward at

145

TABLE 1

Annual Rates of Increase

	Real GNP	Real GDP	Major Crops	Large-Scale Industry
1972–73	7.4	7.0	1.9	11.9
1973–74	6.8	6.8	5.0	7.5
1974–75	2.1	1.9	−5.0	−1.7
1975–76	4.3	3.8	5.1	−0.5
1976–77	1.2	0.5	1.0	−2.0

the assumed rate of population growth.[3] In addition, there were charges during the Bhutto regime that the estimate for the services sector was systematically inflated for several years to make the performance of the economy look better. Ghulam Ishaq's White Paper on the economy points out (perhaps obliquely referring to the point just made) that "[the] overall growth rate during the last five years is at an annual rate of 4.4 per cent. . . .Of this growth, only thirty per cent came from the commodity-producing sectors (agriculture and manufacturing). The balance was contributed by the services sector" (*D* 4 September 1977, 5:2).

The other reason for mistrusting the GNP figures is that they necessarily include income remitted home by Pakistanis working abroad, a subject to which we will return. Since these remittances ("unrequited transfers" is the melancholy term used in balance-of-payments accounting) have grown with speed, their size and increase make GNP look deceptively large, if we think of it as a measure of the health of the domestic economy. For this purpose Gross Domestic Product is a better measure—and it grew significantly less rapidly than GNP after 1974.

Growth has then been minimal. It would be hard to put an exact figure on how much, but it is clearly small, and if we take into account that no one feels that the population is growing at less than three percent per year, then per capita income fell during Bhutto's tenure in office. A sad end for a regime which started to produce a brave new world. How much of this dismal performance can we lay at Bhutto's door? And how much can we ascribe to forces over which he and his regime had no control? What sort of job did the Bhutto regime do in managing the economy? What hope is there for the future? Is Pakistan another basket case, as some have come close to suggesting? The rest of the paper is composed of notes written while groping for an answer to these questions.

Agriculture

In the agricultural sector, the major action of the regime was land reform. In 1972, the ceiling on individual holdings was reduced from 500 irrigated or 1000 unirrigated acres to 150 irrigated or 300 unirrigated acres. (These limits were cut by one third on 5 January 1977, but no further land

TABLE 2

Results of Land Reforms under Ayub and Bhutto

	MLR–64 (1958)	MLR–115 (1972)	MLR–117 (1972)	F.L.C.	Total
No. of owners from whom land was taken	n.a.	2,298	n.a.	n.a.	n.a.
Total area resumed (acres)	1,094,821	1,156,362	521,816	567,322	3,340,321
Amount disposed of	496,384	695,679	267,510	18,000	1,477,573
No. of farmers/tenants given land	48,423	70,851	17,731	n.a.	137,005
Amount of land remaining with Government	598,437	460,683	254,306	549,322	1,862,748

SOURCE: Calculated from the information in Table 12.1 in *Pakistan Economic Survey, 1976–77* (Islamabad, 1977), p. 191. I have rearranged the table to make it clearer, and suppressed the provincial detail. The column labelled "F.L.C." is headed in the original "by FLC in exercise of Suo Moto powers." FLC is the Federal Land Commissioner. MLR–117 resumed land in the Pat Feeder area in Baluchistan.

TABLE 3

Agricultural Production, Major Crops, 1971–72 to 1976–77

	Sugarcane (Tons)	Cotton (Bales)	Wheat (Tons)	Rice (Tons)
		Figures in Thousands		
1971–72	19,648	3,979	6,782	2,226
1972–73	19,632	3,947	7,324	2,293
1973–74	23,533	3,704	7,508	2,416
1974–75	20,916	3,567	7,552	2,277
1975–76	25,143	2,890	8,554	2,576
1976–77	27,709	2,416	9,000	2,589
1976–77 Index (1971–72 = 100)	141.0	60.7	132.7	116.3

SOURCE: *Pakistan Economic Survey 1976–77* (Islamabad, 1977), Ch. 3, *passim.*

seems in fact to have been resumed, and it is not clear that any action was taken after the announcement.) An annual table has appeared in the *Pakistan Economic Survey*, detailing the progress of the reforms, which can fairly be said to be slow and mysterious.[4] Of the 1,678,178 acres resumed by the Bhutto Government, exclusive of those taken recently under Suo Moto powers, only 57 percent had been distributed by March 1977. From the convenience of (at long last) having an accounting of all the acres under both Ayub and Bhutto land reforms, one sees that the Government has more land in hand resumed through the various reforms than it has given away. The National Charter for Peasants of 18 December 1976 promised that all farmers cultivating Government waste could have that land and that "vast areas of cultivatable waste lands are to be distributed, with full ownership rights, among landless peasants and peasants having less than subsistence holdings" (*PES 1976-77*, p. 191) but the government did not explain how much land was in its hands (in addition to that resumed through the reforms) or how much of that was to be distributed to cultivators.

Tantalizingly little information has appeared in the public prints (either officially or otherwise) about what goes on under the land reforms: who gets the land and so on. One could have expected pictures of smiling sons of the soil receiving title to their land from a benevolent Bhutto, Jatoi, or Sheikh Rashid; I saw nothing of the sort, nor has there been anything informative about how small farmers made landowners for the first time have managed to find credit for inputs. Pakistani scholars have told me that the authorities responsible for administering the land reforms were closemouthed with them during the Bhutto days. I do not know what all this means, but I find it strange from a regime which declared over and over its dedication to the small man. The problems of land reform are genuine and difficult, but silence on the part of the Government simply adds to one's feeling that all may not be well.[5]

On the production side, the agricultural picture is mixed, but hardly as dark as the gloomier pundits paint it in Pakistan. Table 3 lays out the production of major crops during the Bhutto period, with 1971–72 as a base-line. The food crops are all at least keeping up with population (no mean achievement) and wheat production is finally nearing self-sufficiency, although there is an occasional disquieting remark on wheat statistics.[6] The present Government is continuing wheat import on a large scale (a million tons in fiscal 1977–78), which either increases one's disquietude or makes one wish to congratulate the Government for ensuring a safe stock situation. (Which?)

The really poor performer is cotton, the major foreign-exchange earner in its various incarnations. Although the *Pakistan Economic Survey* blames "low prices in the international market" for the fall in production (*PES 1967-77*, p. 21), this explanation looks dubious. Acreage has stayed virtually constant since 1973–74, and one would expect most of the effect of price to show up in acreage response. Yield per acre, however, has fallen steadily. It appears as though a sequence of natural disasters, floods and pests, mostly, has been the main culprit. (The only other explanation which leaps to mind is that farmers may be putting on less fertilizer.) Cotton estimates, too, are under fire. Some private estimators apparently think that production was in fact three or four *lakh* bales lower than the dismal level the official figures recorded for 1976-1977.[7]

Industry

The Bhutto regime nationalized in its early days some 18 percent of the industrial capital of the country, according to Government estimate.[8] Other nationalizations followed: ghee, flour milling, rice milling, cotton ginning, life insurance, shipping, banking. How have these sectors fared? We will concentrate on manufacturing units. The information there, although scant, is at least more plentiful than it is for instance for the various trading corporations; the public does not even know if they make or lose money.[9]

The Bhutto administration's releases of information to the public were meager indeed. Tables 4 and 5 reproduce virtually all of it because it is not available elsewhere in one place.

As far as production is concerned, the Government gave only percentage rates of increase over an unspecified base, an old Soviet trick used to convey the impression of substantial achievement when working with small beginnings. (One particularly suspects the automobile corporation.) These figures are available for the eight producing corporations (with 56 producing units) only from 1973–74 onwards. There are several things to note. First is the

TABLE 4
Production of State Enterprises

	Percentage Increases			
	1973–74	1974–75	1975–76	1976–77*
Federal Chemical and Ceramics Corp.	11.7	–10.9	5.2	–11.2
Federal Light Engineering Corp.	24.0	9.9	–2.6	25.2
National Fertilizer Corp.	26.7	–8.2	15.0	4.1
Pakistan Automobile Corp.	83.9	289.0	–12.0	–10.3
Pakistan Industrial Development Corp.	8.5	36.5	–25.2	–14.8
State Cement Corp.	9.5	3.5	–3.4	–1.0
State Heavy Engineering and Machine Tool Corporation	74.0	193.1	100.4	82.5
State Petroleum Refining and Petrochemical Corporation	–5.3	13.0	1.0	–5.3
Overall	31.4	21.8	4.2	2.4

*1976–77 figures are for the increase of July 1976 to March 1977 over the corresponding nine months of the previous fiscal year.

SOURCE: 1976–77 and 1975–76, *PES 1976–77*, p. 45; 1974–75, *PES 1975–76*, p. 39; 1973–74, *PES 1974–75*, p. 46. There appear to be no disaggregated production data available for 1972–73. The overall figures are apparently based on a value-weighted quantity index. The two missing corporations are the Pakistan Steel Mills Corporation, not yet in production, and the National Design and Industrial Services Corporation, not a producing unit.

TABLE 5
Summary Statistics for State Enterprises
(Rupee Figures in Millions)

	1972–73	1973–74	1974–75	1975–76
Sales	1806.0	2956.0	4691.7	5094.8
Percent Increase in Sales	n.a.	63.7	58.7	8.6
Percent Increase in Production	n.a.	31.4	21.8	4.2
Exports	111.0	238.0	345.3	n.a.
Profits	18.0	179.0	286.8	184.0
Profits/Sales	1.0	0.6	6.0	3.6

SOURCE: *Pakistan Economic Survey,* various issues. The State Enterprises involved are those listed in Table 4, all reporting to the Bureau of Industrial Management.

generous sprinkling of minus signs as time goes by. The whole sector seemed close to going into reverse in 1976–77. Second, the disappointing figures for 1976–77 *do not include* the effects of the post-election turmoil in 1977. A third—and countervailing—point: many of the problems were inherited. According to the *Pakistan Economic Survey 1971-72* (p. 29), "Most [most?] of the industries taken over by the Government were in financial difficulties, largely due to mismanagement." Taking over some of the units was no doubt a bad mistake for (ultimate) public relations purposes, since they were unsuccessful and likely to remain so. A number of the units already in state hands before Bhutto were also albatrosses from the beginning. The machine tool complex, for instance, is able to show such delightful rates of increase because it had not been able to produce much of anything earlier, its teething problems lasting well into adolescence. Three cheers for the Bhutto regime if it was able to turn some of these units around; but if it really was, why was it so shy about presenting figures to the public? In particular, why did it studiously avoid matching current figures with figures from the pre-takeover period?[10]

Wild stories abounded on the rumor circuit during the Bhutto years, and the newspapers have carried their share since his fall. For instance, the *Pakistan Times* ran the story that if the public sector ghee mills had been able to earn the same rate of profit as the private sector mills (they all sell at the same controlled price), the public sector would have made profits of Rs 35 *crore* instead of a piddling two *lakh*, all of that contributed by one mill, since the other 21 public sector mills had losses (*PT*, 19 October 1977, 1:3–6). Employment burgeoned in public-sector industries. In Bureau of Industrial Management enterprises, it went from 40,817 in 1972–73 to 61,731 by December 1976.[11] It is of course impossible to tell for sure whether the

workers were needed or not, although one is left with one's doubts, strengthened by the Martial Law Regime's discoveries about cotton ginning. As
Ghulam Ishaq reported:

[The] units on take-over got over-staffed, the number of employees in the ginning
sector alone going up from 25,000 to 51,000 for running half the number of
ginneries compared to the number operated in the private sector before nationalisation (*D* 4 September 1977, 5:7).

Everyone seems to have his own favorite story of malfeasance, misfeasance, or
nonfeasance. Ghulam Ishaq commented with exquisite delicacy on the issue:

It has been alleged that the [State] enterprises have been grossly mismanaged and
these allegations have been denied. The data presented about the operation of these
enterprises and the analysis of the data has been insufficiently refined to support
either view (*D* 4 September 1977, 5:8).

And yet these industries had been nationalized by a regime which emphasized that it was doing so to increase accountability to the people. (I believe
Bhutto even used that now critical word, "accountability.") Accountability
may have been minimal even to higher levels of Government, let alone to the
people. The arrangement of the taken-over industries certainly did not make
it easy to see what was going on, perhaps even for those in "control."

The structure of the bureaucracy looks as though it could have been
designed to conceal information as well as to make decision-making sluggish.
The actual productive units were grouped into coroporations: already we lose
informaton, since the losses of one producing unit can be submerged in the
profits of another. There are ten of these corporations, if we leave out
agricultural processing. The chairmen of the corporations, to whom the
managing directors of the individual units report, are bureaucrats almost
without exception, not managers. Surely we may question whether the set of
skills which enables one to collect land revenue or impose Section 144 equips
one to run modern industrial enterprises. Perhaps so; perhaps brilliant success
is hiding behind the veil of secrecy.

The bureaucratic chairmen then report to something called the Bureau of
Industrial Management. A Ministry was constructed on top of it, and the
Minister and the Chairman of the BIM were made the same person, making
the BIM a "redundant organisation with a small number of functionaries
without any distinct objective," according to Observer, cited above. The
managing director of a given fertilizer plant must clear any major operation
with three higher levels of bureaucracy before he can proceed. Pakistan seems
to be an advanced case of "post-office socialism," as John Kenneth Galbraith
once called it. [12] Even the Russians have learned better than this.

One of the most disturbing aspects of state enterprise has been the
nationalization of various industries serving agriculture. Rice export was
nationalized, cotton export was nationalized, cotton ginning was nation-

alized, rice milling and flour milling were nationalized. It was hard to see what good could come of most of these steps; indeed, it is impossible to know if any has, since none of the corporations in this area issued public reports of any kind. In the case of large-scale undertakings, there is at least a chance that state enterprises could be well run; after all, the general record of Pakistan International Airlines (for all its troubles) is good. But how could the Government conceivably expect to run industries with thousands of units through a bureaucracy of baroque elaboration? How could it dispense with the intricate network of private traders? The Government itself began to come to this view, apparently, towards the end. The Cotton Ginning Corporation found itself unable to cope with buying the flood of raw cotton, even with its 700 units, and the administration was put in the embarrasing position of restoring purchase through the *arhtis*, local middlemen.[13] The government returned 1523 rice huller units to their owners just before Bhutto's downfall, on the announced rationale that their owners were poor. Surely that fact had been apparent beforehand.

The Government could scarcely have thought hard about the nationalization of the gins and mills before it was done. Anyone with knowledge of these industries could have counselled against the takeover. Ghulam Ishaq puts things well in his White Paper:

Dimensions of management problems of agrarian industries are entirely different from those of the organised industrial sector. Small and medium-scale units, as agrarian industries are, their success, by and large, depended on the personal supervision and dedication of owner-managers—a role that could not be adequately performed by State employees and which has resulted in lack of quality control, higher wastage, and damage by weather (*D* 4 September 1977, 5:6).

One assumes that the Government was on some sort of ideological jag.

The argument behind nationalization of the cotton export trade in 1973, putting total amateurs in charge of what is a highly technical business where reaction time is at a premium, is that the private cotton trade had engaged in previous years in various malpractices like going back on contracts for export when the world price rose sharply.[14] The Chairman of the Cotton Export Corporation once made these same arguments before a group of businessmen in Karachi in 1974. When someone asked why it would not be sufficient to have a Government corporation as an *alternative* to sinister private operators, the Chairman had no answer. In fact, the Cotton Export Corporation used private traders to accomplish its goals in any case; it had to.

After considerable public clamor about the nationalized industries, the Martial Law Regime responded in three ways. First, it set up a Commission to review the working of State Enterprises. Ghulam Ishaq announced that the Commission would be established in his White Paper on 3 September, but it was not in fact appointed until 13 October, with N. M. Uquaili, the Chairman of PICIC, as Chairman. The Commission was asked to report by 31 December 1977, but by February 1978 the Commission had met only three times and a report did not seem close. (Why did they make haste so slowly?)

Second—and nearly simultaneously—came various moves of denationalization. The 549 rice-husking units which the Bhutto government had kept when it returned 1523 huller units to their former owners were also returned, as were flour mills and—later—cotton gins. All of these moves were taken before Zia decided in October to postpone elections. Three ghee units were denationalized because of their having foreign-exchange participation, but Zia said that the Government had considered denationalizing the whole ghee industry, but "left it to the next Government" (*D* 2 September 1977, 1:3).

Third came broader considerations of policy. The major problem with all the nationalizations may not lie with the industries nationalized, but with those which were not. The climate established by repeated nationalizations, interspersed with reassurances that there would be no more nationalizations (Bhutto was still giving them as late as March 1977),[15] left the private sector skittish and untrusting—and uninvesting. There would be wide agreement in business circles with the remark of General Habibullah, Adviser to the CMLA on Industrial Affairs, that "nationalisation by the previous Government was not nationalisation but victimisation" (*D* 2 October 1977, 1:8). Industrialists and others called repeatedly for new guidelines of some sort, demarcating private and public spheres of operation. On 17 October, the Government announced that private parties would be allowed to invest in the cement industry (which has of late been on hard times for no clear reason, given the strong demand). On October 30, 11 categories of industry were opened up to private investment, leaving only nine categories of (very) heavy industry exclusively in the public sector. (The complete list was in the newspapers of 31 October.) Reaction has been positive, but it is now (March 1978) too early to tell whether these declarations have borne much fruit; the step is certainly in the right direction.

Gift-Catalogue Government

In terms of general management, Bhutto seems to have made a concerted effort to buy off every organized group, and some of the disorganized, with little attempt to face up to the underlying economic realities. (Not no attempt; little attempt.) Several years ago I commented that one Bhutto budget read like a gift catalogue for the middle class. The performance of the entire regime reads like a gift catalogue for almost everyone, but the crucial question does not seem to have been asked: can you subsidize everything?

Examples. Just after the elections, during the troubles in Spring 1977, the Pay Commission reported, and recommended adjustments in salary levels for all Government employees, although cost-of-living increases, substantial at least at the lower levels, had already been given twice in the administration's history. The awards were well above what the Pay Commission had recommended, reportedly, and will cost the new Government in fiscal 1977–78 a sum of Rs 1808 million, almost ten percent of the previous year's revenue budget. University lecturers earlier got an increase of five increments, producing (no doubt) benign contentment in their ranks. The successive import policies bore gifts as well: consumption goods imports have increased tremendously. Edible oils and wheat bulk large, of course, but even without them the comparison with pre-Bhutto years is not favorable. Land revenue has been abolished for small-holders, but the agricultural income tax has only been announced, not in fact imposed. (Zia has postponed it until June 1978.)

What cornucopia is making all this possible? Has their been some great upswelling of productivity to undergird this distribution of goodies? The answer is no. The economy has grown more slowly than the population. The slow growth cannot be laid at the door of the regime altogether, but it is still the fact. Have the rich been more heavily burdened to help pay for other people's new prosperity? The answer is again no. All this munificence has been made possible by four things: drawing down foreign-exchange reserves, the (somewhat puzzling?) continuing generosity of aid-givers, the immense increase in remittances from abroad, and deficit spending.

Much of what has been going on is revealed in the simple statistics of expots and imports; imports have increased four times as fast as exports. From 1972–73 to 1976–77 imports increased by 141.3 percent, while exports increased by only 34.3 percent (*D* 11 February 1978, 7:3). People comment about how easy it is to purchase many kinds of foreign delights (Danish butter, Japanese watches . . .) almost anywhere in Pakistan. The contrast with the spartan years of the Ayub administration is striking to the returning foreigner. The export performance has been disappointing of course, and for reasons not chargeable to the Bhutto government. The increasing imports have been largely financed through aid.

The amount of aid has risen steadily throughout the Bhutto regime. On 30 June 1976—the latest date for which figures are now available—Pakistan owed $5.7 billion payable in dollars. Apparently something on the order of $3.6 billion of that had been contracted by the Bhutto regime, and the next fiscal year probably added another billion to each of those totals. (The whole GNP in dollar terms is only $13.5 billion!) Many in Pakistan feel edgy about this heady expansion, which now results in debt service payments of 18 percent of foreign-exchange earnings, calculated *after* taking account of the substantial debt rescheduling of recent years.[16] One would not be nervous if one could see productive projects coming along whose foreign-exchange earnings would enable that anticipated debt repayment to take place.[17] The theme of Pakistan with a begging bowl has become familiar in the Pakistani papers. The yearly annual aid inflow is now on the order of $1.2 billion per year. In addition the Bhutto Government spent out of foreign-exchange reserves to a considerable extent; in the single year following 30 June 1976 they were drawn down by nearly two billion rupees (*D* 11 February 1978, 7:2).

Next in line is remittances of overseas Pakistanis, an item in the balance of payments whose performance has been remarkable. Current estimates are that there are a million overseas Pakistanis, who in 1976–77 remitted Rs 5,735 million, moe than triple the amount of the first full year of the Bhutto regime. This sum works out to about 27 percent of foreign-exchange earnings. A good bit comes back through illegal routes as well. Even more spectacular developments are ahead, apparently. For the first four months of fiscal 1977–78, the average monthly rate of remittance was a billion rupees (*PT*, 3 January 1978, 1:2–4). If that rate continues for the year—could it be the result of the return of political stability?—the earnings from manpower export will equal that of goods exports. People express much fear that this earnings boom is somehow artificial or undignified or both; that a family in Hazara District supported by the earnings of a worker in Kuwait is somehow in a different position than if the worker were in Karachi. In any case, the flow of dollars has been a godsend, nicely filling in the gap left by the general disaster in cotton and cotton textiles of the last few years. But it only buys time until the economy and its export performance can once again be firmed up. The rate of increase will be impossible to maintain, although there will no doubt be a large earnings flow for many years to come.[18]

The extent of deficit finance has been a bit frightening: the Government under Bhutto borrowed over Rs 14 billion from the banks, which of course had no choice in the matter.[19] From a position in 1972–73 in which there was a slight budgeted excess of revenue over revenue expenditure of Rs 53 million, the revenue budget was in deficit by Rs 1,535 million in 1976–77. The increase in expenditure for civil administration played a large role here; those expenditures increased by (nearly) a factor of three over the five years. It is hard to see why increases of this order of magnitude were called for. When one bears in mind that the staff Bhutto had at the beginning was designed to conduct the civil administration of a country twice as large as current Pakistan, the increase in expenditure becomes especially alarming. Apparently the Government used jobs as a gigantic system of relief for P.P.P. supporters, a system made easy by the Administrative Reforms, which permitted "lateral entry" into the Central Superior Services. Able people certainly entered Government under the system, but it has come under widespread criticism because of its use as a patronage tool.

The deficits fuelled considerable inflation. The regime stoutly claimed that the inflation was mainly imported from abroad. This seems indefensible. Imports are after all a minor part of Pakistani GNP, and with the magnitude of deficit financing and the expansion in the money supply over the Bhutto years, one does not have far to look to find the cause of the major part of the inflation. The State Bank of Pakistan, at least, has been in no doubt:[20]

Excessive monetary expansion has been the major factor responsible for the sharp rise in prices in recent years. . . .The basic cause of excessive monetary expansion has been the big deficit in Governmental financial transactions.

Evaluation

What do we see in summary, then? We see Bhutto scattering *largesse* in all directions—or rather most directions—and creating claims to resources which are then met by deficit finance, by inflation, by borrowing abroad and dissipating foreign-exchange reserves, and by imports financed by Pakistani workers abroad. The structure looks jerry-built, and it is hard to see how it can last.

Nevertheless, the future picture for Pakistan is not negative, provided that successor governments can restore private investment and control the demands for continuing gift-catalogue government. Agriculture is no doubt dynamic, and can do much; given current yields there is obviously much room for improvement. Pakistani farmers have proved responsive to price incentives and to technological innovation; the problem now is to use the incentives, and to stop subsidizing the urban sector at the expense of the rural. It is not an easy trick, as Anwar Sadat discovered to his pain when he tried to remove food subsidies in Egypt. The Bhutto government did make efforts in its early years, but did not change the support price of wheat after 1974, so now the leap in price may have to be considerable. Farmers are agitating for an increase from Rs 37 per maund to Rs 46, reportedly the current international level (*D* 11 February 1978, 1:4–5). The additional water from Tarbela Dam has probably not yet achieved its maximum effect, and much new fertilizer capacity will help ease balance-of-payments problems; Pakistan expects self-sufficiency by 1980 in nitrogenous fertilizer.

Another major weight around Pakistan's neck has been the import of petroleum. In fiscal 1976–77 imports apparently ran close to $400 million, and one prediction talks of a $488 million burden for fiscal 1977–78 (*D* 20 November 1977, 7:3). But recent domestic discoveries are encouraging, both in oil (Dhodak in December 1976) and natural gas (Pirokh in October 1977). There is talk of the export of liquified natural gas, and there are hopes on the basis of existing discoveries of raising the percentage of self-sufficiency in oil from the current eight to 40.[21] The Bhutto administration clearly pushed exploration in a way in which past administrations had not. Twelve firms have signed agreements for exploration for oil, both offshore and on. In addition, the Government has signed joint venture agreements with two companies, and the World Bank has sent out a mission to deal with the petroleum program.

Cotton is really a major headache, and this was only in part due to Bhutto, apparently. His aggressive policies towards the private sector were certainly no help, but the whirligig that is the world cotton market, combined with natural disaster, were the major factors. The whole cotton set-up, from field to factory, needs strengthening, including some recision in the amount of governmental control and interference.

TABLE 6
Exports in Millions of Rupees

Index: 1972–73 = 100

	1972–73	1975–76	Index
Cotton Group	4,419.8	3,812.1	86
Progressive Group	1,730.5	4,121.9	238
All Else	2,400.9	3,318.9	138
TOTAL	8,551.2	11,252.9	132

Export of Progressive Group

	1972–73	1975–76	Index
Rice	1,136.1	2,479.1	218
Guar & Products	95.7	196.9	206
Tobacco	49.0	160.2	327
Readymade Garments	97.4	328.4	337
Drugs	25.6	107.7	420
Surgical Instruments	45.2	131.4	290
Carpets	281.5	719.2	255
TOTAL	1,730.5	4,121.9	238

SOURCE: Basic data from *Pakistan Economic Survey 1976–77* (Islamabad, 1977), Table 31, "Major Exports." Guar is a legume whose seeds yield mannogalactan, used for paper and textile manufacture and as a thickening agent in foods.

The export picture as a whole is discouraging, but cotton bears major responsibility for that. Total exports in *real* terms have probably fallen, since the increase in value was only about 32 percent from 1972–73 to 1975–76. But the totals conceal much interesting information. Over the period 1972–73 to 1975–76, the performance of cotton and its products was disastrous: a 14 percent fall in the value of shipments. But that fall (in what was in 1972–73 half of Pakistan's exports) masks encouraging increases in a group of other products, which I have labelled the "Progressive Group." Table 6 summarizes their performance. These products have increased by magnificent amounts: 138 percent for the group as a whole, as compared to only 32 percent for all exports. The regime probably deserves no credit for the achievement of these sectors. Some are products whose export in substantial quantity is new: tobacco exports were minuscule before the loss of East Pakistan, for instance. Readymade garments have come from almost nowhere. As recently as 1972–73, the statistical tables of the *Pakistan Economic Survey* listed only two of these Progressive Group products among "Major Exports;" now they are all there. Further, a good many of these products are made by small-scale industry, or at most medium-sized firms. Public-sector exports do not figure in the list at all, unless one counts rice, which is marketed through a Government coroporation.[22] The Progressive Group as a whole accounted for only 18 percent of Pakistan's exports in 1965–66, but was 37 percent by 1975–76. The export sector seems to be diversifying nicely, and if only the cotton sector could be returned to health, export performances would not cause complaint.

The Bhutto regime conducted exploration in the mineral sector with new verve. Export possibilities are substantial, for instance of copper from Baluchistan. Fruitful import-substitution possibilities are several as well: petroleum as mentioned and fertilizer should save a good bit of foreign exchange. These would be especially attractive possibilities if their production could be managed efficiently. Fertilizer seems off to a bad start in that respect, as far as the public-sector units are concerned. If the reported new high levels of wheat production can be maintained by higher prices, then the need for continual import of wheat should vanish.

Future possibilities are still reasonably bright, then, in a number of areas. The major problem is the still-shattered confidence of the private sector, which will certainly need careful nursing. Pakistan needs all the help from the private sector that it can get, and this fact now seems widely recognized. Above all, political stability seems important. Whether the private sector will feel like committing itself when there is the possibility of a return to power of the P.P.P. is another matter, of course. Large-scale industry will be more shy than small, and maybe this fact will lead the Government, whoever controls it, to be more supportive of small- and medium-scale industry.

Notes

1. This paper includes information available only up to March 1978. Two earlier papers of mine are closely related to this one: "Economic Reforms under the Bhutto Regime," *Journal of Asian and African Studies* 8 (July-October 1973): 241–258 and "Economic Problems of Pakistan under Bhutto," *Asian Survey* 16 (April 1976): 364–380.

2. There are several major reviews of the state of the economy for Bhutto's final year. The most comprehensive is of course the *Pakistan Economic Survey 1976-77* (Islamabad, 1977), issued at budget time in June by the Economic Adviser's Wing of the Finance Division. Abdul Hafeez Pirzada's budget speech (in *Dawn*, 12 June 1977) was slightly more up-to-date because of the press time required for the survey. The Martial Law Regime's Secretary-General-in-Chief, Ghulam Ishaq Khan, issued a masterful White Paper on the state of the economy on 3 September, printed in *Dawn* and *Pakistan Times* for the following day. Long excerpts from the State Bank of Pakistan's *Annual Report* are in *Dawn* for 13, 14, 16, and 18 October, but not in *PT*. Finally the Federation of Pakistan Chambers of Commerce and Industry issued a lengthy annual report at the end of the year (*PT* 31 December, 5:1-2). All figures in this article are from the *PES 1976-77* unless otherwise labelled. *Dawn, Pakistan Times, Pakistan Economist*, and *Pakistan Economic Survey* are identified by their initials to economize on space.

3. No one ever seems to comment on the miraculous performance of small-scale industry. Year in, year out, it grows at exactly three percent per year. What constancy of purpose, what determination . . . of course on the part of the Statistical Division, which must produce an estimate, whether there be statistics or no. Their method is quite reasonable: multiply an assumed benchmark, perhaps not radically wrong, by the assumed rate of population growth. The mode of estimation at least has the virtue of not distorting changes in the figure for per capita income. The distressing part is that public officials cite the numbers as though they had meaning. As far as I know, the last benchmark for small-scale industry, as well as for a number of other sectors, is 1960–61.

4. Table 2 in this paper reproduces selected data from the table in the latest *PES*. Two points appear of interest, aside from those made in the text: unlike the similar table in earlier *Surveys*, this table shows 567,322 acres resumed by the Federal Land Commissioner "in exercise of Suo Moto powers." That is much land, and there is no explanation; the number does not appear in the table for the previous year. Second, this table is the first to include the gross results of the Ayub land reforms. What is still lacking is some kind of accounting of the additional amounts of land in Government hands, and some idea of whether any of this remaining land is worth anything without much additional capital investment. It is always alleged that landlords got rid of their unproductive acres. It would also be nice to know where the land is, district by district.

5. There has been virtually no comment on the land reforms by the Martial Law Regime since it took over, either in *Dawn* or in the *Pakistan Times*. Another puzzle.

6. Dr. Amir Mohammad, Adviser to the Chief Martial Law Administrator on Food, Agriculture, and Cooperatives, "said that although he was not satisfied with the method of collecting crop statistics, the general consensus was that the last wheat crop yielded about nine million tons. . . .He said Pakistan requested the United Nations Food and Agriculture Organisation for expert advice on the method of compiling agricultural statistics in a modern and scientific manner. . . ." (*PT* 29 December 1977, 1:7–8). It will certainly be useful to have the crop estimating system looked at, but why does he bring that point up in connection with last year's otherwise rosy estimates? Anwar Aziz Chaudhry, then Federal Minister for Food and Agrarian Managment, said last May, "We are sure there is no possibility of importing wheat. The position is safe and sure in this respect" (*PT* 27 May 1977, 1:7). Yet by December arrangements had been made to import one million tons (see 29 December article cited just above).

7. Animator, "Neglect of Cotton Crop," *D* 5 November 1977, 5:4–6.

8 See my earlier articles for details; there is not enough space for them here.

9. See I. H. Qureshi, letter to the editor, *D* 18 August 1977, 5:7. Other sources of great utility have been the following: Khwaja Amjad Saeed, "Problems of Public Enterprises in Pakistan," *PT* 24 August 1977, 5; Khalique Zuberi, "Denationalisation Debate," *D* 3 September 1977, 5:4–6; Observer, "State Enterprises: Problems and Solutions," *PT* 27 September 1977, 5:1–3; Zafar Iqbal, "Private vs. Public Sector," *D* 31 October 1977, 11:4–6

and 1 November 1977, 7:4–6; Ain Hay, "Public Sector's Performance," D 15 November 1977, 9:3–6; Economist, "A Review of Public Sector," D 1 December 1977, 7:4–6—along with Zafar Iqbal's comment, D 6 December 1977, 5:7; A. Ghani, "Industrial Production," PT 24 January 1978, 4:7–8.

10. In PES 1972-73, pp. 38–39, there is a brief mention of the matter. "Considering the heavy odds, the results achieved by the BIM units has been very encouraging. During 1972–73 (July-March), total sales amounted to Rs 103.5 crore as compared to only Rs 71.4 crore in the corresponding period last year. The profits added up to Rs 5.4 crore as against a loss of Rs 1.3 crore in the comparable period last year. As compared to 1971, the production of 26 BIM units (management of two electric companies was handed over to N.R. division, while 3 were not in production), increased by 6 per cent in 1972." Three observations: (1) the base period for the first comparison includes the first three months of nationalization, so perhaps the loss figure should come as no surprise. It would be much more interesting to know how the figures compared with some "normal" year—if there is one to be found in recent Pakistani history! (2) One wonders why the sales and profit comparisons are for one set of periods and the production figures for another. (3) These figures are not directly comparable with those reported in Table 4, because they do not include the W.P.I.D.C. units.

11. Khwaja Amjad Saeed reports that the average monthly take-home wage in BIM enterprises was Rs 600 per month in 1975-76, having more than quadrupled since 1971–72 (Rs 140). Nice work if you can get it. Saeed, "Problems . . . " PT 24 August 1977, 5:4.

12. One would do well to bear in mind that the system of minute supervision from above of quasi-commercial Government enterprise was imported originally from England. Sir James Cosmo Melvill, the Government director on the Indian railway boards, was asked in 1858, "It is the custom, is it not, with every other department of Government that even the minutest details should pass through the hands of the chief?" Melvill replied, "I think so, and it is a sound principle." One is tempted to note the lack of British success in managing industrial enterprise in the twentieth century. Melvill quote: Report from the Select Committee on East India (Railways), Parliamentary Paper 416 of 1858, question 2952.

13. D 27 October 1976, 5:4–5: "Buying from 'arhtis' is not restoration of system, says Qaim." Qaim Ali Shah was Federal Minister for Agrarian Management.

14. See articles by Nusrat Hasan, Chairman, Cotton Export Corporation, D 31 December 1977, Supplement, I: 1–5 and in D 12 April 1976, 3:6–8.

15. "No Further Nationalisation Says Bhutto," Dawn headline, 29 March 1977, 1:1–3.

16. In May 1972 the Government obtained a short-term debt rescheduling of $233.8 million, followed by another of $107.2 million. A longer-term Memorandum of Understanding of June 1974 provided for a further $650 million of rescheduling for 1974-75 through 1977-78 (PES 1976-77, p. 141). Consequently Pakistan has been relieved temporarily of almost exactly a billion dollars worth of debt servicing since Bhutto came in; in no year has it paid more than 45 percent of what it owed. The balance has merely been postponed, not cancelled. If one put that together with the great increase of debt under Bhutto, one could get nervous about statements like "the ratio of debt service payments to the country's foreign exchange earnings remained within manageable limits" (PES 1976–77, p. 136).

17. The Pakistan Economist commented, "By 1980 Pakistan's heavy industry would be on production line with no domestic customers around" (PE 27 August 1977, 6).

18. The emigration has not been without its problems. Unscrupulous private agents stage-manage much illegal emigration and provide forged documents. Zia originally announced on 1 September 1977 that the new Overseas Employment Corporation Ltd. would have the monopoly on overseas recruitment; on 29 October he stated that the O.E.C. would work side-by-side with the private recruiters (more heavily regulated) in "fair competition." (See Mohsin Ali, "New Channel for Jobs Abroad," D 29 January 1978, 5:4.) The principle cries out for extension to the cotton export trade.

19. State Bank of Pakistan, *Annual Report 1976–77* (Karachi, 1977), p. 7.

20. *Ibid.*, pp. 6–7. The annual report of the State Bank for the last three years of the Bhutto regime was not initially made public on the grounds that since the bank no longer had private stockholders after nationalization, the report was a report to the Government only, and need not be released to the public. The Governor of the State Bank was Ghulam Ishaq Khan, now the Secretary-General-in-Chief of the Martial Law Administration, and a stern opponent of Bhutto on economic policy, in particular on the inflation issue. Apparently there was some legal requirement to publish them, however, since two at least ultimately appeared; they can be found in the *Gazette of Pakistan, Extraordinary* (2 March 1976), not a document of wide circulation. The report for 1973–74 is on pp. 433–484 and that for 1974–75 on pp. 485–548. Commentators in Pakistan do not appear aware that these two reports have been available for some time, and continued to call for their release in late 1977.

21. Dr. Shahzad Sadiq, Secretary, Ministry for Petroleum and Natural Resources, *D* 19 February 1978, 8:4.

22. The residual "other exports" in the table of major exports has also grown rapidly; it would be good to make a closer examination and see what is concealed in that basket category.

The Role of Foreign Capital in Pakistan's Development

M. Mahmood Awan

Foreign capital in its various forms has contributed significantly to the economic growth of many developing countries of the world. It is generally recognized that foreign capital helps relax some of the chronic constraints of a purely economic nature on a growing economy. But purely economic constraints are not the only ones which operate in a developing nation. Perhaps just as significant are the socio-political and administrative bottlenecks. This is probably why the impact of foreign capital inflows varies so sharply from country to country.

In a 1976 study, the author has provided an elaborate theoretical framework for quantitative analysis of the economic impact of foreign capital inflow on the domestic economy with special reference to the allocation of foreign capital to the various sectors of the economy.[1] The objective of this paper is to extend this analysis further and to evaluate the experience of Pakistan in the area of foreign capital utilization, particularly during the sixties and the seventies. A correct appraisal of the past decades should eventually enable us to forecast the emerging trends in the eighties and beyond.

Among the developing countries, Pakistan has been a major recipient of foreign capital. Ever since independence in 1947, she has occupied a very strategic global position and has attracted foreign capital for a variety of reasons. But the flow of foreign resources has not always been either smooth or uniform. The allocation and utilization of foreign resources has been even more erratic. Thus, the impact of foreign capital on such key economic variables as savings, exports, and the growth rate has varied considerably from one period to the next.

In this paper we propose to examine the relevant data in its historical setting and to derive some meaningful conclusions regarding the role and significance of foreign resources for Pakistan's growing economy.

For the purpose of this study, foreign capital is defined as an aggregate of (a) central government transfers, (b) private transfers, (c) central government capital (NIE), and (d) private capital (NIE). This approach is consistent with the categorization provided by the International Monetary Fund. Obviously, foreign capital aggregate differs from the traditional "foreign aid" concept.[2] For a statistical determination of the magnitude of "aid," it will be appropriate to calculate "grant equivalency" of all capital inflows which are in the form of loans. These estimates have been provided by the author in an earlier study.[3] Since not all foreign capital transfers are on concessionary terms, they do not strictly constitute "aid" by traditional standards.

The impact of foreign capital on a country's development may be determined in a variety of ways. First, there are the direct effects of foreign capital transfers on the savings and foreign exchange constraints for the economy. Then, there are many indirect effects based on the market and non-market spillover or "trickle-down" effects. The direct effects are relatively easy to measure but a correct quantification of the indirect and dynamic effects with the ensuing time lags and leakages is extremely difficult. However, such secondary and tertiary effects are crucial in the transformation of the economy. In the case of Pakistan, as we shall see in sections II and III, even though there exists positive correlation between the inflow of foreign capital and domestic savings and growth, there is uncertainty regarding its overall impact. However, it should be pointed out that foreign capital is not the only factor of growth; the roles of labor, natural resources, technological development, institutional framework, political and administrative factors should be juxtaposed with foreign capital. This clarification is needed because several economists have criticized foreign capital transfers without realizing that the nature and extent of foreign capital inflow and its proper utilization primarily depends on the recipient country.[4] In the case of "tied" aid, one can blame the donor countries for the strings attached and their selection of projects can be questioned, but in the case of "untied" assistance, the recipient country bears the major responsibility for correctly assigning foreign capital to its optimum use and for monitoring progress. We shall see in the latter sections of this paper that Pakistan's experience has been quite uneven in this regard and successive Pakistani administrations have faltered in making efficient use of foreign resources for reasons ranging from a lack of political stability to sheer incompetence.

I

Forms and Sources of Foreign Capital: The Nature of Foreign Aid

Pakistan has received foreign capital in various forms. These include loans and credits both from the developed OECD and OPEC countries and from specialized international agencies such as IDA and the World Bank along with grant assistance under specific country programs or special aid conventions such as Food Aid Conventions.[5] Private transfers and capital transfers under private investment schemes constitute yet another category.

Officially, the government lumps together loans and credits and grant assistance under the broad category of foreign aid. Further distinctions are made among project aid, non-project commodity aid, and food aid. Foreign exchange loans generated by project aid are used for procurement of project equipment and services. If these are contracted by the federal government for projects in the public or in the private sector these are termed federal loans. Loans negotiated directly by public or private sector agencies but guaranteed by the federal government for payment of interest and principal are described as "guaranteed loans." Another form of project aid has been local currency counterpart funds which are created by commodity assistance agreements and are made available for specific projects. An example of this is aid furnished under U.S. Public Law 480 (Title I). Commodity aid, itself, is generally used for commercial imports of industrial raw materials, machinery, and consumer goods.

Foreign Capital Input

Except during war periods (or the years immediately following the wars with India) Pakistan has generally had a regular inflow of foreign capital in all the categories mentioned above. In fact, there has been a gradual increase in the commitment of external assistance since the early sixties. Prior to 1955, Pakistan had received total assistance amounting to 372 million dollars, of which 67.5 per cent were grants and 27.2 per cent were loans repayable in foreign exchange.

During the First Five Year Plan (1955-1960) total foreign assistance rose to 993 million dollars, of which 58 per cent were grants and 22.7 per cent were loans repayable in foreign exchange. Corresponding figures for the Second Five Year Plan (1960-1965) were 2,365 million dollars of total assistance, only 17.1 per cent for grants while 78.8 per cent were loans repayable in foreign exchange. During the Third Five Year Plan (1965-1970) there had been a marked decline in foreign aid grants. Although total foreign assistance rose to 2,701 million dollars, only 8.9 per cent of this was in the form of grants. Loans repayable in foreign exchange constituted 91.1 per cent of the total. During the period 1970-1975, total assistance rose to approximately 2,874 million dollars while the relative ratio of grants had declined sharply. During 1975-1976, Pakistan received total assistance of 1,158 million dollars of which only 11.27 million dollars were in the form of grants. According to 1976-1977 budget figures, total assistance is approximately 1,281 million dollars of which only 8.7 million dollars consisted of grant assistance.

Obviously, the cost of foreign capital has risen appreciably in the last two decades. This has resulted in a sharp increase in the annual debt servicing expense. External debt liability is invariably a function of the repayment period, the rate of interest, and the extent of loan tying. This is truly applicable in the case of Pakistan. The calculated debt service to export earnings which was only 9.5 per cent during the Second Plan jumped to 19.4 per cent during the Third Plan and rose to over 30 per cent during the early seventies despite substantial debt rescheduling arrangements with creditors.

This trend of declining foreign aid has serious implications for the productivity of external resources. Increasingly, higher amounts of foreign capital are needed not just for acquiring additional machinery and equipment, supplies and services but also for returning an increasingly higher percentage of gross assistance to foreign lenders in the form of repayment of principal and interest.

Pakistan has been forced to review her borrowing strategy and has started seeking new donors of capital. In recent years, OPEC members like Iran, Saudi Arabia, Abu Dhabi, Libya, Kuwait, and Qatar have provided capital on concessionary terms by way of balance of payments support credits as well as loans for the implementation of priority development projects.

Private Foreign Investment

Pakistan has always welcomed private foreign investment and there is no restriction on the remittance of current profits to the country of investment origin. Similarly, foreign capital in approved industries established after September 1954 can be repatriated at any time to the extent of the original investment, and appreciation of any capital investment under this arrangement is also treated as investment for repatriation purposes. Pakistan maintains investment guarantee arrangements with the United States, Germany, and other countries, under which parent countries provide guarantees against losses which may arise from inconvertability of foreign currency earnings or against expropriation. This has helped provide a favorable climate for multinational corporate activity in Pakistan. Most of the leading West European, North American, and Japanese corporations are marketing their industrial and consumer products quite successfully in Pakistan.[6]

II

Foreign Capital: A Critical Factor in a Changing Economy

During the last three decades, the economy of Pakistan has undergone many changes. Although it is still predominantly an agrarian economy, remarkable progress has taken place in the industrial sector. Foreign capital inflow has generated a considerable industrial infrastructure, even though per capita income and other "equitable growth" indicators have remained generally stagnant in the country. This, however, does not reflect too favorably on those who have managed the allocation of foreign capital and who have administered its use for various sectors of the economy.

Pakistan's economy is highly controlled and perhaps over regulated. Contrary to generally assumed propositions that the inflow of foreign capital results in greater decentralization and liberalization of a country's economy, Pakistan had demonstrated that if appropriate policy actions do not accompany the transfer of resources, an economy may be subject to additional regulatory pressures and controls, thus undermining the price mechanism and market oriented philosophy of foreign capital utilization.

Since her founding, Pakistan's concern for setting highly ambitious targets for investment, savings, and exports has been a characteristic feature of the country. Pakistan established a planning organization in the early fifties with a view to developing the resources of the country as rapidly as possible so as to promote the welfare of the people. . . . provide adquate living standards and social services, secure social justice and equality of opportunity, and aim at the widest and most equitable distribution of income and property. However, due to the lack of any strategic planning, no meaningful decisions could be made for achieving these noble goals. Instead, the Planning Commission, like other ordinary governmental agencies, became bogged down in the routine of excessive paper work concerned mostly with target setting, identifying sources of finance, and proposing additional bureaucratic actions. In a country where managerial skills have been traditionally scarce, the civil service personnel were quick to assert their influence and authority in all phases of public life. The history of Pakistan is replete with examples where economic decision making and policy formulation were done by bureaucrats who were not only incompetant but were also totally oblivious to the country's long range goals.

For example, the projected yearly need for foreign resources increased on the basis of the previous year's actual receipts. There exists an almost functional relationship between the past aid received and the projected needs for the future.[7] Pakistan was cited as a model of development by donor countries during her Second Five Year Plan (1960-1965) for her faithful adherence to pure capital accumulation models of growth and for meeting some self-serving criteria of success in spite of inappropriate selection of priorities. Nevertheless, Pakistan has paid a very heavy price for arbitrarily maintaining a contingency and short-sighted, though politically expedient, development strategy for two decades. On the one hand, this tended to concentrate power in the hands of bureaucrats who failed to make rational allocation of resources because they had little knowledge of the complex problems of economic development. On the other, it created inter-sectorial and inter-regional disparities. In the process, complicated export-import regulations were developed which were neither easily comprehensible nor fully enforceable.[8] Consequently, there arose a triangular concentration of power in the hands of the bureaucracy, the military, and the privileged business elite which sowed the seeds of political and economic discontent in the nation. Obviously, one cannot blame foreign capital inflow, *per se*, for the political and economic malaise in Pakistan. In any other democratic country, where the military and the bureaucratic establishments are subservient to the will of the people, results would have been markedly different.

Due to inefficient planning and lack of political skill, Pakistan has not been able to negotiate her foreign assistance programs to her best advantage. Instead, she has been vulnerable to all sorts of political and economic pressures imposed by the donor countries and institutions. This has meant unnecessary costs to the economy. In a 1972 study, Brecher and Abbas found striking differences between the nominal or stated values and the real cost of loans to Pakistan. In their view, some of the donors of aid to Pakistan actually profited by it.[9] Since much of the aid negotiated by Pakistan was tied to goods and services to be supplied by the donor of aid, it put additional demands on Pakistan's meager foreign exchange holdings. Mohbub-ul-Haq has estimated that the tying of foreign credits since the early sixties has raised the average price of procurements for Pakistan almost fifteen per cent.[10] In fact, a large part of non-agricultural commodity assistance, notably iron and steel imports from the United States, has been overvalued by amounts ranging from 41 to 111 per cent. Even in the case of agricultural assistance, there have been instances where Pakistan had been forced to pay more than market prices for such items as edible oils, cotton, and wheat.

After having recognized the potentially beneficial nature of external resources in the earlier sections of this paper, we do not intend to present a case for their indictment here because of the dual role they have played in Pakistan's economy. However, it is rather unfortunate that in an essentially agricultural country, foreign capital was not adequately allocated or attracted to the rural sector where higher returns were probably possible. It may be acknowledged that private capital moves to areas where it can realize the highest return, but if the government maintains the right to allocate it, then it should be allocated where it is needed most. It is true that huge allocations were made to the water and power sector, especially in the construction of projects such as the Mangla Dam and the Tarbela Dam which were designed to aid the agricultural sector. But these projects have not been sufficient to modernize and to expand this sector to the fullest extent or to raise the productivity of those employed in it.

It may be appropriate at this stage to examine briefly the changes that have occurred over the years in Pakistan's economy. Gross national product has risen substantially and its structure has become more diversified and developed, but because of the mounting population pressures, massive disruptions caused by political upheavals, wars, and occasional natural disasters, the gain in output has not led to an improvement in the standard of living.

The economy lacks an overall design or purpose, even though here and there remarkable progress may be visible.

Over the twenty year period, 1950-1970, GNP increased by 122 per cent, i.e., at an annual rate of 4.1 per cent. The first decade recorded an increase of only 28 per cent, whereas the second decade witnessed a more remarkable growth in GNP of 73 per cent in real terms. However, the growth in per capita income was restricted to only 1.4 per cent per annum over the entire twenty year period. During this period, as the economy was industrialized and urbanized, there has been a marked decline in agricultural production. The structural change in the GNP is significant because the sectoral value added as a percentage of GNP was altered. Consequently, agriculture's share declined from 60 percent in 1949-1950 to 45 per cent in 1969-1970. On the other hand, the manufacturing sector's share doubled from 6 to 12 per cent. Value added in construction probably showed the sharpest change from only 1 per cent of GNP in 1949-1950 to 5 per cent in 1969-1970. Similarly, the shares of the transportation and the trade sectors also increased appreciably, as did the money supply.

In 1951, the money supply available to the economy was 3,698 million rupees.[11] By 1959, this had increased to 5,499 million rupees, and the supply almost doubled during 1966, reaching a level of 10,598 million rupees. This massive growth in the money supply, with its obvious inflationary pressures, continued throughout the late sixties and the seventies, reaching a record level of 34,044 million rupees in 1976.[12] During the early years of her nationhood, Pakistan maintained a favorable balance of foreign trade. But since the mid-fifties, with occasional exceptions, Pakistan has had an unfavorable balance of trade and of payments. In fact, the BOP deficit has increased dramatically over the years because of increasingly higher import needs. In 1956, the goods, services, and transfers deficit was only 166 million dollars. Its size was quadrupled a decade later, and at the end of 1975, Pakistan had a record deficit of 1,052 million dollars.

Insofar as government finance is concerned, the picture is even bleaker. Since 1951, Pakistan has never been able to balance the central budget.[13] In fact, there has been a phenomenal growth in the size of the budgetary deficit. In 1952, the deficit was only 202 million rupees, the 1958 budget year saw a deficit of 1,036 million rupees and by 1967, the budgetary deficit had risen to 3,857 million rupees. Four years later, the 1971 budget showed a deficit of 3,069 million rupees. According to the latest statistics available, the Government of Pakistan had a budgetary deficit of 12,240 million rupees in 1976, with expenditure running at a record level of 22,390 million rupees.[14]

A careful review of fiscal data indicates that the growth in government expenditure has been proportionately higher than the growth in revenues, particularly during the seventies. Because of faulty domestic resource mobilization techniques, Pakistan has never been able to raise enough resources domestically to meet its capital formation needs.[16] Although in the past, every administration has tried to improve the taxation structure in the country, the taxation system has continued to remain unresponsive to the task of development. The level of domestic savings, though it rose appreciably during the early sixties, could not maintain significant growth. This is probably why the financing of governmental activity has been done mostly with borrowing—in large part, foreign borrowing. The extent of foreign borrowing increased sharply during the seventies.

Increasing Indebtedness

The dependence on borrowing as a means of government financing has meant that the nation has been subjected to greater and greater indebtedness over the years. The size of the national debt has grown almost twenty times since 1956. From a 1955 level of only 3,661 million rupees, it stood at 76,533 million rupees at the end of June 1976. It is generally maintained by the purists in the field of development economics that the size of the national debt ought to be examined in proportion to the size of the GNP of a country. The implication is that if a country's GNP is growing much faster than the growth in the national debt, it may not pose any serious problems. Unfortunately, in the case of Pakistan, the problem has already reached alarming proportions. In 1961, the national debt was only 17 per cent of the GNP. By the late sixties, its share had risen by ten percentage points. The seventies have witnessed a phenomenal increase in the ratio of debt to GNP. We produce below some of the recent years' proportion of debt/GNP figures:

Year	1970	1971	1972	1973	1974	1975	1976
Proportion of debt to GNP	.494	.534	.968	.792	.666	.548	.574

Obviously, the absolute size of the debt, and the relative growth of debt in proportion to GNP, are both excessive for a developing country like Pakistan. This must be a matter of great concern for those interested in having inter-generational equity and in eliminating the real cause for scarcity of capital and for alarming inflation rates. Further, the ratio of debt held by international institutions and by foreign governments and banks to total debt has been rising at an abnormal rate. In 1956, the debt held by foreign groups was only 15 per cent of the total debt. By 1964, the foreign share had risen to 31 per cent. During the late sixties, the ratio went up even further. In 1968, 49 per cent of the total debt was held by foreign groups, and by June 30,

1969 their share had reached 52 per cent. In order to have a correct appraisal of the current trends, we are presenting below the data from the seventies:

Year	1970	1971	1972	1973	1974	1975	1976
Proportion of debt held by foreign groups	.516	.527	.680	.664	.698	.654	.641

It should be apparent to the reader how the share of debt held by foreign governments and banks has risen dramatically during this period.[17]

It is necessary to study the debt issue in the comprehensive framework of the overall functioning of the economy. After carefully examining the available data, we find that even though GNP has grown respectably according to "current price" estimate, the size of *real* gross domestic product has not increased appreciably in recent years. What has increased significantly over the period 1960-1976 is the consumption sector, particularly government consumption.

Prior to the secession of East Pakistan in 1971 government consumption was generally less than five billion rupees per year. Normally, one would expect that the size of the government would be curtailed with the elimination of a huge populace from its governance. However, in the case of Pakistan, just the opposite occurred. Government consumption has increased almost three-fold since the separation of East Pakistan. On the other hand, the share of gross fixed capital formation in the GNP went down from 17 per cent in 1965 to only 11 per cent in 1973 and to 12 per cent in 1974. It has stabilized at a not so encouraging level of 15 per cent in recent years.

The growth in industrial production has been noteworthy during the sixties; the index of industrial production was rising by more than six per cent during the mid sixties. But the growth in industrial production has been erratic since 1970. Share prices have been sluggish, while wholesale prices and consumption prices have more than doubled during the period 1970-1976. Pakistan has registered significantly higher export prices, and this has helped raise the value of her exports. But because of the quadrupling of petroleum prices and rising inflation levels in the developed countries; import prices have increased by more than 400 per cent. This has caused a sharp increase in the balance of payments deficit. In the next section, we analyze to what extent foreign capital was able to relax the foreign exchange constraints on the economy. We shall also examine whether foreign capital helped promote savings in Pakistan.

III
Foreign Capital Inflow: A Quantitative Analysis

The economic theory of resource transfers to developing countries remains quite imperfect. It is rather difficult to provide one-to-one direct links between the units of a theoretical structure and the actual performance of an economy. Our objective has been to develop a well-knit framework which will include the key variables involved and which will enable us to analyze quantitatively the impact of foreign capital on savings, investment, and growth.

The Data and Definition of Variables

We have made use of comparable Pakistani time series data covering the nineteen year period of 1956-1974. A number of computations were done to derive additional explanatory variables for estimating regression parameters. In all, the data covers the following thirteen variables:

1. Rate of Growth in Gross Domestic Product (GRO);
2. Per Capital GNP (expressed in log linear form) (1ny);
3. Total Foreign Resource Inflow, as a share of GDP (TFC);
4. Private Transfers (unrequited), as a share of GDP (PTU);
5. Central Government Transfers, as a share of GDP (CGT);
6. Private Capital (NIE), as a share of GDP (PCN);
7. Central Government Capital (NIE), as a share of GDP (CGC);
8. Gross Domestic Savings, as a share of GDP (SAV);
9. Exports, as a share of GDP (EXP);
10. Imports, as a share of GDP (IMP);
11. Investment expenditure (as indicated by Gross Fixed Capital Formation), as a share of GDP (INV);
12. Total Private Consumption, as a share of GDP (CMP); and
13. Real GNP (1970 constant prices) (RGP).

All values taken are for the current time period, assuming that savings, imports, investment, and growth in a particular year are affected by current inflows of foreign resources, and the current level of income. The components of foreign capital inflow, savings, and imports are expressed as respective shares of GDP for getting consistent estimates.

Most of the key magnitudes are expressed as respective shares of GDP to seek estimates of structural change as suggested by Chenery and Strout.[18] The rationale for this is that it allows direct testing of the significance of the changes in variables rather than just the absolute value added in all sectors which usually expands, too, but it is the relative rates of expansion which determine the changes in the structure of production. The share formulation will allow direct testing of the significance of these changes. However, converting the absolute values to shares of GDP might reduce the variance. The coefficient of determination (R^2) could be reduced but it would be more meaningful. In an extreme case where a variable had a trend similar to that of GDP thus leaving its share in the latter almost constant, the coefficient of determination might be very low. The standard error of estimate of the regression and the 't' ratios of the coefficients may then be better statistics for determining the accuracy of the estimates. This will be an important consideration for examining the relative significance of independent variables.

Estimation Problems

There are a number of factors which explain the behavior of savings, investment, and growth in the less developed countries but cannot be quantified directly. Changes in political and administrative structure and in the institutional framework, for example, have an important bearing on savings and on foreign capital utilization in a country. Several elements have to be included as additional explanatory variables in a regression equation identifying the direct and the indirect effects. When only a few variables are included in the regression, their direct effect may be overstated. Therefore, an attempt should be made to isolate the direct effects of the independent variables from the indirect effects of some of the omitted factors. (The residual impact of the additional variables is treated as random.) We have relied on the ordinary least squares (OLS) method for testing various hypotheses.

We have tested and corrected our regression estimates whenever necessary and possible for autocorrelation and for heteroskedasticity using the Durbin-Watson test and the Goldfeld-Quant tests, respectively.

Foreign Capital and Savings

The impact of foreign capital on savings has been a cause of controversy in the recent development literature. Some authors have found a negative association between foreign capital and savings in their regression analyses and have concluded that foreign capital causes a reduction in savings and, hence, is counterproductive in the growth of the economy. However, on the basis of our 1976 study and of the research done by Chenery and Strout, we feel that this conclusion is not warranted.[19]

The appropriate perspective for analyzing the role of foreign capital is to identify the binding constraints on the economy and to examine if it helps fill the savings gap in the economy. The inadequate savings also needs to be examined in relation to the trade gap and overall foreign exchange constraint.[20] When the "expected" trade gap is larger than the "expected" saving gap, foreign capital will serve primarily to fill the larger trade gap. Its impact on the economy will be beneficial because GDP will rise faster than it would without the input of external resources. Thus, this indirect effect should increase savings in the long run (given the marginal propensity to save.) Further, foreign capital has also been provided by donors as compensatory finance to offset the losses suffered by the economy from exogenous events such as wars, natural calamities, and political crises.[21] Under such circumstances, a regression equation based on ex post time series data would show a negative correlation between the inflows of foreign capital and savings, even though foreign capital did not *cause* a reduction in domestic savings. As a matter of fact, by preventing GDP from declining as much as it might have, foreign capital reduced the extent of possible curtailment of domestic savings.

Keeping all these factors in mind, we have undertaken regression analysis of foreign capital and savings. The results indicate that the impact of foreign capital on savings has varied from one period to another. The ex post savings function is specified as follows:[22]

$$S = \alpha_0 + \alpha_1 Y + \alpha_2 F$$

where S = Gross National Saving;
       Y = Gross National Product; and
       F = Net Foreign Capital Inflow.[23]

The above saving function has been estimated with three different data sets, and consistent results have been obtained with various explanatory variables representing income. In the regression equations reproduced below, n indicates the number of observations:

Country	Period	n	Regression Equation 4.1
Pakistan	1956-1974	19	$(SAV)_t = 0.013 - 0.31\,(TFC) + 0.13\,(Y)_t$

$$\begin{array}{ccc} (41.9) & (-3.88) & (4.21) \\ & R^2 = .66 & \\ & \text{D.W.S.} = 1.8 & \end{array}$$

All the regression coeffecients are statistically significant with a 99 per cent level of confidence. The t-ratios are indicated in parentheses. TFC and Y stand, respectively, for total foreign capital inflow and real GNP. The relative significance of income and foreign capital as explanatory variables was changed when per capita GNP (expressed in log form) was used as an independent variable. The results are as follows:

$$(SAV)_t = -0.19 + 0.05\,(lny)_t - 0.77\,(TFC)_t \qquad R^2 = .54$$
$$ -(21.87) \quad (2.94) \quad -(4.23) \qquad \text{D.W.S.} = 1.23$$

The regression coefficients are again statistically significant with a 99 per cent level of confidence. The negative association of foreign capital inflow with savings needs further examination. When we disaggregate foreign capital inflow into its various components, the results are as follows:

Pakistan (1956-1974)

$$(SAV)_t = 0.01 + 1.17\,(PTU)_t + 0.19\,(CGT)_t - 0.61\,(PCN)_t$$

$$\quad\;\;(52.6) \qquad\quad (2.57) \qquad\quad (.42) \qquad\quad -(4.41)$$

$$\quad + 0.76\,(CGC)_t + 0.08\,(Y)_t \qquad R^2 = .83$$

$$\quad\;\;(2.31) \qquad\quad (2.84) \qquad D.W.S. = 2.5$$

The results show that only private capital (PCN) inflow from abroad has a significantly negative association with domestic savings. Also, the evidence is less than significant that governmental transfers were positively associated with domestic savings during this period.

In view of the fact that the flow of external resources did not assume significant dimensions until the beginning of the Second Five Year Plan when an aid-oriented development strategy was adopted, we reduced the time series to the period 1960-1973.[24] The results as to the nature of the association of foreign capital with savings changed dramatically:

Pakistan (1960-1973) n = 14

$$(SAV)_t = -0.16 + 0.011\,(1ny)_t + 0.92\,(TFC)_t \qquad R^2 = .99$$

$$\quad\;-(30.92) \qquad (2.56) \qquad\; (25.81) \qquad D.W.S. = 2.63$$

The regression coefficients are statistically significant with a 99 per cent level of confidence. They indicate that foreign capital had a significantly positive association with savings during this particular period.[25]

Foreign Capital Inflow and Imports

It is common knowledge that foreign capital has been substantially utilized to finance imports. Assuming that exports are exogenously determined, a positive association between foreign capital and imports can be expected.[26] We have specified the import function as follows:

$$IM = \beta_0 + \beta_1 Y + \beta_2 F$$

There can be various versions of this import function. We have modified it whenever a better fit was obtainable. The various estimates of import function are as follows:

Pakistan (1956-1974) n $= 19$

$(IMP)_t = -0.11 + 0.23 \, (1ny)_t - 1.3 \, (TFC)_t$ $R^2 = .89$

$ -(8.\%) \quad\quad (1.14) \quad\quad (5.97) \quad\quad$ D.W.S. $= 2.4$

There is a strong positive association between foreign capital and actual imports. However, the income coefficient is not highly significant. We disaggregated income into its consumption and investment components in order to get their relative impacts on the imports along with foreign capital inflow:

Pakistan (1960-1974)

$(IMP)_t = -0.08 + 0.83 \, (TFC)_t + 0.16 \, (INV)_t \, 0.15 \, (CSP)_t$

$ (2.09) \quad\quad (.47) \quad\quad (2.11)$

$R^2 = .91$
D.W.S. $= 1.91$

Assuming that generally a year's lag is involved in the investment activity in an economy, investment was lagged one year. Subsequently, the following results are obtained:

Pakistan (1956-1974) n $= 19$

$(IMP)_t = -0.09 + 0.58 \, (TFC)_t + 0.19 \, (INV)_{t-1} + 0.21 \, (CSP)_t$

$ -(57.7) \quad\quad (2.64) \quad\quad (.74) \quad\quad (4.58)$

$R^2 = .98$
D.W.S. $= 1.96$

The above regression equation has been estimated after correcting for auto-correlation. It shows that consumption demand was greatly responsible (more so than investment) for imports, although foreign capital inflow and imports were positively associated. When the data for years prior to 1960 are removed from the time series, the results change considerably.[27]

Pakistan (1960-1973) n $= 14$

$(IMP) = 0.02 + 0.64 \, (TFC)_t + 0.11 \, (INV)_{t-1} - 0.013 \, (CSP)_t$

$ (2612.8) \quad\quad (51.41) \quad\quad (5.18) \quad\quad -(4.20)$

$R^2 = .99$
D.W.S. $= 1.21$

Obviously, during this period investment demand and foreign capital inflow played a dominant role in maintaining the high level of imports. It confirms that to keep the installed capacity functioning in the industry additional imports were required. Since the country followed an imports-oriented industrialization strategy, foreign exchange was the more binding constraint, as we have indicated above. A significant positive sign of the coefficient indicates a high marginal propensity to import with respect to foreign capital. An inspection of official statistics further indicates that actual imports often exceeded the planned levels.[28] In general, foreign capital inflow led to greater import liberalization in the country. However, without foreign capital inflow, investment activity would not have proceeded at a strong pace. This is confirmed by a strong positive association of foreign capital inflow with investment in the following regression equation:

Pakistan (1956-1974) n $=$ 19

$(INV)_t = 0.02 + 0.66\,(TFC)_t + 0.12\,(Y)_t\ R^2 = .79$

     (62.1)   (7.02)   (3.82)   D.W.S. $= 1.78$

All the regression coefficients are significant with a 99 per cent level of confidence.

Foreign Capital and Economic Growth

Another important aspect of the impact of foreign capital on the economy is its contribution to growth. There are several ways of examining this contribution. For example, we can include foreign capital in the economy's production function and estimate its marginal productivity. However, in a Cobb-Douglas type production function model, the underlying assumption of relative constancy in the shares of labor and capital (both domestic and foreign) is quite unrealistic. On the other hand, if we recognize that potential growth of the economy is limited by the most restrictive factor, then foreign capital, by relieving the more binding constraint, permits a fuller use of domestic resources and a rate of growth of output will be obtained which is in line with the better endowed factor. As Chenery has pointed out, the growth of total output will be substantially higher than would be permitted by the rate of increase of the restrictive factors(s) of production. In this case, we can specify a Zero Elasticity of Substitution (ZES) production function where imports are treated as a separate variable, just as investment in the production function. An expansion of output would require equal increments of both capital and imports. Thus, in line with two-gap theory, we can write the production function as:

$$Y_t = \min\left[\{\alpha\, K_t, \beta\, IM_t\right]$$

However we cannot regress Y_t on K_t and IM_t without introducing a bias in σ and β because there exists multicolinearity between K_t and IM_t, as is evident from our earlier regressions. Similarly, it will not be very useful to regress the rate of growth directly on foreign capital.[29] Therefore, we need alternative procedures to establish the link between foreign capital and the growth of output.

In an economy like that of Pakistan, which started with a very low income base and a limited scope for capital formation, the absolute measures, such as the increase in the size of GNP or per capita income, may not show the true level of progress attained. When we examine the relative composition of GNP, we find that significant growth has taken place in manufacturing, textiles, cement, chemicals, and in other industries, as well. The country has gradually modernized its entire transportation and communication system. Similarly, agriculture has benefited from better irrigation facilities provided by the construction of huge dams and artificial canals. These sectors could not have grown to this extent if foreign capital had not been available to finance the initial investments. The two-gap framework can probably encompass these developments in the economy better than simple regressions.

Within the two-gap framework, there are two alternative ways to link foreign capital to growth—through the minimum required capital or investment and through minimum required imports—depending on whether the saving gap or the trade gap is binding.

When the saving gap is binding, a simple Harrod-Domar type model of the following type may be utilized:

$$Y_{t-1} - Y_t = 1\,L_t$$
$$S_t = s\,Y_t$$
$$I_t = S_t + F_t$$

where V is incremental capital-output ratio, and s is the average saving rate.

By altering the amount of F, its impact on I and on y can be calculated.

When the trade gap is binding, as is the case with Pakistan, the following import-constrained growth model may be utilized:

$$IM_t = IM_{t-1} + m'\,(Y_t - Y_{t-1})$$
$$Y_t = IM_t - IM_{t-1} + Y_{t-1}$$
$$IM_t = EX_t + Y_{t-1}$$

where IM_t is the level of imports required for Y_t and m' is the marginal (required) import-income ratio. By varying the amount of F in the model, the import of foreign capital on imports and output can be calculated.[30]

We have estimated the values for GNP during 1960-1972 with foreign capital reduced to one-half of its size. The values used for m' and for $\dfrac{\partial IM}{\partial F}$

are respectively 0.10 and 0.83 (based on the regression coefficient estimated in the import functions). We found that when foreign capital was reduced to one-half of its actual level, national output declined anywhere from five per cent in the years 1963-1964 and 1966-1967 to seventeen per cent and nineteen per cent in the years 1961-1962 and 1969-1970, respectively. During the war years, 1964-1965 and 1971-1972, its impact is indeterminate. Over the entire period 1959-1974, the average ratio between the change in foreign capital and the corresponding change in GNP, i.e., $\frac{\Delta Y}{\Delta F}$ is 6.96. This is not an impressive figure, particularly if we take into account the repayment and real interest cost. But it can be argued that even if foreign capital has had a negative association with savings in certain periods, its contribution to the growth of the economy has not been negative. It will be realistic, though, to take the full cost of foreign capital and the alternative means of economic growth into account before passing final judgement on the overall role of foreign capital in Pakistan.

IV
The Impact of Foreign Capital

It is true that purely ideological and sociopolitical reasons were behind the establishment of the state of Pakistan. But the business leaders who were instrumental in the partition of the Indian subcontinent into two states were also interested in maximizing their economic welfare in a new state without the dominance and control of the majority group's entrepreneurs—the Hindu business establishment of India. They found in Pakistan an excellent opportunity for business growth and a permanent market, protected from any major competition by the government which came into being with their blessings. It was, therefore, expected that business expansion would take place smoothly in the new country.

Unfortunately, Pakistan inherited a number of political and administrative problems from the British and did not possess an economic infrastructure which could promote industrialization in a rapid way. However, the business establishment, by utilizing its entrepreneurial talents, quickly took charge of the situation and a number of industries were set up, particularly in the area of consumer goods. As soon as the potential of the Pakistani market was discovered by foreign groups, transfers of foreign capital began and the process of industrialization developed a momentum of its own. It is a noteworthy feature of the Pakistani economy that in spite of all the political problems and natural calamities it had to face over the years it has shown tremendous resiliance, and industrial production has increased by more than 107 per cent since 1951. The index of industrial production during the period 1960-1976 shows that industrial production rose smoothly during the sixties but in the seventies there has been a decline in its growth for reasons unrelated to any decline in foreign capital inflow.

Pakistan has gone through various stages of industrialization from the earlier concentrations on cotton and jute textiles to sugar, cement, paper, and still later to advanced chemical and engineering industries. However, foreign capital was not attracted in sufficient quantity for the establishment of much needed heavy industry. It is only recently that attention has been focussed on developing a viable steel industry in Pakistan. Before the establishment of the Peoples Party regime, private sector investments in various industries were rising on a gradual basis because of strong incentives and fiscal concessions provided by the government. But because of the nationalization of a number of basic industries in 1972, the growth in private sector industrial activity was seriously affected.

During the fifties and the sixties, the industrial sector received a generous allocation of foreign capital at subsidized prices and was awarded favorable terms of trade with respect to the agricultural sector. But the excessive protection and the irrational concessions also encouraged the formation of inefficient industries with very low productivity levels. Some import substitution occurred in consumer goods industries, but imports of industrial products and capital goods have continued to grow. Because of the shortage of spare parts and raw materials, and because of very low labor productivity, the industrial sector has traditionally operated with excess capacity and overall underutilization of facilities.

Public corporations such as PIDC (set up in 1950) and WPSIC (established in 1965) have undertaken ambitious projects in selected industries such as fertilizers, gas, cement, shipbuilding, minerals, sugar, paper and board, and pharmaceuticals. A major part of the financing for these industries came from external borrowings. But the return on investment for public sector industries has been traditionally much lower than that of equivalent industries in the private sector which received financing through public subscriptions and loans from specialized credit institutions like PICIC (formed in 1957) and IDBP (established in 1961). The former institution has also arranged foreign equity participation and foreign loans for the private sector. During the period 1957-1972, PICIC had arranged foreign equity participation to the extent of 122.7 million rupees. It also arranged direct loans from abroad amounting to 488.5 million rupees. In recent years, middle eastern countries like Iran, Libya, and Saudi Arabia have transferred capital to Pakistan for specific projects such as oil refineries, fertilizer plants, cement factories, and textile mills.

With the nationalization of a number of industries, the climate for private business expansion has changed radically from the blueprint envisaged by the business leaders of the forties whom we mentioned earlier. However, foreign resources are still available for the promotion of private enterprise. It should be noted that both the "capacity building" and the "capacity using" needs of industry are being financed by foreign capital which is playing a crucial role in keeping the installed capacity functioning.

Foreign Capital and the Composition of Pakistan's Trade

There has been a gradual change in the direction of trade and in the composition of Pakistani exports and imports during the last three decades which suggests that a transformation is taking place in the economy. As we pointed out earlier, Pakistan's traditional exports have been primarily commodities such as raw cotton, cotton yarn and fabrics, raw hides and skins, rice, etc. that used to be exported to Western Europe and to other markets in developed countries. But in the last decade or so, the direction has been towards Afro-Asian countries and Middle Eastern countries. Pakistan has been able to diversify exports. The production from industries turning out manufactured and semi-manufactured goods, set up with the help of external financing, now constitutes a sizable portion of total exports.

On the imports side, the share of consumer goods is declining. With the aid of a number of state instituted export promotion schemes, the country is moving towards becoming an export-oriented economy. If this positive trend continues, the foreign exchange constraint may not be as binding in the future as it has been in the past. This should create greater opportunities for improving the level of domestic savings in the country. In the past, the inflow of foreign capital has led to insufficient efforts to initiate vigorous domestic savings efforts.

Conclusion

In conclusion, perhaps, it may be in order to offer a few comments on the current phase of Pakistan's economy. Recently, the military regime has initiated the preparation of a fresh five year development plan covering the period 1978-1983 with goal-orientations differing from those of the previous plans. Simultaneously, a re-evaluation of the economic policy-making is under review. At this stage, it may be suggested that a comprehensive study of foreign capital utilization in Pakistan should be undertaken. This paper provides a framework for such an undertaking.

A further study along these lines may provide us with sufficient empirical evidence to prove that the last five years have been probably the worst years in regard to economic stability and growth. Therefore, the economic historians of Pakistan may be tempted to pin the blame on the rulers of this era. But, on the contrary, we hold the view that the economic troubles of Pakistan are much deeper in origin. A thorough examination of the economic record of the last five years would only reinforce our earlier observations about the way Pakistan's economy has been managed in the course of her historical evolution.

It is our view that Pakistan needs to overhaul her fiscal machinery in order to improve the administration and the utilization of foreign capital. Since the smooth flow of foreign resources is far from certain, it may be prudent for the country's planners to explore all possible avenues for maximizing domestic resources. While it may be true that one dollar of foreign exchange has qualitatively greater impact on the economy than a dollar's worth of domestic savings, the cost of procuring that one dollar from abroad, through means other than exports, has been rising rather rapidly. Hence, there arises the need to stabilize the gains already achieved in the economy through past flows of foreign capital and gradually to reduce the country's dependence on foreign capital inflow by maximizing exports.

It is imperative for developing countries like Pakistan to review their development strategies constantly, while taking into account inter-generational equity. In order to reduce the demand for foreign capital at the present time, it may be necessary to ask the present generation to make some sacrifices in the consumption sector. This, however, should have the effect of reducing the burden of spiraling debt payments from the shoulders of generations yet unborn.

The purpose of foreign capital inflow is to supplement domestic efforts towards development. It should not replace or be a substitute for domestic resources mobilization. A proper awareness of this should lead to a more efficient utilization of foreign capital and to a more prudent management of the economy in general.

Notes

1. Awan, Muhammed Mahmood, *Foreign Capital and Development Process: The Pakistani Experience*, University Press of America, Washington, D.C. 1976. The study determined the effect of external resources transfers on various sectors of Pakistani economy and examined the problems of debt servicing.

2. There are many problems associated with defining exactly what constitutes aid. Theoretically, the transfer of real resources from developed countries to the LDCs either in the form of explicit capital movements or through nonmonetary transfers of technical assistance should be considered as aid. But resources can be transferred not only as explicit capital flows but also through disguised forms such as preferential tariff cuts and international liquidity arrangements.

3. Ibid., pp. 108-132.

4. See for instance, Griffin and Enos in the *Economic Development and Cultural Change,* Volume 18 (April 1970) pp. 313-327.

5. Since 1960 Pakistan has received most of its foreign economic assistance through an 'Aid to Pakistan Consortium' created by the IBRD to coordinate and expedite the flow of foreign aid. The Consortium consists of Pakistan's eleven major creditors including Belgium, Canada, France, Italy, Japan, the Netherlands, United Kingdom, United States, West Germany, the IBRD, and the IDA. It generally meets once a year to evaluate Pakistan's economic performance and determine its foreign exchange needs over the coming year. In recent years, the Consortium procedures have had significant lags between project approval and funds disbursements. At the end of 1975, Consortium countries commitments were 68% of total assistance provided to Paksitan. International agencies had contributed 14% and the non-consortium countries' share was 18%.

6. There are at least 105 American companies alone operating in Pakistan. These include banks and insurance companies such as Bank of America, Citibank, American Express Company, Hanover Insurance Company and New Hampshire Insurance Company; manufacturing companies such as Kaiser Industries, American Cyanamid, Color-Tran Industries, Ford Motor Company, Corning Glass Works, General Tire and Rubber Company, International Harvester Company, Johnson & Johnson International, Firestone Tire and Rubber Company, Monsanto Company, IBM, Remington Rand, G.D. Searle & Company, Singer Company, Union Carbide, Litton Industries; a number of chemical and pharmeceutical companies, photographic equipment services, and general consumer companies among them Warner-Lambert, Eastman Kodak, Pfizer International, NCR Corporation, Hercules, Inc., General Mills, Inc., Canada Dry Corporation, Coca-Cola Company; petroleum companies such as Caltex and Exxon; most of the leading American hotel and motion picture companies such as Intercontinental, Hilton and Holiday Inn Hotels corporations, Metro-Goldwyn-Mayer, Inc., Paramount International Films, Warner Brother Pictures, Inc., Universal Films, Inc., Twentieth Century-Fox Film Corporation; and finally air transportation companies such as TWA, and Pan American World Airways, Inc.

7. In projections made during the sixties a number of economists had predicted a gradual decline in foreign capital requirements (and eventual elimination of the need for foreign assistance) based on the targets set in the Perspective Plan Period (1965-1985). See, for instance: Chenery, H.B. and MacEwan, "Optimal Patterns of Growth and Aid: The Case of Pakistan," *Pakistan Development Review,* Summer 1966, p. 241. In actual experience, foreign capital needs have been rising even though growth targest have been scaled down!

8. Pakistan maintained a multiple exchange rate system with serious repercussions. A galaxy of foreign exchange controls were instituted which protected the favored business groups (creating monopoly profits for them), and unnecessarily penalized the others. For an analytical discussion of the issues involved, see: Winston, G., "Overinvoicing, Underutilizations and Distorted Industrial Growth," *Pakistan Development Review,* Volume 10 (Winter, 1970) pp. 405-421.

9. Brecher, I. and Abbas, S.A., *Foreign Aid and Industrial Development in Pakistan,* Cambridge, 1972.

10. Haq, M., "Annual Planning in Pakistan," *Journal of Development Planning,* United Nations, 1970.

11. Pakistan has used multiple exchange rates and has also officially devalued its currency on a few occasions. In 1951, the exchange rate was Pak. Rs. 3.33 = 1 U.S. $. In 1956, it was changed to Rs. 4.762 = 1 U.S. $. After the separation of the East Pakistani province from the country, the currency was devalued further to Rs. 11.03 = 1 U.S. $.

12. The IMF reports indicate that this trend has continued unabated in recent years. Check the various monthly issues of the *International Financial Statistics,* Washington, D.C. for more recent data.

13. 1962 was an exceptional year when the budget showed a surplus of 38 million rupees.

14. I.M.F., *International Financial Statistics*, Vol. XXXI, No. 2 February 1978, Washington, D.C.

15. The original sources for this data are the U.N.O., and various agencies of the Government of Pakistan. Parts of the data are available in some issues of the *International Financial Statistics* published monthly by the International Monetary Fund.

16. It is fair to assume that given the nature of the binding constraints on the economy, it would have been difficult for any developing country to meet its capital accumulation goals without changing the overall economic system and underlying developmental philosophy.

17. As was pointed out earlier in section II, Pakistan has managed to get new lenders of capital in recent years without jeopardizing her credit-worthiness. Although the size of Pakistan's debt should be intimidating to private banks, most foreign banks have not yet turned their faces away from Pakistan primarily because of the tremendous potential for industrial development and absorptive capacity in Pakistan. Further, even though Pakistan has been seeking moratoriums and has asked for periodic postponements of payments on her loans, her record on debt servicing has been better than that of some other developing countries competing for the same funds. That is why her voice is given attentive hearing in international circles concerned with deliberations on the New International Economic Order as visualized by the United Nations.

18. See, Chenery, H.B. and Strout, A.M., 'Foreign Assistance and Economic Development,' *The American Economic Review*, September 1966; also Chenery, H.B. and Bruno, M., 'Development Alternatives in an Open Economy—The Case of Israel,' *The Economic Journal*, Volume 72 (March 1962) pp. 79-103.

19. Ibid.

20. A trade gap (TG) is indicated by the excess of required imports over possible exports and a saving gap (SG) is equivalent to the amount by which potential savings falls short of the investment needs. Although the two gaps are identical in an ex post sense, they can vary in the short run. This generally occurs because of the disequilibrium in developing economies whose production structures take a long time in adjusting to changes in the international markets. Since intended decisions regarding saving, investment, and imports are made by different groups, they may not be mutually consistent.

The process of adjustment which leads to the ex post equality of the saving and trade gaps can follow any of the typical patterns depending on the institutional framework of the economy and the nature of the policy initiatives taken by the government. As far as foreign capital is concerned, it will fill the larger of the two ex ante gaps (though the smaller gap will increase after the equilibrating adjustment has taken place because in an ex post sense the two gaps would be identical). Obviously, the variables whose ex post values will differ most from their ex ante values will be those connected with the smaller, non-binding gap because this bears the weight of adjustment. If the foreign capital is just sufficient to fill the binding gap the ex post levels of the variables connected with this gap will be similar to their ex ante levels. That is to say, when foreign capital is just sufficient to fill the saving gap but exceeds the foreign exchange requirements, ex post imports may exceed the minimum levels needed for the attained level of income or exports may fall short of the ex ante level. On the other hand, if the trade gap is binding and foreign capital is enough to fill that gap, ex post saving may fall short of its potential level or additional investment may take place.

In this case, foreign capital may prove a substitute for domestic saving. (The general situation that realized saving might be below the potential level due to the inflow of foreign capital is widely recognized in the literature but explanations differ as to the causation involved. For example, Kafka (1967) stresses the impact of foreign capital on domestic saving through changes in the marginal efficiency of investment and in the domestic rate of interest, whereas Gurley (1968) and McKinnon (1973) point out the possibility that inflow of foreign capital might keep the bulk of the financial system of a developing country below its optimum size with unfavorable consequences for domestic saving and investment).

If investment does not play an effective role in the process of adjustment of the two gaps, realized saving will be below potential saving by an amount equal to the excess of the *ex ante* trade gap over the *ex ante* saving gap. In case, the saving gap is quite large, foreign capital will be generally a complement to domestic savings. However, when the (ex ante) saving gap is as large as the trade gap, there may not be any substitution between foreign capital inflow and domestic savings. But there will be complete substitution if the saving gap equals zero. We can safely maintain that during years of high exports relative to imports, the saving gap will tend to be binding whereas when exports are low, the trade gap will tend to be the more dominant constraint.

21. See Gustav F. Papanek, "The effect of Aid and Other Resource Transfers on Savings and Growth in Less Developed Countries," *The Economic Journal*, September, 1972, pp. 934-950.

22. Since consumption and saving decisions are based on a weighing of the present benefits derived from current consumption and the future benefits to be derived from the investment of current savings, it is reasonable to postulate that ex post savings will depend on the foreign capital inflow.

23. The equation can be modified to the following form:

$S/Y = a_1 + b_1 \log (Y/P) + b_2 (F/Y)$

where P stands for country's population.

24. Pakistan did receive gross assistance equaling Rs. 5.07 billion during the period 1955-60, but the rate of private saving declined as compared to previous years. The financial saving by households fell to a low level of 2.9% of GNP in 1959-1960. For the period of 1955-1960, the level of public saving was only 0.5% of GNP mainly because of an unstable and inefficient governmental structure which was unable to raise taxes or contain increases in non-development expenditure. It has been recorded that a large portion of foreign assistance was used to import food to meet the domestic shortages and to finance consumption expenditures. Hence, a possible substitution relationship between savings and foreign assistance.

25. For the same period, results from Indian time series data are as follows:

$$India\,(1960\text{-}1973) \quad n = 14$$

$$(SAV)_t = -0.49 + 0.13\,(lny)_t + 0.51\,(TFC)_t$$

$$-(69.5)\,(68.89)\,(35.51)$$

$$R^2 = .99$$

$$D.W.S. = 1.89$$

26. The export propensities may change with the inflow of foreign capital improving particularly the exports of manufactured goods.

27. A comparable regression run on Indian data yielded the following results:

$$(IMP)_t = 0.019 + 0.64\,(TFC) + 0.11\,(INV)_{t-1} - 0.01\,(CSP)_t$$

$$(2440.1) \quad\quad (38.43) \quad\quad (4.24) \quad\quad -(4.36)$$

$$R^2 = .99$$

$$D.W.S. = 1.47$$

The equation has been estimated after correcting for auto-correlation and all the regression coefficients are significant at the 99 per cent level of confidence. The negative association of CSP seems unusual at first. However, if we see the import content of the economy, we find that both India and Pakistan had to import sizable amounts of food and other essential consumer goods. Whenever, the economy was able to provide sufficient amounts of these commodities domestically, the imports from abroad declined.

28. There is some evidence that imports of luxurious items or conspicuous consumption goods increased when additional foreign capital was forthcoming.

29. We did not obtain significant econometric results when we tried to estimate a growth equation with foreign capital as one of the explanatory variables. The estimated equation is as follows:

$$\text{Pakistan} \ (1956\text{-}1974) \ n \ = \ 19$$

$$g \ = \ 0.09\text{-}0.012 \, (y)_t \ + \ 0.89 \, (F)_t \ + \ 0.07 \, (EXP)_t$$

$$(3.37) \qquad - \ (0.60) \qquad (0.61) \qquad (0.05)$$

$$R^2 \ = \ .31$$

$$\text{D.W.S.} \ = \ 1.91$$

where g is the rate of growth of GDP, y stands for per capita income, F is the total foreign capital inflow, and EXP stands for exports. The regression coefficients are statistically insignificant. The earlier results have shown the extent to which foreign capital contributed towards financing imports. We feel that the impact of external resources on the growth of an economy can be judged properly by looking at their contribution towards the mobilization and allocation of the productive resources including (a) the supply of domestic saving, and (b) the supply of imported commodities and services. Since there is considerable evidence that growth is limited by the bottlenecks created by the shortages of foreign exchange (which may be responsible for under-utilization of other available productive factors), foreign capital, by relieving these constraints would make possible fuller use of domestic resources and thus accelerate economic growth.

30. The size of foreign capital inflow (F) can be varied from zero to any percentage of its actual figure because the purpose is to calculate the marginal contribution of F to Y. It is, of course, one of many methods of assessing its contribution.

31. See N. Islam, "Comparative Costs, Factor Proportions, and Industrial Efficiency in Pakistan," the *Pakistan Development Review*, Summer 1967 and Faroog, Q.M. and Winston, G.C., "Shift Working, Employment, and Economic Development: A Study of Industrial Workers in Pakistan," *Economic Development and Cultural Change*, Vol. 26, No. 2, January 1978, pp. 227-244.

Employment Strategies for Economic Stability in Pakistan: New Initiatives

SHAHID JAVED BURKI

Introduction

Discontent with the performance of the economy during the 'sixties was one of the important factors that contributed to the emergence of the Pakistan Peoples' Party (PPP) as a prominent political force in the country.[1] One reason for this discontent was the economy's failure to provide adequate employment opportunities to the growing labor force in the urban sector. This problem was perceived by the PPP: its election manifesto for 1970 promised action by the party in reducing the incidence of unemployment in the urban areas in general and that of the educated unemployed in particular.[2] This perception notwithstanding, once in power, the PPP was not able to alleviate the situation. Its failure to provide opportunities for productive employment to the urban population contributed to the anti-Bhutto campaign in the spring of 1977 and ultimately to the return of the military to politics.

In this paper, I will attempt to seek some answers to the question: why was it that the government of Zulfikar Ali Bhutto failed to formulate effective employment strategies for the country? The paper is divided into four sections: Section I provides an assessment of the political impact of the deterioration of the employment situation during the late 'sixties. Section II presents the employment situation in the early 'seventies, the period during which the PPP gave shape to its economic policies. Section III outlines the policies adopted by the government during the 'seventies for alleviating unemployment and reducing the underutilization of the human resource. Section IV attempts to analyze the economic and political consequences of these policies.

I. Ayubian Economics and its Impact on the Employment Situation

In the 'sixties, Pakistan embarked upon a "busy bee route to development," a route over which the economy was able to move at a fast pace because the planners concentrated on growth as the principal objective of development.[3] Private entrepreneurs, particularly those in the modern sectors (large scale manufacturing, trade and commerce) of the economy, were encouraged to make large profits from their investments and plough back into new enterprises a large proportion of their earnings. Accordingly, during this period, the gross domestic product increased at a rate of 6.1% per annum, a rate of growth to which domestic savings contributed significantly. The manufacturing sector led the way and within it the output of the relatively large scale and relatively more capital intensive industries increased substantially. In 1959–60, on the eve of the Second Five Year Plan (1960–1965), the large scale manufacturing sector contributed 6.9% to the gross domestic produce; ten years later, during the final year of the Third Plan (1965–1970), its share had increased to 19.5%.[4]

The policies that helped to encourage the rapid growth of the modern industrial sector did so by reducing the price of capital goods relative to that of labor. An overpriced rupee, relatively liberal allocation of foreign exchange for the import of industrial goods and availability of relatively cheap financing for the purchase of machinery resulted in the choice of capital intensive technology by the Pakistani entrepreneurs. Accordingly, whereas the output of the large scale manufacturing industry increased at an annual rate of 13.3%, the employment in this sector increased by only 3.5%. Whereas in 1969–70, 78% of the industrial output was being produced by the large scale enterprises, they employed only 25% of the labor force engaged in the sector. In 1969–79, the larger industrial units employed only 650,000 workers, representing an increase of 190,000 over those employed ten years earlier. This means that of the 3.9 million increase in the labor force during the decade of the 'sixties, only 190,000 or 5% was absorbed in the large scale industrial sector. These figures indicate that whereas the manufacturing enterprises may have provided the engine for carrying the Pakistani economy over the path of rapid GDP growth, it did very little to alleviate the country's growing problem of unemployment.

Other modern sectors fared only a little better. Public utilities and transport provided an additional one-half million jobs during the decade of the 'sixties but the two sectors together also claimed a substantial share of public and private savings.

The burden of absorbing the additional labor was shouldered once again by the over-crowded agriculture sector. More than one-third of the additions to the labor force was taken up by this sector; although its share in total employment declined by five percentage points, the number of people engaged in it increased by one and a half million.

The wage differential between the modern sectors and agriculture continued to bring a large number of job seekers from the countryside into towns and cities. While the population increased by a rate of 3.1% during the

TABLE 1
Sectoral Distribution of the Labor Force

	1959–1960		1969–1970		Increase
	No. (million)	%	No. (million)	%	(% per anum)
Sector					
Agriculture	7.9	59.8	9.4	54.9	1.7
Services	2.4	18.4	3.3	19.3	3.2
Manufacturing	1.8	13.6	2.6	15.2	3.7
Construction	0.4	3.0	0.6	3.4	4.2
Public Utilities)			0.2	0.4	
)	0.4		0.9		8.4
Transport)			2.7	4.8	
Unemployed	0.3	2.3	0.3	2.1	0.0
	13.2	100.0	17.1	100.1	2.6

SOURCE: Government of Pakistan, *Composition of the Pakistan Labor Force* (Islamabad: Ministry of Labor, 1975), p. 14.

'sixties, urban population grew by over 5.0% per annum. The inability of the modern sectors to absorb a significant amount of the labor force increase meant that a very large number of new entrants waited for jobs in the non-formal sector of the urban economy, the sector dominated by small, labor-intensive and traditional enterprises. During the 'sixties, the size of the urban labor force grew from 2.7 million to 4.6 million, an increase of 1.9 million. However, of this, about 1.4 million was absorbed in the modern sectors. The remaining half million were added to the already large pool of underemployed work force in the non-formal sectors of the urban economy. By 1969–70, the number of workers in this pool had increased to almost two million.

For economic, social and political reasons, the most ominous aspect of the employment situation in Pakistan concerned the unemployed or under-employed educated youth. The data of Table 2, taken from a number of surveys, provide some estimates of the extent of unemployment amongst the educated youth. The high rates of unemployment in this population group represents a serious economic loss: for instance, in the case of the graduates of the "polytechnic institutes" the government had made a considerable amount of investment to produce skilled manpower. However, the number of gradu-ates far exceeded the ability of the economy to absorb. The result was a high level of unemployment. This high level of unemployment was also politically

TABLE 2
Unemployment Rates Among the Educated

Group	Year	Percent Unemployed
1. Technical Trainees	1968	25
2. Technical Trainees	1971–72	33
3. Technical Training Centre, Karachi	1969	26
4. Swedish-Pakistan Institute of Technology: Landhi, Kaptai, Gujrat	1971	39
5. Agricultural Graduates	1968	16
6. Educated Youth (Matriculates and above)	1969	29

SOURCE: World Bank, *Economic Situation and Prospects of Pakistan, Vol. I* (Washington, D.C., February 1973), p. 15. The World Bank's data is from the Directorate, National Manpower Council, Pakistan.

costly: the modern enterprises are more vulnerable than the traditional to economic stagnation and, as the rate of expansion of the modern sector slowed down in the late 'sixties, the number of skilled and educated unemployed increased. It is perhaps not a coincidence that a political incident involving the students of Rawalpindi Polytechnic Institute in the spring of 1968 triggered off the mass movement that was to result in the fall of the government of Ayub Khan in March 1969.[5]

In sum, the economic policies pursued by the Ayub regime did not help to improve the employment situation. The government depended on "economic processes" to take care of the employment problem. But the "trickle down" assumptions behind the Ayubian model failed and, when Ayub Khan left office in 1969, the employment situation, in terms of the number of people seeking jobs, was much worse than at the time of the *coup d'etat* that had brought him to power.

II. *The Employment Situation in the Early Seventies*

In the foregoing section, we provided some estimates of the changes in the employment situation during Ayub Khan's "development decade." In this section, we will describe the employment situation as it existed in the early 'seventies, the time when Pakistan went back to civilian rule.

The 1972 census estimated Pakistan's population at 65 million and its labor force at 19 million.[6] This suggests a participation rate of only 29.2

percent, considerably lower than the average for the developing countries. The lower rate for Pakistan was due to the very low level of participation for women, a characteristic that Pakistan shares with other Muslim countries of the region.[7] Approximately 540,000 persons were entering the labor force; 140,000 in the urban areas and 400,000 in the countryside.

As in other poor countries, in Pakistan also extended open unemployment could be afforded by only a small fraction of the labor force. Most of those unable to find regular and productive employment worked in the service sector or were self-employed as petty traders. Accordingly, full-time unemployment was measured at just over 2% of the labor force. A Government-sponsored Study Group on Unemployment and Manpower Development estimated open unemployment and the full time equivalent of underemployment at 30% of the labor force.[8] This meant that 5.7 million potential workers were not contributing anything to the country's economy.

The workforce was projected to increase at the rate of 3.0% per annum in the 1970–85 period. A decline in the rate of population increase, if it came about at all, would not affect this rate since the people who would be entering the labor force in this period were already born. On the other hand, a change in social attitudes, particularly those towards the employment of women, could add another percentage point to the rate of labor force growth. Therefore, 3.0% growth in total employment was a minimum goal if the level of unemployment was not to increase any further from its present level. If employment in the already over-crowded agriculture was not to increase any further, a three percent increase in the number of total jobs available to the labor force would imply a 6.6% annual increase in employment in non-agricultural sectors. Experience of other developing countries suggested that productive employment can grow only at the rate of 4.0% per annum, even with GDP growth in the range of 8%. This means, that the bulk of the burden for providing employment to new entrants would fall on the industrial sector: an annual compound rate of 8.0% per annum would be needed for the industrial sector to play this role. But, for this sector to absorb labor at this rate would imply a drastic restructuring in favor of labor-intensive enterprise

An alternative scenario, based on continuing expansion in the size of the labor force engaged in agriculture would, of course, reduce the burden on the manufacturing sector. If agricultural labor was allowed to grow at 1.0% per annum, productive industrial employment needs to grow at only 6.5%; a 2.0% increase in agricultural employment implies a 4.8% increase in the size of the industrial labor force. But to employ productively additional labor in the agriculture sector would mean introducing labor intensive techniques of the type that had received a relatively lower priority during the 'sixties. Either scenario would mean a fundamental restructuring of the economic system that was built by Ayub Khan during his ten and a half years in office. However, when Bhutto came to power and the economic policies of his regime began to unfold, it became clear that he was not going to follow either of these two scenarios.

III. *The Bhutto Regime's Employment Strategies*

Bhutto and his People's Party understood the dimension of the problem of unemployment. They also realized that a PPP government, supported as it was by a number of groups who were unhappy with Ayubian economics, would be expected to move quickly to find ways for providing job opportunities for the unemployed. There was also the recognition that the problem of unemployment needed some drastic solutions, including a fundamental restructuring of the economic system. The PPP's manifesto for the election of 1970 and the speeches made by Bhutto during the election campaign[9] contained not only a number of references to the problem of unemployment but also promised quick action if Bhutto and his political party ever came to power.

Once in power, Bhutto and his government moved quickly. The new government's approach towards the problem of unemployment was to be the direct opposite of that adopted by the Ayub regime. The Ayub regime relied on the private sector to provide employment to the growing labor force. However, no specific incentives were provided to the private entrepreneurs for creating additional jobs. The assumption was that the economy growing rapidly would pick up the employment slack in due course. The Bhutto approach was to tackle the problem of unemployment much more directly. Under him, the government initiated a number of special public sector programs to absorb the unemployed and the underemployed. A Peoples' Public Works Program was launched to provide employment to the large surplus labor force in the countryside. A program was initiated for finding placements in government and non-government bodies for the large reservoir of skilled and semi-skilled unemployed workers in towns and cities, and the export of manpower to the labor short but rapidly growing economies in the Middle East was actively promoted. Of these, only the export of workers to the Middle East had any impact; the other two programs foundered largely because of lack of political support for them.

The Peoples' Public Works Program was patterned after the rural works program that was started by the Ayub government in 1963 but discontinued in the late 'sixties.[10] The new program's main objective was to provide employment opportunities to the rural workers by allocating resources to local bodies for implementing small development schemes such as schools, dispensaries, roads and bridges. It was expected that people not being able to find employment would seek assistance from the government even if the public works program paid wages well below the market rates. It was also expected that the people would come out and work at less than market wages for implementing development projects that would be directly beneficial to them. Accordingly, only a small allocation was made for the program whose official objective was to "absorb the surplus labor in the rural areas."[11] Because of the expectations that people would work at less than market wages and because of the government's inability to create a system of viable local government, the Peoples' Work Program was not implemented on the scale that had been envisaged in the election manifesto or in the First Annual Development Plan[12] issued by the Bhutto government. At best, the program never provided more than 100,000 manyears of additional work to the labor force. Since this is about 2% of the estimated underutilization of the rural work force, the program cannot be said to have made any significant difference to the employment situation.

Despite the rhetoric that the launching of the public works program invited from Bhutto and his political colleagues,[13] this approach to the solution of rural underemployment did not have strong political support. The PPP, particularly its left wing, was much more responsive to the demands of the educated urban unemployed. Since the PPP's left wing was very influential in economic decisionmaking during the early years of the Bhutto regime, the government made a more serious effort to address the problem of the urban unemployed. However, in keeping with the regime's approach towards social problems, it opted in favor of direct measures. These included the creation of a National Development Volunteer Corps (NDVC) and the setting up of a National Development Corporation (NDC). The principal function of NDVC was to provide job opportunities in the public and private sectors to those semi-skilled and skilled unemployed workers who registered with it. A small stipend was to be paid to those who registered with the Corporation for as long as the Corporation was not able to find jobs for them. Because of the financial burden this scheme entailed for the NDVC, the public sector agencies were encouraged to provide jobs to those who registered themselves with the Corporation. Since a very large number of those who applied for jobs through the NDVC had skills that could be used in the construction industry, the government set up the National Development Corporation to undertake large construction projects that were being given a high priority. As in the case of the Peoples' Works Program, the NDVC and NDC operations together had little impact on the employment situation. The NDVC was able to find jobs for 5,000 registered unemployed in a period of over three years, while the contracts won by the NDC provided employment to 15,000 skilled and semi-skilled workers during the best year (1976) of its operation.

Migration of workers to the countries of the Middle East proved to be the most effective "direct intervention" undertaken by the government. While this migration would have occurred even without the government's intervention, a number of government policies helped to increase the flow. These policies included liberal grant of passports, "labor exchange" arrangements with several Middle Eastern countries, special treatment afforded to the migrating labor for bringing back their earnings in the form of consumption and capital goods imports, and special arrangements made by the Pakistan International Airlines and the National Shipping Corporation to service the migrating labor force. By 1978, Pakistan had about 600,000 workers in the Middle East remitting back to their families some $1,000 million of their savings.[14] The impact of this policy on the employment situation in the country was felt in several ways. Serious shortages developed in some of the skills most needed in the Middle East—masons, bricklayers, carpenters, plumbers, and truck drivers migrated in large numbers and the wages demanded by those who remained behind more than doubled in a period of less than three years.

Confident that its direct approach towards the problem of human resource underutilization would produce quick results, the government ignored employment as an objective in its other economic policies. As was suggested above, all of the plausible, employment-providing scenarios allowed an important role to be played by the industrial sector. A scenario with action focused only on the non-agricultural sectors, assumed a rate of growth of 8.0% in industrial employment. Those scenarios that continued to assign some role to the agriculture sector, assumed rates of increase in industrial sector's employment of between 5% to 7%. Given Pakistan's history, any of these scenarios could have been enacted. But they could be enacted only with the active support of the government.

Nationalization of large private firms belonging to ten "basic industries" and appropriation of insurance companies in January 1972; take-over by the government of the vegetable oil industry in August 1973; establishment of the government's monopoly over cotton trade in October 1973; nationalization of private, domestically owned banks in January 1974; and the nationalization of the entire cotton-ginning, rice husking and flour-milling industries in July 1976 were actions designed to increase the role of the public sector in the country's industrial development. The private sector's response to these measures was predictable: as shown in Table 3 below, private sector investment dropped to less than half of its level in 1970–1971.

The data of Table 3 also show that, despite a sharp decline in private sector investment, there was a relatively impressive increase in *total* industrial investment. During the 1971–77 period, total industrial investment increased at the annual rate of 11.2%. This increase was made possible by intense activity in the public sector. In 1976/77, over 70% of the resources going into the industrial development came from the public sector as against only 10% in 1972–73, the first full year of the Bhutto regime. Not only was the public

TABLE 3

Industrial Investment, 1970/71–1976/77

(Million Rupees, constant 1969/70 prices)[1]

| | Private Sector | | | | Total |
	Large and Medium Scale	Small Scale	Total	Public Sector	Industrial Investment
1970/71	1,166	192	1,358	65	1,423
1971/72	876	189	1,065	85	1,150
1972/73	468	157	625	68	693
1973/74	335	157	492	188	680
1974/75	414	187	601	446	1,047
1975/76	503	196	700	1,224	1,924
1976/77	438	213	650	1,563	2,213

SOURCE: Data provided by Central Statistical Office, Government of Pakistan.

[1]Investment in current prices deflated by using price indices of investment goods for the manufacturing sector calculated by the Central Statistical Office.

sector much bigger, it was investing a great deal more than the private sector in terms of the ratio of investment to total value added.

The direct intervention approach that the Bhutto regime used in handling, in particular, the problem of urban unemployment did not influence the establishment of priorities for the public sector industrial investment. In other words, the government did not undertake public sector industrial development in order to produce an impact on the employment situation. The objectives of selecting industrial projects for public sector attention were different: by far the most important of these was making Pakistan independent in intermediate and investment goods. This import substitution strategy in a group of capital intensive industries meant that large government sponsored projects had a very small impact on employment. By the close of the Bhutto period, over 70% of public sector industrial investment was committed to making Pakistan self-sufficient in steel, cement and fertilizer. These three industries had very large capital-labor ratios. For instance, the Karachi Steel Mill requires $100,000 of investment for every job it creates while investments in the large-scale private sector managed enterprises were producing additional jobs for $20,000. The capital-labor ratio for small scale enterprises was estimated to be only $500.[15]

The small scale industrial (SSI) sector could have played a useful role in providing jobs that, in view of the government industrial priorities, were being no longer created in the large scale sector. As shown by the data of

Table 3 above, SSIs showed greater dynamism during the Bhutto period than did the large and medium scale enterprises in the privately managed sectors. Investment in SSIs increased at the rate of about 5.0% per annum during the six years of the Bhutto regime: a modest performance when compared with the public sector but considerably more impressive when compared with other parts of the private sector. Given the availability of investible capital to this sector—a number of large entrepreneurs, no longer comfortable with the idea of setting up of large scale enterprises fearing the possibility of their being appropriated by the government later on, were willing to move in SSIs. Availability of domestic and export markets for the products of SSIs; availability in several parts of the country of the skills required by the enterprises; and ready availability, also, of the raw materials on which a number of the tradiational SSIs were depended made investment in them potentially profitable. However, once again, government policies had the result of discouraging the expansion of this sector.

Although not anticipated by the government, one consequence of the Labor Reforms of 1972, was to discourage the rapid expansion of SSIs. In order to benefit a larger number of industrial workers—an important consti-tuency of the PPP left—the government decided to change the definition of "registered" enterprises from those "employing ten persons and/or using power" to those "employing five or more persons." An enterprise was "regis-tered" by the Provincial Labor Departments to ensure that they were meeting the standards of health, remuneration and non-wage benefits that had been set by various legislations. These benefits were revised by the 1972 labor reforms. The change in the definition of registered enterprises made them applicable to an additional 1.2 million workers. This change in definition caught the owners of affected enterprises—some 155,000 in number by surprise. The small owner's costs increased considerably, for they were now required to modernize their enterprises to meet *all* standards, old or new. There is no doubt that the application of labor legislations to SSIs discour-aged new entrepreneurs from entering this sector.

Considering the support given to the PPP by the small entrepreneurs of the central Punjab, it was expected that the government would encourage the development of SSIs. However, few positive steps were taken by the gov-ernment and the SSIs continued to be discriminated against in a number of ways. Commercial credit, power and water supply, foreign exchange for the import of machinery and raw material and appropriate technical assistance were not readily available to the SSIs. This neglect of the SSIs can perhaps be attributed to the domination of the decisionmaking process by the PPP left. Under the domination of traditional Marxists, the PPP left had little sym-pathy with this sector of the urban economy. Accordingly, while the govern-ment concentrated its attention on the development of the public sector and on protecting the "legitimate rights" of the industrial sector, it left SSIs on their own. Little positive encouragement was provided.

A combination of these policies slowed down the rate of growth of the industrial sector to levels much below those required to absorb the additions to the labor force. At the same time, the government continued to follow the policies that had been pursued by the Ayub regime in the agriculture sector. The large and middle class farmers were encouraged to go in for labor saving, capital intensive technologies. For instance, fairly liberal credit facilities through the state owned Agricultural Development Bank as well as the commercial banks were made available for the purchase of large tractors, threshers and harvesters. The 1972 Agriculture Census estimated the number of tractors owned for farming purposes at 30,500. Four years later, this number was estimated at 40,000. This addition to the stock of tractors was equivalent to a displacement of 100,000 farm workers, about equal in number to additional jobs that were provided by the Peoples' Works Program.

The government, therefore, failed in producing a visible impact on the employment situation. If anything, the situation the country faced was worse in 1976–77 than in 1969–70. Growing at a rate of 2.7% per annum, the country had a labor force of 20.6 million, a net addition of 3.5 million workers. Employment in the agriculture sector did not remain unchanged; it grew at the rate of 1.8% per annum, so that by 1976–77, 10.7 million workers were employed in it. Since the output of the agriculture sector during this period increased by only 1.7% per annum, there was some deterioration in the already low labor productivity. The agriculture sector was now reaching the limit of its absorptive capacity. The output of the industrial sector increased at the rate of 1.9% per annum but there was an increase of only 100,000 in the number of workers. There was a slight decline in the level of employment in the small scale industrial enterprises, from 2.1 million in 1969–70 to just over 2 million in 1976–77. This situation, of course, reflected the government's priorities and its policies that, at best, were indifferent to the SSIs.

A number of other changes in the distribution of the labor force deserve mention. As in most other developing countries the burden of absorbing the large increases in the labor force fell on the service sector in which the rate of employment increased by 5.5% per annum.

The rate of increase in employment in the sector of construction was also more than that of the increase in total labor force, reflecting the priority the government assigned to large scale construction and some shifts in private capital from productive investment to investment in housing and commercial buildings. The increase in the rate of open unemployment reflects, perhaps, the preference of a larger number of people, particularly the urban educated, to wait in line for white-collar jobs rather than commit themselves to low paid jobs in the service sector.

TABLE 4
Changes in the Distribution of the Labor Force
During the Seventies

Sector	1976–1977		Change (1969–70
	No. (million)	%	to 1976–77
			(% per annum)
Agriculture	10.7	51.9	+1.8
Services	4.8	23.3	+5.5
Manufacture	2.7	13.1	+0.5
(Large Scale)	(0.7)	(3.4)	(+2.2)
(Small Scale)	(2.0)	(9.7)	(−1.8)
Construction	0.8	3.9	+4.2
Utilities)			
Transport)	1.1	5.3	+3.0
Unemployed	0.5	2.4	+7.6
Total	20.6	99.9	2.7

SOURCE: Data supplied by the Planning Division, Government of Pakistan.

The most important conclusion to be drawn from the foregoing analysis is that the government, despite its electoral commitment to help solve the problem of employment, succeeded only in making the situation a good deal worse. Its record was considerably worse than that of the Ayub regime that assigned a relatively lower priority to employment in its development policies.

IV. *Some Possible Political Repercussions*

The political repercussions of the economic policies of the Bhutto regime can be described only in speculative terms. No data or information are available at present to relate the anti-Bhutto movement of the spring of 1977 and the policies pursued by his government. Nevertheless, it seems that at least three groups of erstwhile PPP supporters turned against Bhutto largely because of the failure of the regime's economic policies. Industrial labor, particularly in the modern enterprises of Karachi, Lahore, Hyderabad, Lyallpur and Multan played the most important role in maintaining the momentum of the political campaign against the government. Industrial workers had benefited considerably from the labor reforms of 1972. The reforms not only increased minimum wages of industrial workers but only provided them with such non-wage benefits as medical insurance, education subsidy and paid holidays. The result was a quantum jump in the benefits received by the workers; in money terms, the return to the workers was estimated to have increased by 45% as a result of the promulgation of the reforms.

However, with the urban labor force increasing at the rate of 140,000 per year and with the large scale manufacturing sector providing less than 20,000 additional jobs every year, the industrial workers lost a great deal of the gains they had made at the time of the implementation of labor reforms. Competition for jobs in the manufacturing sector reduced the workers' bargaining position and the high rates of inflation eroded the benefits that came laborers' way in 1972. Added to this was the inability of the nationalized sector to generate sufficient profits for meeting the financial burden of the obligation that all entrepreneurs, public or private, had now to meet. It was in their interests to let inflation remove some of this burden. Accordingly, when the opposition to Bhutto took to the streets after the general election of March 7, 1977, it was joined quickly by the industrial workers. In April, with the creation of a national federation of all labor unions,[16] leadership of the anti-Bhutto movement in the principal cities was assumed by industrial workers.

For reasons similar to these, the educated urban unemployed came out in the streets to oppose the government of Bhutto. Those one half million people, growing at the rate of 40 to 50,000 per year, together represent a political dynamite that most governments in developing countries have failed to diffuse. Education makes them politically sophisticated; it also makes it difficult for them to accept jobs in the non-formal sector. However, education does not provide them with the type of skills that are needed by the modern sector. Some of them can be absorbed when the modern sector is growing rapidly; rapid growth moves the queue forward and provides hope to those who are still in line. However, a stagnation in the growth of the modern sector stops the queue from moving and generates frustration. This frustration is quickly translated into political action. This happened in 1968 when the rate of growth of the modern sector slackened a little; it happened again in 1977, after a prolonged stagnation of the modern sector. Because of the close ties that this group had with Bhutto and several factions of his PPP, his political dynamite had a longer fuse. It took longer for it to explode under Bhutto than it did under Ayub Khan.

The third group that had supported Bhutto and the PPP in 1970 but abandoned it in 1977 was made up of small entrepreneurs in towns and cities. They managed one half million small industrial and commercial enterprises that had contributed to the exceptional dynamism of the Pakistani economy during the 'sixties. This group had been won over by Bhutto for the PPP largely because of his promise of modernization: in the restructuring of the economy that Bhutto promised, the small entrepreneurs saw an important role for themselves. The PPP was against big industrial and commercial houses; against big banks and insurance companies that provided capital only to large entrepreneurs; and against the entrenched bureaucracy that managed a system in which the big industrialists, big financiers and big merchants seemed to enjoy protection at the expense of the small shop-keepers, small self-employed industrialists and small money-lenders. The support from this group made PPP's 1970 success possible in a number of towns and small cities of the Punjab and Sind. In the labor reforms of 1972 and in the treatment of SSIs during 1972–76, the small scale entrepreneur saw actions that, willingly or unwittingly, were aimed against them. Accordingly, once the agitation against Bhutto picked up force in the spring of 1977, they joined with the industrial workers and the urban unemployed in an effort to dislodge the PPP and its Chairman.

Pakistan's employment situation would not improve in the future unless the government adopted policies and programs aimed at absorbing new entrants to the labor force as well as clearing some of the backlog. For demographic reasons and also because of some changes in social and cultural environment, the labor force is likely to increase at the rate of 3.2% per annum in the next two decades. By the end of the present century, Pakistan may have a labor force of 42 million, more than twice as large as present. To accommodate an additional 20–22 million workers in productive employment would not only require a rate of growth of over 6% per annum in the gross domestic product but also a total change in investment priorities.

Notes

1. For a discussion of the emergence of the Pakistan People's Party as a political force, see Answar H. Syed, "The Pakistan People's Party: Phases One and Two," in Lawrence Ziring, Ralph Braibanti and Howard Wriggins (eds.), *Pakistan: The Long View* (Durham, N. C.: Duke University Press, 1977), pp. 70–176.

2. Pakistan People's Party, *Manifesto*, (Lahore: 1970).

3. For a detailed account of the type of policies that were adopted during this period, see Gustav F. Papnek, *Pakistan's Development: Social Goals and Private Incentives* (Cambridge, Massachusetts: Harvard University Press, 1968) and for the philosophy of development that was pursued at that time see, Mahbub ul Haq, *The Strategy of Economic Planning* (New York: Oxford University Press, 1963). In a later work, Mahbub ul Haq repudiated this approach as his "convictions clashed with the facts." See his, *The Poverty Curtain: Choices for the Third World* (New York: Columbia University Press, 1976), p. 5.

4. These statistics are from, Government of Pakistan, *Pakistan Economic Survey* (Islamabad: Finance Division, 1977), Statistical Annex, pp. 1–191.

5. For an economic interpretation of the anti-Ayub movement see, Shahid Javed Burki, "Social and Economic Determinants of Political Violence: A Case Study of the Punjab," *The Middle East Journal*, Vol. 25, (Autumn, 1971), pp. 465–480.

6. The census estimates are from the statistical annex of Government of Pakistan, *Pakistan Economic Survey, 1976–77, op. cit.*

7. Dudley Kirk, "A New Demographic Transition,"in Roger Revelle (ed.), *Rapid Population Growth, Vol. 2* (Baltimore, Md.: The John Hopkins Press, 1971), pp. 142–44.

8. Quoted in World Bank, *Economic Situation and Prospects of Pakistan, Vol. 1*, (Washington, D. C.: February 1973), p. 14.

9. These speeches were published by the Government of Pakistan after Bhutto came to power. See, Zulfikar Ali Bhutto, *Awakening the People* (Rawalpindi: Pakistan Publications, n.d.) and *Marching Towards Democracy* (Pakistan Publications, n.d.).

10. For an evaluation of the Rural Works Programme launched by the Ayub regime in 1963 in what was then West Pakistan, see Shahid Javed Burki, "Interest Group Involvement in West Pakistan's Works Program," *Public Policy*, Vol. XIX (Winter, 1971), pp. 167–206. Also see, J. W. Thomas, S. J. Burki, D. G. Davies and R. H. Hook, "Public Works Programs in Developing Countries; A Comparative Analysis," Harvard Institute for International Development, Cambridge, Massachusetts, Development Discussion Paper No. 15, May 1976.

11. Government of Pakistan, *Report of the International Seminar on Integrated Rural Development* (Islamabad: Ministry of Food, 1973), p. 186.

12. Government of Pakistan, *Annual Development Plan*, 1972–73 (Islamabad: Planning Division, 1972), p. 18.

13. Zulfikar Ali Bhutto, *Speeches and Statements, December 20, 1971–March 31, 1972*, (Karachi: Government of Pakistan, The Department of Films and Publications, n.d.), passim.

14. While firm data are available on the quantum of remittances sent by the workers through the banking channels to their families back in Pakistan, there is only speculation about the number of workers who have migrated out of the country.

15. Shahid Javed Burki, Norman Hicks and Mahbub ul Haq, "Pakistan: Operational Implications of Adopting Basic Needs Targets," mimeo, (Washington, D. C.: The World Bank, December 1977). p. 18.

16. For an account of the role played by organized labor against Bhutto in the period between the March 1977 elections and coup d'etat of July 1977, see S. R. Ghauri, "How Street War and Strikes Beat Bhutto," *Far Eastern Economic Review* (July 1, 1977), pp. 10–11.

Foreword

RALPH BRAIBANTI

The recent social development of Pakistan must properly be viewed in the context of a recovery of Islamic identity which is evident throughout the world. Indeed, the relationship of Pakistan to this global trend is a critical one. The euphoria which surrounded the establishment of Pakistan in 1947, thus creating the most populous Muslim state in the world, was certainly a factor in re-directing attention to the importance of Islam in the building of new nations. While several other Muslim states such as Malaysia and Indonesia also gained their independence within the same decade, the Pakistan experience was more important than the others. Whereas the other states included large majorities of non-Muslims, Pakistan became an almost totally Muslim state imbued with the dream of building a truly Islamic society with minimal outside influence.

The 1973 OPEC decision on petroleum pricing was a major event in increasing the power and prestige of the Muslim world. While Pakistan did not contribute in any way to that decision, it increased its network of contacts with Saudi Arabia. Its economy was bolstered by the large Pakistani labor force working in the Middle East. The city of Lyallpur was renamed Faisalabad, and its distinguished Islamicist, Maulana Maudoodi, was the first recipient of the newly-established King Faisal Foundation award for his contributions to Islam. It is not without significance that the High Court of Lahore, in passing judgment on the Bhutto case, used in an *obiter dictum* the argument that Prime Minister Bhutto did not meet the requirements of a virtuous Muslim ruler capable of heading an Islamic state. Under the leadership of General Zia ul-Huq, the trend toward Islamicization has accelerated. Serious efforts were made under the guidance of A.K. Brohi, a distinguished constitutional lawyer and a devout scholar of Islam to revise the legal system in accordance with *Shari'ā*.

It is not a sufficient explanation to state that these changes in the social fabric of Pakistan are merely cosmetic or that they are done for the simple reason of extracting economic benefit from Saudi Arabia. On the contrary, they are part of a larger global movement and they are distinctive in Pakistan because they give reinvigorated expression to deep-seated latent feelings which created the nation but were somewhat in eclipse during the secular-oriented regimes of Ayub, Yayha, and Bhutto.

The following three chapters on population, education, and land reform, should be read in the light of this recovery of Islamic identity. Ghayur and Korson mention Islamicization specifically and conclude that it will affect social groupings and demographic issues. Indeed, it is likely to sedate somewhat the accelerated breaking of constraints on the activities of women which were so characteristic of the Bhutto regime. It will probably also affect the quality of mass education and mass attitudes toward fertility control. While the chapter by Herring does not relate Islamicization with the problems of land reform, we may once again find that there is a relationship. It may well be that a recovery of Islam with deeply-ingrained standards of justice and equality ordained by sacred scripture may be used to facilitate land reform. It is possible, on the other hand, that the effect may be quite the opposite, namely, that Islamicization will conduce to a highly centralized authoritarianism which may strengthen the role of landlords and thus impede the reform of land holdings.

The chapter by Dawn and Rodney Jones on education quite clearly traces the effect of Islamicization on education. Since the writing of this chapter, the trends toward Islamicization have been even more profound and there remains to be seen whether they are merely transitory or will have a more lasting effect inrearranging the warp and woof of Pakistani society.

In sum, contemporary Pakistan is in as much a transitional condition as it was at its establishment. The dynamic of uncontrolled westernization has been considerably sedated but the directions in which the society will move, within the ambit of a strengthened Islamic system, still seem unclear.

The Effects of Population and Urbanization Growth Rates on the Ethnic Tensions in Pakistan

MOHAMMAD ARIF GHAYUR and J. HENRY KORSON

The purpose of this paper is to study the effects of population and urbanization growth rates on the political and social climate in Pakistan. In other words, to what extent do these two variables affect the political behavior of the different cultural and linguistic groups in the country?

The first census taken in British India was in 1871, and was continued on a decennial basis through 1941. Following independence in 1947, the government of Pakistan continued the pattern in 1951 and 1961, but, because of the war in East Pakistan in 1971, the census planned for that year was delayed until September 1972.[1]

TABLE 1

Population and Percent Increase, Pakistan, 1901–1972

Year	Population (In Millions)	Percent Increase
1901	16.576	——
1911	19.382	7.1
1921	21.109	8.9
1931	23.542	11.9
1941	28.282	20.1
1951	33.740	19.3
1961	42.880	27.1
1972	64.892	51.33

SOURCE: Figures up to 1961 were obtained from Government of Pakistan, *Population of Pakistan, Vol. I* (Karachi: Ministry of Home Affairs, 1961) p. II–6. Figures for 1972 were computed from *Census Bulletins,* Vol. 2 Nos. 1, 2, 3, 4 and 5.

Table I shows that the population of what is Pakistan today was only 16,576,000 at the turn of the century and for the first three decades growth was rather slow, reaching 23,542,000 by 1931, an increase of about 46 percent for the period. The major cause of such a slow rate of growth was the relatively high mortality rate for all age cohorts compared with the later decades. The 1941 and 1951 censuses show higher population growth rates than the previous three decades bringing the total population to 33,740,000. However, the most rapid growth was shown by the 1961 and 1972 censuses bringing the population to 42,880,000 and 64,892,000 respectively. Such a rapid growth rate increased the population size by almost 300 percent since 1901. In other words, approximately a four-fold increase (from 16,576,000 to 64,892,000) took place during these seven decades which would be classified as high by any world demographic standards.

Urbanization in Pakistan

Conceptually, urbanization refers to the process of transmission of a region from rural to city characteristics. It connotes a special life style (attitudes, nature of relationships, pace of life, etc.) which is different from Tonnies' "Gemeinschaft" (community-orientation) and C. H. Cooley's primary group relationships. However, as far as the Pakistan census is concerned, it has defined "urban" area in demographic terms as: ". . . a continuous collection of houses inhabited by not less than 5,000 persons designated by the provincial Directors of Census as urban . . ."[2]

In the U.S. any continuous settlement of 2,500 or more is classified as urban.[3] In spite of the fact that in Pakistan a figure twice that of the U.S. is a prerequisite for an area to be classified as urban, most social scientists will agree that many of Pakistan's urban areas as defined by the census takers are not really "urbanized." However, for the purposes of this paper we shall limit the discussion to the 20 largest cities of Pakistan, 19 of which had a population of 100,000 or more in 1972.[4]

As Table 2 shows, the urban growth rate of Pakistan has been quite rapid. Although the total population of the country grew by about 250 percent during the 1901–61 period, the urban population increased by almost 600 percent during the corresponding period. In 1901, the total urban population was only 1,600,000 but by 1961 it reached the 9,700,000 mark. During the 11-year period 1961–72, the urban population further increased by 6.8 percent over the 1961 figure, i.e., from 9,700,000 to 16,600,000. This means that more than a ten-fold increase took place in urban population between 1901–1972 compared with a 600 percent increase in the total population.

Another way to look at the rapid urbanization rate in Pakistan is to compare the figures of the 20 largest cities in the 1961 and 1972 censuses. In 1961, there were 5,876,000 people living in the 20 largest cities and metropolitan areas of Pakistan. But this figure reached the 10,472,000 mark by 1972 for the 20 largest cities. This shows an increase of almost 90 percent

TABLE 2
Urbanization in Pakistan, 1901–72

Year	Urban Population (in millions)	Percent of Pakistan's Population	Total Population (in millions)	Percent Variation
1901	1.6	9.8	16.576	——
1911	1.7	8.7	19.383	+16.9
1921	2.1	9.8	21.109	+ 8.9
1931	2.8	11.8	23.542	+11.5
1941	4.0	14.2	28.282	+20.1
1951	6.0	17.8	33.740	+19.4
1961	9.7	22.5	42.880	+26.9
1972	16.6	26.5	64.892	+66.8

SOURCE: All the figures up to 1961 were taken from Shahid Javed Burki, "Migrations, Urbanization and Politics in Pakistan", in W. Howard Wriggins and James F. Guyot, *Population, Politics, and the Future of Southern Asia* (New York: Columbia University Press, 1973, p. 149), whereas figures for 1972 data were computed from Government of Pakistan, Census Bulletin, 1972, Vol. I and *Census Bulletins,* 1, 2, 3, 4, and 5.

during that 11-year period, and is a significant fact because the largest cities are the most important in the political arena of the country. It is where most of the political meetings and even riots take place. On this point we differ from Burki who believes that it is the towns of 10,000–100,000 population which most determine the political currents of Pakistan.[5]

Table 3 shows that the 20 largest cities comprise 20.2 percent of the country's population, which play an important role in the political life of Pakistan. One out of every five Pakistanis resides in the 20 largest cities, of which 19 had a population of 100,000 or more in 1972. The 1961 and 1972 figures bring another meaningful fact to light: that in 1961 only 12 of the 20 largest cities had a population of 100,000 or more but by 1972 as many as 19 cities could boast of such a figure. This indicates a remarkable increase in the largest cities' population themselves. Karachi, Lahore, Faisalabad (previously Lyallpur)—the three largest cities—showed impressive percentage increases of 81.33, 65.74 and 92.70 respectively (their populations being 3,469,000, 2,148,000 and 820,000 in 1972). Other large cities which increased by at least 50 percent during the 1961–72 period were Rawalpindi (80.88 percent), Gujranwala (86.73 percent), Gujrat (66.66 percent), Bahawalpur (59.52 percent), Sargodha (57.36 percent), Sukkur (54.36 percent), Sahiwal (53.33 percent), Multan (51.95 percent) and Wah Cantt, (194.59 percent)—the last-mentioned was only 37,000 in 1961, thus showing a greater percen-

TABLE 3

Population of Cities/Metropolitan Areas, Pakistan, 1972

Rank In '72	Metropolitan Area	Province	Population in Millions 1961	Population in Millions 1972	Percent Variation 1961–72
1.	Karachi	Sind	1.913	3.469	81.33
2.	Lahore	Punjab	1.296	2.148	65.74
3.	Faisalabad	Punjab	.425	.820	92.70
4.	Hyderabad	Sind	.435	.624	43.44
5.	Rawalpindi	Punjab	.340	.615	80.88
6.	Multan	Punjab	.358	.544	51.95
7.	Gujranwala	Punjab	.196	.366	86.73
8.	Peshawar	NWFP	.219	.273	24.65
9.	Sialkot	Punjab	.164	.212	26.94
10.	Sargodha	Punjab	.129	.203	57.36
11.	Sukkur	Sind	.103	.159	54.36
12.	Quetta	Baluchistan	.107	.156	45.97
13.	Jhang	Punjab	.095	.136	43.15
14.	Bahawalpur	Punjab	.084	.134	59.52
15.	Sahiwal	Punjab	.075	.115	53.33
16.	Mardan	NWFP	.078	.109	39.74
17.	Wah Cantt	Punjab	.037	.109	194.59
18.	Kasur	Punjab	.075	.103	37.33
19.	Gujrat	Punjab	.060	.100	66.66
20.	Islamabad	(F.C.A.)		.077	—

SOURCE: All the figures for 1961 were computed from Government of Pakistan, *Census of Pakistan* Vol. I (Ministry of Home Affairs, 1961) and the 1972 figures were computed from Government of Pakistan, *Census of Pakistan Bulletin 1–5* (Islamabad: Census Organization, 1973).

TABLE 4

Population of Pakistan by Province and Rural-Urban Residence, 1972

Area	Total	Rural		Urban	
		Number	%	Number	%
Punjab	37,743,604	28,486,292	75.5	9,257,312	24.5
Sind	14,007,722	8,307,296	59.3	5,700,426	40.7
N.W.F.P.	8,337,385	7,148,171	85.7	1,189,214	14.3
Baluchistan	2,405,154	2,007,498	83.5	397,656	16.5
Federally Administered Areas	2,485,867	2,472,567	99.5	13,300	0.5
Total	64,979,732	48,421,824	74.5	16,557,908	25.5

SOURCE: Government of Pakistan *Census of Pakistan Bulletin I* (Islambad: Ministry of Interior, 1973) Vol. 1 p. 1.

tage increase. Among the large cities Peshawar registered the least growth of 24.94 percent (from 164,000 to 212,000) between 1961 and 1972 but even this is quite impressive from general standards of urban growth rates throughout the world.

Ethnic Politics in Pakistan

The former East Pakistan is a very homogeneous area linguistically; 98.2 percent population claimed Bengali as their mother-tongue and only 1.8 percent spoke any language other than Bengali.[6] Many foreigners had the impression that once East Pakistan seceded, cultural and linguistic homogeneity would be achieved by the western wing of the country. But this is not so. The 1961 census shows that 58.0 percent of the population of West Pakistan was in the province of Punjab (see Table 4). However, of the rest, 32.28 percent claimed eight other mother-tongues, plus 1.32 percent who were classified as "others."[7]

TABLE 5
Population by Mother-Tongue and by the Number of Speakers of Additional Language, West Pakistan, 1961[a]

Mother-Tongue	No. of Persons	% of Total Population	No. of Speakers of Additional language
1. Punjabi	26,186,586	66.39	465,378
2. Sindhi	4,963,996	12.59	619,684
3. Pushto	3,339,856	8.47	187,088
4. Urdu	2,987,826	7.57	2,871,892
5. Baluchi	982,512	2.49	159,139
6. Brahui	365,557	0.93	87,055
7. Bengali	45,681	0.12	10,127
8. English	17,531	0.04	818,353
9. Persian	26,378	0.07	287,719
10. Arabic	3,334	0.01	189,486
11. Others	523,182	1.32	——
Total	39,442,439	100.00	——

[a] Excluded from the census were 3.4 million persons in the Frontier region of Pakistan.
SOURCE: Government of Pakistan, *Census of Pakistan* (Karachi: Ministry of Home Affairs, 1961) Vol. 1, pp. IV-31, 32.

If all the languages and dialects are included, then their numbers will be at least twice that mentioned above. The data show that Sindhi, Pushto and Urdu with 12.59, 8.47 and 7.57 percent of the population were second, third and fourth in rank as mother-tongues in West Pakistan. Baluchi, Brahui, Persian, English and Arabic had fifth to ninth ranks respectively (see Table 5).

It is unfortunate that data could not be collected on the mother-tongue question in the 1972 census, because language riots had preceded the "Big Count," and it had become an extremely sensitive political issue, therefore, for linguistic grouping statistics for Pakistan one must rely on the 1961 data. However, to a very large extent the four provinces of Pakistan reflect the four (or some say five) major ethnic groups in the country. Table 6 shows that in 1972 the Punjab comprises 57.59 percent of the country's population whereas Sind claims 21.52 percent, N.W.F.P. 12.95 percent and Baluchistan 3.72 percent. Overall, the country's population grew by 51.33 percent in 11 years which means that the rate of growth averaged 3.45 percent per year during the 1961–1972 period. Lee L. Bean says that "such a rate of growth would make Pakistan one of—if not 'the'—fastest growing countries of the world."[8] Most demographers believe that the 1972 census was politicized

TABLE 6
Population of Pakistan by Provinces, 1961 and 1972
(In Thousands)

Locality	Population 1961*	1972	Variation 1961–72 Number	Percent	Proportion 1972 Census
PAKISTAN**	42,880	64,892	22,012	51.33	100.00
North West Frontier Province	5,731	8,402	2,671	46.60	12.95
Centrally Administered Tribal Areas	1,847	2,507	660	35.73	3.86
Federal Capital Territory Islamabad	94	235	141	150.00	0.36
Punjab Province	25,488	37,374	11,886	46.63	57.59
Sind Province	8,367	13,965	5,598	66.90	21.52
Baluchistan Province	1,353	2,409	1,056	78.04	3.72

**Excluding Non-Pakistanis for 1961.
*Data relates to West Pakistan only.
SOURCE: Census Organization, *Population Census of Pakistan, Census Bulletin I* (Islamabad, 1973), p. 1

resulting in some ethnic groups highly exaggerating their numbers. Thus, Bean opined about the 1972 count:

> The original 1971 census was rescheduled as a result of the war, and the actual count was carried out in September of 1972. In addition to the admininstrative and population dislocations created during that period of time, the actual census also coincided with the language riots in the Sind. Because of that coincidence, it may be argued that the language groups in conflict over-reported in order to provide a stronger basis for political representation. Similar arguments could be made in the case of the North West Frontier and Baluchistan Provinces where the National Awami Party leaders were concerned with representational strength relative to the P.P.P. which had its power base in the more populous provinces of the Punjab and the Sind. Such political conflicts led to apparent overcounts in the areas of Muslim-Hindu confrontation during the 1931 Indian census.[9]

Thus, the largest overcount seems to have taken place in Sind and Baluchistan where 66.90 and 78.04 percent population increases were reported during the 1961–72 period. Although part of these extremely high increases of over 4.0 and over 5.0 percent per annum in Sind and Baluchistan can be explained in terms of a high immigration rate, quite definitely some of it would appear to be the result of over-reporting by various linguistic groups for political reasons.

The politics of Pakistan is basically the politics of linguistic groups. Although Pakistan was created (so the masses believe) for the Muslims of the sub-continent, it was hoped that the bond of religion will supersede other bonds (for example, region, language, local culture) among Pakistanis. But when Pakistan came into existence and since there has been no large non-Muslim group to be blamed for real or imagined injustices, the hard realities of daily economic life, plus the aspirations of the growing number of college-educated Pakistanis, it became clear that religion was not enough of a bond to create firm ties of nationalism among the various ethnic groups in West Pakistan, let alone the two culturally diverse wings of West and East Pakistan.[10] The first conflict surfaced as early as 1948 after Jinnah's declaration that only Urdu was to be the national language. When East Pakistan's Mujibur Rahman protested in 1952 he was jailed, which appears to be the first milestone on the road to the creation of Bangladesh in 1971.[11]

In spite of the demise of the eastern wing in 1971 the basic problem of Pakistan still remains the question of national identity; whether Pakistanis consider themselves Pakistanis first and then Sindhis, Baluchis, Punjabis or Pathans, or vice versa. A few among academic observers of Pakistan are inclined to believe that a section of urban intelligentsia is primarily concerned with its regional, linguistic, cultural and ethnic affiliation and only secondarily with Pakistan.[12]

This may be, therefore, an appropriate place to deal with the question of regionalism. This must of necessity be a brief discussion since many scholars have examined the problem in the last generation.

Theodorson and Theodorson define it as the "behavior that emphasized the geographic region . . . stressing the relationship between man and his immediate physical environment. Economic, social, and cultural organizations [are formed] in terms of their interrelationships and functions within the geographic region."[13]

A better definition of regionalism based on language is analyzed by Bernard S. Cohn when he states that regionalism does not just occur but, in fact, emerges when certain special circumstances develop as viewed by rival groups. In his opinion the three important ingredients in the emergence of regionalism are: 1) common symbols, 2) transmission of these symbols within the whole group, and 3) the establishment of regional elites. He defines regionalism as the phenomenon which leads "usually to the conscious or unconscious development of symbols, behavior, and movements which will mark off groups within some geographic boundary from others in other regions for political, economic or cultural ends."[14] However, this paper will deal with the empirical data currently available.

The Case of Sind

Of the four provinces, Sind is the most important as far as the processes of population, migration and urban growth rates are concerned as they affect the ethnic groupings and politics in Pakistan. Before independence, linguistically Sind was a relatively homogeneous province. For instance, according to the 1941 census only 32,000 persons claimed Urdu as their mother-tongue in Sind and Khairpur State in a population of 4,084,000 which is only about .80 percent of the total population.[15] But by 1951, Urdu-speaking Muhajirs (immigrants) made up about 476,000 or 12 percent of the total population of 4,608,514.[16]

Most of the Muhajirs in Sind migrated to Karachi. But at that time Karachi Division was not included in what is today Sind Province since the former was classified as the Federal Capital Area—the seat of the national government, which has since been moved to Islamabad. Had it been included in Sind and Khairpur state statistics, Urdu speakers would have made up about 25 percent of the population. But since Karachi is now counted as part of Sind, it is interesting to look at the language composition for Karachi District in 1961 (see Table 7). The table shows that of a total population of 2,044,044, as many as 1,101,776 or 53.9 percent declared Urdu to be their mother-tongue. Even Punjabi speakers were found more frequently in Karachi (260,747 or 12.8 percent) than Sindhi speakers who numbered only 174,823 or 8.6 percent. In fact, if only the urban population was counted in Karachi District then the third largest linguistic group becomes Gujrati with 152,471 or 7.5 percent of the population and Sindhis would become the fourth, because a substantial number of the 8.6 percent Sindhis lived in "gots" (Sindhi villages) on the outskirts of Karachi city. Baluchis (5.3

percent) and Pathans (5.2 percent) were other important groups in the linguistic mosaic of Karachi.

TABLE 7

Population by Mother-Tongue,
Karachi District, 1961

Mother Tongue	No. of Person	Percent of Total
Brahui	20,263	1.0
English	11,597	0.6
Bengali	25,963	1.3
Gujrati	152,471	7.5
Punjabi	260,747	12.8
Sindhi	174,823	8.6
Urdu	1,101,776	53.9
Baluchi	108,024	5.3
Pushtu	105,482	5.2
Others, not stated	82,898	3.8
Total	2,044,044	100.00

SOURCE: Gov't of Pakistan, *District Census Report: Karachi* (Ministry
of Home Affairs, 1961) Parts I–V, pp. IV–26.

Six other large cities and towns of Sind and Khairpur State also show the
great influx of non-Sindhis (Muhajirs) in the province in 1951 as indicated in
Table 8.

TABLE 8

Populations of Muhajirs vs. Others in
Six Large Cities of Sind, 1951

City	Total	Muhajirs	Other Muslims	Non-Muslims
Hyderabad	241,801	159,805	74,792	7,204
Sukkur	77,026	41,791	33,558	1,677
Shikarpur	45,335	16,087	26,429	2,819
Mirpurkhas	40,412	27,649	10,988	1,775
Nawabshah	34,201	18,742	13,865	1,594
Larkana	33,247	11,767	18,114	3,366

SOURCE: Government of Pakistan, *Census of Pakistan: Sind and Khaipur State* (Karachi:
Ferozesons, 1951) Vol. IV, p. 54.

Muhajirs generally had more formal education than their Sindhi counterparts. Also, as immigrants everywhere, they had a greater tendency to settle in urban areas than in rural areas. Thus, Table 9 shows that most of the Muhajirs were drawn to the urban areas in Sind and Khairpur State. The census also makes another important observation:

The larger increase in its [Sind and Khairpur State] population in 1941–51 decade is mainly due to the influx of Muhajirs whose number in the city [Hyderabad] is 159,805 which is nearly 30 percent of their total in the Province.[17]

In general, Sind and Khairpur State were only 14.9 and 6.8 percent urbanized, respectively.[18] Therefore, the data indicate that the Muhajirs from India and the migrants from the rest of the country settled primarily in urban areas (see Table 9).

TABLE 9

Number of Muhajirs by Urban
and Rural Area Settlement, Sind and Khaipur State, 1951

District	Total Muhajirs	Urban Area	Rural Area
Dadu	20,720	9,194	11,526
Hyderabad	205,641	177,180	28,461
Nawabshah	93,345	41,136	52,209
Sukkur	93,739	66,636	27,103
Tharpurkar	88,765	28,323	60,442
Thatta	5,851	1,813	4,038
Upper Sind Frontier	6,535	3,937	2,598
Larkana	25,682	16,501	9,181
Khairpur State	100,130	48,890	51,240
Total	650,408 (100.00%)	393,610 (61.2%)	246,798 (38.8%)

SOURCE: Government of Pakistan, *Census of Pakistan: Sind and Khairpur State* (Karachi: Ferozesons, 1951) Vol. IV. p. 54.

The Punjab is the least affected area in this respect because of its large population base (57.59 percent of the nation's), and also because it was Punjabis who migrated in the largest number to the three less densely populated provinces. Another favorable element in the case of Punjab was the overwhelming majority of the immigrants from India who came to this Province were Punjabi-speaking from the eastern part of Punjab of the undivided India, many of whom already had some roots and relatives in the western Punjab which joined Pakistan. Thus, they were easily integrated and assimilated in the province. The most important population and urban growth rates occurred in Sind, which, because of the numbers involved have had the greatest effect on the ethnic politics of the country.

N.W.F.P. and Baluchistan fall between the extremes of the Punjab and Sind in this connection. Perhaps Baluchistan is closer to Sind in the continuum of the effect of migration of "outsiders" to the provinces.

Influence of Population and Urban Growth Rates on Ethnic Relations

When a country such as Pakistan is passing through a stage of low economic and industrial development, and, in addition, is confronted with one of the highest population growth rates in the world (approximately 3.45 percent per year), we find that not only are the "push-pull" factors evident in rapid urbanization, but attendant problems, such as the composition of the labor force, unemployment and underemployment soon become political as well as economic problems. Some of these problems will be discussed below. Pakistan is not alone in this matter, as other developing nations with high population and urbanization growth rates are confronted with the same problems.

The ideas of Wriggins and Guyot in their study *Population, Politics and the Future of Southern Asia* (1973) seem to support the data presented in this paper. They believe that if the present rates of population growth continue in that part of the world it could have catastrophic consequences by the turn of this century. Another phenomenon which is taking place simultaneously in the countries of South and Southeast Asia is the rapid growth of urbanization which consists of sprawling "urban villages."

However, once these different cultural groups interact with each other and compete for the limited economic opportunities, then these discontented and frustrated masses are frequently mobilized and politicized by the opportunistic regional leaders resulting in several social and political changes in these societies. They say:

As these peoples of different cultural, ethnic (religious, tribal) and linguistic backgrounds interpenetrate each other's territory, hostilities grow sharply . . . certain ethnic communities may find traditionally low-status groups rising well above them in income, political power, and social standing. Such patterns in ethnic- and status-conscious societies will be resisted or certainly resented, and political or more direct efforts to revenge the consequences can be expected. On the other hand, any conscious constraint of economic growth in the face of such dynamic forces as population growth, political mobilization and larger demands will lead to further intensified stresses.[19]

Now let us examine the data and facts in Pakistan, especially Sind where the problem is more acute. As Sind was "infiltrated" by Muhajirs, Punjabis,

Pathans, Baluchis, Gujratis, and the Tribal people from the north after 1947, it resulted in conflict between the locals and non-locals. There were fewer university-educated people, businessmen and professionals in the ranks of the Sindhis compared to the Urdu and Gujrati-speaking Muhajirs. The Punjabis who came to the cities were also better trained in the sciences, business and the professions than Sindhis. Even those Punjabis who went to the rural Sind as farmers were retired army personnel, aided by the Ayub Khan regime to settle in newer areas, who quickly occupied these lands and prospered.[20]

Other groups, Pathans, Baluchis and Tribal people, limited to lesser skilled jobs who were anxious to find a place in the economic hierarchy, offered almost "unfair" competition to the native Sindhis. This "invasion" by outsiders, (a typical case of ethnocentrism), created considerable resentment among the Sindhis, since work opportunities were extremely limited. But when Sindhis observed that the outsiders were obtaining jobs, setting up businesses, obtaining admission to professional colleges and universities, and were apparently prosperous, this obviously caused conflict. Muhajirs became the main target of attack since they formed the largest groups (about 30 percent of the total) whereas the other linguistic groups combined formed approximately 10 percent of the Sind population.

G. M. Syed, with other members of the Sind United Front, proposed the idea of "Sindhu Desh" suggesting it as the only way to preserve Sindhi culture and the economic independence of Sindhis.[21] It was the growing number of Sindhi college students (the elite, according to Cohn's theory) who saw the doors of career advancement increasingly closed to them because of the competition from Muhajirs and other linguistic groups. By 1959, persons with Urdu as their mother-tongue were a little over one half of Karachi's population but, as Table 10 shows, their higher participation rate in the labor force, particularly in the more lucrative occupations such as administrators, managers, professionals and technicians is evident.

The Sindhi elites' fear of hindrance in career advancement and other economic opportunities is similar to the threat which the locals of Baluchistan and the N.W.F.P. feel from Punjabis who have continually migrated to Quetta, Peshawar and the other cities for the last three decades—and the flow is still continuing. In Baluchistan and the N.W.F.P. hardly any prejudice exists against Muhajirs in spite of the fact that the latter hold good positions in many instances. But the locals feel that Muhajirs do not constitute a threat because the Urdu-speaking population makes up only about two percent of the total in each of these provinces. On the other hand, the Punjabis' proportion in both the provinces is much larger than that of Muhajirs, and the absolute and percentage numbers are expected to increase in the future. This situation causes them to feel more threatened and more hostile to the people from the majority province.

TABLE 10

Natives, Muhajirs and Migrants from the Rest of Pakistan in the Karachi Labor Force, 1959

Occupational Group	Total	Natives	Migrants from rest of Pakistan	Immigrants From India	Immigrants from India as per cent of total
All persons in labor force	573,900	87,125	146,100	329,250	57.4
Professionals & technicians	14,775	2,225	2,250	10,250	69.4
Administrators & Managers	49,300	6,900	6,675	25,650	72.3
Skilled laborers	92,175	7,225	23,000	59,475	64.5
Semiskilled & unskilled	114,150	18,800	45,675	45,300	39.7
Others	303,500	51,950	68,500	178,575	58.88

SOURCE: G.M. Farooq, *The People of Karachi: Economic Characteristics,* Karachi, 1967

Wriggins and Guyot point out the following four phenomena which occur in developing societies like Pakistan when the population is growing at a rapid rate and when "push" factors force people from rural areas and smaller towns to migrate to larger cities where they seek work in the already limited job market for the local people.

1. Political mobilization of the masses.
2. Increased political and economic demands by different groups.
3. Growing unemployment (particularly among the college-educated).
4. Intensified competition and conflict among different ethnic, linguistic, cultural, religious, and tribal groups jockeying for political power and for the very limited economic opportunities. [22]

Now we should like to elaborate these points with reference to data for Pakistan.

1. *Political Mobilization*: Such a political mobilization of the masses took place in East Pakistan culminating in the creation of Bangladesh. In Sind, the United Front, in Baluchistan and the N.W.F.P. the rise of the National Awami Party were indications of such processes. As the number of outsiders increased and they became a substantial proportion of a province's population, the local communal leaders appealed to the latent fears of the masses and of the college-educated elites.

2. *Increased Political and Economic Demands*: Since both locals and non-locals are competing for the same limited economic and job opportunities, some ethnic leaders capitalized on these grievances and put more and more economic as well as political demands of their linguistic groups before the federal government. Mujibur Rahman first demanded parity, then autonomy, and finally independence for his "family," as he used to call his fellow Bengalis. Likewise, G. M. Syed demanded autonomy for Sind, a higher quota of representation for rural Sindhis (where the proportion of Muhajirs is the lowest). Almost all Muhajirs are urban-dwellers. Ghaffar Khan and his son, Wali Khan, demanded the change of the name of their province from N.W.F.P. to Pakhtunistan, agitated against the "invasion" of N.W.F.P. by Punjabis and pressed for the introduction of Pushto as the medium of instruction in the schools in the province. An important aspect of all this is that the greatest support for regional politicians has generally come from the colleges and universities, as students and faculty members traditionally have been quite active politically on the sub-continent. [23]

3. *Growing Unemployment Rate*: Perhaps the most important cause of ethnic tensions in the rapidly growing urban areas is the hard reality of finding a satisfactory job, particularly among the college graduates. Pakistan is a classic example of a surplus of educated unemployed in an underdeveloped society. A recent study showed that the total educated unemployed in Pakistan were close to 400,000. Out of these, 20,000 were unemployed science grad-

uates and 5,000 were graduates of the polytechnic institutions.[24] Such a highly competitive situation for graduates of all linguistic groups leads one to look for scapegoats (other linguistic groups) and the fear of lesser chances for advancement in one's career. That is why colleges and universities are the most active breeding grounds for regional or national political movements. No one can deny the role of Aligarh University in the Pakistan movement, and the same is true of the central role played by the students and faculty of Dacca University in the creation of Bangladesh. The greatest number of devoted supporters of G. M. Syed, Wali Khan and Bizenjo are found on the university campuses at Jamshoro, Peshawar and Quetta than at any other place. These potential elites feel greatly threatened by other ethnic counterparts.[25]

4. *Intensified Competition Among Various Ethnic Groups*: The Bhutto regime, cognizant of the political potential of the college/university-age cohort, responded quite promptly in early 1972 with its *Education Plan, 1972–1980*. An important aspect of this plan was to upgrade some of the colleges to university level, and to open new colleges and universities in various locations around the country. It was felt that by providing additional opportunities to the young for higher education, pressure from this traditional source of political activism would be diffused. This, of course, has done little to provide employment opportunities for university graduates, although the National Development Volunteer Program, also a part of the educational reform, was planned for that purpose.[26] A similar situation prevails for the semi-skilled and unskilled laborers. When the different groups are politicized, it is inevitable that they will jockey for power. Thus, the politics of Pakistan is the politics of ethnic groups on a national as well as on provincial levels. Here we differ from Burki who gives prime importance to the towns of 10,000–100,000 population in the politics of Pakistan.[27]

We believe that the 20 largest cities of 100,000 or over in population provide the more important battleground for the different ethnic groups. It is in these 20 largest cities where they meet, interact, compete and find jobs, or not find them, most of the time. It is in these 20 cities where most of the agitation, demonstrations, and riots took place in 1977 against Mr. Bhutto, in 1969 against Ayub Khan, and against other political leaders before that. Anyone who followed the political events in Pakistan during the last decade will agree that political headquarters, political meetings, riots, demonstrations, firing by police and the army took place in cities like Karachi, (3,469,000), Lahore (2,148,000), Lyallpur (820,000), Hyderabad (640,000), Rawalpindi (615,000) and Multan (544,000). And these are the six largest cities of Pakistan in terms of population. Even the names of the rest of the 14 larger cities are more familiar to any observer of Pakistan than are the towns of 10,000–100,000 to which Burki refers. The other 14 larger cities in order of size are Gujranwala, Peshawar, Sialkot, Sarghodha, Sukkur, Quetta, Jhang,

Bahawalpur, Sahiwal, Mardan, Wah Cantt., Kasur and Islamabad. Obviously, once some of these towns of 10,000–100,000 in size gradually grow in the years to come they will also probably play a more important role in the politics of the country as compared with their importance today. At this point we feel it is well to venture the generalization that the larger the city in terms of population the greater will be the degree of political activism.

Looking Towards the Future: Solutions and Trends

What is in store for the future? Will the forces of rapid population growth and the trend of people migrating from rural areas and smaller towns of 10,000–100,000 to the larger cities, crowding into the already overcrowded job market result in further tensions among the ethnic groups?

We cannot deny the trend of rapid population growth in Pakistan for the next two decades.[28] Even if there should be a decline in the population growth rate of 3.45 percent by the end of the century, the population will have more than doubled in that period. There do not appear to be any projections for the *urban* proportion of the nation's population by the year 2,000. However, from Table 2 we see that in 1901 the urban population made up only 9.8 percent of the total, but by 1972 the percentage had increased two and a half times to 26.5 percent. Consequently, one cannot help assuming that by the year 2,000 an even higher percentage of the population will be living in the cities.

Neither can one be optimistic about the prospects for an improved employment picture, both among those with higher education and the nonprofessionals in the urbanized areas. One potential change in the composition of the labor force might well be an increasing number of women in white collar employment and in the professional/administrative segment of the labor force. This will be discussed in greater detail below. There do appear to be, however, some trends which give rise to some optimism in the future.

1. *Urdu Making Headway*: Despite the fact that there is not a total consensus on Urdu as the national language, there is no denying the fact that it has been voluntarily adopted as the provincial language by the Punjab, Baluchistan and the N.W.F.P. comprising three-fourths (74.26 percent) of the population of the country. And these three provinces have only about two percent of the population with Urdu as their mother-tongue. Paradoxically, Sind, where approximately 30 percent population has Urdu as their mother-tongue, had language riots in 1972. But even here the number of persons knowing Urdu as an *additional* language is on the increase because of the influx of migrants from the Punjab, Baluchistan and the N.W.F.P. They comprise about one-tenth of Sind's population. Also, practically all educated Sindhis know Urdu and as the formal education will be increasingly available

in the future so, one expects, that the number of speakers of Urdu will increase among all Pakistanis. The 1961 census shows (see Table 5) Urdu as the only major language of the country where the number of persons knowing Urdu as an *additional* language (besides their mother-tongue) is almost twice that of any other language. There were 2,963,826 persons with Urdu as their mother-tongue but almost as many (2,871,892) spoke it as an additional language. On the other hand, Punjabi, Sindhi, Baluchi and Brahui have a very poor showing on this score (see Table 5) and cannot claim such a distinction.

In fact, all the major languages of Pakistan have the common Arabic-Persian script and grammar and their nouns have a similar base compared with, for example, Bengali which is written in Sanskrit script. A West Pakistani could not read even the alphabet of Bengali, but this is not the case with the languages spoken in West Pakistan.

Malik analyzes the situation about Sind in a very cogent way. He says:

> The true demographic frontier of Pakistan, however, is Sindh where a new kind of Pakistani is growing out of the social melting pot of Muhajirs, Baluchis, Pathans, Punjabis, and Sindhis. Speaking Pakistani-Urdu with unfamiliar accents, these new Pakistanis will take decades to make an impact, but with their apearance will develop the ethos of a West Pakistan nationalism. No tears need be shed on the demise of the old traditional Sindh while one welcomes the birth of a dynamic demographic frontier in Baluchistan.[29]

2. *Religion*: The breakup of Pakistan and the still continuing "provincialism" in West Pakistan has made it evident that relying on religion alone to be the glue to bind together the four "subnations" in Pakistan will not be adequate. However, one cannot overemphasize the importance of Islam in a traditional society like Pakistan. Religion has great significance in the lives of the masses and even among the middle and upper classes (take, for instance, the popularity of the Jamaat-i-Islami among the educated classes in cities like Karachi, Lahore and Rawalpindi). The basic religious outlook among the masses of Pakistan does mean a uniform value system, common festivals, traditions, a sense of history and the idea of brotherhood and other common symbols which bind people together.

Ahmed very poignantly points out that the role of the ulema in politics of Pakistan will continue and will increase in the future because they are in much closer personal contact with the masses than are the western-style educated leaders in the country.[30] Additionally, these religious leaders have demonstrated their capacity to organize politically during the 1977 elections, as they did in earlier elections. For example, Jamiatul-Ulema-i-Islam formed a coalition government with N.A.P. in N.W.F.P. with Mufti Mahmud as the Chief Minister in 1972. Jamaat-i-Islami has shown strength among the urban educated middle classes in cities like Karachi and Lahore.

In other words, in spite of their traditional political ideologies the religious parties have shown remarkable flexibility in ignoring their doctrinal difference when the need arose. Therefore, Ahmed concludes, if the leadership properly utilizes religion, it can serve as a strong cohesive force for the different linguistic groups of Pakistan.[31] In this connection one may have to take into account the recent measures taken by General Zia-ul-Haq, who has shown even greater enthusiasm for Islamic orthodoxy and practices which may create more of the common symbols for Pakistanis and Pakistani nationalism.

There is no question that the religious leaders, although rarely holders of elective or appointive office, have been taking increasingly stronger positions in terms of developing Pakistan as a truly Islamic state based on the ideology of the Quran. Although previous administrations had paid hardly more than lip service to this ideology in the past, it was interesting to note that even Bhutto submitted to this pressure before his arrest when he announced that Friday, rather than Sunday, would henceforth be observed nationally as the sabbath. Even necessary services would be curtailed on Fridays from noon to 3 P.M. during the regular hours of prayer. The banning of alcoholic beverages for all Muslims is further evidence of the sharp turn to orthodoxy of the national government.

3. *Demographic Rates*: As has been stated above, should the growth rate of 3.45 percent per year continue, the population of Pakistan will more than double before the end of the 20th century. The population growth rate continues to be the nation's most serious socioeconomic problem. Should this rate of increase not be reduced, then cities will continue to grow like "urban villages" and all the above-mentioned problems will be magnified. Although Pakistan was one of the first developing nations in the world to declare family planning as the official policy of the country, its performance record to date is one of the poorest.

Under President Ayub Khan the Government of Pakistan took its first official stand in favor of family planning in 1959. Since that time much foreign aid from several nations, plus appropriations from the national treasury have produced very limited results at best. The most optimistic estimate is a reduction in the growth rate to the more recent 3.45 in 1972.

As a nation founded on Islamic ideology, one of the basic problems has been the "correct" religious interpretation of the Quran. It is here that religious leaders, academicians and other intellectuals fail to agree. As might be expected, conservative Muslims do not believe that any artificial means of fertility control is permitted in Islam. Maulana Maudoodi, a scholar of Islam and leader of the Jamaat-i-Islami, does not believe that use of any contraceptive devices is condoned.[32] However, other more liberal scholars such as Fazlur Rahman believe that fertility control is not against the spirit of Islam

TABLE 11
Sex Ratio of University Students: 1968–69 and 1973–74

University	1968–69				1973–74			
	Males	Percent	Females	Percent	Males	Percent	Females	Percent
Peshawar	374	64	207	36	578	75	190	25
Islamabad	102	92	9	8	413	71	169	29
Punjab	2,258	62	878	38	2,685	74	940	26
Sind	1,696	82	374	18	1,248	83	256	17
Karachi	2,245	66	1,184	34	4,388	63	2,532	37
Baluchistan	—			—	638	92	51	8
Lyallpur	1,787	99.5	8	0.5	2,378	98.6	34	1.4
Eng. Technical Lahore	1,960	99.75	5	0.25	2,636	99.54	12	0.46
Total	10,422		2,665	20.2	14,964		4,184	21.3

SOURCE: *Overseas Weekly Dawn*, Jan. 22, 1978, p. 11. Computed by Education, Planning and Management, Ministry of Education, Islamabad, 1976.

because the Prophet Mohammed himself practiced "azl," otherwise known as Onanism, or withdrawal.[33] Regardless of which position one takes in the controversy, several of the knowledge, attitude and practice (KAP) studies on fertility control that have been done in Pakistan demonstrate that most of the illiterate part of the population do not practice fertility control because they believe "it is against the will of God," or offer similar reasons for their practices. And in more recent months there is no question but that the experience in India of forced sterilization has had a negative effect on the fertility control programs in Pakistan. Should the rate of population growth not be reduced in the near future, it can be safely predicted that all the tensions underlying employment, underemployment and political activism will only be exacerbated.

4. *Women and Politics*: After the March, 1977 elections the P.N.A. charged Mr. Bhutto with rigging the elections. One of the points he made in his own defense for the embarrassingly large margin of victory was that the women electorate had voted for him in overwhelming fashion. The basis of his argument was that during his incumbency women were given more rights, the family laws were strengthened, rather than weakened, (which was one of the demands of the orthodox religious leaders, as well as conservative political leaders), greater opportunities in education were made available to women and, among other reasons, with Begum Nusrat Bhutto at his side, the women electorate and especially their leaders felt they had made considerable progress under the Bhutto regime and didn't want to risk a reversal in their status under a more conservative government. They felt their limited gains were too precious to risk under political leaders who were unsympathetic to their cause.

Although there is no empirical evidence to support Bhutto's claims that the women's support assured his overwhelming victory, there is no question that Pakistani women have made substantial progress in recent years. There is no doubt that women have entered the colleges and universities in large numbers (see Table 11), at least in most of the universities.

Although there was a sizable increase in the *number* of women attending the universities, the proportional increase relative to males was slight. Their entrance into the labor force has evidently increased, from a variety of news reports, and there appears to be a fair amount of consciousness-raising, especially among the educated classes of women.[34]

A number of factors in recent years have contributed to a more liberal outlook. The International Women's Year brought a considerable amount of attention to women leaders from Pakistan, and especialy Begum Bhutto, who led the Pakistan delegation. This was followed by a national conference on the status of women held in Lahore in the fall of 1975.

Before the last political campaign Begum Bhutto was active in the social welfare and education fields, constantly organizing or attending meetings and lending her support to many causes in these fields. Her daughter Benazir has also taken part in the electoral politics of the country. Both have been placed under house arrest from time to time for violating martial law orders against political activity. As we know, Begum Bhutto has been serving as acting chairman of the P.P.P. after her husband's execution.

But the Bhutto women have not held a monopoly on political activity. It is interesting to note that Begum Wali Khan has also served as acting head of her husband's party, and played a very important role in gaining his release from jail. And Begum Asghar Kahn has also been active in addressing rallies on behalf of her husband's political cause. Even women belonging to the more conservative camp (Jamaat-i-Islami) came out of seclusion to take an active part in some of the political campaigning, leading processions and organizing meetings.[35] One of the fears most frequently expressed by women who have been most heavily engaged in political activities in recent years has been the potential loss of the gains made in the area of family laws and the status of women. Ever since the family laws were liberalized more than a decade ago, there has been a continuing struggle on the part of liberal women leaders to maintain their gains against conservative religious and political leaders who have attempted to have the liberalized laws rescinded.

As might be expected, almost all of the above political acitivity has taken place and will continue to take place in the towns and cities of the nation. As education becomes increasingly available to women, it is reasonable to expect that they will not only enter the labor force in larger numbers, but become increasingly active on the political scene. And since the colleges and universities are located in the larger towns and cities, we can expect political activism among women to increase. Perhaps they will become the new and active minority political group seeking recognition for their felt needs— alongside the ethnic groups that continue to play an important role on the political scene.

5. *Mass Education and Mass Culture*: In spite of the fact that it is the elite (college and university educated) which are most consciously sensitive about their rights, and clamor for the few good job opportunities (which, in turn, results in "provincialism") one still cannot deny the importance of educating the masses. It is through mass education that a mass culture can develop in a country where the problem of national identity is acute. Common national symbols, language, outlook, values and traditions can be created with the use of the radio, television, newspapers, books, films, and the classroom. The armed forces, civil service and the universities can also serve as good places for developing national integration.

Conclusion

To sum up, one can say that with the rapid population growth rate in Pakistan and the crowding of large urban centers with educated, unemployed and detribalized rural migrants, we find the ingredients which may make the situation ethnically explosive. However, the numbers of migrants with very strong tribal and *biraderi* (kin-group) feelings and affiliation are now for the first time moving toward an expanded loyalty to their linguistic group—beyond biraderi and the tribe. The authors feel that if these feelings of loyalty to biraderi, the tribe and then to their linguistic group are properly channeled, then these feelings may be extended to the nation-state, Pakistan. In other words, one can look at the phenomenon of provincialism a little more positively if we see that it is just the last step before the final one in achieving a true nationalism. Still, one cannot overemphasize the importance of more planning in the growth of cities and population growth if the politics of discontent on an ethnic basis is to be reduced. Only in this way the ethnicization of politics and the economy can be reduced considerably in Pakistan.

Notes

1. Government of Pakistan, *Census of Pakistan*, Karachi, Ministry of Home Affairs, 1961, Vol. I, II–11.

2. *Ibid.*, p. II–16.

3. William Petersen, *Population*, New York, Macmillan, 1975, p. 471.

4. The influence of the 20 largest cities will be an important topic of discussion in the latter part of this paper.

5. Shahid J. Burki, "Migration, Urbanization and Politics in Pakistan," in W. Howard Wriggins and James F. Guyot, *Population, Politics and the Future of Southern Asia*, New York, 1973, pp. 147–189.

6. Government of Pakistan, *Census of Pakistan*, Karachi, Ministry of Home Affairs, 1961, Vol. 1, p. IV–30.

7. *Ibid.*, IV–33.

8. Lee L. Bean, "The Population of Pakistan: An Evaluation of Recent Statistical Data," in Howard Wriggins, ed., *Pakistan in Transition*, Islamabad, University of Islamabad Press, 1975, p. 2.

9. *Ibid.*, p. 3.

10. Richard F. Nyrop, *Area Handbook for Pakistan* (Washington, D.C.: American University, 1975), pp. 111–125.

11. *The New York Times* published several articles on this development in a number of March, 1971 issues.

12. Nyrop, *op. cit.*

13. George A. Theodorson and Achilles G. Theodorson, *A Modern Dictionary of Sociology*, New York, Crowell, 1969, p. 340.

14. For a full discussion of his theory of regionalism, see his article "Regions, Subjective and Objective: Their Relation to the Study of Modern Indian History and Society." Robert I. Crane, ed., Durham, Duke University Committee on South Asian Studies, 1966, pp. 5–37.

15. Government of Pakistan, *Census of Pakistan Sind and Khairpur State*, Karachi, Ferozesons, 1951, Vol. 6, p. 108.

16. *Ibid.*

17. *Ibid.*, p. 46.

18. *Ibid.*, p. 48.

19. Wriggins and Guyot, *op. cit.*, p. 15.

20. Ayub Khan's land reform made this possible.

21. *Dawn*, Karachi, July 5–7, 1972.

22. Wriggins and Guyot, *op. cit.*

23. J. Henry Korson, *Contemporary Problems of Pakistan*, Leiden, E. J. Brill Co., 1974.

24. Korson, *op. cit.*, p. 128.

25. For an excellent and detailed analysis of the situation in the minority provinces of Pakistan, refer to Hafeez Malik, "Problems of Regionalism in Pakistan," in W. Howard Wriggins, *Pakistan in Transition*, Islamabad, University of Islamabad Press, 1975, pp. 60–132.

26. Korson, *op. cit.*, pp. 128–130.

27. Shahid Javed Burki, "Migration, Urbanization and Politics in Pakistan," in Wriggins and Guyot, *op. cit.*, pp. 147–189.

28. Lee L. Bean, et al., *Population Projections for Pakistan, 1960–2000*, Karachi, Pakistan Institute of Development Economics, Jan. 1968, p. 30.

29. Hafeez Malik, *op. cit.*

30. Manzooruddin Ahmed, "The Political Role of the Ulema in Pakistan," *Journal of Islamic Studies*, Islamabad Institute of Islamic Research, 1967. Note also that both JUI and JI had joined the Zia cabinet during 1978–79, a move which opened a new chapter in Pakistan's history because it was the first time that the ulema became the "power holders" in significant numbers.

31. *Ibid.*

32. Maulana Maudoodi, *Birth Control and Islam*, (translated by Khurshid Ahmed), Karachi, 1958.

33. Fazlur Rahman, a former Director, Research Council on Islamic Ideology, Karachi, is also famous for his liberal views about other issues such as interest on money.

34. Ali Akhtar Baig, "Greater Number of Women Opt for University Education," *Overseas Weekly Dawn*, Karachi, Herald Press, Jan. 22, 1978, p. 11.

35. *The New York Times*, March 13, 1977.

The Policy Logic of Land Reforms in Pakistan
RONALD J. HERRING

Introduction

It is no secret that land reforms in Pakistan have been neither transformational in conceptualization nor effective in practice. Yet both Ayub Khan and Zulfikar Ali Bhutto began their periods of rule with dramatic announcements of land reform. This situation is superficially paradoxical: why should new regimes immediately promulgate "fundamental" agrarian reforms in a nation in which political power has traditionally rested with the landed elite and other propertied classes (and their offspring in the upper echelons of the administrative and military apparatus)? Agrarian reforms worthy of the name transform rural society through alternations in the property structure and production relations, redistributing power and privilege. Such transformations have not been the objectives of regimes in Pakistan, stirring rhetoric to the contrary.

The paradox is superficial because agrarian reforms, like all public policy, are in part a shadow play, serving to distribute political cues, manipulate powerful symbols, all to the end of evoking or maintaining support and compliance from politically active groups, while neutralizing real or potential opposition. Thus it is precisely because Pakistan has remained a society with extreme inequalities of power and privilege, rooted in rural areas in differential access to and control of the land, the primary means of production, that land reforms are a central political issue. The vital elements of symbolic politics — powerful dramaturgy, villains and victims, social justice and modernization — are the very core of land reform. Land as the base of the national economy and land control as the cultural emblem of rural standing, authority and power, privilege and opportunity, charge the policy questions of agrarian reform with special energy and emotion.

The experience of Pakistan with land reforms has been relatively limited. Of the three policy models of land reform which have been dominant in planning theory, political rhetoric and (to a lesser extent) actual policy in the subcontinent, Pakistan has seriously purused only one. These policy models are: (a) tenure reform, in which the state intervenes in and regulates the terms of contracts between landlords and tenants, typically by setting statutory limits on rental exactions and guaranteeing the tenant security of land use rights, (b) the ceiling-redistributive model, in which the state sets a limit, or ceiling, on the amount of land any individual or family can own or possess, appropriating ("resuming") land in excess of the ceiling, with or without compensation to the landowner, for redistribution to landless peasants (sharecroppers, laborers, etc.), (c) land to the tiller, in which landlordism and ground rent are abolished, making the actual cultivator the owner of the land he tills. In various forms and combinations, the subcontinent has seen all of these reform models.[1] In Pakistan, only the ceiling model has been seriously tried.

Taking the South Asian region as a whole, the trend in land reforms has been toward progressive reduction of rural inequalities — at least in law. Tenants have in theory been granted more of the "bundle of rights" we think of as ownership and legal ceilings on land ownership have been legislated and progressively reduced (the notable exception being Ayub Khan's *raising* of the ceiling in East Pakistan while simultaneously imposing a ceiling on West Pakistan's landlords). That practice on the ground has not followed legislation on the books is so clearly established and understood that one need not dwell on the point. The purpose of this chapter is to explicate the policy logic of land reforms in Pakistan, meaning primarily the policy logic of imposing ceilings on land ownership. How were the reforms justified? What does the policy logic imply about the official view of rural society — how does it work and how *should* it work — and about the broader framework of development strategy within which land reforms operate?

That the policy logic of land reform correlates only imperfectly, if at all, with the political motives of ruling elites must be stressed. This chapter is concerned primarily with policy logic, though insights into the politics of land reform flow naturally from comparisons between the justificatory framework of the policy logic and the empirical reality of reform legislation and implementation. For example, the fact that no significant land reforms were made in (West) Pakistan prior to Ayub Khan's 1959 ceiling legislation, contrary to the policy recommendations of the Muslim League's Agrarian Reform Committee and the Planning Board, simultaneously corroborates and is explained by independent evidence of the overwhelming political power of the landlords in the early independence period.

Political constraints on policy are decisive, but policy logic is important in illustrating how those who have power justify their actions to those who matter, both internally and externally. Policy logic thus provides insights into the legitimation functions of the state and regime perceptions of the normative structure on which their authority rests. My argument is that policy logic in Pakistan has supported far more radical and fundamental land reforms than have been legislated or implemented. The gaps between the policy logic and the reality on the ground should be understood in terms of the political power of the rural elite (and the landed interests of elite groups other than landlords) and the imperatives of a full-blown capitalist development strategy.

A capitalist development strategy condones, indeed demands, changes in rural production relations when "feudalism" (as the official rhetoric has termed it) permeates the agrarian social structure: feudal parasites must be replaced with progressive agrarian entrepreneurs. But the attack on the feudal parasites is tempered by the political power of the great landlords and by the core logic of capitalist development: the commitment to inequalities as functional for generating growth, the commitment to unlimited accumulation of private property in the means of production. The resulting contradictions—between imperatives of political stability, national integration, and agricultural modernization on the one hand and the political reality of landlord power and the normative commitment to private property and individual incentives on the other—are reflected in contradictions in policy logic and implementation which have precluded serious agrarian reform in Pakistan. The policy logic supported a frontal assault on the landed magnates; the actual policies have settled for a compromised and qualified nudging of landlords via policy cues and manipulation of symbols in the direction of modernizing and rationalizing the rural economy and polity. Whether future regimes will be able to get away with such temporizing on the agrarian question is moot, but doubtful.

Good Landlords and Bad Landlords

Perhaps the most common adjective attached to "landlord" by advocates of land reform in political and planning documents is "parasitic." The clear implication is that landlords do not do whatever they should do in return for the share of the social surplus which they appropriate. The colonial rulers of South Asia typically distinguished between "good landlords," who invested in the land and provided services to tenants, and "bad landlords," who did neither.[2] Indeed, a major thrust of colonial land revenue and "settlement" policy was designed to create a class of progressive landlords patterned after the English gentry.[3] Nationalist thinking in British India elaborated and developed the critique of the bad landlord; the word "zamindar" (literally "landholder") came to *mean* the parasitic and collaborationist landlord, though there were of course many landlords who were not "zamindars" by title. Jawaharlal Nehru, for example, argued in 1928: "To our misfortune, we have zamindars everywhere, and like a blight they have prevented all healthy growth . . ."[4]

The critique of bad landlords on social and economic grounds was based on the confluence of specific normative and empirical arguments: empirically the landlords were held to be nonproductive and normatively this nonproductive status delegitimized the landlord's claim to rent. In some formulations, nonproductive was escalated to counter-productive. Reflecting a major strand of Congress thinking, Nehru asked rhetorically:

> What does he (the zamindar) do to get his share or deserve it? Nothing at all or practically nothing. He just takes a big share in the produce—his rent—without helping in any way the work of production. He thus becomes a fifth wheel in the coach—not only unnecessary, but an actual encumberance, and a burden on the land.[5]

Nehru termed "the land problem" the "outstanding and overwhelming problem of India" and felt that the "feudal relics" obstructed not only agricultural but also industrial growth, and thus the fundamental prospects of the new nation.[6] Thus the "bad landlord" was considered not only parasitic, but a curse on the rural populace, a dragging "fifth wheel" as Nehru put it.

The same intellectual currents ran in Pakistan, though not so broad or deep. The Hari (sharecropper) Enquiry Committee of Sind (1947–48) quoted approvingly an unnamed American economist to the effect that "next to war, pestilence and famine, the worst thing that can happen to a rural community is absentee landlordism."[7] Indeed, this particular quotation has had fairly wide currency in South Asian agrarian reform circles. But the core meaning of absentee did not necessarily denote physical absence from the land; indeed, the Hari Enquiry Committee noted:

> Absentee landlordism can take two forms, namely, a landlord who does not reside on his lands and a landlord who, though he may reside on his lands, takes little or no interest in its management and development.[8]

The Committee argued that such functionless landlords leave the tenants without aid or direction and subject them to harassment by intermediaries— the *kamgars* of Sind, for example—who manage the land and extract rents.

The landlord who abdicates his responsibilities on the land forfeits his moral claim to privilege in this normative model. The Hari Enquiry Committee stated:

> The advantageous position of the big land-owners in relation to the *haris* which they employ demands that all such zamindars in virtue of the privileges which they enjoy should take a personal and paternal interest and adopt an enlightened and progressive attitude in matters concerned with the welfare of their *haris*.[9]

The good landlord of Sind was thought to be the *zamindar* "of sufficient enterprise and sense of duty to take a paternal interest in his *haris*. . . ."[10] The

landlord class was thus subdivided in official thinking. The West Pakistan
Land Reforms Commission stated in 1959: "We admit that there are progressive landlords, but they are in a minority."[11] This bifurcation, and the
argument that not all landlords are parasitic, opened the possibility of land
reforms with transformational aspects, designed to change undeserving landlords into deserving ones, which would avoid the political costs of a full
confrontation with the landlord class.

The notion of what a landlord should do to deserve his share has varied
over time. In the traditional setting, the "good landlord" provided a range of
functions as the landlord-tenant nexus was frequently of the patron-client
form. The modern "good landlord" was not expected to peform the diffuse,
personalistic non-economic functions of a traditional pattern, but *was* expected to provide such services as modern farm managerial inputs, extension
services and information for technical change, working capital, fixed capital
improvements (tubewells, e.g.), and so on. The traditional good landlord
was to be a patron, the modern good landlord to be an entrepreneur.

The services of the traditional "good landlord" seem to have declined
over time in South Asia for a number of reasons. Perhaps the cynical view has
merit: as courts and a new administrative apparatus in the colonial period
began to enforce contracts and uphold the landlords' property claims, the
necessity of good patron-client relations diminished and with it the services
provided by patrons.[12] Likewise, the extension of the administrative systems
(and political parties in some areas) into rural society obviated the need for
some landlord services.[13] At any rate, at the time of independence, there was
a feeling in both bourgeois ("modernist") intellectual and Marxist circles in
South Asia that the traditional "good landlord" had become parasitic and
anachronistic. The following quotation expresses the view of a leading communist theoretician, twice Chief Minister of the Indian state of Kerala,
E.M.S. Namboodiripad:

> In mediaeval days, landlordism was a social, political, and cultural institution, as
> well as economic. But shorn of all these functions, the Malabar *janmis* (landlords)
> today are only dead corpses of their own forefathers . . .

After figuring the total rent paid by tenants to landlords, he concludes:

> If the payment of this amount goes hand in hand with some social service,
> rendered by the landlords as a class, it would be quite justified.

But contemporary landlords, "shorn of all these functions," the diffuse
traditional social services, must justify their rent by providing economic
services. Namboodiripad asked:

> But does it (the landlord class) justify its economic importance by performing any
> useful function in that sphere as does the entrepreneur in modern capitalist indus-

try? Does it provide capital, either short-term or long-term, to the cultivator who needs it? Does it construct and improve irrigation sources and prevent the preventible drought? Does it carry on any research work to make agriculture up to date and scientific?[14]

After concluding that the landlord class does not perform these (or other) economic functions, and certainly no longer has the social, cultural, political responsibilities of an earlier time, Namboodiripad argues for the abolition of landlordism. There is an interesting point in this conclusion; Namboodiripad's Marxist vision of what modern landlords *should* do to justify rent is the same as that in the avowedly capitalist planning circles of Pakistan. Both agree that the owners of large sections of land must justify their privileges through performance of modern, scientific agricultural functions since the performance of traditional duties has become anachronistic. The disagreement comes in what should be done.

Official policy logic in Pakistan has sought to justify land reforms as policy tools, along with powerful economic incentives, to transform the "feudal" rent-receivers into progressive agricultural capitalists (while simultaneously continuing the colonial policy of putting lands into the hands of new potential entrepreneurs: civil servants and military officers, for example). The "good landlord" is explicitly recognized as the rural counterpart of the urban entrepreneur. This policy model illustrates the recognition in both bourgeois and Marxist thinking the "feudal" relations in agriculture, already disintegrating, must be thoroughly rooted out; the capitalist revolution in agriculture is recognized as a necessary historical stage and a contemporary imperative.

Land Ceilings in Pakistan: The Normative Model

The justification for a ceiling-redistributive reform has as its normative core the notion that existing concentrations of land are unjust. Such an argument is buttressed by the claim that existing landlords do not in some sense *deserve* the special privilege accorded by land control, having come upon their wealth by dubious or even illegitimate means, but the normative case is much more elaborate than a mere rejection of the legitimacy of the landlords' claim to the land. Ofen, the argument is couched in terms of the scarcity of agricultural land and the pressure of population on the land, resulting in a situation in which oligopolistic control of land reources has unfair consequences. The ceiling-redistributive model thus has a double-edge justification: it seems unjust that the primary, and limited, resource of rural society should be concentrated in the hands of a tiny fraction of the population, however they obtained it, and it seems unfair that some—the landless—should be reduced to the levels of poverty, hunger and deprivation which result from the skewed distribution. This double-edged argument can be made in non-economic terms as well—the extreme concentration of land bestows inordinate political and social power on a few whereas a great number—the landless—lack even minimal access to social standing or political rights.

The broader argument for land ceilings includes an economic efficiency justification: the largest estates are too large for proper management and are less than optimally exploited; land reform is thus necessary for production increases. This argument, too, has a double edge. Not only are the largest estates too large to be efficient, but the smallest farms are too small to be efficient; a redistribution creating economically-sized small farms would arguably increase production.[15]

The interaction of these factors was expressed by the West Pakistan Land Reforms Commission (1959) in arguing for ceiling legislation. After reviewing the statistics on land concentration, the Commission noted:

These statistics in themselves do not reflect the real situation. They do reveal vast disparities of wealth and incomes in the rural society, but disparities in wealth are not necessarily a social or economic evil in a system based on private ownership of means of production. It is the peculiar social, economic, and political consequences flowing from what amounts to an institutional monopoly of land in a primarily agrarian society, which is of key importance for our purposes, and we proceed to consider these consequential effects as they operate in the field of landlord-tenant relations and determine the attitudes and behaviors of both the landlord and the tenant.[16]

These effects are then listed. We may note here the extraordinary force given land tenure variables in the policy logic of the paradigm:

(1) Social effects: "Those who do not own land are relegated to a socially inferior position with all the disabilities of that position."

(2) Economic effects:

    (a) Tenants are too impoverished to invest; landlords have the wealth but lack incentives or initiative to invest.

    (b) Tenant incentives are vitiated by the rental arrangements.

    (c) There are diseconomies of small scale.

The net economic effect was stated to be stagnation in total production and a decline in per capita production.

(3) Political effects: "The right of franchise . . . becomes an idle weapon in the hands of many . . . as political power continues to remain with the privileged few."

"An individual may belong to a free society, but if he is economically dependent upon another he is seldom a free agent to exercise his political rights."[17]

The policy logic of the committee is clearly questionable; there is a marked discrepancy between their analysis of the problem (which is quite accurate and disturbing) and the extent and type of response. If the landlord-tenant organization of production results in microeconomic situations which decrease productivity (and the Committee quotes Alfred Marshall to show that this is the case), then size alone is not the problem, and a ceiling is not the answer; a solution would lie in changing the microeconomic situation of the tenants (reduction of rents, for example, a policy explicitly rejected) or vesting land in the tiller. Likewise, if landlessness deprives an individual of his or her fundamental social and political dignity and rights, than sufficient surplus land must be appropriated to eradicate "economic dependence" through imposition of a very low ceiling and a radical redistribution; this the Committee did not seriously consider.

The Committee did not draw the logical conclusions from its inquiry because in the existing political climate to have done so would have been an exercise in futility. Indeed, the *justification* for a ceiling-redistributive reform provides the very reasons for the inadequacy of the policy model, that is, the powerlessness and dependence of the rural poor and the great concentrations of power—political, social, and economic—in the hands of the landed elite.

A skewed distribution of land ownership would not necessarily yield the abject social, political, and economic dependence described by official reports, nor the tenurial disincentives, provided that (a) small holders where economically viable, and were owners, not sharecroppers, and (b) the man-land ratio was such that the landless were not totally dependent on owners for their livelihood. Small holders may be influenced by large owners, but the total dependence which results from lack of independent access to the means of production would not characterize the agrarian system.[18]

Likewise, tenurial defects associated with low productivity are related not to the large size of the owners' holdings, but to extreme competition for opportunities on the land, producing high rents and insecure tenure, as illustrated by more densely populated areas of South Asia such as Sri Lanka and Bangladesh, where all of the social, economic, and political evils mentioned in ceiling models exist without any significant concentration of land in huge holdings. Certainly the available technology, combined with the extremely large size of many estates, made sharecropping the most likely organization of production in Pakistan, but it is less clear that a ceiling on holdings would eliminate the evils attributed to share tenancy. Indeed, the vast majority of Pakistan's share tenants operate holdings for owners of a relatively small size, far below the ceiling limits of the Ayub Khan or Bhutto reforms.[19]

A second issue in the normative case for the ceiling-redistributive policy model is the legitimacy of the original mode of acquisition of the property.

Governments preceding the British Rule 'found it convenient to secure the sword of the brave and the prayer of the pious man, to pacify the deposed chiefs and to reward powerful servants by assigning to them the Ruler's share of the produce of the land in particular villages or tracts.'[22]

The policy was of course continued by the British.

Logically, a number of policy responses to the agrarian defects specified by this normative model were possible. The most direct possible response was a land-to-the-tiller policy. But there were important normative concerns, and of course overwhelming political constraints, which diverted the policy logic into other channels.

The Planning Board of Pakistan, in the *First Five-Year Plan,* noted that East Pakistan had instituted a radical reform in that "it seeks to abolish the institution of landlordship." The Board goes on to justify its recommendation of preserving the existing social organization of production:

We do not advocate the drastic step of abolishing land-ownership in West Pakistan, as it will generate tensions and instability and create a number of difficult problems. Private property is a recognized institution in the community because of the values it enshrines for the individual and social development.[23]

The Land Reforms Commission established by Ayub Khan in 1958 reaffirmed the position. In arguing for regluation of the relations between tenants and landlords — "the institutional framework within which land is used . . . (which) influences . . . opportunities and incentives, enterprise and innovation, and capital formation and productive investment" — the Commission stated:

For the healthy growth of the economy it is essential that private ownership of the means of production is accompanied by free competition and equal opportunities.[24]

Given the prior acceptance of private property in land, "tenancy is inevitable." However:

There is nothing inherently wrong with the institution of tenancy, but if there is no proper adjustment in the terms of tenancy, production incentives are adversely affected . . .[25]

The normative basis of the ceiling model in Pakistan was thus: (a) private property is the legitimate organizing principle for society, particularly because of its provision for individual development, political liberty, etc., (b) radical reform entails serious social costs, particularly with regard to the value of stability, (c) one dominant existing manifestation of private property in agriculture — i.e., landlordism — thus cannot be directly attacked or abolished, but must be transformed along lines congruent with modern, and capitalist, notions of efficiency and rationality.

The policy implications were certainly not laissez-faire, however. The Government of Pakistan in the mid-1950's faced two serious agrarian problems. One was the critical food situation, the other was the unquestioned abuses of landlordism and its lack of agricultural dynamism. The Planning Board concluded that protection of tenants by the Government was necessary in the short-run because of landlord abuses — "the ugliness of prevailing conditions" — but the normative model for the future was classically liberal. Through operation of the ceiling-redistributive model, tenants would be freed from the monopoly hold of landlords on the land and would gain "equality, opportunity, dignity, and freedom." Finally:

We hope that in course of time their relations will come to approximate those prevaliing in the industrially advanced countries. [26]

The normative model is thus that of 19th Century liberalism — relations between capital and labor are to be contractual, the result of free bargaining between (legal) equals. As this equality of status is achieved, the Planning Board noted, there would be less need for government intervention on the side of tenants.

This model — that once concentrations of land were broken up, the government's role in tenant-landlord affairs should revert to a laissez-faire position — was dominant in official policy thinking during the Ayub period. After the reforms of 1959 supposedly achieved this equalization, the Land Commission reported in 1966:

Tenants, who do not discharge their obligations and who do not utilize the land as is customary in the locality, should have no sympathy and cannot be considered worthy of protection from a Government, which is so much interested in the restoration of normal relations between all classes of population and increasing agricultural production. [27]

The ceiling reforms were thus *justified* as moving towards those conditions presupposed by liberal capitalist ideology: contractual bargaining between equals, just as it was presumed to be "in the industrially advanced countries." When this is achieved, rural stability and harmony, as well as agricultural growth, would characterize the agrarian system and the government could revert to its normal laissez-faire role.

The Logic of Setting the Ceiling

The problem of where to set the ceiling depends on the justification for the measure and what it is meant to accomplish. This problem is complicated by the seeming incongruity between restriction or confiscation of landed property and a laissez-faire or protective policy toward industrial and commercial property. How can a case be made for land ceilings in this context? The Planning Board of Pakistan in the *First Five-Year Plan* recognized the difficulty and put forward the following position:

The argument is frequently advanced that if concentration of land ownership is undesirable and in conflict with the social policies of our country, so must also be concentration of ownership of other forms of wealth—factories, urban property, industrial shares, government securities or cash. We consider that the ownership of land is clearly distinguished from other forms of wealth. Landowners who do not manage and cultivate the land themselves, with very few exceptions do little to increase its productivity. By contrast, the owners of most other forms of wealth are usually progressive and provide increasing employment by their activities. They serve an essential purpose in a dynamic economy.[28]

The normative position here is that concentrations of wealth are justified if the result is dynamic economically, creating employment and increasing productivity. In agriculture, this distinction falls between those who actively manage and supervise their lands and those who merely live on the rental income, the absentee rentiers. In both academic and political treatments, this line is said to divide agricultural capitalists from feudal landlords, or entrepreneurs from "social parasites."

The implications for land reform are then clear. Because "feudal" rent-receivers acquired their properties by dubious means and received vast quantities of unearned income therefrom over the years, it was argued that some of their land could be confiscated without compensation. The objective of the land reform, given this normative stance, should be to convert such landowners into rural counterparts of urban entrepreneurs.

Once the desirability of a ceiling is established, what empirical and normative arguments are available to establish rationally the level of the ceiling? Total confiscation—the literal "abolition of feudalism" so frequently mentioned in planning documents—was ruled out both on normative grounds (as private property was an accepted first principle) and for political considerations.[29] Moreover, abolition of the great feudal lords would, in the official view, deprive rural areas of their "natural leadership." Thus the Planning Board recommended a ceiling of 150 acres of irrigated land, 300 acres semi-irrigated, and 450 acres rainfed *(barani)*. The logic was that this ceiling would provide "suitable units of management" for landowners willing to manage their own lands, but would not discourage enterprise. Specific exemptions were recommended for what were in effect primarily capitalist agricultural enterprises—orchards, plantations and estates "already being cultivated with mechanical means."[30]

Despite the cogent official logic in planning circles establishing the case for a mild ceiling reform and redistribution, no purely political regime n Pakistan dared to move against the rural elite. Not until the onset of political immobilism and national crisis, and the imposton of martial law, did the policy logic find its way into law. Almost immediately after seizing power in 1958, Ayub Khan appointed a commission to recommend land reform measures. The Land Reforms Commission for West Pakistan, in setting the ceiling between 500 and 1,000 acres, noted that "looked at from the point of view of social justice alone" the ceiling "will appear large."[31] This certainly seems possible, as more than three-fourths of the agricultural population owned less than 15 acres at the time.[32] Considerations based on social justice were tempered by other imperatives in the policy logic. Specifically, the Commission argued:

> But in determining the extent of the ceiling, social justice has not been the only criterion before us. Even if we were to recommend a much lower ceiling than what we have suggested, the surplus land which would have become available for redistribution among landless tenants would have been too small to secure for each of them a subsistence farm unit. The ends of social justice, in the sense of securing land for the entire landless population, thus being almost unattainable, what we thought was prudent was to fix the ceiling at a level which will on the one hand eradicate the feudalistic elements from the existing tenure structure, and on the other, by causing the minimum disturbance of the social edifice lead to a harmonious changeover and at the same time, by providing incentives at all levels, conduce to greater production.[33]

Evidently, social justice was not taken to mean equality but rather the right of all farmers to own a subsistence holding; even such a restricted notion of justice was, however, unobtainable without setting a ceiling so low (at about 25 acres, by my rough calculations) that there would be "disturbance of the social edifice." In short, a lower ceiling was politically impracticable.[34] But aside from the political situation, the Commission argued that the goals of the land reform, the modernization of agriculture, would be frustrated through a low ceiling:

> We are also anxious that farming as a profession should remain sufficiently lucrative to attract and engage suitable talent on a wholetime basis. It should provide to those engaged in it a standard of living which will compare favorably with that obtainable in other professions. Above all it should offer opportunities for enterprise and leadership which, through precept and example will provide a point of contact between rural conservatism and ignorance and modern ideas and technology.[35]

The conceptualization here is remarkably similar to the British colonial model of a modernizing gentry leading a backward peasantry. The reference group is the top of the rural elite, the professionals, men whose style of life, tastes, and needs preclude occupations in agriculture except under conditions of substantial rewards considerably greater than those available to the average cultivator.

The ceiling policy model had avowedly political objectives as well. A genuine laying of the groundwork for rural democracy through land reform, freeing dependent tenants from their lords, would have been possible only if the ceiling had been set very low, allowing a great deal of land to be redistributed and converting most tenants into owners. Such a low ceiling was politically and normatively ruled out. But there were other political objectives in the reform model. An official report published when Ayub Khan was still in power stated that "the reforms were considered by him to be an absolute necessity for the survival of the system . . ."[36] In announcing the reforms, Ayub Khan stressed their role in creating a politically stable society.[37] The fear for the stability of the system was not so much fear of the political consequences of landlessness and discontent among the rural poor, as was the case in ceiling legislation in India and Sri Lanka in the early 1970's, but was a recognition that the great feudal lords had wielded so much political power that an integrated and stable center was an impossibility.[38] Breaking these concentrations of power through an attack on their landed base was an acknowledged part of the policy model.

With a very high ceiling and numerous loopholes (exemptions, gift and transfer provisions, etc.), the 1959 land reform (Martial Law Regulation 64)[39] did not fundamentally alter the agrarian structure even in theory. Indeed, official publications justifying the reform stated that "even the landlords have benefited from these reforms . . . the Reforms Scheme has not reduced their economic or personal status." The basis for this position is the official claim that the reforms forced landlords to intensify production and thus to "function as a positive factor rather than to remain a negative one," arguing that the feudal lords could not have been happy with their "habits of a drone."[40]

It is difficult to assess this claim empirically. Certainly some larger holders have dramatically modernized, participating fully in the tractor-tubewell and seed-fertilizer technological changes of the mid-1960's which continue today. But other, more powerful, factors were at work, such as the extremely favorable terms on which agricultural capital was made available, including both direct and indirect subsidies (exchange rates, credit terms, price supports, etc.), the absence of an agricultural income tax, and so on.[41] The independent effect of land reform, while not likely to have been great, is virtually impossible to determine.

However, it is worth noting that in 1968 there were 1,495 tractor owners in Pakistan who owned more than 500 acres; these landowners had an *average* of 1,317 acres each and owned 15 percent of the private tractors in Pakistan.[42] While this is a significant concentration of mechanized capital, the number of tractors per owned acre is the lowest of any farm group. Whereas smaller owners possessed a private tractor for every 21 to 150 acres, depending on size of holding, the great landowners averaged only by a little more than one tractor per 1,000 acres owned, not a very intensive use of mechanization. Indeed, that level of tractorization suggests most really huge owners continued to cultivate the bulk of their land with tenants and bullocks. It was the smaller owners who adopted the new tractor technology on a more intensive scale.[43] Owners of more than 200 acres owned about 78 percent of all land held by tractor owners in 1968, but owned only 34 percent of the tractors; owners of between 26 and 100 acres owned only 9.5 percent of the land but 35 percent of the tractors.[44]

These figures are of course not decisive, as land quality and percentage of waste vary by size of holding, but do suggest that the huge landlords have not been the most aggressive agricultural entrepreneurs. That conclusion is bolstered by data on tubewell ownership. Of the tractor owners, those with more than 200 acres of land owned only 14 percent of the tubewells, but 78 percent of the land. Tractor owners with between 13 and 100 acres owned 63 percent of the tubewells on only 21.5 percent of the land. It is thus difficult to argue that the 1959 reforms fully succeeded in creating a class of leading agricultural entrepreneurs from the drone-like feudal landlords.[45]

Despite the contrary normative argument presented in earlier planning documents, compensation was paid the relatively few landlords who were unable to evade the ceiling and had some surplus appropriated. Compensation was paid at 10 times the rental value, capitalized, on a graduated scale inversely proportional to size of holding; this was felt to represent the "economic" or market value.[46] Because of the various loopholes, only 1,902,788 acres was resumed (about 3.9 percent of the land owned) even according to obviously inflated Government estimates, representing about one-fourth of the land in holdings greater than 500 acres each.[47] But even these figures exaggerate the actual impact; because owners were allowed to select the area they would retain, a great deal of the land resumed, and for which compensation was paid, was waste land. In many cases, this was a boon to the landlords.[48] Only 823,062 acres, or 43.2 percent of the total resumed area, was cultivated land; only 537,457 acres, or 28.2 percent of the total area resumed was tenanted land. Despite the negligible benefit to tenants, the burden on the public was significant; compensation to landlords was officially figured as Rs. 89,180,674.13; the annual interest on this amount was Rs. 3,346,669.05[49]

Tenants who received land—and there are yawning discrepancies in official claims as to the number benefited—had to pay for the land, considerably blunting the redistributive impact. The amount owned by those who received land under the reforms totaled Rs. 34,821,620.12, or more than one-third of the total compensation payable. Since the tenants purchased the land at Rs. 8 per Produce Index Unit, and the landlord received from Rs. 1 to Rs. 5 per Produce Index Unit compensation at what was considered the market value, it seems that the "abolition of feudalism" was no bargain for the beneficiaries.[50] One official report noted that some tenants were paying installments to the government as new owners and paying rent to the landlord, still considering themselves "vassals."[51] Moreover, there is clear evidence of fraud and coercion operating at the village level to deprive even those tenants officially counted as beneficiaries from benefiting.

Though compensation payment blunted the 1959 reform's redistributive impact, and was contrary to earlier official policy logic, the Ayub regime considered compensation necessary because "expropriation without compensation would shatter the nation's faith in the institution of private property and enterprise, around which the country's economy was largely built."[53] Ironically enough, it was thus difficult even in theory to thoroughly root out fedualism because of the regime's firm commitment to capitalism.

Bhutto's Land Reforms

In introducing his own ceiling reforms in 1972, President Zulfikar Ali Bhutto termed Ayub Khan's 1959 reforms "a subterfuge," designed "to fool the people in the name of reform" with "all manner of concessions" to "buttress and pamper the landed aristocracy and fatten the favored few."[54] This description is of course rather accurate. Bhutto's own reforms were touted as a means for effecting "the eradication of the curse of feudalism and man's unjust overlordship of the good earth." The agrarian system, which Bhutto termed "oppressive" and "iniquitous," was to be transformed in such a way that the "life and fortunes of the common man" would be affected by the land reform more than by any other measure contemplated by the regime.[55]

In Bhutto's view, the 1959 reforms had eradicated neither feudalism nor oppression because of the concessions made to landed elites. The remaining concentrations had "stunted the growth of a just and harmonious social order;" moreover, it was still the case that "millions of those who produce the wealth of the nation struggle helplessly at a miserable level of existence."[56] Given this analysis, one would expect a rather dramatic reduction in the ceiling. In fact, Martial Law Regulation 115 of 1972 reduced the ceiling by about two-thirds, with no compensation to former owners, though the concentrations of land wealth considered acceptable were substantial relative to the situation of the majority.[57] The ceiling remained high relative to average holdings: with 87 percent of all operated holdings constituting less than 25 acres in 1972, and 44 percent less than 7.5 acres, the ceiling varied nominally between 150 and 300 acres, with a much higher *de facto* ceiling.[58]

The unwillingness to impose a ceiling closer to the average size of holding (about 13 acres) certainly reflects both the political constraints facing the regime,[59] given its power base, and Bhutto's own ambivalence concerning agrarian reform, but also represents an important continuity in the policy model of gentleman farmer capitalists as the vanguard of an agricultural revolution. President Bhutto explained that of the several factors which went into setting the ceiling, the "prime one" was that "agriculture should continue to be an attractive and profitable vocation." He continued:

The size of holding should permit maximum benefit of investment to enable productivity to increase. Enterprising and enlightened farmers should continue to live on the land and give agriculture the sense of purpose it deserves. For these compelling reasons, we are following exactly the same principle for the enlightened entrepreneur. We are as much against the ignorant and tyrannical landlord as we are against the robber barons of industry. We are as much for the creative and humane land-owner as we are for a productive and conscientious owner of industry.[60]

In explaining his ceiling reforms to industrialists in Karachi, Bhutto struck the same note. The ceiling was necessary to break up concentrations of wealth and redistribute some land, but

"at the same time, we have tried to preserve the incentives for the continuation of agriculture as an attractive and profitable vocation for the enterprising and the enlightened farmers."[61]

The policy logic is straight-forward, and shows marked continuity with the agrarian entrepreneurial model of Ayub Khan and the progressive gentry model of colonial administration with which Ayub's vision so clearly resonanted. The operative notion of social justice allows concentration of wealth in land, just as in industry, provided that the owners are "humane," "enlightened," and "enterprising." A very low ceiling, the logic runs, would not be conducive to agricultural progress because it would not attract, indeed would discourage, modern entrepreneurs; the maximum farm size must allow a standard of living comparable to that afforded by alternatives available to the representatives of the stratum which produces agricultural entrepreneurs, a stratum accustomed to high levels of income and privilege. The symbolic expression of the entrepreneurial good landlord is the tractor, and indeed the 1972 ceiling allowed an exemption averaging 50 acres per holding above the ceiling for purchase of a tractor or tubewell.[62]

The 1972 reforms also addressed the problem of converting parasitic bad landlords into entrepreneurial good landlords by mandating a more active role for landowners in production vis-à-vis tenants. Working capital expenses must be split between landlords and tenants and the landlord is made legally responsible for provision of seed in addition to payment of all land taxes and cesses. Thus, in theory, without changing the social organization of production, landlords can be made to play a greater role in modernizing agriculture. The payments legally constituted as obligations in Martial Law Regulation 115 would presumably force the absentee landlord to become involved in agriculture to protect his investment, if for no other reason. Moreover, just as significantly, MLR 115 did *not* regulate rents, nor were new mechanisms put in place to enforce the share rent limitations legislated in the early independence period but never enforced. The landlord was thus offered an additional incentive to modernize operations: additional capital expenditures could be recouped from tenants by raising the rent, and indeed landlords who install tubewells or purchase tractors frequently do just that.

Like the Ayub reforms which they so resemble, the Bhutto reforms did not either in theory or in practice alter the character of the agrarian system of Pakistan. More land was seized and distributed, more tenants were benefited, but the legislation merely nibbled at the margins of the rural distribution of power and privilege. The tenancy provisions in particular were left without effective enforcement mechanisms and were of importance mainly to those tenants already conscious enough and strong enough to question landlord prerogatives. As the 1977 elections approached, Bhutto dusted off the anti-feudal rhetoric and again promised to flay the privileged and powerful lords of the land. The result was, predictably, yet another ceiling reform, with a lower ceiling.

The "second round" of ceilings was announced by Prime Minister Bhutto on January 7, 1977. The ordinance significantly reduced the ceiling (by one third, to 100 acres of irrigated land or 200 acres of unirrigated land. Unlike MLR 115, however, the new ceiling legislation provided for compensation at the rate of Rs. 30 per Produce Index Unit for land resumed by the state. The reaffirmation of the principle of compensation must have offered some reassurance to propertied classes, but the confiscatory element in the new law was still significant, as the compensation falls far short of the market price of land.

The motive behind the second round was clearly tactical and political. The reforms were pushed through the National Assembly on the final day before dissolution for the elections. Bhutto's Pakistan Peoples' Party had played on the symbolism of land reforms as evidence of the party's commitment to the little person, to a redistributionist populism. Throughout the tenure of the regime, land reforms were offered as evidence of a commitment to "socialism." It is thus not surprising that a new round of land reforms, accompanied by introduction of a graduated agricultural income tax and exemption of small farmers from the land revenue tax, should appear on the eve of an important election campaign.

The latest round of reforms was heralded by banner headlines proclaiming: "New Deal for Farmers: Feudal System Comes to an End." The manipulation of symbols resembled that of the 1972 reform. Landlords were threatened with stiff penal sanctions, imprisonment, forfeiture of property (or all of the above) for evasion of the new law (though no one, to my knowledge, had been punished for violation of the earlier law, despite widely acknowledged evasion). The reforms promised social justice as demanded by the "ideology of Pakistan" (invoking the Quaid-i-Azam) and by the requirements of modern agriculture. Bhutto excoriated other politicians who talked of land reform as "dangling promises, raising bogus slogans, faking a concern for the poor only in order to achieve their selfish political ambitions."[63] (Oddly enough, considering the obvious mass political appeal intended in the address, the Prime Minister spoke in elaborate, complex and polished English, elaborating the main points only afterwards in Urdu.)

The Prime Minister defended his latest reforms—which promised to eliminate the last "vestiges of a feudal order in our society"—as "socially just and historically inevitable." There was the familiar concern with "balance," ensuring that the needs of agriculture were met while at the same time providing more land for the landless and further leveling rural inequalities. References in Bhutto's speech also make clear, however, the sense in which the reforms were a preemptive strike, stealing a march on opposition political parties which planned to promise land reforms in their election manifestoes.

The potential impact of the second round of land reforms is difficult to assess. The extreme political instability of the election and post-election period in Pakistan and the change of regimes following the coup have left the status of the reforms in doubt. The new regime informed the Federal Land Commission upon assuming power that the new reforms should be implemented. However, a recent call for a review of land reform implementation suggests that the picture has clouded over once again.[64] The current regime has, of course, shown no great enthusiasm for measures benefiting the poorer classes in general.

If the 1977 ceiling were to be enforced, not very many owners, nor very much land, would be affected. According to land revenue data collected immediately prior to promulgation of the ordinance (and indeed collected to gauge the net impact of the reforms), 46,831 owners possessed land in excess of 100 acres but less than 150 acres, and 56,254 owners possessed holdings greater than 150 acres. These 103,085 owners (a number vastly greater than that suggested by the census) would be allowed to retain in the aggregate 10,308,500 acres of irrigated land or 20,617,000 acres of unirrigated land. The actual amount possessed by the two groups together was 15,039,922 acres, of which only 3,430,045 acres was irrigated. Moreover, 6,157,488 acres of that total, more than one-third, was uncultivated land, and thus almost certainly contained a very high percentage of waste. Since owners are allowed by law to choose the land to be retained within the ceiling, it would seem that very little cultivable land would change hands even if the new law were rigorously enforced.

Such a result was to be expected, of course. Landowners have been aware for some time that land ceilings might be lowered. Indeed, though Bhutto at times promised an end to ceiling legislation, at other times he mentioned future reductions in the land ceiling. Thus rational cultivators have been redistributing (de jure) land among kin, selling land, and making adjustments to avoid losing land should the ceiling be lowered. The incremental logic of ceiling reforms has thus dissipated what little potential for agrarian transformation via land reform survived the mobilization of the landlords—both good and bad—to protect their class privileges—both traditional and modern—throughout the history of independent Pakistan.

Conclusion

Every regime in Pakistan must come to terms with two problems enmeshed in the agrarian system, one actual and chronic, the other merely potential, though increasingly real. The actual chronic problem is that the national economy rests on agriculture; a stagnant agricultural sector produces economic dislocations with severe political ramifications for ruling elites. The second problem is the threat that the direct producers in rural areas, or significant classes thereof, will reject the existing order. Concern about rural disaffection, "disharmony," and "instability" has run like a red thread through the policy logic of land reform in official circles in Pakistan. The two concerns are critically related: a dynamic agriculture can no more be built on a rebellious rural social base than can the colonial ideal of a "contented peasantry" be built on a base of material deprivation. The official policy logic of land reforms in Pakistan has been clear: agrarian relations must be adjusted, though adjusted within a constraining given set of property relations, in order to assure rural "harmony" and a dynamic agriculture simultaneously. A central element in that logic has been the necessity of converting bad landlords to good landlords, parasites to entrepreneurs; that there should be landlords at all has never been seriously challenged in governing circles, in direct contrast to the Indian experience.

But policy logic is one thing, politics another. The transformations suggested in the policy logic would seem politically attractive to ruling elites: it is clear that the interests of both Bhutto and Ayub (and the planning and administrative apparatus) would have been served well by the creation of an agrarian sector in which landlords were "humane" and "enterprising," supervising contented, diligent tenants. The policy means to such an end are not readily apparent, however. To be humane and enterprising does not sit well with every feudal lord, even if it can be demonstrated that higher profits from the land will result. The option of seriously cracking down on landlords has been precluded by the (perceived) balance of political forces; landlords are powerful people who do not like to be pushed around by the state, even by a state which is seeking to guarantee their long-term interests. No regime in Pakistan has mobilized the full power of the state, much less that of the agrarian underclass, to effect structural transformation via land reform. Instead, land reforms in Pakistan have served symbolic political functions and contributed to the arsenal of potential sticks in the array of carrots and sticks available to encourage agricultural rationalization and modernization while simultaneously pursuing regime consolidation ("political stability") and national integration.

Land reform as a symbolic stick (alongside the juicy, sweet carrots of subsidies, low taxes, tractor imports, etc.) can be seen as a signal to landlords that the Government (a) is serious about the need to increase production and circumvent or defuse agrarian unrest, (b) cannot be dominated whimsically by landlords as a personal toy, cannot be ignored or scorned, (c) has the power to fundamentally affect the life chances of individuals and is therefore eminently supportable on rational pragmatic grounds.[65] Simultaneously, and perhaps more importantly, the poicy logic and land reforms themselves serve as symbols to other social groups: a symbol to the left of progressive intent, a symbol of modernist values to urban groups and intellectuals, a symbol of forceful, decisive governance to potential opposition, a symbol of commitment to dynamism and modernity, within a framework of "moderation" and affirmation of class privilege, to industrialists.

The policy logic underlines and strengthens these symbols, signalling the values upon which the regime wishes to build its legitimacy while simultaneously revealing the normative structure of ruling class fractions. The policy logic of land reforms in Pakistan, in contrast to other nations of South Asia, stresses the desirability and possibility of a limited transformation: the landlord-tenant social organization of production on the vast estates was accepted (even institutionalized by Bhutto's tenancy reforms), but the great landlords were put on notice that they must be entrepreneurs, not parasites, good landlords, not brutal feudals, citizens of Pakistan, not autonomous *sardars* or *khans*. The extent to which the land reforms contributed to these goals—despite their loopholes, symbolic posturing, political compromises, and lax implementation—is one of excruciating complexity, fraught with obdurate methodological conundrums, but it also, fortunately, beyond the scope of this brief essay. One conclusion is certain: agrarian reform is on the agenda of Pakistani politics to stay; the regime which ignores the imperatives of social justice and rationalization of production embedded in the policy logic of land reform does so at its own peril.

Notes

1. For an elaboration of the notion of policy logic and the policy models of land reform which have appeared in South Asia, see Ronald J. Herring, "The Policy Logic of Elite Response to the Agrarian Question in South Asia," presented at the Annual Meetings of the Association for Asian Studies, Los Angeles, California, March 31, 1979.

2. For a classic example, see Malcolm L. Darling, *The Punjab Peasant In Prosperity and Debt* (London: 1932), pp. 270-271.

248 Contemporary Pakistan

3. See Eric Stokes, *The English Utilitarians and India* (Oxford: 1959); H.C.L. Merillat, *Land and the Constitution in India* (New York: 1970), p. 15; S. Ambirajan, *Classical Political Economy and British Policy in India* (Cambridge: 1978), especially Chapter 5.

4. The word *zamindar* literally means one who holds the land, but came to mean in political rhetoric a category of proprietor created by British revenue reforms, a pure intermediary, a rentier. It is critical to understand that the term was a land revenue category, defining rights to agricultural income and tax obligations, not a structural-functional category such as "rentier." In the Permanent Settlement areas of India, the *zamindars* were indeed rentiers, sometimes absentee, sometimes not, but both in the *zamindari* areas and elsewhere there were categories of landholders not termed "zamindars" whose tenurial position was equivalent to that of the majority of the *zamindars*. To confuse matters more, "zamindar" in the Punjab, Sind, and other areas could mean anything from a great feudal lord to a small proprietor who cultivated his own land *(kisan)*. Confusing as the revenue terminology is, the tenurial structures were not so esoteric as is often believed, and the major agrarian classes can be fit into generally applicable categories according to function—rentier, supervising landlord, owner-cultivator, leasee, mortgagee, protected tenant, tenant-at-will, attached laborer, casual laborer, etc.—and these categories are of course far more useful than the technical revenue terms. In some ways, the Zamindary Abolition Acts of India were merely revenue reforms, exchanging one group of landlords for another. Nehru's remarks in H.D. Malaviya, *Land Reforms in India* (Economic and Political Research Department, All India Congress Committee, Delhi: 1954) p. 20. On rural property and revenue systems, see B.H. Baden-Powell, *The Land Systems of British India* (Oxford: 1892) Vol. I, Chapters IV-V.

5. Malaviya, op. cit., p. 56.

6. *Ibid.*, pp. 55, 73.

7. Government of Sind, *Report of the Government Hari Enquiry Committee, 1947-48* (No date or place of publication is given; presumably Karachi), p. 19. This extremely interesting report is essentially an apologia for the Sind *zamindars,* and was written by a committee headed by a large *zamindar.* The "hari" is a sharecropper, a tenant-at-will.

8. *Ibid.*, p. 19.

9. *Ibid.*, pp. 20-21.

10. *Ibid.*, p. 21.

11. Government of West Pakistan, *Report of the Land Reforms Commission for West Pakistan* (Lahore: January, 1959) p. 19.

12. For evidence that this was the case in India's Kerala state, see T.C. Verghese, *Agrarian Change and Economic Consequences: Land Tenures in Kerala* (Bombay: 1970), pp. 29, 41, and passim.

13. For a treatment of similar phenomena in an adjoining region, see James C. Scott, "The Erosion of Patron-Client Bonds and Social Change in Rural Southeast Asia," *Journal of Asian Studies,* Vol. 32, November 1972, pp. 5-38. It should be added that consolidation of the state decreased the need for attaching oneself to a patron for physical protection.

14. E.M.S. Namboodiripad, *The Peasant in National Economic Construction* (Delhi: 1954). pp. 19-20.

15. For a paradigmatic treatment, see Peter Dorner, *Land Reform and Economic Development* (London: 1972).

16. *Report of the West Pakistan Land Reforms Commission,* p. 14.

17. *Ibid.*, pp. 14-20.

18. For a superb treatment of these dynamics in rural Punjab, see Hamza Alavi, "The Politics of Dependence: A Village in West Punjab," *South Asian Review* Vol. 4, No. 2 (January 1971) pp. 111-125. Aslo, Saghir Ahmad, *Class and Power in a Punjabi Village* (New York: 1977) especially pp. 91-126.

19. Government of Pakistan, Agricultural Census Organization, *Pakistan Census of Agriculture 1972* (Lahore: no date) Vol. I, Table 7.

20. Government of Pakistan, Planning Board, *First Five Year Plan* (Karachi: 1956), p. 128.

21. *Ibid.*, p. 129.

22. *Report of the West Pakistan Land Reforms Commission*, p. 5.

23. *First Five Year Plan*, p. 128.

24. *Report of the West Pakistan Land Reforms Commission*, pp. 14-15.

25. *Ibid.*, p. 15.

26. *First Five Year Plan*, p. 130.

27. Government of Pakistan, West Pakistan Land Commission, *Implementation of Land Reforms Scheme in West Pakistan*, Appraisal Paper for World Land Reforms Conference, Rome, 1966 (Lahore: 1966), p. 24.

28. *First Five Year Plan*, p. 128.

29. The political power of the great landlords in the 1950's in Pakistan, and their later support for Ayub Khan's regime, is well established. See, for example, Khalid B. Sayeed, *The Political System of Pakistan* (Boston: 1967), pp. 15, 54-55, 114, 240, and passim; M. Shahid Alam, "Economics of the Landed Interests," *Pakistan Economist* (Karachi), August 25, 1973, pp. 14-19; *Implementation of Land Reforms Scheme . . .*, p. 7.

30. *First Five Year Plan*, p. 128.

31. *Report of the West Pakistan Land Reforms Commission*, p. 30.

32. This is a very conservative estimate. We have no exact data. The 1960 *Census of Agriculture* gives no data at all on ownership patterns, only on *operated* size of holding. The West Pakistan Land Reforms Commission compiled existing data on owners, but did not collect data on landless tenants or laborers. Calculations from their *Report* (1959), Appendix I, show that 64.4 percent of all owners owned less than 5 acres, 93.1 percent owned less than 25 acres. Altogether, the owners of less than 5 acres owned about as much land as the owners who held more than 500 acres, though the latter constituted only 0.12 percent of the total number of owners. Pure (totally landless) tenants constituted 34 percent of all rural households in 1972, and landless laborers about 12 percent. The percentage of pure tenants was certainly much higher in the 1950's preceding the Ayub reform. In sum, the figure in the text is an estimate but is certainly no exaggeration and probably understates the case.

33. *Report of the West Pakistan Land Reforms Commission*, p. 30.

34. For sources, see note 29. Also, Nimal Sanderatne, "Landowners and Land Reform in Pakistan," *South Asian Review*, Vol. 7, No. 2, January 1974, p. 123 ff.

35. *Report of the West Pakistan Land Reforms Commission*, p. 30. The point was also emphasized to me by Mr. I.U. Khan, a member of both Ayub Khan's Commission and Bhutto's counterpart. Interview: Rawalpindi, March, 1974.

36. *Implementation of Land Reforms Scheme . . .*, p. 7-8.

37. *Ibid.*, p. 9.

38. This position is also taken by William Bredo, "Land Reform and Development in Pakistan," in Walter Froelich, ed., *Land Tenure, Industrialization and Social Stability* (Milwaukee, Wisconsin: 1961), p. 270. Bredo stresses the role of landlord intrigues and intransigence in the fall of regimes prior to Ayub Khan.

39. See Government of Pakistan, *The Gazette of Pakistan Extraordinary*, Martial Law Regulation No. 64, Notification No. 181/89, March 3, 1969, p. 291. Exemptions from the ceiling are contained in Part III. See also Muhammad Akram, *Manual of Land Reforms* (Lahore: 1973), pp. 60-66 for Rules promulgated under the regulation.

40. *Implementation of Land Reforms Scheme . . .*, p. 25.

41. For a thorough treatment, see Hiromitsu Kaneda, "Economic Implications of the 'Green Revolution' and the Strategy of Agricultural Development in West Pakistan," Pakistan Institute of Development Economics, Report No. 78 (Karachi: 1969); also, Carl Gotsch, "The Distributive Impact of Agricultural Growth: Low Income Farmers and the 'System'," presented to the *Seminar on Small Farmer Development Strategies*, Columbus, Ohio, September

13-15, 1971, mimeo, p. 57 ff.; Keith Griffin, *The Political Economy of Agrarian Change* (London: 1974), p. 211 ff.

42. Government of Pakistan, Ministry of Food and Agriculture, *Report of the Committee on Farm Mechanization,* unpublished but circulated mimeo (Islamabad: 1970), p. 60.

43. Carl Gotsch, in "The Distributive Impact of Agricultural Growth," p. 50, concurs in this assessment, relying heavily on Javed Burki's work. Gotsch also cites examples of large owners selling land to tenants to generate capital to mechanize (p. 60).

44. My calculations, from *Report of the Committee on Farm Mechanization,* p. 60.

45. Data which would allow proper analysis do not exist. Land reforms have distorted the land records, and official data, such as the 1960 *Census of Agriculture,* do not apply to ownership units.

46. For the compensation provisions, see *Martial Law Regulation No. 64,* Part IV; Md. Akram, *Manual of Land Reforms,* p. 67 ff., for *Rules.* Also, Implementation of *Land Reforms Scheme . . . ,* p. 13.

47. My calculations, data from *Implementation of Land Reforms Scheme . . . ,* Appendix I, and *Report of the West Pakistan Land Reforms Commission,* Appendix I.

48. For example, one of the largest landlords of Mardan told me that his family benefitted from the 1959 reforms, as did many large owners he knew, because they were able to dispense with unwanted waste, with compensation from the Government. This same owner, a scientific agriculturalist, lost same good land under the 1972 ceiling law; since all the political parties promised land reforms, he did not take the PPP pledge seriously and had not bothered to make anticipatory transfers as is usually done. Interview: January 13, 1975, Lahore.

49. *Implementation of Land Reforms Scheme,* Appendix G.

50. *Ibid.,* Appendix H and p. 13.

51. *Ibid.,* p. 18.

52. In the village studied by Saghir Ahmad for his doctoral dissertation, of forty-one recorded recipients of land under the reform provisions, only two were actually owners of the land. Ahmad found that local landlords had threatened or bullied other tenants into not accepting land or relinquishing it once accepted. Landlords successfully used control of irrigation water, other tenants and various pressures to blunt the reform. Moreover, the land which was distributed was allocated in such small parcels (well under the official guidelines) that recipients were still dependent on landlords for employment. Saghir Ahmad, *Class and Power in a Punjabi Village,* pp. 37-38. There is good reason to believe that similar dynamics operated during the Bhutto period, but the extent is unknown. Thus the official statistics must be used cautiously, if at all.

53. *Implementation of Land Reform Schemes,* p. 13.

54. Zulfikar Ali Bhutto, "Address to the Nation," March 1, 1972, reprinted by Government of Pakistan, Department of Films and Publications (Karachi: 1972), p. 3.

55. *Ibid.,* p. 1.

56. *Ibid.,* p. 2.

57. A detailed account and analysis of the provisions is available, and will not be reproduced in the text. See Ronald J. Herring and M. Ghaffar Chaudhry, "The 1972 Land Reforms in Pakistan and their Economic Implications: A Preliminary Analysis," *The Pakistan Development Review,* 13, No. 3 (Autumn, 1974), pp. 245-279.

58. Census of Agriculture data, prepared by the Agricultural Census Organization (Lahore) for UNFAO but unpublished. Islamabad, mimeo, February 1975. See Herring and Chaudhry, loc. cit., for a discussion and calculation of operative ceilings.

59. In an interview for *Stern,* June 15, 1972, President Bhutto stated: "I can't nationalize the land. It's not possible. Tomorrow, if someone wants to do it, let him try. At the same time, I can't allow bigger estates to remain. I must cut them down so that production increases and the feudal power is eliminated." Interview published in Government of Pakistan, Department of

Films and Publications, *President of Pakistan Zulfikar Ali Bhutto: Speeches and Statements* (Karachi: 1972), pp. 188-194. See, also, Bruce J. Esposito, "The Politics of Agrarian Reform in Pakistan," *Pakistan Economist* (Karachi), December 1, 1973.

60. "Address to the Nation," March 1, 1972, p. 2.

61. Address of May 23, 1972. Government of Pakistan, *President of Pakistan Zulfikar Ali Bhutto Speeches and Statements* (Karachi: 1972) Vol. II, p. 157.

62. See Herring and Chaudhry, "The 1972 Land Reforms . . .," loc. cit., p. 250, for calculations and discussion.

63. A full text of the speech was printed in *The Pakistan Times* (Rawalpindi) January 6, 1977.

64. *The Pakistan Times,* January 1, 1978. The Government's *White Paper* on the Bhutto period (cited below) makes clear in its discussion of land reforms that the present regime is not committed to redistributive agrarian policies.

65. For documentation of the widely recognized use of land reforms during the Bhutto period as a resource in "ordinary politics" (rewarding supporters, punishing enemies), see Government of Pakistan, *White Paper on the Performance of the Bhutto Regime* (Islamabad: 1979) Vol. IV, The Economy, pp. 10-16.

Educational Policy Developments in Pakistan: Quest For A National Program

DAWN E. JONES and RODNEY W. JONES

Military intervention in Pakistan's politics in mid-1977 not only over-threw the Bhutto regime but reopened fundamental controversies about the goals of education and government responsibilities for shaping educational programs. Although the objectives of the ostensibly caretaker regime of General Zia-ul-Haq have not fully congealed, its early initiatives suggest an effort to reverse the direction of, perhaps even to dismantle, the Bhutto programs unveiled in March 1972. This is one more disconcerting indication that the frequent political upheavals in Pakistan impair a coherent develop-mental approach to education.

Our main purpose is to describe and evaluate the major trends in Paki-stan's educational policies, highlighting controversial themes as well as con-tinuities and discontinuities. The paper is primarily devoted to developments since 1972, combining a preliminary evaluation of the merits and shortcom-ings of Bhutto's programs with a review, at this stage necessarily discursive, of the new military regime's private sector educational initiatives and the debate surrounding them. To put developments after 1972 in perspective, however, we briefly review at the outset the educational policy approaches of the Ayub Khan and interim Yahya Khan regimes, and the political factors which shaped their approaches. [1]

Successive governments in Pakistan have each confronted and usually responded differently to four overlapping types of tension in society and politics that impact directly on the educational system. These are tensions between (1) *religious* and *secular* approaches to nation-building; (2) *elite* and *mass* orientations to organizing politics and distributing the fruits of develop-ment; (3) *private* and *public* responsibility for social and economic enterprise; and (4) *centralized* and *decentralized* approaches to institutional management of the public sector. The last point is further complicated by tensions within government between elected and bureaucratic authorities, and within the civilian bureaucracy between career generalists and laterally-recruited specialists or political functionaries. These broad categories of competing approaches provide us with a starting point for comparing the changes in educational policy in Pakistan.

Part One
Former Approaches to Education

Ayub's Pragmatic Managerialism

Ayub's goals for education differed only marginally from his predecessors' in most respects, but placed more emphasis on modernization and on methods to combat the increasing politicization of education. His concept of modernization was modest and centered on inculcating respect for manual skills and the introduction of more vocational, technical and scientific subjects into the curriculum, together with more rigorous teaching and examination standards. His preference was implicitly for an elite orientation in higher education, with a gradual expansion of public primary education at the base. While his attitude was essentially secularist, he avoided confrontation with religious interests in education by a *laissez-faire* or self-regulatory approach to the burgeoning private sector in the cities.

Ayub's most controversial departures were in the institutional management of public sector education, especially at the university level. He centralized control over the universities and suspended their representative governing bodies (senates), inaugurating an authoritarian atmosphere which aroused student and teacher opposition and contributed to the urban political movement that brought his downfall. The *Sharif Report* of 1959 provided Ayub's rationale for greater discipline in education. It also led to regulations that spelled out how much time university teachers must devote to teaching, preparation and other duties on campus, and to other rules designed to make students work harder and longer for their degrees.[2] A new University Ordinance in 1961 threatened faculty with revocation of degrees or dismissal without appeal on vague grounds intended to cover any kind of political activity. Following student agitation, the Hamoodur Rahman Commission of 1966 investigated grievances in the universities but its recommendations offered no significant hope of redress.[3]

In the later Ayub period, a movement for the reform of private college managing bodies gained momentum under the leadership of the West Pakistan College Teacher's Association (WPCTA, since shortened to PCTA). The Hamid Ahmad Khan Commission of 1968 recommended "democratizing" private college governing bodies by adding representatives of teachers and of other constituencies so as to introduce greater accountability. Ayub's tolerance of decentralization in the private sector extended only to the religious-cum-business elites who owned and ran these colleges, not to the teachers or other affected groups. Hence, he suppressed the publication of the report, adding fuel to the agitation that reached a crescendo and caused Ayub's ouster by General Mohammad Yahya Khan in March 1969.

Nur Khan's Progressive New Education Policy

Yahya Khan's deputy, Air Marshall Nur Khan, formed a braintrust for the generation of new educational ideas, and unveiled a comprehensive New Educational Policy (NEP) for public comment on July 3, 1969.[4] Although Educational expansion at the base had been a long-standing national objective, the NEP made a realistic distributive move, pledging increased spending and reaffirming neglected goals such as the extension of free, universal education up to the fifth class by 1980, and the eventual enrollment of 60 per cent of secondary students in scientific, technical and vocational programs.[5]

A key innovation in the NEP was institutional decentralization and greater professional participation in education decision-making. In the universities, the NEP reinstituted the elected Senates and recommended the repeal of the offensive 1961 University Ordinance,[6] while in the private sector, representative governing bodies were required in the secondary schools and colleges, in effect implementing the still unpublished *Hamid Ahmad Khan Commission Report* and giving teachers their long sought voice in college governance. Universities were authorized to set up "Centres of Excellence" to promote areas of strength and specialized research. At other levels of the educational system, community participation was encouraged to make education more responsive to popular needs.

The NEP was also more receptive to Islamic interests than Ayub's policies had been. The *Nur Khan Report*, for instance, advocated the "inculcation of Islamic values as an instrument of national unity and progress" and as "a dynamic force . . . an inspiration for building a democratic, tolerant, and just society as envisaged in the concept of Pakistan."[7] This endorsement of Islamic values may have been based more on political necessity than widespread Islamic zeal in the Yahya Khan government. There was a need to placate and compensate the private managements for imposing the governing body reforms that those managements successfully resisted as long as Ayub was in power. Nur Khan's Islamic emphasis in education did not go nearly as far as some religiously-oriented managements would have liked.

Some of these differences are illustrated by the criticisms of the NEP by the *Anjuman-i-Himayat-i-Islam* (Trust for the Support of Islam) of Lahore, which had promoted Muslim advancement through education for nearly a century and at the time managed three colleges, a medical school, eleven other schools and two orphanages. The Lahore *Anjuman* was a leading proponent of an *Islam-passand* viewpoint which seeks a synthesis of orthodox Islam with modern knowledge and should be distinguished from fundamentalist or traditionalist strains of Islamic thought. The *Anjuman* advocated censoring of textbooks to ensure that all anti-Islamic content would be purged, and similar regulation of teachers obliging those who were Muslims to affirm their faith and all teachers to pledge never to engage in "un-Islamic or anti-Islamic activities."[8] Contrary to the NEP premise that falling educational standards were caused in part by restrictions on academic freedom, the *Anjuman* insisted that controls on educational content were necessary to ensure the propagation of common values. Thus, while Nur Khan's policy and the *Anjuman* position both claimed to find their inspiration in Islam, the former reasoned its way toward academic freedom and democratic institutions and the latter towards a more authoritarian (and self-serving) control over pedagogy and curricular content.

A practical evaluation of Nur Khan's NEP is not possible because it was never fully implemented, being rapidly overtaken by events. The dismemberment of Pakistan was followed by the transfer of power in December 1971 from Yahya Khan to the leadership of Zulfiqar Ali Bhutto and the Pakistan People's Party (PPP) which had won a majority of National Assembly seats in the western wing in the 1970 elections and thus had the best claim to govern the truncated country.

Bhutto's Eclectic Socialism

Educational policy was one means the PPP could use to impress the nation with its populist commitment to both Islam and socialism. Because Nur Khan's educational progressivism had stolen some of its thunder, the PPP needed dramatic gestures to solidify the support of teachers' associations, leftist groups and other urban constituencies. Minister for Education Abdul Hafiz Pirzada, described as an "energetic bombshell" by one foreign consultant, was charged with coordinating the PPP approach. Ideas for the PPP's *Education Policy, 1972-80*, announced in broad outline in March 1972, were drawn from an intensive ten-week canvas of educational circles and conferences in Islamabad representing the full spectrum of educational administrators and teachers, as well as college and university students.[9] Participation of all interested groups was a keynote of the PPP approach to education from the start, though the initial burst of enthusiasm soon wore off.

The PPP claimed that its educational reforms would be redistributive in nature, going beyond a much needed expansion of the educational system to restructuring it to eradicate the control of the privileged classes and to make education fully available to the poor. In fact, the Bhutto government made only marginal progress in this direction and in retrospect there is doubt about its commitment to socialist objectives. Two PPP initiatives—the nationalizaton of private education and the provision of free textbooks—were formally socialist measures, but neither was significantly redistributive in actual results.

Nationalization of all private colleges and schools was announced in March 1972, to take effect the following September in colleges, and over the next two years in schools. Tuition fees were eliminated in the nationalized schools, and standardized (usually a reduction) in nationalized colleges at the levels already charged in government colleges. Since virtually all the nationalized institutions were located in urban areas, this policy had almost no relevance to the bulk of the nation's poor who live in rural areas. Theoretically, access to education for the urban poor was improved but, for a variety of practical reasons, not greatly improved. The major beneficiaries of the abolished school fees and reduced college fees resulting from nationalization were urban upper and middle class families who could most easily pay for their education, and formerly did in most cases.

A more important purpose of educational nationalization was actually distributive, on behalf of private teachers who sought the security of employment, fringe benefits, status and advancement opportunities of teachers already in government service. This they found out was a mixed blessing, though on balance advantageous.

Government distribution of free textbooks began in 1974 in the first primary classes, with plans to extend them in stages to all primary classes. This measure was intended to relieve poor families of the costs of buying books for their children and to make "free education" actually free. Its disadvantages were that it robbed funds from other programs and that the free textbooks, which were printed on cheap pulp paper, did not stand up for more than a few weeks of use. When replacements were needed, families had to pay for them out of pocket, negating the original purpose. To compound matters, the free textbooks were inefficiently distributed leaving some schools without them well into the school year.

In some respects, the PPP educational programs were conceptually innovative and experimentalist. In an effort to overcome the huge "wastage" (drop-out) problem in the first years of school, the government ordered automatic promotions of students regardless of performance, reversing the Ayub emphasis on rigorous criteria for promotion. The Bhutto government reasoned that educational effectiveness should be achieved less by examination results than by improving curricular materials and libraries, and by reorienting pedagogical methods from rote learning to the development of concepts, skills and the relationship of knowledge to life experience. To cope with illiteracy which had actually risen in the 1960's, the government proposed establishing over 9,000 Adult Education Centers by 1980, primarily for women and rural inhabitants. To soak up educated unemployment, a National Development Volunteer Program (NDVP) was established. A People's Open University was founded to provide part-time and correspondence course education in vocational subjects outside the conventional structure. And the PPP attempted to institutionalize public participation in formulating and revising educational policy by provision for educational advisory councils at each tier of government and also within local institutions. But to make these essentially modernist reforms palatable, the PPP also reaffirmed Islamic education by requiring all levels of the educational system and even formerly non-Muslim nationalized schools to introduce compulsory courses in *Islamiyaat* (Islamic studies).

Although the present Zia-ul-Haq government has begun to dissociate itself from the Bhutto regime educational philosophies, some of the PPP programs may conceivably continue. We can only report on the most fragmentary assessments of their performance. In the Punjab recently, 6,273 Adult Education Centers were functioning, though less than satisfactorily because, according to one study, they were based on outdated approaches and materials, suffered from insufficient funds and were badly organized and administered.[10] On the other hand, the NDVP program has virtually collapsed. Its poorly-paid but educated "volunteers" were supposed to become more employable in the open job market, but their experience has been just the reverse, and only the most desperate still volunteer. The advisory Educational Councils were all but defunct by 1974.

The People's Open University (POU), on the other hand, has picked up momentum. Courses are offered in shorthand and typing, Arabic, and teacher training, and a general education cycle is starting after one abortive attempt.[11] It remains to be seen whether the teacher training courses will be effective. The latest three-year push is to give in-service training to 150,000 primary school teachers at a considerable savings in cost and time. Each teacher is to receive and digest over a six month period 9 books covering all the subjects taught at this level, with guidance from local study centers and weekly radio broadcasts. The expected cost is Rs. 200 per teacher instead of Rs. 1,250 in the conventional mode. The first batch through in early 1977 numbered 5,600 and the goal for the second session is 14,000 newly trained teachers.[12] While this rapid processing of primary teaching credentials will undoubtedly fill spaces in newly opened schools, we have our doubts that the classes will be well served by teachers trained in so remote a manner.

Part Two
The Merits of Private Education

Zia's Revival of the Private Sector

Prior to nationalization, the private educational sector in Pakistan was large and influential. Private colleges and high schools, although concentrated primarily in the urban areas, outnumbered their public counterparts nationally. In the large cities of Karachi and Lahore, private institutions predominated even at the primary level. Government schools were numerous in the rural areas where free education was necessary. But in the cities private schools proliferated because the middle class preferred them and was willing to pay for them. Some private institutions were set up by minority groups such as the Muslim and Parsi merchant communities, Urdu-speaking refugees from India, the Ahmadiyya sect and Christians, to cater to their own communities. Among the latter, the prestigious missionary-founded schools and colleges had trained an impressive quotient of the nation's political and professional elite. It should come as no surprise, therefore, that there is pressure in the wake of Bhutto's overthrow to undo the nationalization policy.

Zia's military intervention was initially described as an interim measure to ensure that fresh elections could be held in 1977 under impartial supervision. Those elections have been postponed, however, and are unlikely to occur for at least a year or two. As time passes, administrative pressures mount on the Zia regime to give up the caretaker facade and address substantive policy issues. Certain striking policy developments have already occurred in the educational sector. The PPP's relatively secular approach has been discarded in favor of a reaffirmation of orthodox Islamic values. The policy of nationalization in education has been questioned and even threatened with reversal. And the participation of teachers' associations in the formulation of educational policy has been sharply curtailed. There is a new ascendancy of those social groups who were displaced by the teachers' movement and who now threaten teachers' interests again. The present vulnerability of teachers was demonstrated in mid-1978 when the entire leadership of Lahore's PCTA was transferred out of the city to colleges widely dispersed throughout Punjab province. These transfers affected about 200 college teachers along with officers of the Nationalized School Teachers' Association, and represent a formidable blow to the strong tradition of teacher activism radiating from Lahore since the early 1960s.[12a]

The main unifying theme for the Pakistan National Alliance (PNA), which combined in 1977 to oppose the PPP, was the pledge to govern according to the *Nizam-i-Mustafa*("Order of the Prophet").[13] Useful as an ideological club against socialistic trends, the theocratic connotations of *Nizam-i-Mustafa* are also congenial to the Army leadership. There has been a process of social change at work in the armed forces. The original western-educated (Sandhurst) elite, exemplified by Ayub Khan, is giving way to officers educated entirely in Pakistan's schools, with their roots in the relatively conservative urban middle class of Punjab, which is increasingly weighted towards newly urbanized families from agricultural backgrounds. Among the rising officers, there is a genuine albeit somewhat naively articulated reverence for Islamic priniciples. General Zia himself represents the *Islam-passand* viewpoint. Though he denies being political ("I am terribly against this."), he has remarked that it is good that most college students now identify with the Jamiat-I-Tuleba (student wing of the Jama'at-i-Islami) and that advantage should be taken of this fortuitous situation.[14]

Seeing this changed climate, managerial interests have pressed with some success for the restoration of the private educational sector. As early as June 1977, the Sind government began approving the opening of new private schools up to matriculation.[15] PNA leader Professor Ghafoor Ahmad called for a new private sector, but without denationalizing the previously taken-over schools.[16] Then in August the Karachi Martial Law Administrator actually denationalized two institutions, the Anjuman Islamia Secondary School and the Jinnah Polytechnic Institute.[17] The announcement came at the inauguration of a new library sponsored by the *Anjuman Islamia,* apparently as a reward for this contribution of philanthropic resources to the educational system. There was an outcry by the affected teachers who feared that their service conditions would be degraded. But only the PCTA addressed the larger issues, reminding the authorities that these particular managements had had bad records before nationalization and that "permission to open new schools by private parties should be given under a properly drafted law after ensuring that the interests of teachers and students were protected."[18] As this piecemeal erosion of nationalization ensued, a fresh debate among teachers' associations began. The Sind Lecturers' Association and the Rawalpindi PCTA spoke out against denationalization. They observed that while standards had fallen since nationalization, the policy was not at fault so much as poor facilities, the outdated examination system and unfavorable teacher-student ratios.[19]

Denationalization became a key issue at the government-sponsored Education Conference of October 3–5, 1977, to which many high level educationists and bureaucrats were invited as well as leading members of other professions such as law and journalism. In contrast to the PPP's 1972 conferences on education, however, neither the practicing teachers nor their associational representatives were invited. In opening the conference and setting the theme for its deliberations, General Zia said, "I think the time has come when we should offer good private enterprise in the educational institutions. . . ."[20] The conferees agreed two days later that "denationalisation of selected institutions may be examined on merit on [a] case-to-case basis." But they also recommended safeguards for the protection of teachers' service conditions, salary and advancement, and regular consultation between schools and the government over the setting of fees.[21]

Teachers' associations voiced immediate opposition. The Rawalpindi PCTA declared that the conference recommendations had "shocked the teachers of nationalised institutions all over Pakistan because they dreaded the return of the dark days of pre-nationalisation."[22] The College Principals' Association called for the nationalization of all the exempted English-medium schools as a measure to complete the social equalization of the nationalization policy instead of reversing it.[23] A rumor that the government intended to denationalize Islamia College of the *Anjuman-i-Himayat-i-Islam* brought a sharp reaction from Dr. Mubashir Hassan, formerly General-Secretary of the PPP. He accused the Anjuman of fifty years of profiteering and corrupt management and suggested that it would be a travesty to restore to it control of any institution.[24]

For the time being, the Zia government has apparently decided not to denationalize further, but only to encourage the formation of a new private sector in education.[25] On November 20, Zia authorized the opening of new private schools up through the high school level and assured any would-be managements there would be no future nationalization.[26] Assurances against nationalization are almost meaningless, of course, because successive governments will make their own decisions, even changing the constitution if they have to—just as the PPP did earlier. But the creation of a new private sector will eventually require the government to face the issue of monitoring private establishments to ensure that teachers' working conditions are adequately protected. This brings the issue full circle since, from the teachers' point of view, effective government regulation of managements would have made nationalization unnecessary in the first place. It is doubtful now that teachers will support the creation of a new private sector; they fear that the government will defer too much to private managerial wishes at the teachers' expense. If the private sector is revived, a new set of private teachers' associations will probably also arise in due course.

The Zia regime also seems to be reverting to the Ayub pattern of purging politics from the educational system by fiat. The exclusion of teachers' representation from the educational conference is one example. Another more ominous indication is the appearance on November 12 of Martial Law Regulation (MLR) No. 28, which prohibits elections to student and professional organizations or associations. The maximum penalty for violating MLR 28 is three years of rigorous imprisonment and/or a whipping of up to ten lashes.[27] The rationale may be two-fold, to stifle the electioneering in organizations that so frequently spills over into anti-government agitation, and to ensure that the student unions remain largely under the control of the *Jamiat-i-Tuleba* or other *Islam-passand* groups. In any case, MLR 28 is an effort to put the lid on educational organizations rather than to integrate them into the governmental process, and lids build up pressure.

Issues of Public and Private Education

The official justification most emphasized by the PPP for the nationalization of private education was that it would end the rampant commercialism that allegedly existed.[28] Many private schools were said to be operated for profit at the expense of teachers, students and the quality of the product. Teachers suffered from overwork, meager pay, insecure tenure and little or no provision for retirement. Students suffered because private managers failed to invest in adequate buildings, laboratories and libraries, and because the morale of their teachers was low. Nationalized schools, by contrast, would be efficiently managed and adequately financed by the government—with no precious resources siphoned off for private profit. Their teachers would enjoy the status of government servants, job security and pay commensurate with their qualifications. Their students would receive more attention and have better facilities. And the quality of education would be raised across the board to match the established standards of government colleges and schools.[29]

With the benefit of hindsight, the PPP rationale for nationalization appears somewhat shaky on its own terms. While teachers did gain better conditions of service, there is little evidence that nationalization improved the quality of education significantly. On the contrary, in the better private institutions, it seems to have declined. Moreover, the PPP overlooked the positive advantages of private education and neglected to examine or reached hasty conclusions on a number of important issues. On the question of resources, while the PPP assumed the private sector was improvident, there is some counter-evidence that the private sector is comparatively efficient and, in addition, actually generates revenue for education that would not otherwise be available. On the question of educational quality, the PPP failed to take into consideration that the best of the private schools were pacesetters for the system as a whole and provided independent standards against which public schools could be measured and induced to improve. Although the PPP stressed the importance of fostering innovation, experimental approaches and creative thinking in education, its assumption that nationalized schools would be more conducive to these developments than private schools has not been borne out. Nationalization has bureaucratized the schools in question and stifled educational innovation. Finally, while the PPP was convinced that nationalization was an egalitarian measure, it worked perversely, injuring the interests of certain social minorities, notably Christians. Although there is insufficient evidence to settle these issues here, there is some suggestive new information coming to light in current debates.

The proponents of nationalization were badly in error on the costs of goverment take-over. They appear to have assumed that because private schools and colleges not only charged higher tuition fees than their government counterparts but also received government subsidies, that they were making enormous hidden profits and were simply milking the government and the public at the same time. If this was corrected by government management, it was assumed, the additional burden on the government would be small—especially if the government expropriated the physical assets of the schools in question without paying compensation to the owners. The ultimate effect, some believed, would be to enlarge radically the resource base for education.[30]

This view was extraordinarily short-sighted or ill-informed. It failed to calculate the systemic loss of revenue that would result from abolishing school and reducing college tuition fees in nationalized institutions, or the new drain on revenues that regularizing and upgrading the salaries of teachers in those institutions would entail. Ultimately, it overlooked a rather important implication that added costs of nationalization would draw more money into urban schools and reduce the share of revenues available for the opening of new government schools in rural areas where the need was probably greater.[31] In short, nationalizaton was arguably a misconceived reform that benefited the urban middle class at the expense of rural development.

The Zia government is making an effort to revive the private sector to cope with the demand for new schools that the government cannot fill.[32] Although there is a note of desperation in this shift in policy, given the difficulty in raising taxes, it may be the most practical way to generate new commitments of educational resources.[33] The cost to government of educating citizens in private institutions is much lower than in public institutions. Figures gathered on costs for education in Karachi colleges before 1972 showed that the government laid out an average of Rs. 323 thousand for each government college and an average of only Rs. 32 thousand, about one tenth, for each private college. Each government college student there cost the government about Rs. 600 per year, about fifteen times the Rs. 40 the government put down in subsidy to educate a private college student.[34]

There are some complexities in comparative costs that these figures do not address. Private colleges could be run more cheaply because they paid lower salaries, which is partly why private teachers' associations became a powerful lobby for nationalization. Private colleges were also predominantly arts colleges, which are much less expensive to operate than science colleges or technical institutions, and it was usually left to the government to provide the latter. But even on this last point, the picture is mixed. Some data show that the government share of the operating costs of government *arts* colleges in West Pakistan increased more sharply than the average government support for all public institutions from 1961 to 1970. Moreover, in that period, the average government subsidies to *private* colleges and schools increased *less rapidly* than the government support for public institutions.[35]

From a strictly economic standpoint, private education would seem to be a good deal for the government. If so, the more educational demand can be met by private efforts, the freer the government should be to channel any uncommited public resources into types of education and areas of the country where the private sector is unlikely to lead. And within the private sector, the government could concentrate more easily on stimulating through subsidies the relatively expensive scientific and technical varieties of education that development seems to require.[36]

Nationalization together with the increased emphasis on Islam in education has made the position of Christians, the only substantial non-Muslim minority in Pakistan, rather uncomfortable. The Pakistani Christian community is rather unusual in that while the bulk of it is lower class, it also contains a disproportionately influential professional middle class, with prominent representatives in administrative and military officer circles. This has been due in part to the promotion of education and creation of excellent schools by foreign missionaries. Most of these schools did not cater exclusively to Christians. Their enrollments have always been predominantly Muslim. But Christian schools usually gave poorer Christian students financial assistance and guaranteed the availability of education to those who were qualified for admission. In some cases, an informal quota system may have existed. Christian institutions also provided an attractive employment avenue for educated Christian professionals. Nationalization of so-called "missionary institutions" threw Christian teachers and students into unshielded competition with the Muslim majority. If advancement in Pakistan depended primarily on merit, this competition might be equitable and healthy. But in fact, competition is based increasingly on ascriptive factors. Shorn of control of educational institutions, the predominantly lower class Christians are ill-equipped to defend their interests in a society where the very foundation for the existence of the nation is Islamic.[37]

For the Christian minority, the Zia government's interest in reviving private education could be some source of comfort, though as yet it is too early too tell. The *Nizam-i-Mustafa* theme is a potential source of trouble. The martial law regime's October 1977 Educational Conference recommended, for instance, that:

For recruiting members of the teaching staff for our educational institutions some mechanism [will] be evolved so that besides stressing. . .academic standards, the moral character and devotion to principles and practice of Islam [will] also be taken into account.[38]

Taken literally, this would put overwhelming pressure on Christian would-be teachers to convert. Not surprisingly, Christian leaders have been seeking modifications of government policy. In the same conference, Dr. Anwar Barkat, Principal of Forman (Christian) College, succeeded in persuading the delegates to amend the proposal for compulsory Islamic studies to allow minority students to take alternative courses based on their own religious traditions.[39] Dr. Barkat also led a delegation to General Zia in September 1977 to lobby for minority rights, and Zia assured the delegation that his government would protect such rights.[40] Islamic traditions do in fact provide for the protection and autonomy of minorities. Only time will tell whether these traditions are vital in Pakistan. The 1974 upheaval and resulting constitutional amendment directed against the heterodox Ahmadiyya community does not augur well for any sectarian minority in Pakistan.

Nationalization has also had adverse effects on educational management. In private institutions, principals and headmasters had considerable flexibility in allocating resources internally. Under the new regulations, there is a myriad of bureaucratic controls designed to ensure accountability and minimize corruption. But these controls also stifle initiative and make it difficult to get things done, whether it be the repair of a building, the procurement of furniture or the appointment of teachers. There are widespread complaints about petty bureaucratic interference and there is some evidence that regulations and financial transactions are manipulated to provide material or political pay-offs to authorities at various levels in the hierarchy. Nationalization may have put an end to "private profit," but it may also be that public veniality has simply taken its place, and it is not at all clear that this is a change for the better.

The effects of bureaucratism and over-centralization have reached comic proportions in the area of personnel. There was a tendency even before nationalizaton to delay promotions and the permanent filling of vacancies for indefinite periods. A newspaper article carried the graphic headline, "Dead Lecturers Promoted," and explained: "Twenty-five lecturers who are no longer alive were promoted last week to Junior Class I by the West Pakistan Education Department. . . . Their promotions were due since 1959 and they died awaiting the decision of the Department." Promotions for twenty-five *retired* teachers were also announced at the same time.[41]

More recently, these abuses have become so common the term "*ad-hocism*" has been coined for them. When vacancies occur, the Public Service Commission often fails to act promptly on them. In the interim, institutions appoint teachers on an *ad hoc* basis. This takes the urgency out of the situation for the Public Service Commission, but it strings teachers along for years without security of service—giving rise to conditions not unlike those in the private sector that fueled the movement for nationalization. Sometimes real hardships or arbitrary discrimination result. For example, while all the lecturers in Punjab region colleges appointed *ad hoc* between 1970 and 1975 were eventually regularized, those appointed *ad hoc* since 1975 were referred to the Public Service Commission and the Commission abruptly dismissed 80 per cent of them.[42]

Conclusions

At present, the thrust of educational policy in Pakistan is unclear. Zia's government is uncertain of what direction to take, having second thoughts about denationalization and no coherent program for stimulating a new private sector. Such recent proposals as that for the use of mosques and religious leaders as nuclei of new primary schools are indicative of a poverty of distinctive ideas and clarity of purpose. Yet this lack of preconceived approach may not be so bad. Existing educational institutions continue to function even without a clarity of goals; the virtue of the bureaucratic machinery is that it keeps routine programs going. Moreover, there is now an opportunity for Pakistan's leaders to take stock, to evaluate past efforts and conduct a search for more effective policy concepts and organizational approaches.

It would be unfortunate if, in seeking alternative remedies, the present regime discarded the sensitivity to egalitarian and redistributive values that has been engendered by the Nur Khan and PPP educational programs, whatever the misconceptions or shortcomings of the policy measures intended to embody those values. Nationalization may have been misdirected, but some of the problems that inspired it were real. Still, the hesitation of the new regime over the issue of nationalization is healthy and raises a basic question: what can the government most effectively do to provide for the nation's educational needs? There are no satisfactory short answers to this question, but in the interest of stimulating reflection and discourse, we suggest the following points.

Government planning in education is inescapable, but how much should the government *qua* government be directly involved in the educational enterprise? Available resources limit the capacity of the government to meet all educational demand directly. A reasonable role for the government, therefore, is to employ incentives to stimulate and regulate the private sector to meet as much of the demand as it can, freeing the government to concentrate on supplementary needs. The public sector's major direct concern should be with the expansion of primary and secondary education in the rural areas. There is much more to social equality than education, but there is probably nothing so integral to egalitarianism as the spread of literacy.

As regards the private sector, the government is better equipped to regulate in some areas than others. Rules can and have been written to regulate financial management and personnel standards and practices and it is appropriate both that they be enforced and revised as circumstances change— with mechanisms devised for professional input so that change can be monitored and interpreted routinely rather than as a result of pent-up political pressures. The requirement of governing boards in individual schools and colleges would go a long way towards effective supervision of government regulations, particularly if the representation of teachers is elective and gives them a meaningful voice.

On the other hand, the government is ill-equipped to program educational content or enforce educational standards. These matters should be decentralized and left almost exclusively to professionals, in the public as well as private sectors. This is proposed not because today's professionals are so excellent—indeed, they leave much to be desired—but because only by being made responsible for these matters will they have much incentive to improve themselves, what they teach and those they teach.

Now that the Islamic education issue has become so prominent and explosive, it will be politically difficult for any government to relinquish it, but that is exactly what should be done. There is no way in Pakistan to set central standards for Islamic education that will produce any consensus. Using an Islamic appeal as the guiding force for education could conceivably lead to such misdirected efforts as enforcement of the Ideology Council's recommendation that Arabic be made compulsory in a system that is already overloaded with rival languages.[43] Individual institutions should be left to find their own solutions to this issue of Islamic focus, though government protection may be needed for some that reach unpopular positions.

Standards and content are prescribed throughout Pakistan's educational system. There are three possible ways to modify the system so as to reduce the role of the government and increase the role of professionals in both areas. One would be to compose the curricular and examination-setting committees of the Boards of Intermediate and Secondary Education primarily of teachers, and to make the selection of teacher members elective rather than appointive. The same could be done for the counterpart committees of the universities which control the curricular content and examination standards for all recognized degree colleges. The second modification would be to encourage the spread of the "semester system" which is now used in Karachi University and is being contemplated for the remainder of the universities. At the University of Engineering and Technology in Lahore, the system is already working well, but only because a teacher-student committee worked out a system of regulations which they have been able to maintain, including a rule against awarding grace marks, and another affirming that those who are qualified to teach are also qualified to examine.[44] The third modification would be to detach some degree colleges by stages from the university's control over curriculum and examinations, and to give either individual detached colleges or clusters of colleges full responsibility for designing their own curriculums and examinations, setting their own standards and awarding their own degrees. This would best be begun with colleges that already have traditions of excellence.

The principle that would come into play would be the effects of the marketplace. Independent colleges or groups of colleges that achieved distinction by producing exceptional graduates would eventually be recognized. To the extent that diversity and innovation in educational content made this possible, the lesson would filter back to those preparing students at the secondary and intermediate levels, and the revision of curricular content and standards would be influenced accordingly. The universities which have not been noted for educational leadership would be faced with a salutary competition, probably forcing introspection, ferment and eventual improvement.

Over a longer time span, consideration could be given to further decentralization of the administration of the secondary and intermediate schools to produce a similar kind of competition among educational divisions, districts or groups of schools. Community interest might be awakened eventually to force more educational responsiveness to grass-roots concerns.

Out of the diversification of educational institutions and approaches that we envision here, we see a more functional response to two basic problems, the need for trained manpower that is adapted to the developmental needs of society and the organic evolution of a sense of national identity. Highly-regimented bureaucratic societies can program for manpower requirements with partial success, but most societies, particularly those with unstable governments such as Pakistan's, cannot. The alternative is to let the employment demand created by such economic growth and moderization as occurs influence the producing sector, i.e., the educational system. The more flexible the educational system is, the more effectively it will respond to employment demand. The more diverse and decentralized the educational system is, the more flexible it will be.

There is another advantage of flexibility in education for a regionally and linguistically pluralistic society like Pakistan. Islam is the only national common denominator, but it is too contentious a subject to rely on exclusively. While the regions of Pakistan are sharply different, each has a culture which can be cultivated through education. There is the obvious risk that permitting this would exacerbate political separatism. But a contrary case can be made for the promotion of regional self-assurance as the most reliable foundation for spontaneously evolving national links—aided by a free process of political participation which gives localities a stake in the decisions of the center. The advantage of educational diversity within regions is that it also fosters pluralism within those regions and makes regional interests less monolithic and potentially less dangerous to the goal of national unity.

Notes

1. These factors, and those that underlie the educational programs of Bhutto, are analyzed in more depth in our "Nationalizing Education in Pakistan: Teachers' Associations and the People's Party," in *Pacific Affairs*, Vol. 50. No, 4 (Winter 1977–78), pp. 581-603, and in expanded form in our monograph, *Private Power and Educational Politics in Pakistan: The Politics of Nationalization*, (University of Texas at Austin, Center for Asian Studies, March 1978).

2. Government of Pakistan, Ministry of Education, *Report of the Commission on National Education* (Karachi: Government of Pakistan Press, 1959).

3. Government of Pakistan, Ministry of Education, *Report of the Commission on Student Problems and Welfare* (Karachi: Government of Pakistan Press, 1966).

4. Government of Pakistan, Ministry of Education and Scientific Research, *The New Education Policy of the Government of Pakistan* (Islamabad: March 1970), also known as the *Nur Khan Report*.

5. *Nur Khan Report*, pp. 3, 11.

6. The latter was actually not accomplished until the advent of the Bhutto regime.

7. *Nur Khan Report*, pp. 1, 15.

8. *Pakistan Times*, August 28, 1969.

9. "Educational Minister Press Conference," *Education for the Masses; The New Policy* (Karachi: Department of Films and Publicatins, Government of Pakistan), p. 15. The press conference was held on March 16, 1972.

10. Nasim Ahmad, "Problems of Adult Education," *Pakistan Times*, Oct. 4, 1977.

11. *Pakistan Times*, Aug. 8, 1977.

12. *Ibid.*

12a. "Squeeze on Teachers' Union," *Viewpoint* (Lahore), June 18, 1978, p. 14; "Teachers: Crisis Unresolved," *Viewpoint,* June 25, 1978, p. 11.

13. *Nizam-i-Mustafa* refers to the original Islamic social and political order, and the principles of justice, imputed to the rule of the Prophet Muhammad in Mecca and Medina. The term is suggestive of a golden era of social and economic justice. But how this would be translated into a contemporary constitution for Pakistan has not been elaborated.

14. Zia's remark was made at the Islamabad Educational Conference of Oct. 3–5, 1977. See *Dawn*, Oct. 4, 1977.

15. *Dawn* editorial, Aug. 28, 1977.

16. *Ibid.*

17. *Dawn*, Aug. 14, 1977.

18. *Ibid.*, Aug. 17, 1977.

19. *Ibid.*, Sept. 6, 1977; *Pakistan Times*, Sept. 9, 1977.

20. *Pakistan Times*, Oct. 4, 1977.

21. *Ibid.*, Oct. 6, 1977.

22. *Ibid.*, Oct. 9, 1977.

23. *Dawn*, Oct. 13, 1977.

24. *Pakistan Times*, Oct. 21, 1977.

25. *Ibid.*, Oct. 22, 1977.

26. *Ibid.*, Nov. 21, 1977.

27. *Dawn*, Nov. 13, 1977.

28. Other justifications were offered as well, including the socialist argument that some private institutions perpetuated class differences and social inequality by discriminating against the poor. Nationalization was supposed to ensure that any student, regardless of social standing or ability to pay, would gain admission.

29. For a survey of pro-nationalization arguments, see Dr. W. M. Zaki, Compiler, *End of Misery*, Ministry of Education and Provincial Co-ordination (Islamabad: Printing Corporation of Pakistan Press, 1972).

30. See K. F. Yusuf, "Better Education, Lesser Cost," in *End of Misery*, p. 31.

31. A recent *Dawn* editorial observed that the government was not opening new schools because it was struggling to keep up with the needs of nationalized schools. *Dawn*, Oct. 25, 1977.

32. *Pakistan Times*, Oct. 4, 1977.

33. For a discussion of constraints on taxation for education, see Charles S. Benson, *Finance of Education: Training and Related Service in the Public Sector*, Planning Commission, Government of Pakistan (April, 1970), p. 22.